CW00501804

Fighting

Fighting Words

Religion, Violence, and the
Interpretation of Sacred Texts

Edited by

John Renard

UNIVERSITY OF CALIFORNIA PRESS

Berkeley   Los Angeles   London

University of California Press, one of the most distinguished university presses in the United States, enriches lives around the world by advancing scholarship in the humanities, social sciences, and natural sciences. Its activities are supported by the UC Press Foundation and by philanthropic contributions from individuals and institutions. For more information, visit www.ucpress.edu.

University of California Press
Berkeley and Los Angeles, California

University of California Press, Ltd.
London, England

© 2012 by The Regents of the University of California

Library of Congress Cataloging-in-Publication Data

Fighting words : religion, violence, and the interpretation of sacred texts / edited by John Renard.
    p.   cm.
  Includes bibliographical references and index.
   ISBN 978-0-520-25831-0 (cloth : alk. paper) — ISBN 978-0-520-27419-8 (pbk. : alk. paper) — ISBN 978-0-520-95408-3 (ebook)
   1. Violence—Religious aspects. 2. Sacred books—History and criticism. 3. Religions—Relations. I. Renard, John, 1944–
   BL65.V55F64   2012
   201'.76332—dc23   2012029403

Manufactured in the United States of America

21 20 19 18 17 16 15 14 13 12
10 9 8 7 6 5 4 3 2 1

In keeping with a commitment to support environmentally responsible and sustainable printing practices, UC Press has printed this book on 50-pound Enterprise, a 30% post-consumer-waste, recycled, deinked fiber that is processed chlorine-free. It is acid-free and meets all ANSI/NISO (Z 39.48) requirements.

CONTENTS

PREFACE

My goal here has been to assemble a collection of essays designed to provide representative samples of an enormous subject: how various sacred texts deal with the subject of violence and how exegetical specialists in a variety of religious traditions have interpreted those texts. Given the libraries full of sacred texts and commentary thereon, such a vast topic as this one can only sample cursorily in a single volume. But the unfortunate topicality of questions of allegedly religious justification of carnage in our time makes all the more pressing the need to provide access to some explicit approach to the subject, however partial or fragmentary the results.

I offer my gratitude to the final cohort of colleagues who persevered through the vicissitudes of a process that began in 2006. I believe their generous and very patient collective effort will provide a useful contribution to broader understanding of a major religious theme in the lives and belief of so many millions of our fellow human beings.

I am grateful to Jared Goff and Alex Giltner, of Saint Louis University, for their valuable editorial assistance at various stages of the project; to Jacob Van Sickle, also of Saint Louis University, for his help in a variety of editorial matters, compiling the glossary, and generally preparing the final manuscript for delivery to the press, as well as for help in proofreading the final pages. I thank also Barbara Roos for compiling the index. Special thanks to Reed Malcolm, religious studies editor of the University of California Press, for his flexibility and patience in the completion of this project; and to UCP project editor Rose Vekony and copy editor Robert Demke for their very able editorial assistance in the book's latter stages. And as always, my deepest gratitude to my spouse, Mary Pat, for her unfailing support and good humor through the ups and downs of this protracted project.

Exegesis and Violence

Texts, Contexts, and Hermeneutical Concerns

John Renard

Thomas Hobbes famously observed in his *Leviathan* that human life is "nasty, brutish, and short." He and other influential philosophers have identified violence as virtually a "state of nature" that humankind has struggled endlessly to ameliorate, and with precious little success. Religious authors in every age and culture have likewise filled libraries with their analyses of the roots and remedies of this scourge, this "mark of Cain." Every credible religious or ethical system condemns murder, yet sacred texts claimed by adherents of most (if not all) religious traditions describe in often grisly detail how believers have had recourse to divinely sanctioned violent means in defense of a "people" or to spread the sacred message. For millennia, preachers and teachers of religious values have discerned in their scriptures a divine logic both for and against engaging in large-scale violence, yet confusion among religious believers remains pervasive.

Many people across the globe find themselves asking whether "religion" is not in fact more of a catalyst than a cure for much of the violence in our world. Unfortunately, when the scale tilts toward blaming religion as a major (or even the chief) contributing cause of mayhem, the blame is too often ladled out exclusively against "them." Religionists are too seldom willing to entertain the possibility that their own faith tradition is as much a contributor to the problem as a counterforce. Adherents of a given tradition often insist on how it could scarcely be more obvious that someone else's sacred text and historical record are rife with a divine mandate for the indiscriminate slaughter of unbelievers and all they hold dear, while claiming that their own revealed patrimony sanctions only self-defense. The present collection of essays invites readers to explore these vexing questions by mining the sacred texts and exegetical traditions for important examples of scriptured communities of faith.

BACKGROUND AND METHODOLOGICAL ISSUES

Comparative studies of the world's religious traditions take countless different forms, depending on their guiding purpose. Many books survey the full range of aspects of multiple traditions, including sacred texts, basic beliefs and rituals, schools of thought or "denominations," organizational features, and paradigmatic figures. Narrower in scope, a number of studies have dedicated themselves to a general comparison of the sacred texts of many traditions in a single volume.[1] Work in the relatively new subdiscipline bridging religious studies and theology known as Comparative Theology typically focuses on explicitly "theological" themes across two, or occasionally three or more, traditions. Several recent comparative works have focused on violence in the name of religion.[2] But general studies of the vast topics of scripture as a category or of violence as a theme seldom assist the reader in understanding the logic behind marshaling sacred texts in support of or against resorting to violent action, the widespread practice of decontextualizing those texts in service of extremist interpretations, or the range of exegetical methods evidenced in the history of a given text's interpretation.

Why Exegesis and Violence?

One of the critical issues in interreligious relations today is the connection, both actual and perceived, between sacred sources and the justification of violent acts. Unfortunately the connection has been relatively little studied in a way that makes solid text-based scholarship accessible to the general public. The present volume begins with the premise that a balanced approach to religious pluralism in our world must build on a measured, well-informed response to the increasingly publicized and, sadly, sensationalized association of terrorism and other forms of large-scale violence with religion.[3]

Such a measured response must begin with the sacred texts so often cited as inspiration and justification for every kind of violence, from individual assassination to mass murder to the total obliteration of a society. In pursuing a balanced approach to this complex topic, this book is not merely about the religious sanction of violence. It is fundamentally about the diverse ways in which interpreters of the various sacred sources have handled texts that appear either to prescribe or to describe violence, including interpretations that militate against violence. The desired result is a representative overview of the virtually universal phenomenon of variant methods of interpreting sacred texts that sanction, mandate, or explicitly rule out violent means. "Scripturally sanctioned [or forbidden] violence" is clearly an expansive and ideologically loaded term. The present collection uses the category as a general organizing concept that embraces a wide range of scriptural traditions, exegetical methods, and hermeneutical concerns.

Two major underlying assumptions motivated the development of this project, and though they are background issues, it is essential to state them up front. First, concern with issues of violence, vengeance, war and peace, and claims to religiously legitimate wrath is a demonstrable current running through parts of the texts and commentaries of many of the world's faith communities. Secondly, however, persons of faith are not to be held accountable for violence committed by those who claim, without warrant, to speak for them.

Scope and Method of the Volume

A widespread assumption seems to be that religiously sanctioned violence is characteristic of, perhaps even unique to, the so-called Abrahamic traditions: Judaism, Christianity, and Islam. An important goal of this volume is to demonstrate that, however a tradition's "core" teachings concerning violence are perceived, interpreters from many major traditions have had to deal with references to violence in those sources. Whether prescriptive or descriptive, such references are by no means monopolized by Abrahamic or West Asian traditions.

Essays by eight specialists in the scriptural and exegetical sources of seven scriptured faith traditions explore a wide variety of approaches to the complex subject. They address three broad areas of concern: key relationships between sacred text and context, major strands of exegesis within and among the traditions represented, and historically significant examples of exegesis in practice.

The essays focus on one or more texts from their respective tradition's sacred scriptures that relate in some important way (whether by sanction or repudiation) to the use of violent means by divine mandate, considering both the immediate and broader context of the scripture(s) in question. Most of these texts have been cited throughout the centuries as justification for the violent actions of members of the tradition in question. The essays also examine major exegetical trends, underscoring the historical fact of alternative readings within each faith tradition. Thus, an important function of the collection is to highlight alternative interpretations or methods of exegesis evidenced in the various traditions. Overarching questions include: What exegetical resources have been espoused—even if only by a historical minority—for advancing a moderating approach to the use of violent means? And how, precisely, have interpreters read particular texts as justification for recourse to violence?

AN OVERVIEW OF THE MAJOR SCRIPTURAL TRADITIONS

A brief general introduction to the sacred texts and the remarkable variety of exegesis manifest in each of the faith communities treated in these essays will offer students and other nonspecialist readers essential general background.

Judaism and the Hebrew Bible

According to a traditional Jewish reckoning, the Hebrew Bible is a collection of twenty-four "books" divided into three main groupings: Torah, Prophets, and Writings. Jews, as well as Christians generally, identify five books of Torah: Genesis, Exodus, Leviticus, Numbers, and Deuteronomy. These books are also known as the Pentateuch, from the Greek meaning "five vessels" or "scrolls." In the category of "Prophets" *(Nevi'im),* Jewish tradition includes eight books. Joshua, Judges, 1 and 2 Samuel as one book, and 1 and 2 Kings as another together comprise the four "former prophets." The four "latter" prophets are Isaiah, Jeremiah, Ezekiel, and the collection of the twelve "minor prophets" *(trei-assar* in Jewish [Aramaic] parlance, including Hosea, Joel, Amos, Obadiah, Jonah, Micah, Nahum, Habakkuk, Zephaniah, Haggai, Zechariah, and Malachi—"minor" because they are shorter texts). Under the heading of "Writings" *(Khetuvim)* are a total of eleven books, with Ezra and Nehemiah considered as one, as well as 1 and 2 Chronicles. The "Five Scrolls" *(megillot)* include the Song of Songs, Ruth, Lamentations, Ecclesiastes, and Esther. Psalms, Proverbs, Job, and Daniel complete the Writings. Taken together the *Torah, Nevi'im,* and *Khetuvim* are designated by the acronym *TaNaKh.*

An important theme in Jewish thought is the complex relationship between the "written" and "oral" Torah. *Torah* is a Hebrew word generally translated as "teaching," "instruction," or "custom." It is sometimes used to refer to the first five books, Genesis through Deuteronomy. According to tradition, Moses himself composed the whole of the Torah under divine inspiration. This ancient attribution lends maximum authority to these sacred texts by association with the man most identified with the divine revelation that shaped Judaism. But Torah also has a broader meaning. In its larger sense, Torah means revealed or divine Law, that is, all that God requires of Jews, and this meaning applies to a larger corpus of literature than the Pentateuch or even the entire Hebrew Bible. The historical evolution of the Hebrew scriptures is far longer and more complex than the present shape of the Bible might lead one to suspect. The editing that eventuated in the final shape of the Pentateuch alone represented already multilayered interpretative developments. In a sense, the "later" books of the Hebrew Bible represent early forms of exegesis of the earlier texts.

Jewish extrabiblical literature is vast and expansive. Two large bodies of literature are generally known as Talmud and Midrash. Talmud consists of the systematization of successive waves of originally oral commentary by religious scholars on sacred scripture. First, views of earlier generations of rabbis were codified in the Mishna. Subsequent generations further commented on the Mishnaic material, and that was brought together in the Gemara. Then the Mishna and Gemara were combined in the Talmud, which was produced in two versions, the Jerusalem or Palestinian Talmud and the considerably larger Babylonian Talmud.

Medieval European rabbinical scholars devised still more comprehensive and elaborate exegetical frameworks. Perhaps the most famous is summed up in the acronym *PaRDeS* (an ancient Persian term meaning "Paradise"). Each of the upper case consonants stands for a Hebrew term referring to one of the four principal levels or methods of exegesis. *Peshat* is the literal sense and the kind of interpretation prevalent in oral Torah, *remez* looks for the allegorical meaning, *derash* (study) derives the homiletical or ethical significance, and *sod* (more) unveils the mystical significance of a text. Jewish exegesis has devised highly sophisticated methods of drawing out the various meanings of the sacred text and has preserved the results in an enormous library known as Rabbinical literature.

Much of the content of the Talmud is described by the term *halakhah,* a word that means literally "proceeding, walking." It refers to the bulk of Talmud and more generally to the literature interpreting the specific rules and legislation found in the scripture. The plural of the term, *halakhot,* came to mean all the specific laws derived through exegesis, even if not explicitly mentioned in scripture. Halakhic literature peers into every conceivable nook and cranny of Jewish daily life, prescribing in minutest detail how the Torah should be used as a guide here and now. The term *midrash* means "study, commentary, amplification" and originally meant the method used by all scholars of sacred scripture. Hence, much Talmudic material is midrashic, for example. But eventually midrash came to be more popularly identified with the non-halakhic material in the Talmud and with another type of literature called *aggadah* (or *haggadah,* meaning "narrative"). Works of aggadic midrash, like halakhic works, primarily comment on scripture. But unlike *halakhah, aggadah* is more concerned with reading between the lines. Aggadic works tell the story behind the story and say little about specific legal implications. As such, *aggadah* is generally much more appealing and entertaining, offering interpretations that are frequently very moving, charming, and droll.

Against this broad backdrop, Reuven Firestone's "A Brief History of War in the Hebrew Bible and the Jewish Interpretive Tradition" explores a number of critical junctures in biblical history, highlighting the divine initiative and support of violent means in ancient Israel's dealings with other peoples. Firestone identifies as a key element the early transition from a sort of revolving henotheism to monotheism, and from a tribal to a universal theology. In this context, prominent historical moments include especially the extended period of initial conquest of Canaan, expansion under the monarchy, restoration during the Second Temple Period, and various revolts against Roman rule during that period and after the destruction of the Temple in 70 C.E. An especially important turn away from any possibility of "offensive" war characterized rabbinical thought during subsequent centuries. Twentieth-century events again turned Jewish concerns back toward greater willingness to understand the use of violent means as rooted in a theological reading of Israel's history and the right to continued existence as an unfolding of the modern Zionist project. In the course of his chapter, Firestone provides a broad overview of both a range of literary exegetical genres and diverse ways of interpreting the biblical library.

Christianity and the Old Testament

Christian communities identify and enumerate the canon of the "Old Testament" differently both from mainstream Jewish tradition and, in some instances, from one another. In theory, Christian churches agree in dividing the whole corpus into the Law, the Prophets, and the Writings, but they count their books differently and thus arrive at a total of thirty-nine. But for pedagogical purposes, one could argue, Christian biblical studies distinguish the Pentateuch (the Jewish Torah), the Historical books, Prophets strictly so-called, and Wisdom literature. The Historical books include a group known to some Christians and Jews also as the "former prophets" (Joshua, Judges, 1 and 2 Samuel, and 1 and 2 Kings), along with the books of Chronicles, Ezra, and Nehemiah. Among the "latter prophets," known to most Christians simply as the prophetic texts, are the three major prophetic books, Isaiah, Jeremiah, and Ezekiel; the twelve "minor" (so-called because they are "shorter") prophets counted as one in the Hebrew scriptures; and Daniel. Finally, among those books known to Jews as the Writings is a set of works some Christians call "Wisdom literature," some traditionally attributed to David and his son Solomon, and the minianthology called the Five Scrolls (or *megillot*). Protestant versions call "apocryphal" seven texts that are part of Catholic versions of the Bible. Among these are the "historical" Books of Maccabees and the "wisdom" books Ecclesiasticus and Wisdom. Finally, Protestants and Catholics both call "apocryphal" three other short works, III and IV Esdras (Ezra) and the Prayer of Manasseh.

From the very beginning, the emergence of Christianity as a distinct tradition depended on the young community's exegesis of the Hebrew scriptures. Since the majority of the earliest Christians were Jewish by birth and education, they naturally regarded the Hebrew Bible as their own authoritative divine revelation. But the tradition of messianic expectation that had evolved especially in the later writings evoked continual scrutiny and reexamination among Jews everywhere: When would the Messiah come? And how was one to identify Him? Largely on the basis of their reading of scripture, the early followers of Jesus found the answers in Jesus. By a process that would come to be known as "typological exegesis," early Christians saw in numerous Old Testament personages, events, and institutions anticipations or "types" of Christ. Abraham, for example, was a type of God the Father in his willingness to sacrifice his only son, Isaac, who was in turn a type of Christ. Jonah's emergence from the belly of the whale was a type of Christ's resurrection from the grave. Typological exegetes saw in Jesus the perfection of realities only adumbrated in the Hebrew scriptures. Aaron's priesthood, for example, was merely temporary (as evidenced by the destruction of the Temple), but that of Christ is eternal (Hebrews 7). In addition to discerning these and other typological antecedents of Christ, interpreters saw in many prophetic writings veiled allusions to the Christ who was to come. In the "suffering servant" texts of Deutero-Isaiah, for example, early Christians detected such striking parallels to what they believed were the very essence of the life and death of Jesus that the prophet could only have been referring to this Messiah.[4] In the New Testament, Jesus suggests a parallel between himself and Isaiah's references to a Spirit-filled anointed one who preaches good news to the poor, frees the imprisoned, and heals the blind, and he likens himself to Elijah and Elisha (Luke 4:16–30). These are only a few of the ways in which early Christians found legitimacy for their views in Jewish tradition.

Since Christians consider the Old Testament integral to their revealed message, biblical exegetes have struggled to make sense of countless texts originally associated with the history of Israel. Even for Christians who have considered themselves the "New Israel," appropriating much of the historical record's specificity with respect to real estate, political power (or the lack thereof), and enemies long defunct requires more than a little exegetical dexterity. In "Annihilate Amalek: Christian Perspectives on 1 Samuel 15," Bernhard Asen explores Christian interpretations of an important Old Testament "text of terror" that mandates uncompromising violence against a perennial nemesis of Israel. He begins with an analysis of the context of 1 Samuel 15 before taking up the phenomenon of "total warfare" as articulated there and interpreted in subsequent scripture and tradition. He then reflects on how Christians have dealt, and might in the future deal, with the patrimony of such texts. In the process, Asen offers a fine example of how focusing on a single, arresting text exegetically can generate further reflection on the reality of large-scale violence in service of what religious communities might consider a divinely revealed mandate. Asen concludes with a reflection on related New Testament themes in a way that provides a transition to Leo Lefebure's essay.

Christianity and the New Testament

Two broad types of literature comprise the bulk of the uniquely Christian scripture. Among the earliest documents are the letters of Paul of Tarsus. Tradition attributes fourteen of the New Testament's twenty-seven "books" to Paul, but several were actually penned by later followers of Paul in his name as "letters from the dead." These writings function as a medium by which Paul could remain active "in spirit" among the Christian community. The largest and most important of the texts are addressed to local Christian communities collectively (Romans, 1 and 2 Corinthians, Galatians, Ephesians, Colossians, 1 and 2 Thessalonians, and Philippians). Four are addressed to individual Christian leaders with whom Paul worked (1 and 2 Timothy, Titus, Philemon). The addressees of the Letter to the Hebrews, almost certainly not written by Paul, are curiously diffuse and not geographically identifiable as the local churches are. These epistles provide a great deal of information about the spread and organization of the early Church, and, to a lesser degree, about the personality of this man of prodigious energy called Paul, a man some regard as the true "founder" of Christianity. Seven other letters, two attributed to Peter, three to John, one to James, and one to Jude, afford small glimpses into the variety of theological and practical issues facing the Christian "diaspora," the communities developing beyond the central Middle East.

At the heart of the Christian scriptures are four documents called "gospels" (from the Greek *euangelion,* "good news"). Mark's gospel, likely the earliest, is also the shortest of the four. Matthew's, addressed chiefly to those of Jewish background, and Luke's, addressed to a largely Gentile or Hellenistic readership, followed within the next twenty to thirty years. Luke's gospel also has the distinction of being part of the only consciously crafted two-volume work in the New Testament, since it is completed by Luke's account of the post-Jesus church in the Acts of the Apostles. Because of their similarity of perspective and emphases, the Gospels of Matthew, Mark, and Luke are called the "synoptic" Gospels. John's Gospel, often referred to as the most theological of the four, was almost certainly written later, around the end of the first century C.E. Last but not least is the Book of Revelation or the Apocalypse.

Christians believe the sacred texts collectively called the New Testament are divinely inspired, but composed by human authors. Some take that a step further, insisting that divine inspiration consisted of a literal transmission from God through the author, who communicated the message unaltered. As I have suggested above, early Christian exegesis of the Hebrew scriptures had already moved beyond merely literal interpretation. Though the literal meaning of the sacred text naturally remained the bedrock of exegesis, typological understandings of Jewish tradition soon developed into more specific varieties of figurative exegesis to be applied to the Greek as well as the Hebrew scriptures. Within a few generations of the death of the last people who actually lived during the time of Jesus, Christian literature gives evidence of what would eventually develop into the "literal" and the "spiritual" senses, the latter then branching into three types. Taken together, the four senses are the literal meaning *(historia);* the symbolic or figurative meaning *(allegoria);* the moral or ethical implication *(tropologia);* and the eschatological parallels, that is, what the text suggests about the goal of human life *(anagogia).* A simple but useful mnemonic rhyme helps keep the four levels of meaning straight: what our forebears did (history), where our faith is hid (allegory), rules for daily life (tropology), where we end our strife (anagogy). A good example of how major early Christian interpreters applied the four senses might be the four rivers of Paradise mentioned in Genesis 2:10–14. Their literal meaning is simply that of historical identity—the Pishon, Gihon, Tigris, and Euphrates rivers. On the figurative level, the rivers might symbolize the four gospels, the divine revelation fanning out to all the world's four directions. In addition, one might understand these four streams as the four cardinal virtues, prudence, justice, fortitude, and temperance. And finally, the earthly rivers have their heavenly counterparts in the Paradise awaiting true believers.

When Christians study their scriptures, they can take any of a number of approaches, as already suggested. A common pastoral approach nowadays reads the scriptures almost entirely as if they are addressed to twentieth-century Christians. They are thus in a way "timeless" and not subject to historical conditions. Another approach tries to get behind the words as much as possible to understand their meaning in their original context. This second approach by no means disregards the personal, pastoral, and deeply spiritual implications of the sacred text. Historical-critical scholarship looks, for example, at the differences in how even texts as generally concordant as the synoptic gospels show divergences in vocabulary, major themes, and the order of events in the life of Jesus, and points of view tailored to different audiences. It notes how the inspired authors, as much editors as original writers, interwove Jesus's words and actions, telescoping time and space. As skilled literary communicators, the inspired writers also made use of stylized scenes that followed predictable patterns in their description of the main actors, actions, and crowd responses. Combining analyses of the literary, linguistic, and historical elements, the historical-critical method seeks insight into how these documents, two millennia and many layers of culture removed from us, appear to speak in so many distinct voices about the same great spiritual reality. Underlying it all, the method suggests, are the unique theological insights granted to each of the sacred authors. Each offers a characteristic reflection on the deeper meaning of the "good news" and of Jesus the Christ. For Mark, Jesus was most of all the Suffering Servant; for Matthew, the Messiah; for Luke, the Savior guided through his life by the Holy Spirit; and for John, the Divine Son. These are not exclusive, but complementary insights. Unlike a predominantly spiritualized or pastoral method of interpretation, whose immediate concern is to deal with apparent inconsistencies among the sacred authors by "harmonizing" them into a seamless historical reconstruction, the historical-critical method seeks to understand the text in its original language as clearly as possible across an enormous chasm of time, space, and culture.

Against the backdrop of Christian ambivalence and a certain scriptural ambiguity with respect to violence, Leo Lefebure's "Violence in the New Testament and the History of Interpretation" examines a series of key texts within the major bodies of New Testament scripture. Beginning with the Synoptic gospels and moving through the Johannine literature, the Acts of the Apostles, the Pauline Epistles, and the Revelation, Lefebure pursues the theme of conflict, especially between the followers of Jesus and the prevailing religious establishment. Here a key theological element is the evolving Christian understanding of the relationship between the "new" revelation of the New Testament and the Mosaic/prophetic dispensation embodied in the Hebrew scriptures. In the second part of his essay, Lefebure addresses exegetical questions raised in the course of two millennia of Christian encounters with Jews, Muslims, and heretics. He concludes with a reflection on prospects for "Jews and Christians reading the New Testament together."

Islam, Qur'an, and Hadith

In about the year 610, Muhammad began to deliver orally the messages he believed were of divine origin. The Prophet's followers initially memorized his enunciations of the revelation, and, according to traditional accounts, the Qur'an was not produced in full written form until some years after Muhammad's death in 632. What began as "an Arabic recitation" retained that name even after it was written down, and the resulting book is still known as "The Recitation" or Qur'an.

The sacred scripture contains about 6200 verses, roughly equivalent in length to the New Testament, arranged in 114 sections called *suras*. Muhammad's earliest revelations tend to be short, rhetorically potent utterances in an ancient form of rhymed prose similar to the preferred idiom of pre-Islamic seers and soothsayers. Later suras tend to be lengthier and less poetic, and often take up more practical concerns. Suras are arranged in more or less descending order of length, so that many of the earlier sections are actually found in the latter part of the book. The heading of each sura contains the title, the number of verses, and an indication as to whether it was revealed at Mecca or Medina. Interpreters consider it very important to place each text historically, for the "circumstances of the revelation" are critical in unwrapping its original meaning. Tradition has identified the suras, or the portions of them where it is clear that a single sura is actually a composite, as either early, middle, or late Meccan (610–22), or Medinan (622–32). Muslims generally believe the Qur'an is the direct, literal word of God, unmodified in any way by the Prophet who uttered them at God's bidding.

Since the Islamic interpretation of history overlaps in significant ways with those of Judaism and Christianity, one should not be surprised to find that some material in the Qur'an parallels biblical material. Some narrative treatments of various biblical patriarchs and kings, whom the Qur'an identifies as prophets and messengers, immediately recall aspects of biblical accounts. But there are also interesting variations in the stories. Adam and Eve's fall, for example, is sometimes connected with eating from a forbidden tree, but alternatively with eating an ear of wheat. Sprinkled throughout the scripture are references to Abraham's near sacrifice of his son (whom Islamic tradition takes to be Ishmael rather than Isaac) and to Moses's mission to Pharaoh, David's musical gifts, Solomon's royal grandeur, and other variant narratives. Perhaps the single most important parallel is the story of Joseph. Sura 12 of the Qur'an retells the tale found in Genesis 39–50 with its own distinctive flavor and variations in detail. Only Joseph's story is told in its entirety, and all in a single sura dedicated solely to it.

Jewish and Christian readers have often concluded that Muhammad "borrowed" from the Bible, but Muslim tradition views the situation very differently. The way the Qur'an tells the stories, mostly in short excerpts and allusions, suggests that Muhammad's listeners must have been already familiar with at least the general drift of the narratives. There are also some accounts of nonbiblical prophetic figures, called Hūd, Sālih, and Shuayb, which are in some ways unique to the Arabian peninsula. It is important to note that Muslim tradition has discerned in both the Old and New Testaments references to the coming of Islam's prophet. God promised to raise up for Israel a prophet like Moses (Deuteronomy 18:18), namely Muhammad. The prophet Isaiah sees two riders approaching, one on a donkey and the other on a camel: Jesus and Muhammad. Jesus promised to send a *parakletos* ("advocate," John 14:16), but Muslim commentators argue that with the correct vowels, the Greek word is *periklutos,* meaning "highly praised," the exact meaning of *muhammad* in Arabic.[5]

Second only to the Qur'an in both authority and antiquity is the large body of works containing sayings attributed to Muhammad, along with hundreds of anecdotes about him. This material is known collectively as Hadith (sayings or traditions). When Muhammad died, neither the scripture nor the Prophet's words and deeds had been formally committed to writing. And even long after the Qur'an had been carefully edited, Muslims hesitated to produce written versions of Muhammad's sayings. Custodians of these Prophetic Traditions kept them by heart, much as the earliest followers had preserved the Qur'an.

Not until some two centuries after Muhammad died did his community deem it necessary to gather and edit the Hadith on a large scale into "canonical" collections. The impetus to do so came in part from legal scholars, who believed that the only way to interpret the spirit of the Qur'an faithfully in cases not explicitly treated in the scripture was to have a sound testimony of the Prophet's own views. Through much of the ninth century, Muslim religious scholars undertook the massive task of traveling widely and gathering and recording thousands of Hadiths from countless individuals known for their reliable memories. These scholars, often working independently and at some distance in time and space, then sifted through what they had gathered. Since the very existence of this treasure trove depended on its oral transmission from one generation to another, scholars looked first at the chains of transmission to see whether all the individuals listed were trustworthy. If they were not, one could reasonably dismiss the Hadith itself as not entirely reliable. By the end of the ninth century, half a dozen authoritative collections of the Hadith were available (and many lesser ones as well), complete with scholarly evaluation of the relative soundness of each saying and anecdote. Muslims traditionally consider the content of the Hadith to be divinely inspired, though expressed in Muhammad's own words, unlike the Qur'an, which is in God's own diction.[6]

Discussion of the Qur'an is a regular activity in most mosques, usually in connection with the Friday congregational prayer (which, in the United States, is also sometimes held on Sundays). One or more discussion leaders might present a text and then open the floor to comments and questions. The first concern is generally to establish the "circumstances of the revelation." What was the specific occasion on which this particular text was revealed to Muhammad? Was it revealed in connection with any unusual or momentous event? Was it a direct response to some question or predicament that had arisen in the early Muslim community? Contemporary Muslims can dip into an enormous reservoir of traditional scholarship for help in interpreting the Qur'an. Exegetes began compiling detailed and extensive commentaries on the sacred scripture at least as early as the eighth century. They refined the tools of a specialty called *tafsir*, "explanation, elaboration." Scores of multivolume works in Arabic (plus countless more in various other languages) of great antiquity and authority are still widely available from publishers of Islamic books, and many are now being translated into Western languages. Classical commentators and modern-day interpreters alike look first to the Hadith for help on obscure passages of the Qur'an, for Muhammad himself often responded to questions about specific texts. Careful study of Arabic grammar and a wide knowledge of other works of Arabic literature for purposes of comparison are also essential background for professional exegetes. In addition to elucidating the basic or literal meanings of a sacred text, Qur'an commentary can also probe into further levels of meaning. Muslim mystics especially have written allegorical or symbolic interpretations, often referred to as *ta'wil* (from a root connoting "retrieval of original meanings"), to uncover the deeper spiritual implications of the scripture.[7]

Most readers of this volume will be aware of a variety of narratives that underscore "distinctively Islamic" views of religiously sanctioned violence. An essential element in such narratives concerns the identity of those whom Muslims are purportedly enjoined to despise, fight, or kill. Michael Sells's chapter, "Finhās of Medina: Islam, 'The Jews,' and the Construction of Religious Militancy," addresses the assumptions that drive militant interpretations of the Islamic teachings regarding Jews. As a test case, Sells explores two qur'anic statements that some contemporary Muslim militants view as divine condemnation of Jews. The first part of Q 5:64 reads, "The Yahūd say the hand of God is bound. May their hands be bound and may they be cursed by [through, on account of] what they said"; and the first part of Q 3:181 reads, "We have heard the words of those who said we are rich and

God is poor." Sells begins by asking about the text's "frame of reference." Early historical reports passed down from the companions of Muhammad suggest that it was one man named Finhās, or that it was Finhās in conjunction with a few others, who uttered the two statements quoted and criticized in the Qur'an. Sells argues that the Finhās reports provide an influential frame of reference in qur'anic exegesis over a period of several hundred years. Even exegetes with an anti-Jewish agenda reproduced these reports that radically undermine the notion of a generic divine condemnation of Jews as a people by specifying one or a handful of Jewish elders as those subject to the divine rebuke. Even if we doubt the authenticity of the Finhās reports, Sells suggests, we are left with the question: what then was the frame of reference? When the original frame of reference is forgotten, Sells demonstrates, the way is paved for militant interpretations that portray sacred texts as propounding divinely ordained conflict between unchanging, monolithic groups—in this instance, between Muslims and Jews. The consequences of forgetting that group names are spoken (even within divine revelation) under specific conditions and with specific frames of reference are, Sells argues, enormous.

Baha'i Tradition

On May 23, 1844, a young Persian (Iranian) merchant named Sayyid Ali Muhammad (1819–50) proclaimed himself the recipient of a long-promised divine message. He assumed the title of the Bab (Arabic for "gate" or "door") and announced that his mission was to prepare the way for the fulfillment of this world-transforming revelation. In his principal writing, the *Bayan* (Clarification, Elucidation), the Bab announced or foretold the imminent arrival of a new and more important messenger who would teach a way of reform and reconciliation to the world's major faith traditions. His religious mission also involved bringing Islam to its fulfillment while superseding the Qur'an's injunctions. Despite understanding himself as the messenger for the advent of another, greater teacher, the Bab's followers and those who would identify themselves later as Baha'is saw the Bab's revelation as a distinct and independent, though short-lived, revelation. During his brief public ministry, the Bab's message elicited considerable opposition. He was imprisoned in 1847 and was executed three years later, becoming a martyr of the new "Babi" tradition or "dispensation." One of the Bab's crucial texts, composed in proclamation of his mission in 1844, is his commentary on the qur'anic story of the prophet Joseph (sura 12), on which Todd Lawson comments in his chapter.

At a gathering in 1849, a follower of the Bab named Mirza Husayn Ali (1817–92) took the name Baha' (later to become known as Baha' Allah, Splendor of God). After assuming a leadership role among the Babis following the Bab's imprisonment, Baha' (Mirza Husayn Ali) had to contend with the increasing persecution of the community by Persian authorities. He endured imprisonment in Tehran when he gave himself as ransom for the Babi community, and went into exile in Baghdad in 1853. There the Babi community grew under his tutelage, and there he wrote the Persian "Book of Certitude" *(Kitab-i Iqan)*. In 1863, Baha' publicly identified himself as the messenger whom the Bab had predicted. Once again, opposition forced him into a five-year exile in Turkey, during which he wrote a major Arabic text, the "Most Holy Book" *(al-Kitab al-Aqdas)*. Released from confinement, Baha' migrated to what is now northern Israel/Palestine (in the environs of Haifa, the site of the world headquarters of the Baha'i faith), where he would spend the rest of his life. Before his death in 1892, Baha' appointed his eldest son, Abd al-Baha' (1844–1921), who according to tradition was born on the very day that the Bab announced that he had been called to proclaim a new message of truth, as the center of his cause and its final authority. Also known as Abbas Effendi, Abd al-Baha' presided over major developments in Baha'i religion, including the spread of the faith to Europe and America. Among his major writings are the fourteen-part Tablets of the Divine Plan, addressed to the growing American Baha'i community. Like his father, Abd al-Baha' suffered seasons of persecution and died in Haifa.

Abd al-Baha's grandson Shoghi Effendi (1857–1957), the first and only "Guardian of the Cause of God" *(wali amr Allah),* was largely responsible for the translation and dissemination of Baha'i sacred texts, the consolidation and growth of the international Baha'i community, and the beautification of the Baha'i holy places in Haifa and its environs. All Baha'is have access to the core writings in the form of books and numerous compilations and anthologies excerpting letters, proclamations, prayers, and testimonies of the foundational figures, much of which has been translated into dozens of the major languages of the world. Today, the affairs of the Baha'i faith are the responsibility of a three-level administrative system: Local Spiritual Assemblies, National Spiritual Assemblies, and, at the top, the Universal House of Justice, whose headquarters is in Haifa.[8]

Todd Lawson's essay, "The Return of Joseph and the Peaceable Imagination," studies the Baha'i scriptural theme of peace in the face of violence. Baha'i tradition stands out in the present context in that a central theme in its earliest texts is the promotion of harmony. Ironically, the original teaching suggests, religion itself is all too often the cause of disharmony. Sacred sources understand violence writ large as a key to the scenario of divine engagement with humanity through a long succession of prophets, continuing through the Bab, all of whom were violently rejected by a majority of the people to whom God sent them. In the first section of his contribution, Lawson provides a literary-theological overview of key ingredients in the Baha'i vision of the prophetic mission. He introduces the reader to the distinctively Baha'i understanding of a divinely inspired mode of living in the world, with explicit reference to the tradition's dramatic response to the classic Islamic concept of justifiable struggle *(jihād)*. The second section of the essay illustrates an intriguing aspect of Baha'i "exegesis" of the qur'anic story of the prophet Joseph, the ultimate human symbol of the divine qualities of patience, forbearance, and wisdom. Lawson follows up by exploring Baha'i tradition's further explicit analysis of Joseph as the paradigm of the "true" *mujahid,* understood not as "warrior" but as "seeker." He concludes with reflections on Baha'i interpretation of the larger global setting, again with reference to the classic Islamic juxtaposition of the era of *jahl* (the world before final revelation) and the age blessed with the Baha'i reinterpretation of divine disclosure.

Zoroastrianism

The core beliefs that have come to be identified as Zoroastrianism date even from before the Achaemenid monarchy (c. 550–330 B.C.E.), which many Iranians still associate with the origins of their nation. Visitors to the ruins of Persepolis today can still see 2500-year-old icons of the Zoroastrian faith, such as images of the winged human figure of the deity Ahura Mazda. The roots of Zoroastrian tradition, however, go back considerably further in time and farther to the northeast geographically. Scholars generally consider a "prophet" named Zarathushtra (Zoroaster, modern Persian Zardosht) the tradition's foundational figure, and date him to between 1800 and 1500 B.C.E. In what is now northwestern Central Asia and northern Afghanistan, amid a culture of warrior-heroes (whose stories are still vividly recounted), cattle, goat, and sheep herding pastoralists, and settled agriculturalists in the Bactrian Bronze Age, Zarathushtra preached against practices designed to stoke the ire of men bound for combat. Unlike other cults of the surrounding region, Zoroastrian theology evolved as a blend of monotheism and dualism.

The principal textual collection that comprises the main Zoroastrian scripture is a complex anthology called the Avesta. Assembled finally sometime between 300 and 500 C.E., but reflecting a much older and well-preserved oral tradition, the Avesta includes a variety of genres and themes in its four large parts and half a dozen minor texts. First is a collection of liturgical hymns called the Yasna (sacrifice, or worshipful deeds), within which is a set of seventeen hymns attributed directly to Zarathushtra, called the Gāthās. Part 2 of the Avesta, the Yashts, hymns the praises of twenty-one lofty beings, including divine powers, angels, and ancient Iranian heroes. Mithra, who went on to become the center of a major cult in parts of the Roman Empire, stands out among these figures. A twenty-two-chapter work known as the Videvdad comprises a set of instructions for warding off evil forces *(daivas).* Among the several lesser texts is an assortment of hymns, litanies, a month's worth of daily prayers, and blessings. Perhaps the most important of these is the Khorda, known as the "Little (or Short) Avesta," because it gathers selections of prayers from elsewhere in the larger scriptural anthology. Scholars suggest that the canon was set around 325 C.E.

In addition to the core scriptures, a small library of texts in the Middle Persian language known as the Pahlavi books was collected in western Iran between the ninth and twelfth centuries C.E. by magi or Zoroastrian priests. Their goal was twofold: to preserve their hitherto orally transmitted exegetical traditions; and to answer new concerns arising among the laity and priesthood as Zoroastrianism (formerly the demographically dominant faith in Iran) dwindled to a minority religion under the Islamic caliphates. The principal Middle Persian texts include a major source of exegetical material called the Zand (interpretation), dating from centuries before the Pahlavi books, as well as elaborations of cosmogonic, cosmological, and eschatological myth and theory. One of these texts referred to prominently in Jamsheed Choksy's contribution to this volume is the Bundahishn, a cosmogonic text. Zoroastrian texts in a variety of other languages developed among the minority communities in Iran as well as the diaspora communities of India.

Although the relatively small number of Zoroastrians living today too often leaves the tradition out of consideration in surveys of "world religions," important Zoroastrian concepts have made their way into the theological lexicons of other traditions, particularly the Abrahamic ones. During important developmental and transitional periods of Zoroastrianism's history, the tradition influenced Jewish, Christian, and Islamic thought. Prominent among cross-traditional concepts are eschatological themes and related notions of retribution, apocalyptic scenarios, and characterizations of good and evil forces such as angels and demons.[9]

In "Justifiable Force and Holy War in Zoroastrianism," Jamsheed Choksy introduces the reader to an important theme in the tradition's sacred texts, as well as to the major elements in the broader historical and theological contexts essential to the interpretation of that theme. Coming to the fore are teachings of Zarathushtra's principal spiritual descendants, the magi, concerning the contest of cosmic forces of good and evil, particularly as represented respectively by the deity Ahura Mazda and Angra Mainyu, the leader of the hordes of chaos. Drawing from all the formative periods of Zoroastrian history, from Achaemenid times through Late Antiquity and medieval times, Choksy provides a superb overview of the tradition, concluding with a brief reflection on implications for adherents of the faith in our time.

Hinduism

At the origins of the long history of Hindu scriptures stands a set of texts called the Vedas. They consist of four distinct collections of texts, each with its own distinctive purpose. The name *Veda* comes from a Sanskrit root meaning "wisdom" or "vision," the same root that gives us English words like *video*. According to tradition, "seers," called *rishis,* composed the texts and communicated them orally. The *rishis* were able to see the truths revealed to them because they were also "hearers" of the sacred word. In fact, Hindu tradition groups the most sacred of its scriptures in the category of "that which is heard" *(shruti)* to distinguish them from a secondary level of revelation called "that which is remembered" *(smriti)*. The Vedas evolved over a period of centuries, and religious specialists eventually wrote them down in an ancient form of Sanskrit. The earliest and most important of the four scriptures is called the Rig Veda, an anthology of more than a thousand hymns to various deities. A second collection, called the Sama Veda, includes material from the Rig edited for ease of ritual use according to melodies and poetic meters. In the Yajur Veda, the early priesthood gathered the most important sacred mantras. A final collection of ritual incantations makes up the Atharva Veda. Many of the Vedic hymns are especially beautiful and offer a unique insight into how the early ritual specialists who made up the priesthood sought to understand and affect their world through contact with forces beyond human control.

Over a span of perhaps two thousand years (c. 3000 to 1000 B.C.E., according to some Indian scholars), Hindu ritual specialists produced a substantial body of sacred literature by way of commentary and reflection on the Vedas. The earliest of these works, the Brahmanas, were manuals for priests, which were each attached to one of the four Vedas. These texts elaborated on the mythic stories to which the Vedic hymns often had made only passing allusions, expanding on the tradition much as the early Jewish rabbis had developed the oral Torah. The Brahmanas served the practical purpose of recording for posterity precise directions for correct ritual performance. Still another layer of scriptural development gave rise to a series of works called Aranyakas, "Forest Treatises." Composed by and for hermits, these texts offered further commentary on the Vedas meant to foster the contemplative life. Aranyakas were connected with the Brahmanas much as the Brahmanas were linked to the various Vedas. With their emphasis on inward reflection, the Aranyakas signal an important turn away from the ancient Vedic and Brahmanical reliance on external ritual. Another type of sacred text called the Upanishads evolved from about 1500 to 500 B.C.E. The name *upa-ni-shad* means, loosely, "sitting at the feet of" a mentor. These remarkable documents, many in the form of a dialogue between teacher and student, reflect deeply on the nature of the divine and of the self. Life's true meaning rests not primarily in dealing with forces beyond human control, but in understanding both the ultimate causes of all things and the relationship of the self to those causes. The Upanishads represent major developments known collectively as Vedanta, the "end or culmination of the Vedas."

During the so-called Classical Period (500 B.C.E. to 500 C.E.) especially, various denominations developed their own distinctive sacred texts called *sutras* (threads, aphorisms), *shastras* (treatise, rule), and *agamas* (what has come down). Sutras often take the form of commentary on earlier major texts and are key sources for the six philosophical schools called the *darshanas* (views). Some philosophical texts are called *shastras,* but this category is best known as a vehicle for treatments of religious law. *Agamas* belonging to the various sects often include material ranging from the mythic to the epic to the philosophical. Shaivites generally use the term *agama* to describe their twenty-eight canonical works, while Vaishnavite communities often call their unique scriptures *samhitas* (collections) and Shakta groups prefer the term *Tantra.*[10]

Laurie Patton's contribution to this volume focuses on a sacred text that has long been a central feature of the religious traditions of India's Vaishnavite communities. The Bhagavad Gita (Song of the Blessed Lord) is now nestled within the Mahabharata (Great India), one of Hinduism's two major epics—yet another important category of sacred Hindu texts. The Gita was a particular favorite, and long-time spiritual focus, of Mahatma Gandhi, who made it his task to explain how a sacred text set in the context of war represented an invitation to peace. In the context of the history of variant approaches to the meaning of the Gita, in which the supreme deity enjoins killing even one's kin for the sake of duty *(dharma),* Patton explores the underpinnings of Gandhi's complex attempt to reconcile deity and destruction by means of allegorical/metaphorical exegesis, and concludes that such an approach is ultimately less than convincing. She proposes in its place an "ethical interpretive dynamism around the question of necessary force," and "an alternative hermeneutic that moves away from Indian philosophical approaches and is grounded instead in Indian aesthetic theory." In the process, Patton points indirectly to a problem shared by interpreters of virtually all the great scriptural traditions: to what extent can one credibly resort to spiritualized readings of sacred texts rendered morally ambiguous—or downright scandalous—by changing religious and cultural contexts?

Sikh Tradition

Sikh tradition began in the late fifteenth century in the region of Punjab, which now comprises both a major Pakistani province and an important northwestern Indian state. In an era of increasing Muslim-Hindu tension and violence, various religious leaders of the Sant (poet-saints) tradition of North India struggled to forge links between the two major traditions. Nanak (1469–1539) was born in a religious environment suffused with the thought of the North Indian Sants along with the Hindu and Islamic traditions. He shared both the mystic and iconoclastic tendencies of Sants such as Kabir (1398–1448), Ravidas (1450–1520), and Namdev (1270–1350). Reared in the Hindu Khatri (or Kshatriya, "warrior caste") tradition, Nanak rejected certain aspects of traditional Hindu structures of authority, including the centrality of the Vedas and the caste system. His first pronouncement after his mystical experience was: "There is no Hindu, there is no Muslim." To a society torn with conflict, he brought a vision of common humanity and intercommunal harmony.

Nanak gradually acquired a following of his own that became the core of the original Sikh community. He was acknowledged as the first of what would be a succession of ten "Gurus" whose teachings form the foundations of Sikh teaching. Nanak's devotional songs *(shabads)* and the poetic *Japji* (recitation), which functions as a summary of Sikh principles, came to form part of the chief sacred text, the Adi (first) Granth (or Guru Granth Sahib) written chiefly in Punjabi. Poetic-musical works by Nanak's first four successor Gurus form the second major segment of the scripture. Part 3 of the Adi Granth is in effect an anthology of short works that comment on the musical *ragas* of part 2, and that include devotional hymns from Hindu *bhakti* and Sufi traditions. It enshrines poems of Kabir as well as the works of poets from as early as the twelfth century and as late as Tegh Bahadur (1621–75), the ninth Sikh Guru. In addition to the Adi Granth, Sikhs revere a secondary collection of quasi-hagiographic narratives attributed to Gobind Singh, the Tenth Guru (1666–1708), known as the Dasam (tenth) Granth.

Sikh tradition constructs the principal framework of scriptural revelation and interpretation as an unbroken succession of the Ten Gurus. Within that framework, Sikhs (literally, "disciples") understand the Adi Granth as itself a "guru" in written book form. Each of the living gurus represents the highest echelon in religious teaching authority for the individual seeker. Together the succession of Gurus establishes a pattern that recommends to each believer the need of expert guidance in the interpretation of the sacred sources and the path of *bhakti*, intense devotion to God alone. Under the first four Gurus, Nanak, Angad (1504–52), Amar Das (1479–1574), and Ram Das (1534–81), Sikh tradition recommended practices such as vegetarianism, and the role of the Guru tended to be rather private and devoted to spiritual pursuits, though there is ample evidence that the Gurus often spoke out unambiguously against the injustices of the ruling Muslim dynasts. Arjun (1563–1606), who compiled the Adi Granth around 1604, worked more publicly to establish the Sikh community financially and institutionally, thereby enabling it to assert itself more forcefully when necessary. His involvement in mundane affairs roused the enmity of the Muslim Mughal ruler Jahangir and landed Arjun in prison, where he died. According to some readings of traditional sources, before his imprisonment Arjun succeeded in setting his son Hargobind (1595–1644) on a more activist path, including a distinctly martial bent.

Gurus seven and eight—Har Rai (1630–61) and Harkrishan (1656–64)—soft-pedaled the militaristic tone in the interest of avoiding conflict with the emperor Aurangzeb. That tone once again tilted toward greater militancy when Hindu pleas persuaded Tegh Bahadur to confront the Mughal ruler, who had the ninth Guru imprisoned and executed. Finally, Guru Gobind Singh's signal role involved turning the Sikh spirit more wholeheartedly to the defense of justice and the community into a formidable military force. Symbolizing that transformation, Guru Gobind inaugurated the Khalsa (the pure) and instructed all male Sikhs to take the surname Singh (lion). Gobind Singh initiated an elite into the Khalsa through investiture with a set of five symbols and a regime of dietary and ethical principles befitting warriors. In the end, he proclaimed himself to be the last of Ten Gurus.[11]

In "Words as Weapons: Theory and Practice of a Righteous War in Sikh Texts," Pashaura Singh takes the reader on a brief tour through the genealogical history of the Gurus with examples of their contributions to, and interpretation of, the sacred texts. He explores several sacred sources beyond the two Granths, embracing a wide range of literary forms and theological perspectives, anchoring his analysis in the broader context of Mughal political history. Singh traces developing Sikh understandings of violence, one of the "four rivers of fire" (along with attachment, greed, and anger), as the community's complex relationships with political power evolved over several centuries. In a marvelous minisurvey of the late medieval and early modern history of South Asia, Pashaura Singh brings out the intriguing range of metaphorical language Sikh author-teachers fashioned to address the hard realities of a world in which outward physical violence too often threatened to distract religious seekers from the essential inward struggle of the spiritual quest. He ends the body of his study with a brief discussion of "five varieties of exegesis" that aptly sums up his main themes and highlights the complexities and multiple, often competing narratives of Sikh history.

GLIMPSES OF SHARED FEATURES
IN THE SCRIPTURED TRADITIONS

Three large unifying features emerge from this broad overview of diverse scriptures and exegetical traditions: first, several thematic characteristics evident in scriptural treatments of violence; second, common literary genres and forms within both holy writ and exegetical traditions; and finally, several shared methodological concerns.

Function and Theme: The Language of Violence in Scripture

Broadly speaking, one can identify two large categories of texts concerning violence in scriptural traditions: descriptive and prescriptive/prohibitive. *Descriptive* texts include a variety of genres that, in general, involve three sorts of scenario. First, mythical struggles attending a religion's cosmogony typically feature divine or elemental powers in conflict, as in some major texts of both the Zoroastrian and Hindu traditions. Second, stories of "historical" wars and battles considered essential to a faith community's master narrative of emergence and establishment are key elements in, for example, Jewish and Sikh texts and, in a slightly different key, the Qur'an's recounting of the often violent rejection of prophetic messengers over the millennia. Third, descriptions of gathering, imminent, or otherwise inevitable conflagration on a cosmic scale constitute a characteristic ingredient of many eschatological or apocalyptic visions in traditions such as Christianity, Islam, and Zoroastrianism. Texts of this kind do not necessarily condone *or* condemn recourse to violence as such. Sacred sources typically describe cosmogonic and apocalyptic conflicts as simply the way things are, necessary facts of existence in the great divine dispensation. Description of historical conflict, on the other hand, may go beyond mere chronicling of a faith community's struggles by emphasizing divine guidance, approval, or disapproval (as I will discuss shortly), or by identifying participation in violent conflict as a necessary element in the community's existence. Given its essential role, such violence is often characterized as a laudable, heroic mark of cooperation with the divine plan.

By contrast, some key texts are *prescriptive or prohibitive.* All of the traditions represented in this collection address the complex questions of whether, under what circumstances, to what extent, and by what means the community of believers is to resort to the use of violence in service of their religious beliefs. This is often couched in terms of *sacrality,* one's sacred or ritual obligations. In several of these traditions (e.g., Jewish, Islamic, Hindu, and Zoroastrian), violence in sacred scripture is intimately connected to intimations of the deity as sovereign in every respect, including the freedom to enjoin violence under a variety of circumstances for the deity's own inscrutable purposes.

From both descriptive and prescriptive texts, one can discern common thematic threads running through the many scripture traditions. From among these I will highlight as an example the way some scriptures tend to characterize those engaged in violence divinely sanctioned. There is a consistent and widespread tendency to devise a language by which to characterize in precise terms the religious status of those who wade into the fray in service of their faith and especially the status of those who die in the process. Some traditions call these agents "holy warriors," or some rough equivalent thereof, and those who sacrifice their lives are "martyrs" or "heroes." Zoroastrian tradition, for example, with its elevation of many divine and human beings as great warriors in the cosmic battle against evil, illustrates this point vividly.

Not surprisingly, the "other," the enemy in each context, is typically identified in some way as an embodiment of evil. Scriptures often couch this assessment in the language of the deity's broad dispensation, in which the "other" functions as an object of retribution, divine justice, or apocalyptic scourge. Three other important thematic elements are worth brief mention here. In some traditions, violence has a sacral function, such as appeasing the divinity in the ritual sacrifices of Judaism, or cosmic purging in Zoroastrianism and some traditions of Christianity, or even spiritual growth or elevation, as in the Bhagavad Gita of Hinduism. In other instances, such as in the Baha'i and early Christian traditions, it is nonviolence that most embodies the sacred. In either case, a fundamental theme for these traditions within their sacred writ is the sacral nature of violence. In addition, violence is often connected to *revelation*. Religiously legitimated violence (too often unhelpfully reduced to the concept of "holy war") naturally appears frequently in these chapters and the scriptures about which they write. It is this "revealed" authority that so often underlies recourse to such "texts of terror" throughout history. This theme is intimately related to that of "othering" so often encountered in sacred texts, and Sells addresses the issue directly with respect to the precise identity of *al-Yahūd* in his central qur'anic text. Sells explores from an Islamic perspective a question raised in Asen's essay—namely the tendency to identify a group named in scripture (in this instance, the Amalekites) as the quintessential enemy who reappears in other guises throughout history. Finally, as Patton and Choksy (among others) suggest, the language of violence is often couched in narrative frameworks that give meaning and structure to the violence. Some traditions, in other words, see certain forms of violence as a dramatic—even performative—aspect of the larger cosmogonic process.

Genre and Form in Scripture and Exegesis

The sacred texts of the world's scriptured traditions embrace a broad range of literary genres, both in the scriptures themselves and in their often extensive libraries of exegetical literature. The following is only a sample of the more prominent of these genres.

First, narrative forms (typically in prose) include a rich variety of "historical" texts. Within the Hebrew scriptures/Old Testament, prime examples are the five books of the Torah/Pentateuch, and the "historical" books, as well as the "apocryphal" books of Maccabees. The Christian tradition's central texts are largely narrative in structure—the four gospels, Acts of the Apostles, and Revelation all fall into this category. Important segments of the Qur'an—composed largely in a distinctive literary type somewhere between prose and poetry known as "rhymed prose" *(saj')*—provide narratives of previous prophets' roles in the divine dispensation. These texts are generally short ad hoc homiletical exempla rather than detailed expositions of sacred history. Of special note are the distinctively Islamic genres of Hadith and *Sīra* (prophetic biography), whose exegetical sections include many narrative segments employed in discussions of the "occasions of revelation."

In general, the kind of *descriptive* violence so abundant in Jewish historical and Christian and Zoroastrian mythic/apocalyptic accounts is rare in the Qur'an. Narrative forms play an important role in Hindu tradition as well, especially as represented by the two major epics, the Ramayana and the Mahabharata, both filled with episodes of conflict. Finally, a number of frankly "hagiographic" texts find a place in the larger category of narrative. Here the Sikh, Zoroastrian, and Baha'i traditions are especially well represented.

Second, we find across the world's scriptures a rich variety of poetic compositions. In this context, the Psalms, along with extensive sections of the "latter" prophets and "wisdom" literature ("Writings") in the Hebrew Bible/Old Testament, devote considerable attention to questions of war and peace. Virtually the whole of the New Testament is prose, but poetic forms are represented in Hinduism's Vedas, Zoroastrian devotional Gāthās and Yashts, and Sikh Guru Nanak's prayerful songs. An important component of the scriptures of all these traditions are hymns, typically poetic in form, and almost always functioning as prayers, chiefly of praise but also of supplication.

A third essential genre is what one might call homiletical or predicatory discourse. A good example of this is the prophetic literature from the Hebrew Bible (such as Samuel's chastisement of Saul, which is discussed in Asen's article). Later Hebrew prophetic texts whose theme is violence (such as Isaiah, which is discussed in Firestone's article) also exemplify this genre.

In a number of traditions' scriptures, one also encounters texts either explicitly legal in themselves or directly implicated in the community's elaboration of legal and ethical codes. The books of the Torah/Pentateuch, particularly the books of Exodus, Leviticus, and Deuteronomy, are rich in such texts. Christian scriptures, on the other hand, include relatively few legal texts, with the possible exception of more generally ethical gospel texts such as the Beatitudes or segments of the epistolary texts such as Romans and Corinthians. Some texts in the Qur'an, in particular some of the later "Medinan" suras, provide explicit prescriptive guidance in daily personal comportment as well as community governance and ritual.

Many traditions regard scripture as the first and best commentary on itself, but nearly all of those represented here have witnessed the evolution of interpretive traditions, some quite voluminous and still growing. Beyond the scriptural corpora strictly so-called are the often vast collections of expressly "exegetical" literature. Of the seven historic traditions represented here, four stand out for the breadth and depth of their production of exegetical literature. Beginning relatively soon after the definitive formation and closure of their "canons" and extending over many centuries, Judaism, Christianity, Islam, and Hinduism have all generated vast libraries of texts dedicated to the sole purpose of elaborating on a set of divinely originated scriptures. Over nearly two millennia, Jewish scholars recorded their reflections on Tanakh. Early on, these were organized in thematic works of the sort that turned into the Mishna and eventually the Talmud. Commentary organized more directly according to the texts of individual books of scripture emerged in creations such as the Midrash Rabbah, for example, in which one commentary is dedicated to each of the five books of Moses, and in which there is another set of midrashim on the five Megillot (scrolls, part of the Writings). Line-by-line commentary followed, particularly during medieval times, in the works of outstanding exegetes such as Rashi.

Christian authors similarly began commenting on their sacred texts thematically during the early Patristic period, but by the fourth and fifth century, Church Fathers such as Origen, Hippolytus, and Augustine began the tradition of producing exegetical works on individual biblical books. That tradition continued through medieval and Reformation times with major classics such as those by Thomas Aquinas, Martin Luther, and John Calvin. The seventeenth century was even more prolific than the sixteenth in this regard, and the production of exegetical literature continues unabated to this day. In Islamic tradition, the earliest specific commentary on the Qur'an came in the form of Muhammad's responses to queries about the meaning of specific texts, responses enshrined in the Hadith.[12] Muslim exegetes, it appears, had recourse to verse-by-verse commentary perhaps earlier in their history than either Jews or Christians. Michael Sells addresses exegetical sources, along with the importance of an early sacred biography, the *Sira* or Life story of Muhammad.

Hinduism, representing as it does one of the most expansive and variegated of all scriptural traditions, has produced a commentarial literature equally vast. With respect to the text studied here in Laurie Patton's essay, commentaries devoted to the relatively brief Bhagavad Gita have been penned by virtually all the great theologians, even through our own time. By contrast, the Zoroastrian, Baha'i, and Sikh traditions have developed comparably fewer explicitly "commentarial" forms through which to plumb the depths of texts understood more narrowly as "scripture." As Todd Lawson points out in his essay, Baha'i sacred sources themselves arguably compose a kind of unique exegesis of Islamic texts, both the Qur'an and Hadith. Zoroastrian exegetical commentary is especially represented in the work entitled the *Zand,* "Interpretation."

The Many Senses of Scripture: Hermeneutics and Exegetical Styles

One can find evidence of a number of similar hermeneutical principles and exegetical "types" across several major traditions. Perhaps the most pertinent exegetical modes in relation to this volume's central topic are variations on "literal" or historical interpretation, on the one hand, and the several kinds of "spiritual" or symbolic interpretation such as the typological, allegorical, ethical, or teleological/eschatological, on the other. Literalist or historical interpretations of scriptural texts on religiously sanctioned warfare, whatever the faith tradition, deal rather straightforwardly with the question of when and under what circumstances the use of large-scale violence was and is justified. As Firestone, for example, indicates, the rabbis addressed the problem by defining war as either "discretionary" (or defensive) or "commanded" (or offensive). They then argued that according to the (Palestinian) Talmud, the latter type was no longer possible because it applied only to Joshua's wars of conquest. Twentieth-century circumstances dramatically altered views of war. Muslim exegetes argued the question of legitimacy through premodern times, adducing similar reasons for restraint in general; but in our day, the recognition of constraints has again fallen victim to larger geopolitical dynamics.

An important variant on the quest for literal, historical, or outward/apparent meanings is the phenomenon of legal or juristic exegesis, which draws out implications for behavior required of, or to be avoided by, believers in defense of the faith or in imposing it on others. Firestone shows how Rabbinic Judaism made use of this technique in understanding its own relation to violence in the wake of historical events by making the legal requirements of war nearly impossible to fulfill. He shows, in addition, how that legal understanding was overturned during the founding of modern Israel as a nation-state. Material in this volume's chapter on Islam also resonates with the question of whether a reference to "the Jew" is to be identified as a specific person or a collective. A related exegetical concern is that of connecting specific texts with historical circumstances and making that connection the fulcrum of one's interpretation.

Christian interpreters of the Old Testament have, not surprisingly, taken a different approach to the scripture's "texts of terror," with their predominantly descriptive violence, as well as to apparently prescriptive texts. Though Christians over the centuries have expended great energy developing theories of "just war," the "literal" meanings of biblical warfare have been of lesser importance to Christians. In addition to discussing various theological implications of violence and power in the context of Israel's emerging monarchy, Bernhard Asen's essay introduces (at least implicitly) a "spiritual" reading of scriptural violence by exploring Christian exegesis of the prophets Malachi, Zechariah, and, in particular, Isaiah. One can also discern a hint of typological exegesis that sees in the Old Testament arch-nemesis Amalek a "biblical type" of modern "antitypes" personified in the implacable enemies of God and faithful believers in our time. Christian exegetes, as Leo Lefebure's essay suggests, also used a kind of typological interpretation when they characterized Jews as Christ-killers and Muslims as followers of a "type" of the Antichrist, Muhammad.

Leo Lefebure introduces yet another mode of exegesis with the expressly *allegorical* Christian reading of the Old Testament figures Sarah and Hagar as representatives of the "two covenants." Christians are well acquainted with Paul's clearly metaphorical use of martial imagery as he recommends that believers equip themselves with the sword of the spirit, the shield of faith, and the breastplate of righteousness. Allegorical or metaphorical exegesis also forms a main theme in Laurie Patton's discussion of Gandhi's desire to confront the enormous moral dilemma posed by the Bhagavad Gita. Todd Lawson's essay on Baha'i tradition describes an interpretation of the thoroughly irenic prophet Joseph as the ideal "warrior," via what one could argue is a blend of typological and allegorical exegesis.

Finally, *apocalyptic/eschatological* exegesis, known in Christian sources by the technical term *anagogical,* represents another significant thread bridging scriptured traditions. Just as Jewish interpreters understood Israel's military defeats and subjugations as divine punishments for their infidelity, so some Christian exegetes identified various threatening forces, Muslims in particular, as divine recompense for their faithlessness. More importantly, perhaps, several scriptured traditions, including the Baha'i and Zoroastrian as well as Christian and Islamic, include an ultimate sacred combat in their end-time scenarios. Lefebure's essay shows how apocalyptic texts such as 2 Thessalonians 2 have been interpreted throughout Christian history, especially to promote violence against the Jews.

. . .

Small investigations of huge topics, however well focused they may be, often raise more questions than they answer. Several such questions turn on the perceived association of specific acts of violence, and the express or imputed motivations behind them, with particular faith traditions. Are we ever justified in identifying particular deeds or patterns of action as "Christian," "Islamic," "Hindu," or "Jewish" violence? If so, what criteria might one use, and under what circumstances is such identification justifiable? In another vein, if one can judge from anecdotal reports of conventional speech about this subject, it appears that many Europeans and Americans (and likely also citizens of many lands across the globe) take it for granted that specific threats, or even a generalized sense of danger, from a perceived enemy are more ominous when the enemy is identified as avowedly religious than as nonreligious. But are aggressors who claim religious justification inherently more fearsome, inescapable, and insidious than, say, those who allege that they are acting out of purely political or economic motives? Are the express intentions of, say, drug cartels to wipe out all obstacles or competitors to their grim trade any less to be feared than claims of "religious" warriors that their motive stems from a divine mandate to "total war"?

Finally, two variations on the Golden Rule might offer a way of stepping back and gaining a bit of perspective on these and other such difficult dilemmas. First, the Golden Rule of Ethical Pluralism: if your own faith or ethical tradition unequivocally condemns a certain course of action, it is never fair to assume that another tradition condones it. And since our subject here is the complex activity called the exegesis of sacred texts, I suggest that the Golden Rule of Scriptural Interpretation is worthy of reflection: if you don't want members of another faith to interpret your scriptures as only the extremists among your community would, do not interpret their scripture as only the extremists among them would.

NOTES

1. See, e.g., Frederick Denny and Rodney Taylor, eds., *The Holy Book in Comparative Perspective* (Columbia: University of South Carolina, 1985); Harold Coward, *Sacred Word and Sacred Text: Scripture in World Religions* (Maryknoll, NY: Orbis, 1988); William Graham, *Beyond the Written Word: Oral Aspects of Scripture in the History of Religion* (Cambridge: Cambridge University Press, 1987); Jane D. McAuliffe, Barry Walfish, and Joseph Goering, eds., *With Reverence for the Word: Medieval Scriptural Exegesis in Judaism, Christianity, and Islam* (New York: Oxford, 2003). For anthologies of sacred texts, see, e.g., Ninian Smart and Richard Hecht, eds., *Sacred Texts of the World* (New York: Herder, 1984); Kenneth Kramer, *World Scriptures: An Introduction to Comparative Religions* (Mahwah, NJ: Paulist, 1986); Joan Price, *Sacred Scriptures of the World Religions: An Introduction* (New York: Continuum, 2010).

2. These works include Mark Juergensmeyer, *Terror in the Mind of God* (Berkeley: University of California Press, 2003); Oliver McTiernan, *Violence in God's Name: Religion in an Age of Conflict* (Maryknoll, NY: Orbis, 2003); and Charles Selengut, *Sacred Fury: Understanding Religious Violence* (Walnut Creek, CA: Altamira, 2003). On the other side of the issue, one finds a small handful of approaches such as Daniel Smith-Christopher, ed., *Subverting Hatred: The Challenge of Nonviolence in Religious Traditions* (Maryknoll, NY: Orbis, 1998). Studies of individual traditions or comparative studies of two or three (most commonly in various combinations of the Abrahamic faiths) include such works as James Brundage, *The Crusades, Holy War, and Canon Law* (Surrey, UK: Gower, 1991); Penny Cole, *The Preaching of the Crusades to the Holy Land, 1095–1270* (Cambridge, MA: Medieval Academy of America, 1991); Phyllis Tribble, *Texts of Terror: Literary-Feminist Readings of Biblical Narratives* (Minneapolis: Augsburg, 2003). Also of interest here is the work of René Girard on religion and violence, such as his *Violence and the Sacred* (New York: Continuum, 2005) and *The Scapegoat* (Baltimore: Johns Hopkins University Press, 1989).

3. See, e.g., Christopher Hitchens, *God is Not Great: How Organized Religion Poisons Everything* (New York: Twelve, 2009).

4. Exegetes have long understood Isaiah as consisting of works by more than one author, with "deutero-(second) Isaiah" including chapters 40–66, or in some readings 40–55, with chapters 56–66 attributed to a "trito-(third) Isaiah."

5. See, e.g., Gabriel Said Reynolds, *The Qur'an and its Biblical Subtext* (New York: Routledge, 2010); G. S. Reynolds, ed., *The Qur'an in Its Historical Context* (New York: Routledge, 2007); Angelika Neuwirth, Nicolai Sinai, and Michael Marx, eds., *The Qur'an in Context: Historical and Literary Investigations into the Qur'anic Milieu* (Leiden: Brill, 2010).

6. See, e.g., John Burton, *An Introduction to the Hadith* (Edinburgh: Edinburgh University Press, 1994).

7. See, e.g., Hussein Abdul-Raof, *Schools of Qur'anic Exegesis: Genesis and Development* (New York: Routledge, 2010).

8. See e.g., Michael Sours, *Word without Syllable or Sound: The World's Sacred Scriptures in the Baha'i Faith* (Los Angeles: Kalimat, 2000); [Baha'i Publishing], *Meditations: Selections from Baha'i Scripture* (Wilmette, IL: Baha'i Publishing, 2008).

9. On the influences on Abrahamic tradition, see Jamsheed Choksy, "Hagiography and Monotheism in History: Doctrinal Encounters between Zoroastrianism, Judaism, and Christianity," *Islam and Christian-Muslim Relations* 14, no. 4 (2003): 407–415. Further on Zoroastrian scriptures, see Jamsheed Choksy, "Zoroastrianism," in *Encyclopedia of Religion*, 2nd ed. (New York: Macmillan, 2005), 14:9988–10008; Mary Boyce, *Zoroastrians: their Religious Beliefs and Practices* (New York: Routledge, 2001) and *Textual Sources for the Study of Zoroastrianism* (Chicago: University of Chicago Press, 1990).

10. For useful overviews, see, e.g., Barbara Powell, *Windows into the Infinite: A Guide to the Hindu Scriptures* (Freemont, CA: Jain Publishing, 1996); Dominic Goodall, ed., *Hindu Scriptures* (Berkeley: University of California Press, 1996). On the Bhagavad Gita, see, e.g., Irina Gajjar, *The Gita: A New Translation of Hindu Sacred Scripture* (Edinburg, VA: Axios, 2007).

11. See, e.g., Gurinder Singh Mann, *The Making of Sikh Scripture* (New York: Oxford University Press, 2001); Christopher Shackle and Arvind Mandair, *Teachings of the Sikh Gurus: Selections from the Sikh Scriptures* (New York: Routledge, 2005).

12. See, e.g., Marston R. Speight, "The Function of Hadith as Commentary on the Qur'an, as Seen in the Six Authoritative Collections," in *Approaches to the History of the Interpretation of the Qur'an,* ed. Andrew Rippin (Oxford: Clarendon, 1988), 63–81.

2

A Brief History of War in the Hebrew Bible and the Jewish Interpretive Tradition

Reuven Firestone

The Hebrew Bible is a collection of diverse kinds of literature, reflecting many wide-ranging aspects of human culture and society, and spanning up to a thousand years of human experience.[1] Within this anthology one can find numerous stories depicting violence, battles, and all-out wars between individuals, families, tribes, and national communities. Some legal material also treats rules of behavior in war. These all reflect the social and political reality of the ancient Near East, where war and violent acts were considered to be normal, effective, and acceptable tools within the political repertoire available to family, tribal, and national leaderships. Israel[2] emerged as a community in the ancient Near East during a period when empires had weakened and when the communities and peoples living in what is today's Israel, Palestine, Lebanon, and Jordan competed rather equally in the early Iron Age of the late thirteenth and twelfth centuries B.C.E. (Iron 1).[3] War was not only necessary for survival; it was also permissible under certain conditions for community benefit.

The worldviews represented by the Hebrew Bible all assume the overarching guidance, or at least scrutiny, of a great monotheistic creator God. This is both the God of Israel (Genesis 33:20; Exodus 32:27; and so on) and the God of the universe (Genesis 14:22; Psalms 115:15; and so on) who watches over and often guides or requires certain behaviors in relations between human individuals and groups. The Hebrew Bible conveys the general message that, while war is not something to be glorified and while peace is the long-term goal for both Israel and the world as a whole, war does have its place, may in fact be a divine obligation, and can bring benefit to the community of Israel. Violence and wars between sectors of the larger Israelite community and between Israel and other nations are often couched in terms of God's command, or at least God's sanction.

Despite the setbacks that Israel experienced through its violent conflicts with other communities, even including the destruction of the Jerusalem Temple at the hand of the Babylonian Empire in 586 B.C.E., war and violence remained important and respected instruments in the Israelite political arsenal during the biblical period (roughly 1000–300 B.C.E.). Israel profited from war as well as suffered from war. War was simply a basic, normal, and often necessary part of the landscape of the ancient world, and Israel lived within it. Even in visions of the End of Days, when the wolf shall lay with the lamb, God "shall strike down the land with the rod of his mouth and slay the wicked with the breath of his lips" (Isaiah 11:1–9).[4]

It eventually became apparent, however, that what many had considered to be divinely authorized fighting against Israel's enemies was no longer of real benefit. By the late Second Temple Period (roughly 200 B.C.E.—70 C.E.), the enemies of Israel were no longer local tribal communities or far-away empires, but Greek and Roman Empires that not only conquered and extorted resources, but remained and colonized and simply could not be eliminated or removed from the Land of Israel. Rising up against the Romans proved to be so catastrophic that an exegetical program emerged among the survivors that redefined the meaning and applicability of divinely authorized war. Through interpretation, the rabbis of the Mishna and Talmud virtually eliminated the option of divinely sanctioned war from applicability in contemporary history. War had become too dangerous, too self-destructive.[5] This exegetical program remained in place for nearly two millennia until, after the reestablishment of a Jewish polity in the twentieth century, a new exegetical layer, for some Jews, revived the notion of divinely authorized war.

THE BIBLICAL CONTEXT

According to the epigraphic evidence, the association of gods with fighting and war appears to have been a fundamental part of life among most if not all peoples in the ancient Near East. Not only does the Hebrew Bible refer to most wars as divinely authorized, but so do many extrabiblical texts ranging from the region of ancient Canaan to Mesopotamia, Anatolia, Egypt, and points in between. The "Moabite Stone," for example, refers to battles of the Moabite King Mesha against the Israelites in the mid to late ninth century B.C.E. Written in the name of the king, it associates the early weakness of Moab with the anger of the Moabite god Kemosh against "his land." King Mesha became victorious against Israel only after Kemosh commanded him to fight: "And Kemosh said to me, 'Go, take Nebo from Israel!' So I went by night and fought against it from the break of dawn until noon, taking it and slaying all, seven thousand men, boys, women, girls and maid-servants, for I had devoted them to destruction for [the god] Ashtar-Kemosh. And I took from there the [. . .] of Yahweh, dragging them before Kemosh . . . . Kemosh drove [the king of Israel] out from before me."[6] Community identity in the ancient

Near East was based on kinship, and large kinship groups such as tribes or tribal confederations considered themselves to have special relationships with tribal deities. Just as Kemosh was the tribal deity of the Moabite people, Milkom was the tribal god of the Ammonites, Dagon the god of the Philistines, Ashtoret the goddess of the Phoenicians, and so forth.[7] When communities went to battle against their enemies, they hoped that their gods would support them.

Some depictions of war couch authority for fighting in terms of divine sanction or even command, as noted from the Moabite text cited here. Sometimes the deity entered directly into the fray itself. The God of Israel, for example, defeated the armies of the great and powerful Egypt without any of the Israelites actually engaging in the battle (Exodus 14). And in the primary biblical text detailing the rules of military engagement, the priest is instructed to address the assembled troops before battle and assure them that "it is the Lord your God who marches with you to do battle for you against your enemy, to bring you victory" (Deuteronomy 20:4).

War was a common and oft-used instrument in the political tool kit of the ancient Near East. All communities engaged in fighting when it would benefit the community materially or in defense of the community when attacked. During the periods depicted in the Bible, such as those of the patriarchs and the judges and the early kings, Israel played out its political life on a basically even political and military playing field where "you win some and you lose some." And because the God of Israel along with the gods of other tribal communities was such a ubiquitous part of life, fighting and winning or losing was naturally associated with the deities. When gods get involved in war, whether by personally engaging in the fray or by sanctioning or commanding aggression, we are discussing "holy war." According to this definition, virtually all wars in the ancient Near East were "holy wars."

In this environment, when a great power such as Assyria, Babylonia, or Greece conquered smaller communities, the gods of the great powers tended to supersede or merge with and dominate the deities of the local communities. Requiring offerings to the gods of the conquerors was a means of demanding political loyalty, and conquered people may have been willing to do so for their own transcendent, as well as political, protection. Making offerings to the gods of the conquerors was therefore a way of hedging one's bets in a situation of stress caused by being conquered by a much more powerful political entity represented by a presumably more powerful god (or gods).

TRANSITION TO MONOTHEISM

In the earliest period of Israel's existence, its tribal god, like the gods of other tribes in the region, seems to have been known and referred to among the Israelites by his personal name.[8] Israel, however, eventually came to understand its deity not merely as a limited tribal god like those of its neighbors but as the one and only great creator-God who was master over the entire world and the heavens around it. With the transition from a polytheistic or henotheistic worldview to one of true monotheism, it evidently seemed absurd or impossible for weak and vulnerable humans to address an all-powerful God through a personal name,[9] so the personal name dropped out of use and God was referred to as *"the God" (ha'elohim)* and often referenced simply as "our great Lord" *(adonai).*[10]

It appears to be around this point in the evolving theological and cosmological perspectives of Israel that the old notion of a limited tribal god fighting on behalf of the tribe was transformed into the all-powerful God of the universe protecting his "chosen" community.[11] That is, the emotional particularity of imminence in the tribal deity remained even after the intellectual transition to universal transcendence of the great creator-God. Despite God's universal nature, God therefore continued to have a special relationship with "His people Israel" (Judges 11:23; 1 Kings 8:49; and so on).[12] Although the "God of Israel" (Exodus 5:1, 24:10; Numbers 16:9; and so on)[13] became the one and only "God of all,"[14] he retained a special relationship with Israel that was unique and eternal and often defined in terms of "chosenness," even after the Israelites considered their God to be the God of all creation.[15]

From the perspective of the Israelites themselves, this may not have appeared problematic or contradictory, since they understood all of humanity to worship the false gods of the old tribal system. Whether they made offerings to Milkom or to Marduk, all communities living in their world engaged in the same generic religion of polytheism, a worldview and form of worship that was forbidden and hated by the God of Israel who was, simultaneously, the God of the universe. Because only Israel worshipped the one true God, it was thus logical to presume that the one true, universal God would privilege the one particular human collective that recognized him.

As the once-tribal theology of Israel evolved into a universal theology, it naturally retained its ancient cultural assumptions about God's special relationship with the people of Israel and God's special love for the only tribal community that recognized the truth of monotheism and, therefore, of God. It was thus natural for the community to presume that God would continue to fight Israel's battles. After all, Israel was the only human collective that recognized God, even if it would backslide on a number of occasions and fail to fully realize God's will.

Because God powered the entire world and nothing within it was beyond divine reach, when Israel was attacked or even defeated by foreign warriors it was assumed that this, too, was God's design. Rather than a statement of weakness of the God of Israel (who was simultaneously the universal God) at the hand of a more powerful foreign god, a defeat for Israel had to be understood as a sign of God's anger against his chosen people (Leviticus 26, Deuteronomy 28). Military defeat was thus understood as divine punishment wrought by or at least acquiesced to by the one great God of the world.

> In the second year of King Pekah son of Remaliah of Israel, Jotham son of King Uzziah of Judah became king. He was twenty-five years old when he became king, and he reigned sixteen years in Jerusalem. . . . He did what was pleasing to the Lord, just as his father Uzziah had done. However, the cult places were not removed; the people continued to sacrifice and make offerings at the cult places. . . . In those days, the Lord began to incite King Rezin of Aram and Pekah son of Remaliah against Judah. (2 Kings 15:32–37)

When the Northern Kingdom of Israel (also called Samaria and often referred to in the Bible also as Ephraim) was destroyed by the Assyrians in 723 B.C.E., prophets such as Isaiah and Hosea were depicted as having prophesied its doom as a result of its collective sins.

> Israel is a ravaged vine and its fruit is like it. When his fruit was plentiful he made altars aplenty; when his land was bountiful cult pillars abounded. . . . The inhabitants of Samaria fear for the calf of the house of delusion; indeed its people and priestlings, whose joy it once was, mourn over it for the glory that is departed from it. It too shall be brought to Assyria as tribute to a patron king; Ephraim shall be chagrined, Israel shall be dismayed because of his plans. (Hosea 10:1–6)[16]

The Southern Kingdom of Judah was destroyed by the Babylonian Empire a century and a half later, and this defeat was also considered to have been the work of God.

> Zedekiah was twenty-one years old when he became king, and he reigned eleven years in Jerusalem. He did what was displeasing to the Lord his God . . . he stiffened his neck and hardened his heart so as not to turn to the Lord God of Israel. All the officers of the priests and the people committed many trespasses, following all the abominable practices of the nations. . . . The Lord God of their fathers had sent word to them through His messengers daily without fail, for He had pity on His people and His dwelling-place [Jerusalem]. But they mocked the messengers of God and disdained His words and taunted His prophets until the wrath of the Lord against His people grew beyond remedy. He therefore brought the king of the Chaldeans upon them. . . . They burned the House of God and tore down the wall of Jerusalem, burned down all its mansions, and consigned all its precious objects to destruction. Those who survived the sword he [the Chaldean king] exiled to Babylon, and they became his and his son's servants. (2 Chronicles 36:11–20)

But some seventy years after the Babylonian destruction and subsequent exile, soon after the Persians destroyed the Babylonians and took over their holdings, God was depicted as causing the Persian king not only to bring the Jews back to their homeland in Judea, but to rebuild the Jerusalem Temple: "The Lord roused the spirit of King Cyrus of Persia to issue a proclamation throughout his realm by word of mouth and in writing, as follows: 'Thus said King Cyrus of Persia: The Lord God of Heaven has given me all the kingdoms of the earth, and has charged me with building Him a House in Jerusalem, which is in Judah. Any one of you of all His people, the Lord his God be with him and let him go up" (2 Chronicles 36:22–23).

JEWISH HOLY WAR IN HISTORY

According to the perspective expressed repeatedly in the Hebrew Bible, the community of Israel succeeded in its wars when it obeyed God, while it failed in war when it was collectively disobedient. This assumptive observation may have developed as a means to retain the notion of God's special concern for Israel simultaneously with the notion of God's universal role as the one great God of the world. The formula in which obedience to God resulted in victory while disobedience caused Israel's defeat was one of a number of teleological assumptions embedded in the biblical view of history. Because of this powerful teleology in conjunction with the lack of corroborative sources for most historical description in the Bible, it remains unclear whether many of the wars depicted there even occurred. In any event, the equation of obedience = victory // disobedience = failure became an article of faith among many Jews during the Second Temple Period (536 B.C.E.—70 C.E.) and beyond.

After the rebuilding of the Jerusalem Temple, we know little about Israelite history from the Bible itself, and few extrabiblical sources provide much additional information. As a client of the larger Persian Empire from the sixth to the fourth centuries B.C.E., the Jewish province of Judea (called Jehud by the Persians) certainly engaged in military activities, but we have virtually no information about them. Alexander conquered the Middle East in 330s B.C.E., but the unified empire of Alexander soon split into fluid and feuding Hellenistic dynasties whose major centers were in Ptolemaic Egypt and in Seleucid Syria. The next major war of Israel after the Babylonian destruction was the Hasmonean Revolt against the Seleucid Greeks in the second century B.C.E., a historical event that was recorded and discussed in Jewish works that were not included in the canon of the Hebrew Bible.[17] It was followed some time later by two major Jewish revolts against the Romans referenced by Josephus and Rabbinic literature, one in the first century C.E., and the second some seventy years later. In all three, the leadership among the fighters (or their publicists, at the very least) believed that they were engaged in "holy wars" in which their piety and obedience to God's will would bring eventual victory. The Hasmonean Revolt resulted in Jewish victory, even against what seems to have been overwhelming odds. The following two wars, however, met with overwhelming defeat and catastrophic destruction.

THE HASMONEAN REVOLT AGAINST THE SELEUCIDS

The Hasmonean Revolt occurred under the rule of the Seleucid king Antiochus IV (r. 168–61 B.C.E.) and was led by a priestly family called the Hasmoneans, also known as the "Maccabees," whose name was applied to four independent writings called the "Books of the Maccabees." The first two of these writings treat the Hasmonean Revolt, while the third and fourth treat other issues. First Maccabees is an anonymous work written originally in Hebrew but preserved only in Greek.[18] It notes repeatedly how God favored the zealotry of the Jewish military uprising against the pagan Hellenistic Syrians (the Seleucids), and suggests throughout that God assured the success of the war because of the piety and heroic fortitude of the Hasmonean family. Despite many setbacks, including the deaths of the sons of the patriarchal Mattathias who began the revolt, the piety, bravery, and perseverance of the fighters earned them ultimate collective success. Their leaders regularly prayed to God for help before going into battle, equating their fighting with the battles of the biblical heroes (1 Maccabees 3:46–53; 4:8–11, 30–34; 7:40–42). One unmistakably intended correspondence is the 1 Maccabees 3:55–56 parallel with the rules of war outlined in Deuteronomy 20, referring specifically to the deferments that could be taken to remove oneself from fighting. The work unmistakably expresses the conviction that divine favor would assure ultimate military success.

First Maccabees rarely includes outright divine miracles in the sense of direct supernatural intervention,[19] nor does it claim that its contemporary history was a fulfillment of prophesy. On the other hand, it describes events in a way that would suggest the likelihood of divine intervention, such as the agonizing death of the Hellenizing Jewish priest Alcimus after he had begun demolition of part of the Temple (9:54–56). The hero Judah is depicted as relying entirely on God's deliverance in his battles against overwhelming odds, exclaiming, for example, "It is easy for many to be delivered into the hands of few. Heaven sees no difference in gaining victory through many or through a few, because victory in war does not lie in the weight of numbers, but rather strength comes from Heaven" (1 Maccabees 3:18–19). First Maccabees expresses the conviction that divine favor assured the ultimate military success of the Hasmoneans, and the Hasmonean House did indeed prevail in what appears to have been an unbalanced war that logic would suggest should have ended in failure for the Judean fighters. The victory was celebrated with a ceremony to rededicate the newly purified Jerusalem Temple that had been defiled by the pagans (1 Maccabees 4:47–60). A commemorative ceremony was instituted thereafter as an annual religious celebration called *Hanukah,* meaning "dedication."

Second Maccabees is an entirely different work, written by a Jew originally in Greek and in the style of Greek historians. Unlike the sober prose with occasional poetic inserts of 1 Maccabees, 2 Maccabees is highly emotional throughout, and despite its obviously Greek cultural setting, it expresses a strong condemnation of Hellenization. Martyrdom, for example, has a measure of efficacy, for the acts of martyrdom are depicted as having a positive effect on the Hasmonean victories. In contrast to 1 Maccabees, 2 Maccabees includes many miracles and repeatedly mentions a belief in resurrection.[20] Judas and his soldiers are portrayed as scrupulously observing the divine commandments and as praying for and receiving divine aid, which is repeatedly depicted as the cause of Judas's many victories. Both books associate military victory with God's providence. Pious zealotry is rewarded with divinely wrought military victory, which in turn brings about the purification of God's Temple and, eventually, national independence. This is all possible because of the pious activism of Jewish heroes.

But pious militancy is not the only tactical position found in these two sources. Other strategies are employed as well. There are devout quietists who oppose the militant activism of the Hasmonean family and retreat to the desert, hoping to escape the evil decrees of Antiochus rather than fight against them (1 Maccabees 2:29–38; 2 Maccabees 6:11). Unlike the militants who escape to the mountains lightly packed and ready for action, these militants flee to the desert, burdened with their entire families and even cattle. They choose neither to desecrate the Sabbath nor to defend themselves against the Greek army detachment sent out to destroy them. As a result of their massacre, 1 Maccabees draws the conclusion that Jews must, contrary to contemporary practice, fight defensively on the Sabbath (1 Maccabees 2:39–41).

THE FAILED REVOLTS AGAINST ROME

Jews rose up repeatedly against the Roman Empire's control of Judea, finally renamed Syria Palestine in 135 by Hadrian in an attempt to de-Judaize the region after the costly Jewish revolts. A "zealot movement" had previously emerged in the year 6 C.E. when Judea was first incorporated into the Roman Empire under Emperor Augustus.[21] A man named Judah the Galilean had already participated in the widespread disturbances that followed Herod's death in 4 C.E. and succeeded in seizing control of a government armory in Sepphoris. Josephus considered Judah and his followers to be outside the three main sects or Judean philosophies, the Pharisees, Sadducees, and Essenes. He usually refers to them as *leistai* (brigands)[22] or *sicarii* (dagger-men), but he occasionally calls them by the name they used to refer to themselves, *kana'im* (zealots), and finally lists them as a fourth philosophic sect.[23]

There was much dissatisfaction and resistance to the Roman occupation among the Jews, and two major Jewish revolts erupted that were extremely costly for Rome, and catastrophic for the Jewish Judea. The first broke out in the year 66 C.E. when Jews destroyed a Roman garrison in Jerusalem and ended the usual sacrificial offerings for the welfare of the Roman people and emperor. They set up a provisional Jewish government that attempted to unify the traditional Land of Israel under its rule.

The Roman response under Emperor Nero was overwhelming: he dispatched Vespasian with an immense army to crush the rebellion. Internal complications accompanying the death of Nero in 68 and Vespasian's victorious succession a year later delayed much of the fighting. By the year 70, however, the Jerusalem Temple had been burned to the ground by Vespasian's son Titus, and the only lingering active resistance remained in the desert fortress of Masada, which held out until 73.

The Jewish fighters presumed that they were fighting for God and his Temple, and that God would intervene as in ancient days.[24] But the Jews were divided into political or religious (or political-religious) factions at the time that were also influenced by geography and class.[25] The difference between the groups that favored fighting and those that devoted their energies to nonmilitant resistance is sometimes described in Jewish sources as the difference between Rabbi Yochanan Ben Zakkai and the Zealots, or between Yavneh and Jerusalem.[26]

The story of how Rabbi Yochanan Ben Zakkai was spirited out of Jerusalem under Roman siege by his students in a coffin appears several times in Rabbinic literature.[27] The sources maintain that the subterfuge was the only way for him to pass the guards of the city gates without being killed for treason by Jewish zealots. As Jerusalem was making its last stand against Rome, this rabbi negotiated with General Vespasian for permission to build an academy in the Judean town of Yavneh (Jamnia). At the end of the day, it was not the zealots, but Yochanan Ben Zakkai and his students who survived the destruction and reestablished Jewish life in the Land of Israel, guaranteeing its survival there and elsewhere, even if as a depressed people and under the dictatorial rule of Rome. Yochanan Ben Zakkai's strategy, as constructed by Rabbinic tradition, held that if political and military efforts endangered the survival of the people and its religious system, they must be abandoned.

The devastation wrought in Jerusalem by the Roman military did not end Jewish militancy or military uprisings. The next and last Jewish uprising against Rome began nearly seventy years after the destruction of the Second Temple in an unmistakable parallel to the rise of the Persian Empire and its destruction of the Babylonian Empire nearly seventy years after the Babylonian demolition of the First Temple. Bar Kokhba is the popular name of the military leader who commanded the Jewish revolt against Rome in 132–35 C.E. The details of the revolt do not concern us here aside from the fact that it was serious enough to have been a source of significant concern to the Roman rulers.[28] It precipitated a Roman response designed to prevent any future attempts to revolt. Terrible destruction ensued in its aftermath for the Jews of Judea at the hand of Rome.[29] Statistics from ancient reports are notoriously unreliable, but it is likely that tens or perhaps even hundreds of thousands of Jews were killed in the fighting or died from starvation and illness in the chaos that followed.

Outraged by Jewish defiance, the Romans obliterated the most notable historic markers by which Jews identified their land. Judea was renamed Syria-Palestina (meaning the Palestine of Syria), thus dropping Jewish national identity from official reference to the land. Jerusalem was depopulated of Jews, and its sacred shrine, which had already been destroyed in the Great Revolt of 66–70 C.E., was replaced with a temple to Jupiter. The city was turned into a pagan Roman colony and the ancient name by which the city had been known was replaced by Aelia Capitolina, after the Emperor Titus Aelius Hadrianus. Jewish practices such as circumcision, Torah study, and even prayer were evidently banned for a short period.

Most Jewish survivors in Judea were forced to emigrate because of a combination of Roman military and political restrictions and economic destitution. By an act of the Roman Senate, it was decreed "that it is forbidden to all circumcised persons to enter and to stay within the territory of Aelia Capitolina; any person contravening this prohibition shall be put to death."[30] Many Jews moved to Persia or Galilee, and Jewish Judea never completely recovered until the modern period. The revolt is remembered in Jewish sources both in references to its military leader, Bar Kokhba, and to the location of his last stand in the city of Beitar. The ultimate failure of the revolt and its disastrous results were of such importance to the evolving Rabbinic self-concept that it was listed in the Mishna along with four other great disasters that befell the Jews on the ninth day of the Jewish month of Av, the quintessential day of calamity and mourning for the Jewish people.[31]

The Bar Kokhba Revolt was the last great Jewish military action until the advent of modern Zionism in the twentieth century.[32] It was commanded by a military leader with the backing if not coleadership of Rabbi Akiba, arguably the most important religious leader of his generation.[33] The very name Bar Kokhba, meaning "son of the star," hints at the messianic associations with the revolt. According to the Palestinian Talmud (Ta'anit 4:5)[34] and Midrash Lamentations Rabba (2:4),[35] Rabbi Akiba referred to Bar Kokhba as the King Messiah *(malka meshicha)* and supported his view with an interpretation of Numbers 24:17 that is understood by the rabbis to be an unambiguous messianic statement.[36]

> Rabbi Shim'on b. Yohai[37] taught: "Akiba my teacher would expound (Numbers 24:17): *A star will step forth out of Jacob*[38] as follows: Koziba will step forth from Jacob. Rabbi Akiba, when he saw Bar Koziba, would say: 'This is the King Messiah.'" R. Yochanan b. Torta[39] said to him: "Akiba, weeds will grow out of your cheeks and the son of David will still not have come!"[40]

The star *(kokhav)* rising out of the Jacob was none other than Bar Kokhba, according to Rabbi Akiba, and the name Bar Kokhba in Aramaic means exactly that:

son of the star—"star man." Moreover, the Edom referred to in the continuation of the Numbers passage is a code throughout Rabbinic literature for Rome.[41] According to Akiba's understanding, then, Bar Kokhba was destined by divine authority to lead the Jewish people in a successful revolt to retake possession of the Roman holdings in the Land of Israel, if not to destroy the evil empire of Rome itself. Akiba's view is countered in this source by that of Rabbi Yohanan ben Torta, an otherwise insignificant contemporary, who does not take Bar Kokhba to be a messianic figure.[42] Bar Kokhba is twice referred to in the passage as "Bar Koziba." In fact, neither Bar Kokhba nor Bar Koziba was the general's real name.

We know that his actual name was Shim'on Bar Kosva or Bar Kosiva. Two puns seem to have evolved in relation to the name, depending on how he was viewed: Bar Kokhba ("son of the star" or "star man") among those who attributed messianic status to him (in relation to Numbers 24:17),[43] and Bar Koziba ("son of lies" or "man of lies," meaning "liar") among those who opposed him and, later, those who suffered from the failure of the revolt. In traditional Jewish literature, his name is written Bar Koziba, reflecting the obvious conclusion reached by the rabbis that he was a false messiah who brought great destruction to his people.[44]

The Bar Kokhba Rebellion marks a watershed in both the history of Israel and the history of Jewish thought. After its horrendous failure, the Jewish activists who engaged in guerrilla activities henceforth would be described in Rabbinic literature as criminals *(listim, biryonim)* rather than freedom fighters *(qana'im)*.[45] From this day forward, Rabbinic Jewish wisdom would teach consistently that it is not physical acts of war that protect Israel from its enemies, but rather spiritual concentration in righteousness and prayer. The militant messianic uprisings and military confrontations that occurred from the Maccabees to Bar Kokhba were superseded by a far more quietistic messianism represented by Rabbi Yohanan bar Nappacha of Tiberias and his school of thought.[46] Consequently, the Rabbinic sources that emerged after the failed revolt teach that it was the pious sage and not the great warrior who was the true hero of Israel, and that his heirs among the rabbis rather than the mighty warriors would henceforth lead the people of Israel and bring them eventually to redemption.

THE ABOLITION OF A BIBLICAL INSTITUTION

The rabbis succeeded in their suppression of militancy by emphasizing two symbolic paradigms that counter the expectation of divinely authorized military success. One defined divinely authorized warring ("holy war") in a way that made it virtually impossible to apply. The other constructed a delicate relationship between exile and redemption in which the Jews had virtually no option other than to accept their divinely ordained fate to live under the political hegemony of Gentiles.

In the first construct, found at the end of the eighth chapter of Mishna Sotah, the rabbis distill the dense, complex, and varied expressions of holy war in the Bible into two sentences, and in those two sentences they distill them into two types: "discretionary war" *(milchemet r^eshut)* and "commanded war" or "war of *mitzvah*" *(milchemet mitzvah)*. This construct established extremely narrow parameters for discussion of war in Rabbinic Judaism. However one reads the two Talmuds' slight expansion of the Mishna, the dangerous wild card of divinely authorized war ("war of *mitzvah*") could no longer be initiated by Israel because *initiated* holy war, by definition in the Talmud, is limited to the divinely commanded wars of conquest led by Joshua.[47] Henceforth, the only possible kind of Jewish holy war is defensive, but even that option is articulated only in the Palestinian Talmud and is absent from the Babylonian Talmud, the latter being the authoritative work upon which Jewish law is constructed.[48] What had proven to be the terrifying wild card of holy war was thus effectively removed from the active repertoire of Rabbinic Judaism.[49]

The second construct that emerged from the Rabbinic repertoire is the "Three Vows," through which the rabbis discouraged mass movements that might instigate a violent backlash by the Gentile powers under which the Jews lived. These vows refer to a phrase occurring three times in the Song of Songs, *I make you swear, O daughters of Jerusalem, by the gazelles and by the hinds of the field, do not wake or rouse love until it is wished.*[50]

By general consensus, the rabbis understand this verse to mean that God is making the daughters of Jerusalem, a metaphor for Israel, swear not to wake or rouse love—understood as attempting to bring the messiah—until it is wished, meaning until God decides the time is right. God will bring the messiah when God wills. Attempting to bring the messiah by human means through rebellion, war, or revolution rather than through waiting patiently for God to bring the messiah himself is sometimes called "forcing God's hand." This came to be considered an act of disobedience that would only bring further divine wrath and additional disasters for the Jewish people.

Combined, the two positions were understood in classical Rabbinic thought to convey the divine command that Israel not ascend to the Land of Israel en masse to attempt to reestablish Jewish rule there through arms nor rebel against their inferior position under the rule of Gentiles.[51] In response, God will not allow the Gentiles to persecute the Jews "overly much" *(yoter midday)*. When God determines the time is right for the messiah, God will bring the messiah himself. In the meantime, Jews must continue to live in a state of exile, but they need not be entirely passive. They can hasten the coming of the messiah by means of obedience to the divine will through proper religious observance and acts of human compassion. If Jews did not agree to these terms, then they would be subject to divinely sanctioned violence at the hand of the Gentiles, permitting their "flesh [to be consumed] like [that of] gazelles or hinds of the field."

The biblical construct of Israel's wars succeeding when they obeyed God but failing when they refused to heed the divine will (obedience = success // disobedience = failure) was thus retained in Rabbinic Judaism, but with one major innovation. That innovation was, in essence, a lesson derived from history. After the destruction of the Second Temple and the failure of the Bar Kokhba Rebellion, Jewish leaders were no longer to be considered qualified to determine when the time is ripe for war. War is still theoretically possible, but practically impossible. That is to say, a "Jewish default position" would judge Jews incapable of knowing whether or not they were spiritually fit enough to engage the enemy successfully. The rabbis ruled, therefore, even if somewhat indirectly, that wars initiated by Jews, for all intents and purposes, were no longer an option. The only authority capable of deciding when the time is ripe for war or mass movement is God, and "the time" is represented by the coming of the messiah. Human initiative in this direction was an attempt at "forcing God's hand" to bring the messiah, which would result in possibly catastrophic divine punishment. Active messianic movements were thus condemned, and when they occasionally appeared such as under the leadership of Sabbatai Zevi,[52] their catastrophic outcomes encouraged Rabbinic leadership to work hard to prevent their formation. This Rabbinic reformulation of the biblical position on war and violence held sway for nearly two millennia, but like many aspects of Jewish life and perspective, these were altered under the powerful pressure of modernity.

MODERNITY CHANGES THE RULES
AND MODIFIES PRIOR ASSUMPTIONS

The complex forces of modernity and the equally complex Jewish responses to them are subjects of much scholarship that cannot be distilled adequately here.[53] We direct our attention rather abruptly to three related subjects that have profoundly affected Jewish attitudes toward war and violence. These are the development of the Jewish national movement known as Zionism resulting in the establishment of a Jewish political state, the overwhelming horror of the Holocaust, and the great growth of messianic thinking among many Jews since the 1960s.

European Jewish identity was profoundly affected by modernity as Jews began to be integrated into the larger societies in which (or alongside of which) they had lived for centuries. One nagging aspect of identity constantly pulling at modern Jews was the problem of how to integrate their identity as Jews into the patterns of identity that were articulated by modern Europeans. We have observed above that religious identity among biblical monotheists, like their polytheist neighbors in the ancient Near East, was profoundly affected by their tribal identity. Religion in the ancient Near East was a tribal affair, and tribal communities were loyal to their tribal deities. Throughout the ages, Israel never moved entirely away from their kinship consciousness. Although Jews are as ethnically and racially diverse as Christians or Muslims, they always identified as a religious people (or nation, or polity, or society). But as a universal religious identity, being Jewish was never limited to a single tribe, race, nation, or kinship unit, and non-Jews have joined the "Jewish people" through conversion for thousands of years. Quite contrary to European Christian identity, therefore, Jewish identity was both a religious marker and a marker of peoplehood or nation.[54]

In the West, Jews were eventually integrated into society at large in the nineteenth century by discarding or reducing the "national" aspect of their identity and joining the French, British, and Dutch nations as believers in the "Jewish faith." In Eastern Europe, their emancipation was much slower and by the turn of the twentieth century was hardly a reality. When Jews attempted to join the national movements working toward political independence from Czarist Russia or the Austro-Hungarian Empire, they were rejected as foreign nationals by virtue of their Jewish identity. It was inconceivable to the nationalists that they could be both Jews and Poles, Jews and Ukrainians, and so forth. Profoundly influenced by their rejection from modern national movements at the same time that national identity was becoming a profound force for determining modern identity, some Jews took the path of discarding or reducing the "religious" aspect of their identity and joining with other Jews to work toward their own independent political future. That national movement eventually became Zionism.[55]

Zionism was founded by secularists, Jews who had rejected their religious identity and considered themselves a Jewish nation. Most religious Jews rejected Zionism and refused to join or support the movement because it was considered a dangerous attempt to rebel against the divine command that Israel not ascend to the Land of Israel en masse nor rebel against their inferior position under the rule of Gentiles.[56] The few religious Jews who supported Zionism attempted to dissociate the movement from any sense of messianism and argued that immigration to Palestine was not a mass movement and not associated with expectations of a final divine redemption.[57] Nevertheless, a small but significant community of Religious Zionists has participated in the movement to establish a Jewish homeland since the inception of modern Jewish nationalism. Among them were some who believed that establishing a Jewish homeland in Palestine had transcendent meaning, particularly those who were influenced by the first Ashkenazi Chief Rabbi under the British Mandate, Rabbi Abraham Isaac Kook.[58]

To the secular Jews who led and largely populated the Zionism Movement, the issues of divinely authorized war and the Three Vows were meaningless. Secular Jews worked to bring large numbers of Jewish immigrants to Palestine under the

Ottomans and later under the British Mandate Authority. When frictions with local Arab populations resulted in violence against the Jewish colonists, they defended themselves with arms and eventually, when war was considered inevitable, they initiated military actions. This was a significant change from the war policy established by the rabbis of the Talmud, but again, it was mostly secular Jews who were fighting.[59]

The escalation in militancy within the Jewish population of Palestine spiked in response to the Arab Revolt of 1936–39. By the time the revolt had subsided, World War II and the Holocaust had begun. With the outbreak of the war and the growing reports about the fate of the Jews of Europe, the Zionist leadership concluded that it had to be fully prepared for military solutions to political problems. Moreover, with Field Marshall Rommel's penetration of Egypt and the possibility of a German conquest of Palestine, Palestinian Jews mobilized to defend their communities. These were decisions and actions of the secular Jewish leadership. They were unconcerned with religious law and felt no obligation toward it. As the Jewish community of Palestine continued to grow after the end of the war and before the establishment of the State of Israel, however, more and more religious Jews arrived from Europe and the Middle East and North Africa as refugees. They were ready and often eager to fight for the establishment of a Jewish nation-state that would protect them from present and future danger, and they were ready particularly after the fate of millions of Jews who were not able to fight became known. But they were confronted with the problem of the Rabbinic enactment that made mass mobilization for war virtually impossible.

When war between Jews and Arabs seemed inevitable in 1947, Rabbi Isaac HaLevi Herzog (d. 1959), the Chief Rabbi of Palestine under the British Mandate and the first Chief Ashkenazic rabbi of the State of Israel, wrote a legal responsum to the question of whether the Three Vows remain in force. He wrote that the decision of the League of Nations to allow the establishment of a Jewish state removed the problem of "rebelling against the nations" because the nations had already sanctioned a Jewish state.[60] Herzog thus opened the way for Orthodox Jews to volunteer to train and fight in an organized Jewish army. Later, he authorized a military draft, including Orthodox Jews, on Jewish legal grounds based on the argument that a war of defense lies within the category of Commanded War. The wars for Israel's national independence were conceived purely as wars of defense. Moreover, Herzog concluded that Israel had been released from its vows because the nations of the world had long before transgressed *their* vow "not to oppress Israel too much."[61] His responsa were influential, but his views were nevertheless opposed by a powerful force of anti-Zionist religious leaders.[62] Note that his arguments had no messianic reference or logic. It would take another major development to thoroughly revitalize religiously sanctioned war for many religious Jews.

THE MIRACULOUS "SIX-DAY WAR"
AND THE REVIVAL OF JEWISH MESSIANISM

On May 12, 1967, the eve of Independence Day, just one day before the beginning of the crisis leading up to the Six-Day War, the only son of Rabbi Abraham Isaac Kook, Rabbi Tzvi Yehudah Kook, delivered a sermon in which he bewailed the partition of the biblical Land of Israel during the 1948 War, as a result of which Jews were unable to visit the holy cities of Hebron and Nablus: "Yes, where is our Hebron—are we forgetting this? Where is our Nablus, and our Jericho? Where—have they been forgotten? And all the far side of the Jordan—it is ours, every clod of earth, every square inch, every district of the land and plot of land that belongs to the Land of Israel—are we allowed to give up even one millimeter of them?"[63] Rabbi Tzvi Yehudah Kook was the head of the most important Religious Zionist yeshiva in Israel and the larger Jewish world. Three weeks after the sermon, his students would consider his words truly, not merely metaphorically, prophetic.

Part of the reason for their prophetic assessment of his message lies in the astonishing events of the following weeks, which led up to the outbreak of war on June 5. Israel found itself surrounded by millions of Arabs who were being exhorted to destroy it. Egypt's President Gamal Abdul Nasser had received and absorbed massive Soviet military armament during the previous decade. With the blessing of the USSR, he expelled the United Nations' Expeditionary Force (UNEF) that had been established in the Sinai Peninsula after the 1956 War, concentrated over a hundred thousand troops in the Sinai Peninsula, and closed the Straits of Tiran to Israeli shipping. He persuaded Syria and Jordan to join the preparations for war, and even Iraq, Morocco, Tunisia, and Saudi Arabia offered at least token use of their armies and communications.[64]

It appeared to the Israeli public that the United Nations cared little about the military buildup and the possible invasion, and Europe seemed to express little interest in the pressure building up in the region. The year 1967 was only twenty-two years after World War II. More than one quarter of the Israeli population at that time had survived the horrors of the Holocaust as refugees or had lost close relatives to the systematic Nazi genocide. There was palpable fear that another holocaust was in the making. As part of the war preparations in Tel Aviv, mass graves were dug in the main football stadium.[65]

Nasser gave speech after speech exhorting his people and soldiers to be ready for the onslaught. The Jews would be destroyed. Tel Aviv would be emptied of its inhabitants. The Zionist entity would exist no more. Whether Nasser had the actual intention to invade or was simply attempting to gain politically through an act of military bravado, he gave every impression to Israel that he was serious. And Israel took him seriously. The Israeli chief of staff, Yitzhak Rabin, broke down temporarily over the stress, and the entire Jewish world held its breath, with terrible fear and dread over the future of Israel.[66]

But in one day the war was essentially over. Israel managed to destroy the air forces of all the neighboring Arab nations within hours. With Israeli control of the skies, the war was won. It ended formally six days later. To the Jews of Israel and the world, who were terrified at what seemed to them to be an impending massacre, the quick and relatively painless victory was miraculous. To many in the Religious Zionist world, it was not merely a metaphor but was indeed a divine miracle. One must keep in mind the fresh and overwhelmingly powerful memory of the Holocaust among Israelis and Jews everywhere. It was natural to consider the astonishingly swift and nearly painless victory to be a sign of the approaching messianic redemption, a signpost along the path to a final divine deliverance after so much suffering. Even staunchly secular Jews found themselves drawn toward their religious roots.[67]

In addition to the presumed miracle of Jewish survival against all odds was the miracle of Jewish conquest of the most sacred sites of the Bible. The war brought virtually all the important biblical sites under Jewish rule, which was the first time in two millennia that Jews were in political control of the ancient homeland. This was noted immediately and clearly, and many Religious Zionists considered this to be powerful evidence in support of the divinely authorized redemptive nature of Zionism and the Jewish state.[68] Zionism and Israel were instruments of God through which he was now and finally bringing about the messianic redemption.

The 1967 War marks a larger historical watershed indicating a change in conception of the Israel-Arab/Palestinian conflict. What had been articulated previously as a national conflict between Israelis and the Arabs of Palestine began to be articulated by partisans of both sides in increasingly religious and apocalyptic terms. After the messianic suggestion associated with the conquest of most of the biblical Land of Israel in the 1967 War, many Orthodox religious scholars, and particularly Religious Zionist activists and thinkers, became deeply invested in legitimating the right of Israel to control those territories and in the legitimacy of Jewish militancy in general. The causes of this are complex, but it is clear that many Orthodox thinkers began, only after 1967, to discover and cite a range of premodern thinkers and arguments that support the messianic nature of the State of Israel.[69] The chief rabbi of the Israel Defense Forces and later the chief Ashkenazi rabbi of Israel, Shelomo Goren (d. 1995), provided a series of reasons for the cancellation of the force of the Three Vows.[70]

The "miraculous" nature of the 1967 War enabled Religious Zionists to articulate publicly the messianic nature of Zionism. It was the 1973 War, however, that served to invigorate The Settler Movement and encourage an increasingly militant and military approach to political control of the territories captured by Israel during the 1967 War. Those territories, which had quickly come to be considered a biblical patrimony, were nearly lost in the 1973 War. This was a terrifying sign to some Religiously Orthodox Jews that the Israeli government was willing to negotiate away biblical holy sites captured in 1967, which they viewed as a move against God. Based on the traditional Jewish view that Israel (or the Jewish people) succeeded in war when it obeyed God while it failed in war when it was collectively disobedient, the near disaster of the 1973 War was viewed as a sign of God warning that Jews must do everything humanly possible to settle and control the area through force if necessary, and that the imperative to do so trumped both international law and even the laws of the State of Israel.

It was the aftermath of the 1973 War that stimulated the activist movement of settlers called "Gush Emunim," which eventually gave way to what is called simply "The Settler Movement."[71] The old biblical notion of "conquest" was invigorated through a religious nationalist narrative that emerged to explain the extraordinary success of the 1967 War and almost calamitous near-failure of the 1973 War. By the mid-1980s, particularly among the more activist groups within The Settler Movement, conquest had taken on an aggressive and militant tone, to such an extent that it had become transformed into a biblical sense of divinely ordained, aggressive, unlimited military conquest of the Land of Israel. Indeed, and ironically, the very act of conquest itself had become one sign of the coming divine redemption.

As with most any topic of discussion within the greater Jewish community, there is no overall consensus about when war should or must be waged and what constitutes its limits. Religious leaders and scholars continue to take a variety of positions on the issues of settlement, force, and violence, and some movements such as Oz Ve-shalom/Netivot Shalom and Meimad have formed from within the Orthodox Jewish community of Israel to counter the growing militant aggressiveness of Religious Zionism.[72] Thus, while the Orthodox community is not all of one mind on the issues, for the large majority of traditional Jews today the impediments to divinely authorized war that were so successfully established by the Rabbinic sages of the Talmud have been removed to allow Jewish "holy war" to reenter history. The language and the idea of military conquest has increasingly infiltrated the language of thinkers and teachers that make up The Settler Movement and its supporters and, subsequently, Zionist discourse in general. Stuart Cohen notes how the Israel Defense Forces incorporates Jewish religious terminology, symbols, and collective myths into its training and troop education in order to create a unified fighting force out of the divergent populations of religious and secular Jews of widely different backgrounds, which has a significant impact on the citizens of the state as a whole, given the profound impact of the IDF on the personal lives of Israel's citizenry.[73] Key Religious Zionist thinkers have written major works claiming any war fought by the Jews of Israel to be divinely sanctioned or holy war (*milchamot hashem*, "wars of God").[74]

The increased investment in linking Israel's modern wars to divinely sanctioned or even commanded war parallels the intensification of belief that divine redemption is imminent, and the signs of the approaching Redemption became increasingly obvious and more frequent. By the 1980s, but from 1967 if not earlier among some observers, it had become possible to observe the historical signposts of Redemption in seemingly odd ways.

It is simply that a series of historic events have brought the Jewish people into a position in which it is impossible not to feel that we are on the road that must lead to redemption. We have only to think of some of the events of the post-war era, following the apocalyptic terrors of Nazi Europe, to see how pregnant they are with significance. Had the necessity for free Jewish immigration into Palestine after 1945 not met with the implacable hostility of the Arabs, there might not have been a Jewish State in our time. Had President Truman's suggestion in 1946 to admit one hundred thousand displaced persons to Palestine been accepted by Britain and the Arabs, there would have been no UN Resolution. Had the Arabs not resisted that UN Resolution of 1947 the new Israel would have remained a tiny, truncated, insignificant pocket-state. Had Hussein in 1967 not thrown in his lot with the Arab anti-Israel confederacy (in defiance of Israel's plea), Judea and Samaria and Jerusalem might still have remained outside Jewish care and influence. Is it any wonder that believing Jews see in all this process the working of the Hand of God? History is bearing down on us. . . . Inexorably, if we have eyes to see and a heart to understand, we are led to acknowledge that, after two thousand years of wandering in the by-ways of exile, we have emerged on the high road of history which, however long it may yet be, must lead us eventually to Redemption. It is in this sense that we describe our own era as "*Reshit Zemichat Geulatenu* [the beginning of the flowering of our Redemption]."[75]

The perception of divine signs and notion of divinely sanctioned or even commanded war became generalized by the 1980s to the extent that for many it could fit virtually any definition of the conflict between Israel and the Palestinians and neighboring countries. This represents a revival of holy war, particularly among an influential and activist community of Orthodox Jews. Of course not all Jews (or all Orthodox Jews) agree with the conclusions and pronouncements of zealous rabbis and activists. But virtually all traditionally minded Jews and most Jews living in Israel, whether religiously observant or not, have become familiar with the discourse of holy war in Jewish terms. The revival of the old holy war paradigm was not a conscious program or political goal, but rather the product of an attempt to make sense of sacred text and tradition in light of contemporary events. It was the result of a religious and human response to a reality that was confusing and frightening, and also a response to social and political forces both locally and internationally that were beyond the ability of the political leadership of the state to manage.

NOTES

1. For a historical study of divinely authorized war in Judaism, see Reuven Firestone, *Holy War in Judaism: The Fall and Rise of a Controversial Idea* (New York: Oxford University Press, 2012). Research for this essay was made possible by a grant from the National Endowment for the Humanities for research in Israel during the 2000–01 academic year.

2. The traditional Jewish term, *Israel,* is a shortened form of "the People of Israel" (*'am yisra'el* or *beney yisra'el),* not a reference to a modern nation-state. The actual name of the modern Jewish state is *medinat yisra'el,* "the State of [the People of] Israel." In this essay I use the traditional term *Israel* to refer to the Jewish people from the biblical period (for which a common parallel reference is *Israelite*) to the modern period for which the term *Jews* is the more common term.

3. Ann Killebrew, *Biblical Peoples and Ethnicity* (Atlanta: Society of Biblical Literature, 2005), 13–14, 21–92.

4. In the days to come, when "the Mount of the Lord's House shall stand firm above the mountains and tower above the hills; and all the nations shall gaze on it with joy" (Isaiah 2:2–4). God "will execute judgment among the nations and rebuke the many peoples so that they shall beat their swords into plowshares and their spears into pruning hooks" (Micah 4:1–3). This parallel citation from Isaiah and Micah may not reflect as benign an operational program as we tend to read in these phrases, for God's executing judgment and rebuke is not a very peaceful scene (cf. 2 Samuel 7:14; Job 33:19), and one must keep in mind that it is "they" who shall beat their weapons into weapons of production. Israel is not necessarily included in this scenario.

5. It is interesting to note a similar phenomenon in early Christianity, where Christians both observed and experienced the destructive results of Jews rising up against the Roman authorities early on, and thus learned from their reading of scripture that such behaviors are wrong. However, after the empire was Christianized, a reverse strategy emerged to justify the use of military force and imperial armies in order to enforce, sometimes with brutal violence and cruelty, the authority of the Church.

6. James Pritchard, ed., *The Ancient Near East* (Princeton: Princeton University Press, 1957), 1:209–210. For a biblical version of the same conflict, see 2 Kings 3:4–27.

7. Judges 16:23; 1 Kings 11:5–7, 33; 2 Kings 1:3; 18:34; 23:13; Judges 10:6; and so on. Loyalty to a tribal deity did not keep people from relating to other deities that served roles in myth or nature.

8. The divine name was conveyed in writing by the four consonants Y.H.W.H., which some scholars, using the work of Wilhelm Gesenius, believe was pronounced "Yahweh." See William Smith, *A Dictionary of the Bible* (Boston: Little, Brown, 1863), 1:954–55; available at http://books.google.com/books?id=4a8eAQAAIAAJ.

9. In many if not most cultures, it is common to address equals or those on a lower social status by name, while addressing one's social superiors with special forms of address. Royalty are often addressed as "your highness" or other such epithets to ensure the necessary acknowledgment of separation between those with great power and those without. Such a psychology may lie behind the loss of the "personal name" of God in the Hebrew Bible (see Mishnah Yomah 6:2 to see discussion of an annual sacred rite at the Jerusalem Temple in which the true "personal name" of God was uttered by the high priest).

10. *Elohim* is "god" in a plural form, but the plural form denotes greatness rather than plurality. *Adonai* is also in the plural form, meaning literally, "our lords," and it is that plural form that suggests the grandeur. When humans in the Hebrew Bible refer to a superior as "my lord," it appears in the singular form, *adoni* (Genesis 23:6; 24:37; Exodus 32:22; 1 Samuel 25:41; Ruth 2:13; and so on)

11. Reuven Firestone, *Who Are the Real Chosen People? The Meaning of Chosenness in Judaism, Christianity, and Islam* (Woodstock, VT: Skylight Paths, 2008), 19–30.

12. While these particular references may reflect premonotheism sensibilities, the retention of the term *God of Israel* through the canonization process around the first century C.E. is no accident.

13. Some texts are careful to note that Y.H.W.H. is the God of Israel (Exodus 32:27; 34:23; it is very common in Joshua, Samuel, Kings, and so on). See Mark S. Smith, *The Early History of God: Yahweh and the Other Deities in Ancient Israel* (Grand Rapids, MI: Eerdmans, 2002).

14. Usually rendered as "God (or possessor) of the heavens and earth" (Genesis 14:19, 22; 24:3, 7) or God of the entire world (Isaiah 54:5) but also "God of the spirits of all flesh" (Exodus 16:22).

15. The transition to a confident monotheism took many years, but seems to have been completed by the end of the period of the classical prophets. Nili Fox, "The Concepts of God in Israel and the Question of Monotheism," in *Text, Artifact, and Image: Revealing Ancient Israelite Religion*, ed. G. Beckman and T. Lewis (Providence: Brown Judaic Studies, 2006), 341–43. Note how some biblical passages express a certain anxiety about the problem of how a universal God of all creation could have a unique relationship with only one small community of God's human creatures (Deuteronomy 7:6–11; Isaiah 19:24; Amos 3:2; 9:7).

16. Second Kings is more direct: "In the ninth year of Hoshea, the king of Assyria captured Samaria. He deported the Israelites to Assyria and settled them in Halah, at the [River] Habor, and in the towns of Media. This happened because the Israelites sinned against the Lord their God, who had freed them from the land of Egypt, from the hand of Pharaoh king of Egypt. . . . They committed wicked acts to vex the Lord, and they worshiped fetishes concerning which the Lord had said to them, 'You must not do this.' . . . The Lord was incensed at Israel and He banished them from His presence; none was left but the tribe of Judah alone" (2 Kings 17:6–18).

17. Some biblical references are considered by scholars to reflect aspects of this war. See Uriel Rappaport, *The First Book of Maccabees: Introduction, Hebrew Translation, and Commentary* (Jerusalem, Yad Ben-Zvi, 2004), 65–66; H. L. Ginzberg, "Dates and Characteristics of the Parts [of the Book of Daniel]," *Encyclopedia Judaica* 5:1281–1286. Arnaldo Momigliano supposes Daniel to refer to Antiochus IV's desecration of the Jerusalem Temple in Daniel's "abomination of desolation" (Daniel 9:27; 11:31; 12:11 in parallel with 1 Maccabees 1:54). See Arnaldo Momiglano, "The Romans and the Maccabees," in *Jewish History: Essays in Honour of Chimen Abramsky*, ed. Ada Rapoport-Alber and Steven Zipperstein (London: Peter Halban), 231–44.

18. Rappaport, *The First Book of Maccabees*, 1–2, 9–10.

19. A notable exception is a reference in Judah's prayer found in 1 Maccabees 7:41, where he calls on God to crush the enemy like God's angel struck down 185,000 blaspheming followers of a certain king.

20. For a good comparison of the two, see Jonathan Goldstein, *1 Maccabees*, The Anchor Bible 41 (New York: Doubleday, 1976), 3–36.

21. See Martin Hengel, *The Zealots: Investigations into the Jewish Freedom Movement in the Period from Herod I until A.D. 70*, trans. David W. Smith (Edinburgh: T & T Clark, 1989).

22. Seth Schwartz, *Imperialism and Jewish Society, 200 B.C.E. to 640 C.E.* (Princeton: Princeton University Press, 2001), 89–90. Modern scholarship is not in agreement over what category of troublemakers this term refers to. The arguments vary from political revolutionaries to social bandits, Robin Hood-like heroes of the downtrodden, desperate people who have fallen through the cracks of a strained economy, or a combination of these.

23. On Judah the Galilean and the Fourth Philosophy, see Hengel, *The Zealots*, 76–145. On Josephus's reference to what the zealots called themselves, see *Wars* 4:3, trans. William Whiston (Grand Rapids: Kregel, 1960). Cf. Mary Smallwood, "Bandits, Terrorists, Sicarii and Zealots," appendix A in Josephus, *The Jewish War*, trans. G. A. Williamson (New York: Dorset, 1981), 461–62.

24. Hengel, *The Zealots*, 282–90.

25. This point is made repeatedly and demonstrated convincingly by Schwartz, *Imperialism and Jewish Society*.

26. Another faction or set of factions with textual traditions to support their positions are those known from the texts discovered in the caves near Qumran and the Dead Sea, commonly known as the "Dead Sea Scrolls." They are not included here because they are noncanonical and it is not yet clear what communities they represent.

27. *Avot deRabbi Natan* (ARN[1] chapter 4, ARN[2] chapter 6), BT. *Gittin* 56a-b, *Lamentations Rabba* 1:5, no. 31, *Midrash Mishle* 15, which is virtually identical to ARN[2].

28. According to the Roman historian Cassius Dio, the Roman forces suffered so many losses that "Hadrian in writing to the senate did not employ the opening phrase commonly affected by the emperors, 'If you and your children are in health, it is well; I and the legions are in health.'" Dio Cassius, *Roman History* 69, 12:1–14:3, quoted in Menahem Stern, *Greek and Latin Authors on Jews and Judaism* (Jerusalem: Israel Academy of Sciences, 1974–84), 2:391–93.

29. For a variety of perspectives on the history of the rebellion, see Geza Vermes and Fergus Millar's revision of Emil Schurer, *The History of the Jewish People in the Age of Jesus Christ* (New York: Continuum, 1987); Yigal Yadin, *Bar Kokhba* (New York: Random House, 1971); Shimon Applebaum, *Prolegomena to the Study of the Second Jewish Revolt* (Oxford: British Archaeological Reports, 1976); Aharon Oppenheimer, *Mered bar Kokhva* [The Bar Kokhba Revolt] (Jerusalem: Zalman Shazar Center, 1980); Aharon Oppenheimer and Uriel Rappaport, *The Bar Kokhba Revolt: New Studies* (Jerusalem: Zalman Shazar Center, 1984); Menachem Mor, *The Bar Kokhba Revolt: Its Extent and Effect* (Jerusalem: Yad Ben-Tzvi, 1991); Peter Schäfer, *The Bar Kokhba War Reconsidered: New Perspectives on the Second Jewish Revolt Against Rome* (Tübingen: Mohr/Siebeck, 2003). On views regarding the image of Bar Kokhba in Rabbinic literature, see Ephraim Urbach, *The Sages* (Cambridge, MA: Harvard University Press, 1987), 593–603; Richard G. Marks, *The Image of Bar Kokhba in Traditional Jewish Literature* (University Park: Pennsylvania State University Press, 1994).

30. Michael Avi-Yona, *The Jews of Palestine: A Political History from the Bar Kokhba War to the Arab Conquest* (New York: Schocken, 1976), 50.

31. Mishna Ta'anit 4:6.

32. There were, of course, a few small Jewish military actions that had no historical impact, such as the uprising against the Caliphate by Abu 'Isa al-Isfahani in the eighth century. See Aaron Aescoly, *Hatenu'ot hameshichiyyot beyisra'el* [Jewish messianic movements] (Jerusalem: Bialik Institute, 1956), 123–24, 139–41; Salo Baron, *A Social and Religious History of the Jews* (New York: Columbia University Press, 1952–83), 5:184–94; Steven Wasserstrom, *Between Muslim and Jew* (Princeton: Princeton University Press, 1995), 71–82. On the militant Jewish Khazar nation, the Jewishness of which is still uncertain and which had virtually no impact on Jewish history per se, see Douglas Dunlop, *The History of the Jewish Khazars* (Princeton: Princeton University Press, 1954); Peter B. Golden, *Khazar Studies* (Budapest: Akadémiai Kiadó, 1980).

33. Israeli scholars have generally assumed that most if not all the Rabbinical leadership of the time backed the rebellion. See Y. Ben-Shalom, "Ma'mado shel bar-kokhva karosh ha'umah utemikhat hachkhamim bamered" [The status of Bar Kokhba at the head of the nation and the support of the sages for the rebellion], *Cathedra* 29 (1984): 13–28; Gedaliah Alon, *The Jews in Their Land in the Talmudic Age*, trans. Gershon Levi (Cambridge, MA: Harvard University Press, 1996), 630. This is unlikely. As mentioned above, Seth Schwartz (in *Imperialism and Jewish Society*) has shown that the amount of power and influence of the rabbis at this time is really unclear, and it is likely that the community was divided just as it was during earlier periods of military conflict with imperial powers. See Schäfer, "The Causes of the Bar Kokhba Revolt," 93–94.

34. This is the Standard English name for this work, which is called the "Jerusalem Talmud" in Hebrew *(talmud yerushulmi)*.

35. On Lamentations Rabba, see Galit Hasan-Rokem, *Web of Life: Folklore and Midrash in Rabbinic Literature* (Stanford: Stanford University Press, 2000), 8–9, 12–15.

36. See Targum Onkelos and Pseudo Yonatan s.v., Num.24:17.

37. He was a mid-second-century-c.e. sage in the Land of Israel and one of only four students of Rabbi Akiba who survived the Bar Kokhba Revolt (BT *Yevamot* 62b). According to the traditions attributed to him, his hatred of the Romans remained with him throughout his life.

38. A more complete rendering of Numbers 24:17 is *I see it, but not now, I behold it, but it is not near: a star [kokhav] will step forth out of Jacob, a scepter will rise out of Israel. It will smash the brow of Moab, the foundation of all the children of Seth. Edom will become its possession.*

39. Little is known of this man aside from his opposition to Akiba over the status of Bar Kokhba given in this passage. The only other statement given in his name gives the reasons for the destruction of the two Temples (*Tosefta, Menahot* [Tzukermandel Ed.] 13:22; BT *Yoma* 9a-b).

40. For a careful textual analysis of Rabbinic literature on Bar Kokhba, see Peter Schäfer, "Bar Kokhba and the Rabbis," in Schäfer, *The Bar Kokhba War Reconsidered*, 1–7.

41. Gerson Cohen considers the origin of the association of Esau/Edom with Rome to be the Bar Kokhba Revolt and identifies Rabbi Akiba as the likely source. Gerson Cohen, "Esau as Symbol in Early Medieval Thought," in *Jewish Medieval and Renaissance Studies*, ed. Alexander Altmann (Cambridge, MA: Harvard University Press, 1967), 20–22. Louis Feldman sees that identification already in Josephus, and perhaps even in the Testaments of the Twelve Patriarchs. Louis Feldman, *"Remember Amalek": Vengence, Zealotry, and Group Destruction in the Bible According to Philo, Pseudo-Philo and Josephus* (Cincinnati: Hebrew Union College Press, 2004), 63–64. After the Christianization of the Roman Empire in the fourth century, Edom became a Rabbinic code name for Christianity.

42. The earliest reference to Bar Kokhba by his messianic name is found in a contemporary, Justin Martyr, who wrote in Greek and seems not to have known that it was his *nom de guerre*. Richard Bauckham, "Jews and Jewish Christians in the Land of Israel at the Time of the Bar Kochba War, with Special Reference to the *Apocalypse of Peter*," in *Tolerance and Intolerance in Early Judaism and Christianity*, ed. Graham Stanton and Guy Stroumsa (Cambridge: Cambridge University Press, 2008), 228–29.

43. Bauckham concludes from Justin Martyr's innocent reference to him by his messianic nickname that it was standard usage and that Jewish support for the revolt was virtually universal except for Jewish Christians. But it seems unlikely that support for Bar Kokhba would have been so overwhelming given the fractious nature of the Jewish community during this period, the variety of positions held by Jews regarding the earlier Great Revolt of 66 c.e. observable in Josephus and Rabbinic literature, and the harsh Rabbinic critique found in the texts cited here, which, although edited from earlier messianic material by later redactors, conform to points of view that would be contemporary to Akiba and Bar Kokhba.

44. Yael Zerubavel, "Bar Kokhba's Image in Modern Israeli Culture," in Schäfer, *The Bar Kokhba War Reconsidered*, 281.

45. Aharon Openheimer, "Kedushat hachayyim vacheruf hanefesh be'iqvot mered bar-kochva" [Sanctity of life and martyrdom in the wake of the Bar Kokhba Revolt], in *Kedushat hachayyim vecheruf hanefesh* [Sanctity of life and martyrdom], ed. Yesha'ya Gafni and Aviezer Ravitzky (Jerusalem: Zalman Shazar Center, 1993), 89.

46. Nahum Glatzer, "The Attitude toward Rome in Third-Century Judaism," in *Essays in Jewish Thought* (Tuscaloosa: University of Alabama, 1978), 1–15. On messianism in Judaism, see Urbach, *The Sages*, 649–90; Abba Hillel Silver, *The History of Messianic Speculations in Israel* (New York: Macmillan, 1927); Joseph Klausner, *The Messianic Idea in Israel* (New York: Macmillan, 1955); Aaron Aescoly, *Hatenu'ot hameshichiyot beyisra'el;* Arie Morgenstern, *Hastening Redemption: Messianism and the Settlement of the Land of Israel* (New York: Oxford University Press, 2006); Aviezer Ravitzky, *Mes-*

sianism, Zionism, and Jewish Religious Radicalism (Chicago: University of Chicago Press, 1996); Dov Schwartz, *Meshichiut: Faith at the Crossroads: A Theological Profile of Religious Zionism,* trans. Batya Stein (Leiden: Brill, 2002).

47. The terminology in the two Talmuds is quite specific: *milchamot yehoshua likhbosh* (the wars of Joshua to conquer) in the Babylonian Talmud, *Sota* 44b, and *milchemet yehoshua* (Joshua's war) in the PT. *Sota* 8:1.

48. Maimonides (d. 1204) nevertheless formalizes the notion of defensive war as a category of *mitzvah* war in his *Mishneh Torah, melakhim* 5:1.

49. Holy war remained alive and well in the fantasy world of Rabbinic Judaism, but hardly a real possibility. But as noted above, there were occasional historical exceptions to the Jewish rejection of organized military adventures, such as the militant Khazar kingdom and the messianic warrior Abu Isa al-Isfahani, but neither seem to have been part of the world of Rabbinic Judaism, and neither had a noticeable impact on the development of war ideas in Judaism.

50. *Song of Songs* 2:7; 3:5; 8:4. The last rendering of the sentence, in 8:4, does not include "by the gazelles and by the hinds of the field," but the rabbis include it there also by analogy.

51. "Ascension" or "going up" refers to moving from outside the Land of Israel to within the biblical borders (which is where the modern Hebrew term for emigration to the State of Israel, *'aliyah,* comes from). This was considered a collective prohibition but not a prohibition against individuals who wished to move their families to the Land of Israel.

52. Gershom Scholem, *Sabbatai Sevi: The Mystical Messiah* (Princeton: Princeton University Press, 1973).

53. See S. Ettinger, "The Modern Period," in *A History of the Jewish People,* ed. H. H. Ben-Sasson (Cambridge, MA: Harvard University Press, 1994), 727–1040; Paul Mendes-Flohr and Jehuda Reinharz, eds., *The Jew in the Modern World: A Documentary History,* 2nd ed. (New York: Oxford University Press, 1995); Arthur Hertzberg, *The Zionist Idea* (New York: Harper & Row, 1966).

54. On the nature of modern national identity, including its religious component, see Benedict Anderson, *Imagined Communities* (New York: Verso, 1991).

55. Walter Laqueur, *A History of Zionism* (New York: Schocken, 1976); Hertzberg, *The Zionist Idea.*

56. Ravitzky, *Messianism, Zionism, and Jewish Religious Radicalism;* Reuven Firestone, "Holy War in Modern Judaism? 'Mitzvah War' and the Problem of the 'Three Vows,'" *Journal of the American Academy of Religion* 74, no. 4 (December 2006): 954–82.

57. Ravitzky, *Messianism, Zionism, and Jewish Religious Radicalism,* 11, 221. In retrospect, it is possible to see hints of messianic thinking associated with even the religious Zionist leaders that argued for the dissociation of Zionism with messianism. See also Firestone, *Holy War in Judaism.*

58. For English-language works on Abraham Isaac Kook, see Jacob Agus, *Banner of Jerusalem: The Life, Times and Thought of Abraham Isaac Kuk* (New York: Bloch, 1946); Isadore Epstein, *Abraham Yitzhak Hacohen Kook: His Life and Works* (Jerusalem: Torah Ve'Avodah Library, 1951); Zvi Yaron, *The Philosophy of Rabbi Kook,* trans. Avner Tomaschoff (Jerusalem: World Zionist Organization, 1991); Benjamin Ish-Shalom, *Rav Avraham Itzhak HaCohen Kook: Between Rationalism and Mysticism,* trans. Ora Wiskind Elper (Albany: SUNY Press, 1993); Abraham Isaac Kook, *Orot,* trans. Bezalel Naor (Northvale: Jason Aaronson, 1993); Lawrence Kaplan and David Shatz, eds., *Rabbi Abraham Isaac Kook and Jewish Spirituality* (New York: New York University Press, 1995); Simcha Raz, *An Angel among Men: Impressions from the Life of Rav Avraham Yitzchak Hakohen Kook,* trans. Moshe Lichtman (Jerusalem: Kol Mevaser, 2003).

59. Some religious Jews also engaged in fighting and the use of arms, but they were a small minority and they tended to consider their actions as entirely defensive and thus justified by Rabbinic tradition.

60. *Kol kitvey maran haga'on rabbi yitzhaq Isaac Halevi Hertzog* [The collected writings of Rabbi Yitzhaq Isaac HaLevi Herzog] (Jerusalem: Mosad HaRav Kook/Yad HaRav Herzog, n.d.), 1:121. This responsum appears in slightly different version in Herzog, "Al haqamat hamedinah umilchamoteha" [On the establishment of the state and its wars], *Techumin* 4 (1983): 13; Yitzhak Refael and S. Z. Shragai, eds., *Sefer HaTzionut HaDatit* [The book of Religious Zionism] (Jerusalem: Mosad HaRav Kook, 1977), 1:60–61.

61. Refael and Shragai, *Sefer hatziyonut HaDatit*, 1:62–3.

62. Ravitzky, *Messianism, Zionism, and Jewish Religious Radicalism*, 40–78.

63. Tzvi Yehudah Kook, "Qedushat 'am qadosh 'al admat haqodesh" [The sanctity of the holy people on the sacred land], *Shanah Beshanah* (1976): 268 (originally delivered orally in 1967); Ehud Sprinzak, *The Ascendance of Israel's Radical Right* (New York: Oxford University Press, 1991), 44.

64. Howard Sachar, *A History of Israel: From the Rise of Zionism to Our Time*, 3rd ed. (New York: Alfred A. Knopf, 2007), 622–35; Segev Oren and Walter Lacqueur, *The Road to War 1967: The Origins of the Arab-Israeli Conflict* (London: Weidenfeld and Nicolson, 1969) 136–37.

65. Michael Bar Zohar, *Hachodesh ha'arokh beyoter* [The longest month] (Tel Aviv: Levin Epstein, 1968), 153–54.

66. For the period leading up to the 1967 War, see Oren and Lacqueur, *The Road to War 1967*; Nadav Safran, *From War to War: The Arab Israeli Confrontation, 1948–1967* (New York: Pegasus, 1967).

67. Sachar, *History of Israel*, 614. "[Moshe Dayan] would even refer to the Six-Day War of 1967 as an expression of the nation's yearning for the land of its forefathers, rather than as a war of survival." Ibid., 479.

68. The newsletter of the Religious Kibbutz Movement, a source of much Religious Zionist activism in the 1950s and '60s, was full of messianic images and speculation in the immediate aftermath of the 1967 War (No. 256; 15, no. 10 [June 1967]). See Menahem Friedman, "Jewish Zealots: Conservative versus Innovative," in *Jewish Fundamentalism in Comparative Perspective*, ed. Laurence Silberstein (New York: New York University Press, 1993), 148–63.

69. Shelomo Aviner, *Am Kelavi'* [A national like a lion cub] (Jerusalem, 1983), 2:114–15, 119–20; Meir Blumenfeld, "Bidvar hashevu'ah shelo ya'alu bachomah" [On the vow not to go up as a wall], *Shanah BeShanah* (1974): 151–55; Menachem Kasher, "Da'at torah 'al hashevu'ah shelo ya'alu yisra'el bachomah le'eretz yisra'el" [Torah position on the vow that Israel not go up as a wall to the Land of Israel], *Shanah BeShanah* (1977): 213–28; Moshe Tzvi Neriah , "Zekhuteynu 'al eretz yisra'el" [Our right to the Land of Israel], *Torah sheBe'al-Peh* (1974): 149–80.

70. Shelomo Goren, *Torat HaMedinah* (Jerusalem: Chemed, 1996), 36–42.

71. Janet O'Dea, "Gush Emunim: Roots and Ambiguities: The Perspective of the Sociology of Religion," *Forum on the Jewish People, Zionism and Israel* 2, no. 25 (1976): 39–50; Kevin Avruch, "Traditionalizing Israeli Nationalism: The Development of Gush Emunim," *Political Psychology* 1, no. 1 (1979): 47–57; Janet Aviad, "The Contemporary Israeli Pursuit of the Millennium," *Religion* 14 (1984): 199–222; Eliezer Don Yehiya, "Jewish Messianism, Religious Zionism, and Israeli Politics: The Impact and Origins of Gush Emunim," *Middle Eastern Studies* 23, no. 2 (1987): 215–34. See also Roger Friedland and Richard D. Hecht, "The Politics of Sacred Place: Jerusalem's Temple Mount/al-haram al-sharif," in *Sacred Places and Profane Spaces*, ed. Jamie Scott and Pauls Simpson-Houseley (New York: Greenwood, 1991), 21–61.

72. Dov Schwartz, "Religious Zionism III: Since 1948," in *Encyclopaedia of Judaism* (Leiden: Brill, 2005), 4:2315–16; www.netivot-shalom.org.il/index.php. But while a peace movement has formed within the ranks of Orthodox Zionists, it has been largely sidelined by more militant voices that are overwhelmingly dominant.

73. Stuart Cohen, *The Scroll or the Sword* (Amsterdam: Harwood, 1997), 42–56.

74. Yehudah Amital, *Hama'a lot mima'amaqim* [From out of the depths] (Jerusalem Alon-Shevut:

Har Etzion Association, 1986); Yitzhak Kaufman, *Hatzavah kahalakhah: hilkhot milchamah vetzavah* [The army according to halakhah: Laws of war and army] (Jerusalem: n.p., 1992), 2–10; Yakov Ariel, "Da'at haramban bekibbush ha'aretz" [The view of Nahmanides on conquest of the land], *Tehumin* 5 (1984): 174–79; idem, *Be'ohalah shel torah* [In the canopy of Torah: Responsa] (Kefar Darom: n.p., 2003), 26–32.

75. Bernard M. Casper, *"Reshit Zemichat Geulatenu,"* in *Religious Zionism after Forty Years of Statehood,* ed. Shubert Spero and Yitzchak Pessin (Jerusalem: Mesilot, 1989), 66–69.

3

Annihilate Amalek!

Christian Perspectives on 1 Samuel 15

Bernhard A. Asen

In the Academy Award winning movie *Patton,* starring George C. Scott, an important scene finds General Patton frustrated by bad weather. He summons the Third Army division chaplain and requests a "weather prayer." Patton: "I want a prayer, a weather prayer." Chaplain: "A weather prayer, sir?" Patton: "Yes, let's see if you can't get God working with us." Chaplain: "Gonna take a thick rug for that kind of praying." Patton: "I don't care if it takes a flying carpet." Chaplain: "I don't know how this will be received, general. Praying for good weather so we can kill our fellow man." Patton: "I assure you, because of my relations with the Almighty if you write a good prayer, we'll have good weather. And I expect that prayer within an hour." Chaplain: "Yes, sir."[1]

In the next scene Patton walks in the blowing snow, accompanied by a series of background images: violent explosions and flamethrowers spewing fire. As he strolls, battle helmet under arm, he reads aloud the chaplain's prayer: "Almighty and most merciful Father we humbly beseech Thee of Thy great goodness to restrain this immoderate weather with which we've had to contend. Grant us fair weather for battle. Graciously hearken to us as soldiers who call upon Thee that armed with Thy power we may advance from victory to victory and crush the oppression and wickedness of our enemies and establish Thy justice among men and nations. Amen."[2] After the weather clears, Patton says to his aide: "God, get me that chaplain. He's in good with the Lord and I want to decorate him."

These "fighting words" for help in battle can be found throughout human history and raise the age-old question of the relationship between God and violence in human experience. The following essay discusses one incident in that vast history that also involved a chaplain and a military commander. In 1 Samuel 15,

55

Samuel, a priest, prophet, and judge confronts Saul, Israel's first king, who is preparing for war against the Amalekites. Samuel instructs Saul to attack Amalek and "utterly destroy *[herem]* all that they have . . . [and to] not spare them, but kill both man and woman, child and infant, ox and sheep, camel and donkey" (1 Samuel 15:3). Saul's army defeated the Amalekites but "Saul and the people spared [King] Agag, and the best of the sheep and of the cattle and of the fatlings, and the lambs, and all that was valuable, and would not utterly destroy them; all that was despised and worthless they utterly destroyed" (1 Samuel 15:8–9). Samuel subsequently confronts Saul, charging him with disobedience for not fully carrying out Yahweh's command. He stresses the importance of obedience (1 Samuel 15:22) and says, "Because you [Saul] have rejected the word of Yahweh, he has also rejected you from being king" (1 Samuel 15:23). After Samuel has "hewed Agag in pieces before Yahweh in Gilgal" (1 Samuel 15:33), he and Saul part company, never to see each other again. The incident concludes with the words: "And Yahweh was sorry that he had made Saul king over Israel" (1 Samuel 15:35).

This Amalek narrative is only one of many so-called texts of terror in the Hebrew Bible (cf., e.g., Psalm 83:4; Isaiah 19:1–10; Exodus 17:8–16, Joshua 8:24–25). Raymund Schwager estimates that the Old Testament contains "over six hundred passages that explicitly talk about nations, kings, or individuals attacking, destroying and killing others."[3] How are we to understand such texts? Can we ignore them? Can we simply write them off as "typically Old Testament"? Sometimes Christians confine themselves to the New Testament and say that the texts of the Hebrew Bible have been "abrogated" by the New Testament. But do not Christians claim that the Old Testament is also the charter of *their* faith? Furthermore, such texts of terror also occur in the New Testament. Is not the Parable of the Pounds that Jesus tells also in the Christian Bible? "But as for these enemies of mine who did not want me to be king over them—bring them here and slaughter them in my presence" (Luke 19:27). And what about Acts 5:1–11 or Revelation 14?[4]

Many attempts have been made in recent years to come to terms with the issue of God and violence in human culture and the Bible. One thinks, for example, of the work of René Girard, Hector Avalos, and Mark Juergensmeyer, and in biblical studies the work of Susan Niditch, Terence Fretheim, Philip Stern, and others.[5] These attempts have been admirable. However, Jonathan Klawans contends that "extravagant theorizing on the origins of religious violence will rarely stand up to scrutiny, for scrutiny after all requires evidence, and grandiose theorizing about such origins, by its nature, reaches beyond what the evidence can soundly support."[6] Klawans's advice is to "focus instead on ways in which religion in general (and for our purposes biblical scriptures and beliefs in particular) serve to accentuate, exaggerate and otherwise bring about acts of human violence *in specific documented historical contexts*. This mode of analysis begins with clear (and meaningful) definitions. It proceeds to work with historical data, and considers context. It then comes to grips with the religious and social dynamics in play, attending to the variables that lead to the manifestation of scripturally-justified biblical violence."[7]

Here I will follow the general contours of Klawans's advice and (1) consider 1 Samuel 15 in the context of the rise of kingship and the establishment of statehood in Israel; (2) explore the biblical concept of "utter destruction" or the "ban" (which is subsumed under the general idea of "holy war") in 1 Samuel 15 and its trajectory into the latter prophets, Rabbinic literature, and the LXX; and (3) conclude with some comments on violence in the New Testament and how Christians might understand and come to terms with the specific text of terror that is 1 Samuel 15.

1 SAMUEL 15: CONTEXT

The Book of 1 Samuel highlights two major events in Israel's history: (1) the establishment of the monarchy (chs. 8–12), and (2) preparing the way for David's rise to power (chs. 16–31).[8] Furthermore, 1 Samuel also establishes the principle that Israel's king is to be subject "to the prophet through whom God conveys his word. In other words, the obedience to the word of God is the necessary condition for a king acceptable to the God of Israel."[9]

David Jobling calls 1 Samuel 12 through 2 Samuel 7 the "Book of the Everlasting [i.e., unconditional] Covenant."[10] The covenant operative up to 1 Samuel 13, however, is conditional. First Samuel 12:25 concludes: "But *if* you still do wickedly you shall be swept away, both you and your king." First Samuel 13 begins the "everlasting covenant" with the house of David, which is central "to the Israelite consciousness (and, through the theology of Jesus as Messiah, the Christian consciousness)."[11] It ends with 2 Samuel 7 and the succession narrative, with the promise that David's "throne shall be established forever" (2 Samuel 7:16). This promise is denied to Saul from the beginning of his kingship in two episodes, 1 Samuel 13:8–15 and 1 Samuel 15, both involving cultic offenses where Samuel confronts Saul.

According to David Tsumura, since "Wellhausen's *Prolegomena* (1878), there has been a general tendency to view these passages [13:8–15; 15:1–34] as doublets, that is two versions of the same incident".[12] they report Saul's offense at Gilgal, emphasize obedience to Yahweh, and "are similar in structure."[13] The basic difference between the two episodes is that Saul's transgression in 1 Samuel 13 is not as "explicit as we might like."[14] Did Saul usurp Samuel's role as priest, or was his failure that he did not wait long enough for Samuel to arrive? It appears that Saul usurped priestly authority by making offerings that Samuel, the chaplain, was to have made. In the transition from the institution of judgeship to prophecy, and from the institution of judgeship to kingship,[15] clear boundaries needed to be established among the institutions of leadership. General Patton could very well have written that weather prayer himself, but he did not. He followed military protocol and, so it appears, Saul should have done so regarding the sacrifices in 1 Samuel 13.

The precise nature of Saul's transgression in 1 Samuel 13 has been the subject of considerable discussion. According to Klein, "Sacrifices were normally offered before a holy war (1 Samuel 7:9), and God's permission was frequently sought (cf. Judges 20:23, 27; 1 Samuel 7:9; 14:8–10; 14:37; 23:2, 4, 9–12; 28:6; 30:7–8; 2 Samuel 5:19, 23)."[16] Samuel, of course, was initially opposed to kingship (1 Samuel 8:6). His opposition had been "tempered by a new system in which the charismatic savior's (or judge's) responsibilities were assigned to the king (in leading the troops) and to the prophet (who had to communicate to the king Yahweh's authorization for war)."[17] Another view is that Saul was in effect combining the roles of priest and king. In any event, Saul's "foolishness" (1 Samuel 13:13) may not have been that he actually offered the sacrifices but that he failed to acknowledge Samuel's "higher role as the divine messenger and to listen to the word of God."[18]

In 1 Samuel 15, on the other hand, Saul's transgression is very clear and explicit. He fails to be obedient down to the last detail in instituting the *herem* and annihilating the Amalekites. Consequently, Saul is rejected as king. Now, it is true that when Samuel confronts Saul in 15:14 about the bleating sheep and lowing cattle, Saul does say, "*They* have brought them from the Amalekites; for the people spared the best of the sheep and the cattle, to sacrifice to Yahweh your God but the rest *we* have utterly destroyed" (15:15). The problem is that to sacrifice and to carry out the ban were not one and the same thing. Sacrifice usually implied that some of the meat was set aside for human consumption. The command was to devote everything to God. If, in fact, Saul believes he had carried out the ban to its fullest extent, why does he say *they* have brought and *we* have utterly destroyed, instead of *I*?

DEFINING THE WORD *HEREM*

Because the root *hrm* has a broad range of semantic meanings, there is no single generally accepted scholarly definition of the term. According to Brekelmans, the noun *herem* occurs twenty-nine times in the Old Testament. The root *hrm* "referred originally to that which is forbidden either because it is accursed and should be destroyed *(res exsecranda)* or because it is very holy *(res sacrosancta)*."[19] Philip Stern's discussion of the philological background of the root *hrm* emphasizes that *hrm* denotes a separation between "that which is God's and that which is human matched by a corresponding physical action or course of action making and marking the separation."[20] The *herem*, then, is a "consecration through destruction (to a deity) of a designated enemy, with some or all of the spoils of victory set apart to the deity by destruction, not subject to the usual division among the army."[21] Susan Niditch succinctly defines the *herem* simply as "God's portion."[22]

Saul's transgression in 1 Samuel 15 is his failure to give the most valuable portion of the booty from the attack on the Amalekites to God. As Niditch puts it, "To mix humans, the highest of God's breathing creations, with sickly or less valuable animals is to break the whole concept of the ban as sacrifice."[23] Furthermore, sparing King Agag from the destruction meant that the most prized part of the booty was not offered to God, which was contrary to the whole idea of the ban.

THE *HEREM* AS SACRIFICE

Leviticus 27:28 states that "every devoted thing is most holy to Yahweh." Here, as well as in Leviticus 27:21, the words *qodesh* (holy) and *herem* (devoted to destruction) are juxtaposed. In these instances the *herem* is not an object or person that has been destroyed, but something devoted and sacrificed for the benefit of God or the priests.[24] While Stern thinks that these Levitical references are later, "domesticated" uses of the term *herem,* Niditch believes the lateness of these texts "proves only that the sacrificial nuance of the ban is alive and well in late biblical works."[25]

Consider, for example, the interesting "honey incident" just before our text in 1 Samuel 15. In 1 Samuel 14:24, we read that Saul "committed a very rash act on that day. He had laid an oath on the troops, saying, 'Cursed be anyone who eats food before it is evening and I have been avenged on my enemies.' So none of the troop tasted food" (v. 24), except, that is, for Saul's son Jonathan who ate some honey (14:27–29). Some of Saul's troops slaughtered the sheep, oxen, and calves taken from Michmash and "ate them with the blood" (14:32). Saul, hearing what his troops had done, hastily built an altar where the animals were slaughtered and their blood sacrificially burned.

When Saul decided to attack the Philistines once again, he this time "inquired of God" (14:37), unlike in 1 Samuel 13; but he received no answer, perhaps implying God's anger because of the previous violations of Saul's oath on the part of Jonathan and some of the troops. Attempting to find out how the situation had unraveled, Saul swore that even if his own son Jonathan were responsible, that person would die. The lot was cast and pointed to Jonathan and Saul. Saul ordered the lot to be cast once more and this time it fell to Jonathan, who readily admitted he had eaten some honey and was prepared to die (14:44). Fortunately, the people "ransomed Jonathan, and he did not die" (14:45). The point of this narrative is that vows made to God are clearly a matter of "do or die." What is set apart, holy, devoted to God must be wholly regarded as such.

DIVINE PARTICIPATION IN AND
IMPLEMENTATION OF THE *HEREM*

Patton said to his division chaplain, "Let's see if you can't get God working with us." In Israel's concept of holy war, the "sanction and active participation of the national god" was a presupposition for war.[26] We are told that when Saul "saw any strong or valiant warrior, he took him into his service" (1 Samuel 14:52). In fact, however, the number of warriors was irrelevant because "nothing [could] hinder Yahweh from saving by many or by few" (1 Samuel 14:6). The warriors do not war alone. When Saul gives his eldest daughter, Merab, to be David's wife, he tells David, "only be valiant for me and fight Yahweh's battles" (1 Samuel 18:17).

Indeed, Exodus 15:3 states, "Yahweh is a warrior; Yahweh is his name."[27] In one of the oldest known fragments of Hebrew poetry in the Old Testament, the so-called Song of Miriam (Exodus 15:1–18), Yahweh is the one who "triumphed gloriously" and threw "horse and rider into the sea" (v. 1). For Israel, more often than not, it was Yahweh who conducted war. During Israel's journey to Sinai after the Exodus from Egypt, they were attacked by the Amalekites at Rephidim (Exodus 17). The Hebrew people prevailed not because of their military prowess but because of Yahweh's power and because *Yahweh* would "have war with Amalek from generation to generation" (Exodus 17:16).

Before the rise of the monarchy, the Hebrew Bible tends to avoid the idea of human beings conducting war with the support of the deity and instead sees God himself in charge of war.[28] For example, in Joshua 10 it was Yahweh who "threw" the Amorites "into a panic" and Yahweh who "chased" them and "threw down huge stones from heaven upon them" (vv. 10–11). It was Yahweh who "gave the Amorites over to the Israelites" (v. 12). Indeed, Joshua even enlisted the sun and the moon (v. 12) until victory was won. Similarly, in the Song of Deborah (Judges 5), the "stars fought from heaven . . . against Sisera" (v. 20) and "the torrent Kishon swept them away" (v. 21). There are also numerous instances where "Yahweh's spirit" *(ruach)* comes to the rescue (cf. Judges 6:34, for Gideon; 14:6, for Samson) or where the enemy is routed because the enemy is frightened by Israel's God (cf. Judges 7:22; 1 Samuel 7:10; 14:15).

It is the transition to the monarchy when the people demand to have a king who will "go before us and fight our battles" (1 Samuel 8:20). However, never in Israel's history does Yahweh appear to be a mere spectator or figurehead with regard to national politics or military affairs. In the ideology of kingship, it is clear that it is not the king but Yahweh who is the subject of war and victory. It is God who strikes the king's enemies "on the cheek" and breaks "the teeth of the wicked" (Psalm 3:7), and God "who sits in the heavens and laughs" (Psalm 2:4) and breaks the nations "with a rod of iron" and dashes them "in pieces like a potter's vessel" (v. 9).

In addition to divine leadership and sanction, a "holy war" also required the support of religious officials. In the protocols of holy war outlined in Deuteronomy 20 the instruction is given, "Before you engage in battle, the priest shall come forward and speak to the troops, and shall say to them: 'Hear, O Israel! Today you are drawing near to do battle against your enemies. Do not lose heart, or be afraid, or panic, or be in dread of them; for it is Yahweh your God who goes with you, to fight for you against your enemies, to give you victory'" (vv. 3–4).

A desire to "get God working with us" was not confined to Israel. The Mesha Stone, dating from the ninth century B.C.E., speaks about how King Mesha liberated his land and people from the sovereignty of Israel's kings with the help of the god Chemosh.[29] The stone reports how Mesha viciously carried out "ethnic cleansing" of Israelite settlements: "Now the men of Gad had always dwelt in the land of Ataroth, and the king of Israel has built Ataroth for them: but I fought against the town and took it and slew all the people of the town as satiation [intoxication] for Chemosh and Moab. And I brought back from there Arel [or Oriel], its chieftain, dragging him before Chemosh in Keriotl, and I settled there men of Sharon and men of Maharith."[30] While the concept of the "ban" does not appear here, it seems to be implied. The inhabitants were eradicated completely for the sake of Chemosh, and all of the remaining material possessions (houses, land, household goods), thanks to Chemosh, fell into the hands of the Moabites. The text continues: "And Chemosh said to me, 'Go, take Nebo from Israel!' So I went by night and fought against it from the break of dawn until noon, taking and slaying all, seven thousand men, boys, women, girls and maidservants, for I had devoted them to destruction *[herem]* for (the god) Ashtar-Chemosh. And I took from there the [. . .] of Yahweh, dragging them before Chemosh. And the king of Israel had built Jahaz, and he dwelt there while he was fighting against me, but Chemosh drove him out before me."[31] Here, again, the extermination of the population is mentioned. But in this instance, the women also are included and the word *ban (herem)* is used (the same word as in Hebrew). Everything is dedicated to the god Chemosh, whose task it was to give land and to guide people in times of war.[32]

In addition to the Mesha Stone, there are further parallels to genocidal actions among the Hittites and in some ancient Greek and Roman literature.[33] The Mesha Stone, however, is clearly the "closest parallel to the biblical command against Amalek."[34] The difference is that the context of the Mesha Stone is set within a dream and, unlike the biblical injunction, it is not commanded by a god.

Did Israel, then, like its neighbors, actually practice this kind of holy war? Can 1 Samuel 15 be considered, per Klawans's advice above, a *specific documented historical context* of holy war? These are difficult questions to answer definitively because of the paucity of the data. The Book of Deuteronomy provides us with only a handful of texts concerning the conduct of the *herem* in Israel. Deuteronomy 7:1–2 unequivocally states that when Yahweh brings the people into the land, he will clear away "many nations," including the "Hittites, the Girgashites, the Amorites, the Canaanites, the Perizzites, the Hivites, and the Jebusites," and when he does, these nations are to be "utterly destroyed." Not all wars, however, resulted in the *herem*. Deuteronomy 20 sees at least three possible outcomes of war: (1) If a city accepts terms of peace and surrender, all the people in it "shall serve you at forced labor" (v. 10). (2) If the terms of peace are rejected and the people continue to fight, the city is besieged and all the males are put "to the sword" (v. 13), but the "women, the children, livestock, and everything else in the town, all its spoil" (v. 14) is taken as plunder. (3) However, the cities of the "people that Yahweh your God is giving you as an inheritance" (v. 16) are to be "annihilated" *[herem]* . . . so that they may not teach you to do all the abhorrent things that they do (v. 18). The only exception to annihilation is the trees that produce food (vv. 19–20).

Deuteronomy 21:10–14 mentions that marriage to captured women is possible, but if, after a time, the husband is not "satisfied with her" (v. 14), he is to set her free and not sell her like a slave. Apparently, the military camps where Israel was billeted were considered sacred space. Deuteronomy 23:9–14 speaks about guarding against "any impropriety" (v. 9), including nocturnal emissions and the disposal of bodily excrement (vv. 10–12), because "Yahweh your God travels along with your camp" (v. 14). Furthermore, a newly married man "shall not go out with the army or be charged with any related duty. He shall be free at home one year, to be happy with the wife whom he has married" (24:5).

Whether or not Israel actually implemented the ban is also a controversial issue. According to Moshe Weinfeld, the ban in Deuteronomy is a "utopian program," a *Kulturkampf* against the gods of the Canaanites and the "abhorrent things that they do for their gods, and [by which] you thus sin against Yahweh your God" (Deuteronomy 20:18).[35] In her study of war ideology in the Hebrew Bible, Susan Niditch maintains that "the ban in its ferocity cannot simply be rejected as a later accretion or an untrue reflection of the real religion of Israel."[36] And C. Brekelmans concludes that "one cannot prove that the *herem* was a permanent element of the holy war. It was apparently promised and executed only in particular crises in order to assure God's aid (cf. Numbers 21:2ff.; Judges 1:17)."[37]

An important related matter is the dating of 1 Samuel 15. McCarter assigns 1 Samuel 15 to a middle, though still pre-Deuternomistic, prophetic strand,[38] while Stern thinks 1 Samuel 15 goes "back to the earliest part of the Samuel traditions, certainly no later than the ninth century B.C."[39] Zevit claims that the "literary sources conveying the story [1 Samuel 15] date to the ninth-eighth century (Exodus), and the seventh (Deuteronomy, 1 Samuel), while the narratives concern events that occurred, according to the historiographic tradition, in the twelfth, eleventh, and tenth centuries BCE."[40] Other scholars consider 1 Samuel 15 to be the beginning of a hypothetical source called the History of David's Rise (HDR), which attempts to explain Saul's rejection and David's subsequent rise.[41] According to Klein, because the HDR is a hypothetical document "whose exact limits cannot be determined, the purpose or intended audience of the document may never be determined to everyone's satisfaction"[42] In the end, there is no certain date that can be assigned to 1 Samuel 15. Its composition could have happened any time from the reign of Josiah (640–609 B.C.E.) to the postexilic era (550 B.C.E.).[43]

Is 1 Samuel 15, then, a *specific documented historical* text? It is difficult to say with certainty, but surely the narrator of 1 Samuel 15 presents it as historical. The ban was considered to be "God's portion,"[44] and involved "rooting out the cancerous and contagious 'other,' that which is unclean because of sin."[45] Saul was assigned the task of rooting out the Amalekites and giving God his required "portion"; but he failed and thus was rejected as king, and the "spirit" *(ruach)* of YHWH departed from Saul, and an evil spirit from God began tormenting him (1 Samuel 16:14). One wonders whether in those moments when David was playing the lyre to dispel that evil spirit from Saul (1 Samuel 16:23), Saul may have thought, Why? Why did God bring Saul so far only to cast him off?

According to Walter Dietrich and Christian Link, there may have been three possible reasons:[46]

1. The biblical narrator had to come to terms with a basic datum of the beginning of the monarchy where the sovereignty of Saul, the Benjaminite, and his family had to be transferred to the Judean, David, and his successors. Such transference of sovereignty was not typical of the monarchical system, and the biblical historiographers did not have an adequate explanation for it. They were certain, however, that God was involved in this fundamental change. Saul's rise, then, could not go counter to God's will; he had to blaze the trail to make way for David.

2. According to the biblical account, God was forced to initiate and allow the monarchy, and had not freely agreed to it or freely instituted it. Before Saul ever entered the scene, it was "all the elders" who came to Samuel and insisted that he "appoint for us, then, a king to govern us, like other nations" (1 Samuel 8:5; cf. 8:19–20). Samuel considered the request "evil" (ra'); God himself perceived it as a dethronement. God would not or could not prevent Israel from doing something so dangerous and wrongheaded. Consequently, God even helped the people by providing in Saul a suitable candidate for kingship (1 Samuel 9:1–10, 16). Indeed, God had "chosen" Saul to be king (1 Samuel 10:24), but it was a chosenness joined to specific expectations: Saul was to fulfill his responsibilities and entrust himself to Samuel's leadership. Instead, he began to make decisions solely on his own and those decisions became increasingly catastrophic. A second reason, then, why God rejected

Saul as king was that God wanted the best for Israel, and Saul was not the best Israel had.

3. An omnipotent and omniscient God should have known whom he was choosing to be king, and whether that person was capable of performing the task. The Saul narrative shows that "in this sense the God of the bible is not omniscient and omnipotent. He will or must allow human beings and relationships to develop in unexpected and even negative directions."[47] Saul was not, essentially, an evil person. Had he followed protocol and strictly adhered to the rules of the game, he might have been an effective ruler. When that did not happen, God intervened to protect Israel from ruination. Was Saul, then, a victim of the failure of divine foresight? No. "Rather, Saul was an admonitory example of the freedom of human beings (who are entrusted with enormous power) to act faithlessly toward God and their fellows, and for the freedom of God to counter such faithlessness."[48]

Dealing with Amalek would now be left to a "neighbor" of Saul's, a "better man" (1 Samuel 15:28), named David. As the Book of 1 Samuel nears the end, the Amalekites reappear in chapter 30, but this time it is not Saul who has to deal with them, but David. Had Saul carried out the *herem* against the Amalekites back in chapter 15, this second battle would not be necessary. As chapter 30 opens, the Amalekites have successfully raided, burned, and looted Ziklag, and have carried off David's two wives, Ahinoam and Abigail (v. 5). Before pursuing the raiders, however, David, in direct contrast to Saul, seeks "strength in the Lord his God" by consulting with the priest, Abiathar. Permission is granted to pursue the raiders (v. 8) and David eventually recovers everything the Amalekites had taken, including his two wives (v. 18). In the process of attacking, "four hundred young [Amalekite] men" mount camels and get away (v. 17). Consequently, not even David completely annihilates the Amalekites. At least four hundred of them live to fight another day.

The fate of the Amalekites after David's time is mentioned briefly in 1 Chronicles 4:42–43, where we are informed that "five hundred men of the Simeonites . . . destroyed the remnant of the Amalekites that had escaped." According to 1 Chronicles 4:41, this incident occurred "in the days of Hezekiah," which would have been sometime in the eighth century B.C.E.

The very first verse of 2 Samuel begins: "After the death of Saul, when David had returned from defeating the Amalekites, David remained two days in Ziklag." During this time, a young man came and reported the deaths of Saul and Jonathan to David (cf. 1 Samuel 31). The young man confesses to having killed Saul, and twice tells David that he is an Amalekite (vv. 7, 13). Finally, David has the young man killed, not because he was an Amalekite, but because he "killed Yahweh's anointed" (v. 15). According to Feldman, Pseudo-Philo 65.4 identifies the young messenger as "Edabus, the son of Agag, the king of the Amalekites whom Saul had spared, thus stressing the lesson that Saul had to pay for his failure to carry out the divine command."[49]

WHO WERE THE AMALEKITES?

Why was it so important that the Amalekites be destroyed? Why were they such a hated and intractable enemy? Genesis 36 provides a genealogy of Esau's descendants. According to Genesis 36:11, 12 and 1 Chronicles 1:36, Amalek was born to Timna, the concubine of Eliphaz, Esau's son. While not mentioned by name in any extrabiblical source, they were probably nomads and, as the Bible describes them, Israel's most despised enemy. The Amalekites were not considered part of the Canaanite population, but were probably a western branch of the Edomites (Genesis 36:12; Psalm 83:7–8) active somewhere in the Negev (cf. Genesis 14:7; 1 Samuel 27:8).[50] Starting at Genesis 14:5, the story is told how in the "fourteenth year Chedorlaomer and the kings who were with him came and subdued . . . all the country of the Amalekites."[51] While Numbers 13:29 records that they lived in "the land of the Negeb," their nomadic travels, according to 1 Samuel 15:7, extended "from Havilah as far as Shur, which is east of Egypt." What their precise relationship was to the Israelites and why they were so despised is difficult to determine. First Samuel 15:2 says they were to be punished "for what they did in opposing the Israelites when [they] came up out of Egypt." Exactly what they did, however, is never mentioned. Deuteronomy 25:17–19 implies that the Amalekites attacked the Israelites when they were "faint and weary, and struck down all who lagged behind." Ziony Zevit translates Deuteronomy 25:18 as "and he 'untailed' in you all stumblers behind you," implying that the Amalekites attacked "stragglers behind the main group from the rear."[52]

The Amalekite king, Agag, is mentioned seven times in 1 Samuel 15. A king named Agag also appears in Balaam's oracle in Numbers 24:7. In that same oracle, Amalek is mentioned twice in v. 20, but, according to Feldman, Balaam's oracle is "apparently deliberately ambiguous as to whose responsibility it is to eliminate the Amalekites."[53] The word *Agagite* also appears as a Gentilic name for Haman, the hated enemy of the Jews in the Book of Esther (3:1, 10; 8:3, 5; 9:24).[54] In the only other reference to Amalek, Exodus 17:8–13 says that he "came and fought with Israel at Rephidim" (v. 8), but does not call him a king. This is the well-known episode where Aaron and Hur held up Moses's weary hands "until the sun set. And Joshua defeated Amalek and his people with the sword" (vv. 12–13).

Finally, 2 Samuel 8:4 indicates that "Yahweh gave victory to David wherever he went." Amalek is listed in 2 Samuel 8:12 as one of the nations that David "subdued" (v. 11), and after the days of Saul and David, as mentioned above, the Amalekites were "no longer named as serious opponents."[55]

THE AMALEKITES AND *HEREM* IN THE PROPHETS,
RABBINIC LITERATURE, AND THE LXX

While the concept of the *herem* and the threat of the Amalekites play important roles in the stories of Saul's decline and David's rise, they do not figure prominently in the rest of the Hebrew Bible. Israel's prophets use the word *herem* very sparingly in their oracles, and do not mention Amalek at all. One might wonder, for example, why Amalek is not at the top of Amos's list in his oracles against the nations (1:1–2:8). Stern is no doubt correct when he says: "It would be futile to speculate as to why the earlier prophets, such as Amos, Hosea, and Isaiah, did not choose to employ the *herem* as part of their formidable rhetorical arsenals."[56] And where the prophets do use the word *herem,* they tend to use it in a figurative, metaphorical sense.[57]

In Isaiah 34:2, 5 (which has not been clearly dated to the exilic or postexilic period), the poet writes: "For Yahweh is enraged against all the nations and furious against all their hordes; he has doomed them, has given them over for slaughter *[herem]. . . .* When my sword has drunk its fill in the heavens, lo, it will descend upon Edom, upon the people I have doomed to judgment *[herem]*." Here the deuteronomic concept of the *herem* extends to all nations. The loss of identity in the exilic and postexilic era becomes almost delusional,[58] and the idea of the *herem* is reinstituted in its harshest form in order to denounce all forms of non-Yahwistic, nonorthodox thinking in the sharpest terms. "One can, perhaps must, be startled by such uncompromising harshness. However, one should not overlook that what might be present here is a bloody, painful self-critique."[59]

In Malachi 3:24 (English RSV: 4:6) and Zechariah 14:11, the word *herem* is used as a metonym for war and wrath. Malachi ends with the words: "He will turn the hearts of parents to their children and the hearts of children to their parents, so that I will not come and strike the land with a ban of utter destruction *[herem]*." The land was Yahweh's and access to the land depended on "family harmony,"[60] and if such harmony was not achieved, "Yahweh would smite the land *herem,* meaning that he would remove the land from the human sphere by force, for the world order could not be achieved by YHWH's word alone."[61] Zechariah 14:11 then states: "And it [Jerusalem] shall be inhabited, for never again shall it be doomed to destruction *[herem]*; Jerusalem shall abide in security."

Later, in Rabbinic literature, the demand to eradicate the Amalekites still applied. However, according to Feldman, the rabbis "left considerable latitude as to when the eradication of the Amalekites will be carried out."[62] The tendency among the rabbis was to place the final elimination of the Amalekites not in history but at the end of time.

In one of the Dead Sea Scroll fragments, 4Q252, Col IV, we read: "It was he whom Saul sl[ew], as he said through Moses in respect of the last days, 'I will erase the memory of Amaleq from under the heavens.' "[63] The scroll fragment here is no doubt commenting on Deuteronomy 25:19: "Therefore when Yahweh your God has given you rest from all your enemies on every hand, in the land that Yahweh your God is giving you as an inheritance to possess, you shall blot out the remembrance of Amalek from under heaven; do not forget." However, the scroll fragment substitutes "in respect of the last days" for "when Yahweh your God has given you rest from all your enemies on every hand."[64] This appears to be in harmony with the Rabbinic idea that Amalek's final destruction will not happen in history but at the eschaton.

It is most interesting that when the LXX deals with Old Testament passages that speak of Yahweh as a warrior God, the translators drastically alter the texts. For example, Exodus 15:3, "Yahweh is a man of war," becomes "the Lord brings wars to nothing" in the LXX; and Isaiah 42:13, "Yahweh goes forth like a soldier, like a warrior he stirs up his wrath," reads, "the Lord crushes war." According to William Klassen, "apparently influential members of the Jewish community sought to minimize the bellicose depictions of Yahweh."[65] Why or what circumstances prompted such a change is unknown. Yahweh is described as a god of war, and if he has the power to wage war, he also has the power to destroy it.

CHRISTIAN MODES OF REFLECTION ON THE BIBLICAL RECORD

At the beginning of this essay, I noted that Christians cannot simply evade or ignore texts of terror like 1 Samuel 15, because the Old Testament is also the charter of the Christian faith. Nonetheless, those of us who walk daily into a classroom or face a Sunday morning Bible class know the challenge of trying to answer questions about "that Old Testament God" who is not only involved in but commands violence and the total destruction of entire peoples and nations. According to Raymund Schwager, "No other human activity or experience is mentioned as often, be it the world of work or trade, of family and sexuality, or that of knowledge and the experience of nature. For the biblical authors, the most impressive and distressing experience seems to have been that human beings war with and kill one another."[66]

In his "Concluding Reflections on Religion and Violence: Conflict, Subversion and Sacrifice," Stephen Marini writes, "Our students always ask why religion seems to be such a cause of violence, when it proclaims universal values of peace and harmony. . . . From a cultural and historical perspective, it is certainly difficult to deny that religion is indeed a major source of human violence."[67]

How, then, do we deal with it all, make some sense of the senseless violence? Do we suppress it, avoid it, explain it away? Attempting to spiritualize, historically adjust, idealize, view as metaphor, or reduce to "God's mysterious ways" such tough texts is dishonest.[68] Somehow we have to come to terms with it. How, then, might Christians come to terms with the "fighting words" that are 1 Samuel 15?

First, one needs to remember that 1 Samuel 15 is situated in the context of establishing a national identity. At such a time, it is not impossible to imagine invoking God's help. It is also easy to invoke God's help when that national identity is shattered and lost, as it was in the exilic and postexilic era. According to Psalm 72, Israel's kings were responsible not only for the military protection and defense of God's people, but also for establishing justice in the land. The psalmist proclaims: "Give the king your justice, O God, and righteousness to a king's son. May he judge your people with righteousness, and your poor with justice. May the mountains yield prosperity for the people, and the hills, in righteousness. May he defend the cause of the poor people, give deliverance to the needy, and crush the oppressor" (vv. 1–4). And in Third Isaiah's hopeful description of the coming of God, the redeemer and transformer of Zion, we are told that "Peace" will be appointed the overseer and "Righteousness" the taskmaster: "Violence shall no more be heard in your land, devastation or destruction within your borders; you shall call your walls Salvation and your gates Praise" (60:17–18). As Fretheim puts it, "Such a resolute divine *opposition* to human violence is important to remember in reflecting upon divine violence. In sum: if there were no human violence, there would be no divine violence."[69]

Second, one might cite a more contemporary example: the terror of Auschwitz. In this regard, Dietrich and Link provide the following scenario.[70] What if a legion of well-trained Allied soldiers—or a legion of angels—had gathered together the torturers and murderers of the Nazi concentration camps and invoked Deuteronomy 20:13, 16: "You shall put all its males to the sword. . . . You must not let anything that breathes remain alive." How might the victims of the Shoah have reacted to that? Might they not also have affirmed and shouted the words of Psalm 58:11: "People will say, 'Surely there is a reward for the righteous; surely there is a God who judges on earth?'"

We know that no avenging soldiers—or angels—appeared at Auschwitz or any of the other death camps. By the time the Allies did arrive to liberate the concentration camps it was too late. Violence had taken its course—but on the *other* side.[71]

Third, while the idea of the *herem* is not present per se in the New Testament, it would be incorrect to claim that the New Testament does not have a concept of divinely sanctioned war. According to Sigmund Mowinckel, there is mention in Rabbinic literature of a Messiah ben Joseph, who will defeat Gog at the end of time.[72] This "War-Messiah" was thought by some to be even more warlike than the expected Davidic messiah.

Furthermore, as Terence Fretheim states, "The New Testament especially, with its talk about hell, even envisions an eternal violence, in which God is very much involved (e.g., Matthew 13:36–50; Revelation 14:9–11)."[73] Christians should not overlook that the Book of Revelation contains considerable violence. In Revelation 19, for example, the rider on the white horse, the Lamb (Jesus Christ), initiates the final, decisive battle against evil. The rider is described as "clothed in a robe dipped in blood.... [with] the armies of heaven, wearing fine linen, white and pure, ... following him on white horses" (19:13–14). This imagery is very reminiscent of Isaiah 63, where Yahweh's robes are red with the blood of the Edomites (the descendants of Esau), whose "juice splattered" on Yahweh's garments and "stained all his robes" (v. 3). The "armies of heaven" (Revelation 19:14) recall numerous Old Testament texts that extol the deeds of Yahweh of hosts (literally, Yahweh of the armies) and speak of his wrath (cf., e.g., Isaiah 9:19; 10:23; 13:4, 13; 31:4). However, according to Wilfrid Harrington, "In all of this Christians endure—they do not take violent action against the worshipers of the beast. The message of Revelation is, in its apocalyptic dress, the message of Jesus. There must be a response to injustice, to oppression. That courageous response which may and can demand the ultimate sacrifice, is always non-violent."[74]

Fourth, and most important, however, is that the Old Testament shadow of violence and brutality follows Jesus himself from the beginning to the end of his earthly life, which finds its denouement in a passion story.[75] It is the story of a violent death, which, yes, happens with God's permission. Jesus is crucified between two criminals (Luke 23:33). However, long before this final act of violence, the gospels narrate Jesus's entire life under that shadow of violence. His life began with the flight into Egypt, where the infant Jesus narrowly escaped Herod's genocide in Bethlehem (Matthew 2:13–15), and the connection is made with the Exodus from Egypt, which certainly would have recalled the death of the firstborn in the tenth and final plague (Exodus 11:4–8; 12:29–30).

Then, at the midpoint of Jesus's earthly career, a voice from heaven reminiscent of another foundational event in the Old Testament called out. The words "This is my beloved Son, in whom I am well pleased" (Matthew 3:17) surely would have called to mind Abraham's son, Isaac, who also is described as "your son, your only son Isaac, whom you love," and who was to be offered "as a burnt offering" (Genesis 22:2). The passion history records an event where God permits what, at the last moment, God did not permit in the Abraham/Isaac story. God, as Paul says, citing Genesis 22:16, "did not withhold his own Son, but gave him up for all of us."[76]

In Mark 14 (cf. Matthew 26; John 18), after Jesus finished praying in the garden of Gethsemane, Judas arrived with a crowd of people who were carrying swords and clubs. Jesus was betrayed and arrested, and then "one of those who stood near [John 18:10 identifies this person as Peter] drew his sword and struck the slave of the high priest, cutting off his ear" (v. 47). In Matthew's account of this incident, Jesus does say, "Do you think that I cannot appeal to my Father, and he will at once send more than twelve legions of angels? But how then would the scriptures be fulfilled, which say it must happen in this way?" (Matthew 26:53–54).

The violence continues when Jesus is spat upon, blindfolded, struck, and beaten (Mark 14:65). A crown of thorns is placed on his head and he is struck with a reed

(Mark 15:18). A murderer, Barabbas, is chosen to be set free instead of Jesus, who had done no evil (Mark 15:6–15).

In the final scene of the gospel passion account, Christ is crucified between two criminals and all of the violent history of the past is cast in a new light. According to Luke, one of the convicts crucified with Jesus says, "And we indeed have been condemned justly, for we are getting what we deserve for our deeds, but this man has done nothing wrong" (23:41). This, by the way, may have been how the Old Testament writers thought about the condemnation of the Amalekites. They were receiving just punishment for their oppression of the Hebrew people. However, for the New Testament witnesses, Jesus's crucifixion was not just, and even Pilate could find no fault in him (Luke 24:4, 14; John 18:38; 19:4, 6). In the crucifixion, God himself stepped into the world's violent web and put his divinity on the line. Christians confess that God became human in the form of his only son, Jesus, when the good of his creatures was threatened by violence.

Christians do not have easy answers or quick remedies to the problems of war and violence. God's history with his people has not yet reached its goal. There is still suffering, death, and tears. And, sad to say, there is always another Amalek out there that someone wants to annihilate. Nations, like individuals, have long memories and they bear grudges. On the one hand, it is understandable that Israel would want to retaliate. After all, when the people were leaving Egypt, the Amalekites attacked from the rear, terrorizing the "faint and weary," those who lagged behind (Deuteronomy 25:17–18). Such violence against the most vulnerable and helpless of the refugees could not go unpunished. As the story is told, it would have to wait until a later time, but there would be retaliation. Christians and others continue to identify their nemeses as Amalekites. You might Google the words "modern day Amalekites" sometime. I found 21,700 results, associating everybody from Ahmadinejad to Zionists, from Al-Qaeda to the Palestinians, as well as every evil from the sins of the "flesh" and spiritual lethargy to gay and lesbian lifestyles, with the ancient cohorts of Amalek. Such searching for Amalek only compounds the violence and deepens the bitterness. All faith traditions call upon their communities to reject violence and to cease looking for Amalek. Christians certainly are summoned not only to reject violence but to "let the same mind" be in them that was in Christ Jesus, "who emptied himself, took on the form of a slave, and became obedient to death—even death on a cross" (Philippians 2:6–8).

. . .

In the very last scene of the movie *Patton*, Patton (George C. Scott) recalls the tradition of Roman conquerors who rode in a triumphal chariot while a slave stood behind the conqueror holding a golden crown and whispering in his ear a warning that *all glory is fleeting*.[77]

Saul's glory was indeed fleeting. As Jobling puts it, "if the Bible has a figure comparable to the tragic heroes of Greek drama that figure is King Saul."[78] He may have "killed his thousands," but David killed his "ten thousands" (1 Samuel 18:7) and in every sense became the "engine of Israel's imagination."[79] In the end, there is no glory in violence. None. It was not Saul's glory, or David's, that mattered, but Yahweh's. Centuries later, another Benjaminite named Saul, "also known as Paul" (Acts 13:9), himself no stranger to violence and persecution (cf. Galatians 1:13, 23; Philippians 3:6; 1 Corinthians 15:9; Acts 8:1), would draw attention to that glory when he spoke to the Christians in Rome:

> Do not repay anyone evil for evil, but take thought for what is noble in the sight of all. If it is possible, so far as it depends on you, live peaceably with all. Beloved, never avenge yourselves, but leave room for the wrath of God; for it is written, "Vengeance is mine, I will repay, says the Lord," [cf. Proverbs 20:22; 24:29]. No, "if your enemies are hungry, feed them; if they are thirsty, give them something to drink; for by doing this you will heap burning coals on their heads." Do not be overcome by evil, but overcome evil with good. (Romans 12:17–21)

NOTES

1. www.script-o-rama.com/movie-scripts/p/patton-script-transcript-george-scott.html.

2. See Msgr. James H. O'Neill, "The True Story of The Patton Prayer," www.pattonhq.com/prayer.html.

3. Raymund Schwager, *Must There Be Scapegoats? Violence and Redemption in the Bible,* trans. Maria L. Assad (San Francisco: Harper & Row, 1987), 47. All Biblical citations are from HarperCollins Study Bible, New Revised Standard Version With the Apocryphal and Deuterocanonical Books (New York: HarperCollins Publishers, 1993).

4. For a discussion of religious violence and some New Testament texts, see David Frankfurter, "The Legacy of Sectarian Rage: Vengeance Fantasies in the New Testament," in *Religion and Violence: The Biblical Heritage: Proceedings of a Conference Held at Wellesley College and Boston University, February 19–20, 2006,* ed. David A. Bernat and Jonathan Klawans (Sheffield: Sheffield Phoenix Press, 2007), 114–28; A. Y. Collins, *The Combat Myth in the Book of Revelation* (Missoula: Scholars Press, 1976); idem, *Crisis and Catharsis: The Power of the Apocalypse* (Philadelphia: Westminster Press, 1984); Tremper Longman III, "The Divine Warrior: The New Testament Use of an Old Testament Motif," *Westminster Theological Journal* 44 (1982): 290–307; Robert G. Hammerton-Kelly, *Sacred Violence: Paul's Hermeneutic of the Cross* (Minneapolis: Fortress, 1992). For books, articles, and essays on various aspects of religion and emotion in religious traditions, see John Corrigan, ed., *Religion and Emotion: Approaches and Interpretations* (New York: Oxford University Press, 2004); John Corrigan, Eric Crump, and John Kloos, *Emotion and Religion: A Critical Assessment and Annotated Bibliography* (Westport, Connecticut, 2000). For a general discussion of human and divine anger in the Old Testament, see Bruce Edward Baloian, *Anger in the Old Testament* (New York: Peter Lang, 1992).

5. René Girard, *Violence and the Sacred* (Baltimore: Johns Hopkins University Press, 1977); idem, *Things Hidden Since the Foundation of the World,* trans. Stephen Baunn and Michael Metteer (Stanford: Stanford University Press, 1987); idem, *The Scapegoat,* trans. Yvonne Freccero (Baltimore: Johns Hopkins University Press, 1986); Hector Avalos, *Fighting Words: The Origins of Religious Violence* (Amherst: Prometheus, 2005); Mark Juergensmeyer, *Terror in the Mind of God: The Global Rise of*

Religious Violence, 3rd ed. (Berkeley: University of California Press, 2003); Susan Niditch, *War in the Hebrew Bible: A Study in the Ethics of Violence* (New York: Oxford University Press, 1993); Terence Fretheim, "God and Violence in the Old Testament," *Word & World* 24, no. 1 (Winter 2004): 18–28; idem, "Theological Reflections on the Wrath of God in the Old Testament," *Horizons in Biblical Theology* 24 (2002): 14–17; idem, "'I Was Only a Little Angry': Divine Violence in the Prophets," *Interpretation* 58 (2004): 365–75; Philip Stern, *The Biblical Herem: A Window on Israel's Religious Experience* (Atlanta: Scholars, 1991).

6. Jonathan Klawans, "Introduction: Religion, Violence, and the Bible," in Bernat and Klawans, *Religion and Violence*, 14.

7. Ibid., 14–15. Italics in original.

8. David Tsumura, *The First Book of Samuel* (Grand Rapids, MI: William B. Eerdmans, 2007), 73. For a general discussion of the date, authorship, and religious background of 1 Samuel, see pp. 11–46.

9. Ibid.

10. David Jobling, *1 Samuel* (Collegeville: Liturgical Press, 1998), 78.

11. Ibid. Other "everlasting covenants" include Noah (Genesis 9), Abraham (Genesis 17), and Phineas (Numbers 25).

12. Tsumura, *The First Book of Samuel*, 387. See also P. Kyle McCarter, Jr., *I Samuel: A New Translation with Introduction, Notes, and Commentary,* The Anchor Bible Commentary (Garden City: Anchor, 1980), 270–71, n. 4.

13. Tsumura, *The First Book of Samuel,* 387. See also Ralph W. Klein, *1 Samuel,* Word Biblical Commentary (Waco, TX: Word, 1983), 123.

14. Tsumura, *The First Book of Samuel,* 128.

15. For a discussion of leadership roles in ancient Israel, see Joseph Blenkinsopp, *Sage, Priest, Prophet: Religious and Intellectual Leadership in Ancient Israel* (Louisville: Westminster John Knox, 1995). See also, Robert Wilson, *Prophecy and Society in Ancient Israel* (Philadelphia: Fortress, 1980).

16. Klein, *1 Samuel,* 127.

17. Ibid.

18. Tsumura, *The First Book of Samuel,* 348.

19. Ernst Jenni and Claus Westermann, eds., *Theological Lexicon of the Old Testament,* trans. Mark E. Biddle (Peabody: Hendrickson, 1997), 474.

20. Stern, *The Biblical Herem,* 16.

21. Ibid.,1.

22. Niditch, *War in the Hebrew Bible,* 30.

23. Ibid., 61–62.

24. Ibid., 29.

25. Ibid., 30–31.

26. L. E. Toombs, "War, ideas of," in *The Interpreter's Dictionary of the Bible,* ed. George A. Buttrick and Keith R. Crim (New York: Abingdon, 1962), 4:797.

27. For a discussion of the divine warrior in the Ancient Near East, see Theodore Hiebert, "Warrior, Divine," in *The Anchor Bible Dictionary* (New York: Doubleday, 1992), 6:876–80. See also P. D. Miller, Jr. *The Divine Warrior in Early Israel* (Cambridge, MA: Harvard University Press, 1973). According to Miller, "The conception of God as a warrior played a fundamental role in the religious and military experiences of Israel. . . . One can only go so far in describing the history of Israel, or its religion, or the theology of the Old Testament without encountering the wars of Yahweh. In prose and poetry, early and later material alike, the view that Yahweh fought for or against his people stands forth prominently. The centrality of that conviction and its historical, cultic, literary and theological ramifications can hardly be overestimated" (264). See also Frank M. Cross, "The Divine Warrior," in

his *Canaanite Myth and Hebrew Epic* (Cambridge, MA: Harvard University, 1973); Peter C. Craigie, *The Problem of War in the Old Testament* (Grand Rapids, MI: Eerdmans, 1978); Millard C. Lind, *Yahweh Is a Warrior* (Scottsdale, PA: Herald, 1980); Gerhard von Rad, *Holy War In Ancient Israel*, ed. and trans. Marva J. Dawn (Grand Rapids, MI: Eerdmans, 1991); Rudolf Smend, *Yahweh War and Tribal Confederation: Reflections upon Israel's Earliest History*, trans. Max Gray Roberts (Nashville: Abingdon, 1970).

28. Walter Dietrich and Christian Link, *Die Dunklen Seiten Gottes*, vol. 1: *Willkür und Gewalt*; vol. 2: *Allmacht und Ohnmacht* (Neukirchen-Vluyn: Neukirchener, 2000), 190. All references, translations, and summaries throughout this essay of these two volumes are mine.

29. For an extensive discussion of the Mesha Stone, see Stern, *The Biblical Herem*, 19–56. See also J. Andrew Dearman and Gerald L. Mattingly, "Mesha Stele," in *The Anchor Bible Dictionary*, 4:708–9.

30. James B. Pritchard, ed., *Ancient Near Eastern Texts Relating to the Old Testament* (New Jersey: Princeton University Press, 1950), 320–21.

31. Ibid.

32. Gerald L. Mattingly, "CHEMOSH," in *The Anchor Bible Dictionary*, 1:896–97.

33. See Louis H. Feldman, *"Remember Amalek!": Vengeance, Zealotry, and Group Destruction in the Bible According to Philo, Pseudo-Philo, and Josephus* (Cincinnati: Hebrew Union College Press, 2004), 2–7.

34. Ibid., 7.

35. "Deuteronomy, Book of," in *The Anchor Bible Dictionary*, 2:179. See also Gerhard von Rad, *Deuteronomy* (Philadelphia: Westminster, 1966).

36. Niditch, *War in the Hebrew Bible*, 9.

37. Jenni and Westermann, *Theological Lexicon of the Old Testament*, 2:476.

38. McCarter, *1 Samuel*, 15.

39. Stern, *The Biblical Herem*, 169.

40. Ziony Zevit, "The Search for Violence in Israelite Culture and in the Bible," in *Religion and Violence: The Biblical Heritage*, ed. David A. Bernat and Jonathan Klawans (Sheffield: Sheffield Phoenix Press, 2007), 34.

41. See, e.g., Tsumura, *The First Book of Samuel*, 13 and n. 55; Klein, *1 Samuel*, xxxi–xxxii.

42. Klein, *1 Samuel*, xxxi–xxxii and 147–148.

43. See the discussion of the date and authorship of 1 Samuel in Tsumura, *The First Book of Samuel*, 11–322, esp. 16–19.

44. Niditch, *War in the Hebrew Bible*, 28ff.

45. Ibid., 60.

46. Dietrich and Link, *Die Dunklen Seiten Gottes*, 2:72ff.

47. Ibid., 73.

48. Ibid.

49. Feldman, *"Remember Amalek!,"* 219.

50. See Zevit, "The Search for Violence," 33.

51. For a discussion of how a "country of Amalekites" could have existed in the time before Esau, see Gerald M. Mattingly, "Amalek," in *The Anchor Bible Dictionary*, 1:169.

52. Zevit, "The Search for Violence," 33. Stern makes the observation that the Hebrew word *zanab* (tail) might have suggested "some monstrous animal (the Chaos-monster) pursuing Israel's stragglers" (174–75).

53. Feldman, *"Remember Amalek!,"* 10.

54. See the entries on "Agag," and "Agagite" by Duane L. Christensen and Mark J. Fretz in *The Anchor Bible Dictionary*, 1:88–89.

55. Mattingly, "Amalek," 171.

56. Stern, *The Biblical Herem,* 207.

57. Ibid., 190.

58. Dietrich and Link, *Die Dunklen Seiten Gottes,* 2:201.

59. Ibid.

60. Ibid., 206.

61. Ibid.

62. Feldman, *"Remember Amalek!,"* 52.

63. *The Dead Sea Scrolls Translated,* ed. Florentino García Martínez, trans. Wilfred G. E. Watson, 2nd ed. (Grand Rapids, MI: Eerdmans, 1992), 214.

64. Feldman, *"Remember Amalek!,"* 54.

65. William Klassen, "War in the NT," in *The Anchor Bible Dictionary,* 6:869–70.

66. Schwager, *Must There Be Scapegoats?,* 47.

67. Stephen Marini, "Concluding Reflection on Religion and Violence: Conflict, Subversion, and Sacrifice," in Bernat and Klawans, *Religion and Violence,* 129–34, quote at 132.

68. Terence Fretheim, "God and Violence in the Old Testament," 18–19.

69. Ibid., 21.

70. Dietrich and Link, *Die Dunklen Seiten Gottes,* 1:201–202.

71. Ibid.

72. Sigmund Mowinckel, *He That Cometh: The Messiah in the Old Testament of Later Judaism,* trans. G. W. Anderson (Nashville: Abingdon, 1954), 290–91.

73. Fretheim, "God and Violence in the Old Testament," 18–19. On the theme of violence in the New Testament generally, see footnote 1 on p. 18 of Fretheim's article. See also Fretheim, "Is the Biblical Portrayal of God Always Trustworthy?," in *The Bible as Word of God in a Postmodern Age,* ed. T. E. Fretheim and Karlfried Froehlich (Minneapolis: Fortress, 1998), 97–11.

74. Wilfrid Harrington, *Revelation,* Sacra Pagina Series (Collegeville: Liturgical Press, 1993), 16:195.

75. In what follows, I am indebted to the discussion on the "militant God" and the "shadow of violence" in Dietrich and Link, *Die Dunklen Seiten Gottes,* 1:187–220.

76. Dietrich and Link, *Die Dunklen Seiten Gottes,* 1:218.

77. www.script-o-rama.com/movie-scripts/p/patton-script-transcript-george-scott.html. Italics mine.

78. Jobling, *1 Samuel,* 250.

79. Walter Brueggemann, *David's Truth in Israel's Imagination and Memory,* 2nd ed. (Minneapolis: Augsburg, 2002), 2.

4

Violence in the New Testament
and the History of Interpretation

Leo D. Lefebure

Even though Jesus proclaimed a gospel of peace (Matthew 10:12–13; Luke 10:5; John 14:27; 20:19, 21, 26), Christians have repeatedly engaged in violent conflicts both with their neighbors in other religious traditions and with other Christians. Christian warriors have worn the sign of the cross in battle and have often seen themselves as fighting on behalf of God's cause; they have cited biblical passages to justify violent assaults, inquisitions, and persecutions. Christians have also invoked the Bible to place limits on violence or to end violence altogether.

The roots of this ambivalence lie in the ambiguities of the Christian scriptures and the Jewish heritage from which they emerge. The earliest followers of Jesus continued to read the Jewish scriptures in the Hebrew Bible and the Greek Septuagint, which present both Isaiah's moving call to transform swords into plough-shares and cease training for war (Isaiah 2:4), and the brutal divine command to exterminate all the inhabitants of the Promised Land without exception lest they tempt Israelites to idolatry (Deuteronomy 20:16–18). While Jesus commands his followers to love their enemies (Matthew 5:44) and respond nonviolently to evil (Matthew 5:38–42), he also engages in fierce controversies: "Do not think that I have come to bring peace to the earth; I have not come to bring peace, but a sword" (Matthew 10:34).[1]

Scriptural hermeneutics has always been embedded in the life-forms and practices of the Christian community, with multiple assumptions lurking in the background of every act of interpretation. The explanation of any individual verse presupposes a sense of the entire Bible, of the practice of the Christian life, and of the relation between Christianity and other religious traditions. From Origen (d. c. 254) and Augustine (d. 430) to the Second Vatican Council (1962–65), Christian interpreters have insisted that any particular verse must be understood in light of the whole corpus of biblical texts and the life of the Church; Origen and Augustine warned against literal interpretations that would violate Jesus's fundamental principle of love.[2] The father of modern hermeneutics, the Protestant theologian Friedrich Schleiermacher (d. 1834), stressed the twofold hermeneutical movement from the interpretation of a part to the interpretation of the whole. We interpret the part in light of the whole, and then we reinterpret the whole in light of our new understanding of the part.[3]

With varying degrees of self-reflection, every generation and every community of Christians decides which biblical passages to place in the foreground and which in the background. This principle is of particular importance concerning biblical passages regarding peace and violence. Rabbi Jonathan Sacks expresses the challenge:

> Every scriptural canon has within it texts which, read literally, can be taken to endorse narrow particularism, suspicion of strangers, and intolerance toward those who believe differently than we do. Each also has within it sources that emphasize kinship with the stranger, empathy with the outsider, the courage that leads people to extend a hand across boundaries of estrangement or hostility. The choice is ours. Will the generous texts of our tradition serve as interpretive keys to the rest, or will the abrasive passages determine our ideas of what we are and what we are called on to do?[4]

Complicating the task of biblical interpreters is the unresolved question of what books should be included in the Christian scriptures. The Book of Revelation, which presents the influential combat myth of the divine warrior, was rejected by many in the early Church; and the Byzantine Orthodox tradition to this day does not read this book in the liturgy.[5] After centuries of debates over which books would be accepted as scripture, today most Christians accept the same canon of the New Testament, but differences persist concerning what books constitute the First (or Old) Testament of the Christian Bible.

Tragically, Christians have frequently had violent relationships with those to whom they are most closely bound by history, geography, and theology: Jews, Muslims, and other Christians. This essay will examine the interpretation of New Testament passages that have been of special importance in the conflicts with the Jewish and Muslim communities and with Christians deemed heretical. The discussion will begin by surveying New Testament texts that would later be understood to justify violence, particularly those passages regarding the conflicts of Jesus and his followers with their contemporaries, especially other Jews. Because of the extensive scholarship on the New Testament, this discussion can offer only the most cursory overview of some of these texts in their original setting. The second section of this chapter will examine the later history of interpretation of the New Testament in relation to Jews, Muslims, and dissenting Christians, with particular attention to two themes that fueled historical Christian animosity toward Jews and Muslims: (1) the condemnation, passion, and crucifixion of Jesus, which influenced Christian attitudes toward Jews for centuries; and (2) sacred combat and the figure of the Antichrist in New Testament apocalyptic texts, which shaped many Christian views of Muslims from the seventh century to the present. The final section will explore the hermeneutical situation of Christians reading the New Testament in dialogue with Jews in the wake of the Holocaust and in light of shifts in historical scholarship regarding the origins of Christianity and Rabbinic Judaism.

CONFLICTS IN THE NEW TESTAMENT: TEXTS IN THEIR ORIGINAL CONTEXT

Synoptic Gospels: Matthew, Mark, and Luke

In the synoptic gospels, Jesus repeatedly engages in fierce polemics against the Scribes and Pharisees. When they challenge him for allowing his disciples to eat without washing their hands, he calls them "Hypocrites!" and severely chastises them (Matthew 15:3–9; Mark 7:1–8). Jesus cautions his disciples against the "yeast" of the Pharisees and Sadducees, that is, their evil corruption (Matthew 16:5–12). Jesus warns the crowds in Jerusalem against the example of the Scribes and Pharisees, again accusing them of hypocrisy; they are "blind guides" (Matthew 23:16, 24). Jesus angrily foretells the suffering that will come upon the Scribes and Pharisees:

> You snakes, you brood of vipers! How can you escape being sentenced to hell? Therefore I send you prophets, sages, and scribes, some of whom you will kill and crucify, and some you will flog in your synagogues and pursue from town to town, so that upon you may come all the righteous blood shed on earth, from the blood of righteous Abel to the blood of Zechariah son of Barachiah, whom you murdered between the sanctuary and the altar. (Matthew 23:33–36)

Jesus also laments the infidelity of the inhabitants of Jerusalem and foretells the coming destruction of their city (Matthew 23:37–24:2; Mark 13:2; Luke 13:34–35; 21:20). Donald Senior comments on the context of Jesus's polemic against the Jewish leaders in Matthew 23: "Matthew's strong critique of the Jewish leaders in this passage and elsewhere in the gospel also reflects the tension between his largely Jewish Christian community and the Pharisaic leadership of formative Judaism, as both communities were attempting to define themselves in the period prior to and contemporary with the composition of the gospel. Such tension and debate, while often hostile in tone, remained essentially an intra-Jewish debate and cannot be understood as 'anti-Semitic' in the sense the term is used today."[6]

At a meal in the home of a prominent Pharisee, Jesus tells a parable of a great royal feast to which many persons are invited. After all the original invited guests decline the invitation, the master of the house orders a servant to "bring in the poor, the crippled, the blind, and the lame" (Luke 14:21). The servant does so and reports that there still is room. "Then the master said to the slave, 'Go out into the roads and lanes, and compel people to come in, so that my house may be filled' " (Luke 14:23). In the original context Jesus addresses the warning to the Pharisees and lawyers with whom he is dining, hoping to gain their acceptance of his message lest they, like the original invitees in the parable, find themselves excluded because of their own decision. Joseph Fitzmyer comments on the admonition: "Those who are excluded from the banquet have only themselves to thank; God will not drag the unwilling into it against their will."[7] While Jesus is here in an adversarial relationship with the Pharisees, it is important to note that not all Jews reject Jesus: "Luke is at pains to show that some of the Palestinian contemporaries of Jesus did accept him."[8] Of greatest importance for the later Christian tradition was the master's command to compel people to enter the feast. Fitzmyer explains that in its original context the command to make people come to the dinner "means merely that the poor and others will understandably resist in their modesty such an invitation, until they are gently taken and led into the house."[9]

The synoptic gospels were composed before the clear differentiation and separation of Jews and Christians into two distinct religions.[10] Many of the first followers of Jesus were Jews who accepted Jesus as Lord and Messiah; they did not see themselves as leaving the religion of Judaism in order to join another religion. Jesus's vigorous debates over Torah with Pharisees, Scribes, and Sadducees reflect the Jewish context of his day; fierce disagreements and sharp rhetoric were characteristic of Jewish halakhic (legal) debates before, during, and after the time of Jesus.[11] As Amy-Jill Levine notes, "Jesus himself was a Jew speaking to other Jews. His teachings comport with the tradition of Israel's prophets. Judaism has always had a self-critical component."[12] In his study of the historical Jesus, John Meier notes that despite the usual adversarial tone, there are indications that some Pharisees were open to Jesus's message and that their interactions were not all negative.[13] In the context of the ministry of Jesus and of the synoptic gospels, it is not anti-Jewish for Jesus to debate with other Jews about Jewish practice.

Similarly, E. P. Sanders sums up the image of Jesus in the synoptic gospels: "There is no good evidence that Jesus was an anti-Jewish Jew. . . . The evidence from the Gospels, however, indicates that Jesus accepted the Jewish version of ancient religion, as well as the common belief that illness and mental problems were often caused by demonic possession. He probably did criticize and argue with some of his contemporaries, but the criticisms that we find in the Gospels are rather modest in comparison to the words that some of the biblical prophets, such as Amos and Hosea, directed against their contemporaries."[14] The culmination of Jesus's conflict with other Jews comes at the end of his life, when, the gospels report, Jewish leaders plotted against him and a Jewish crowd in Jerusalem demanded his death. In the most infamous scene of all, according to the gospel of Matthew Pilate is reluctant to accept responsibility for the execution of Jesus (Matthew 27:24); in response, the crowd in Jerusalem demands the death of Jesus of Nazareth. When Pilate demurs, "the people as a whole answered, 'His blood be on us and on our children!'" (Matthew 27:25). Regarding the involvement of Jews in the condemnation and crucifixion of Jesus, Raymond Brown comments: "In the Christian picture of what was done to Jesus, at first there was nothing anti-Jewish in depicting the role of the Jewish authorities in his death; for Jesus and his disciples on one side and the Jerusalem Sanhedrin authorities on the other were all Jews. The depiction of those Jews opposed to Jesus as plotting evil was not different from the OT depiction of the wicked plotting against the innocent."[15]

This does not mean that there are no tensions. Daniel Harrington notes that some scholars seek to minimize the problem posed by Matthew 27:25 by interpreting it as referring only to a relatively small gathering of Jews in Jerusalem; however, Harrington observes: "But in Matt 27:25 he switches to *pas ho laos* ("all the people"). Elsewhere in his Gospel, Matthew uses *laos* to refer to the Jewish people taken as a collectivity. Matthew meant more than the small group of Jews who gathered around Pilate's judgment seat at Passover time in A.D. 30. . . . Given Matthew's concern for Christian identity within Judaism, it seems likely that for him 'all the people' represented the Jewish opponents of the Church."[16] The synoptic gospels proclaim that Jesus is the Messiah, the Christ, the fulfillment of the hopes of ancient Israel. In its original context, this is not a denunciation of Judaism as a religion; but it did mean a vigorous debate with other Jews who rejected the claims made about Jesus by his disciples.

The Johannine Tradition

Some of the fiercest controversies between Jesus and Jewish leaders occur in the gospel of John, where Jesus repeatedly disputes with "*hoi iudaeoi*," which is usually translated as "the Jews." In the climax of the argument, Jesus pointedly asserts to them: "You are from your father the devil, and you choose to do your father's desires. He was a murderer from the beginning and does not stand in the truth, because there is no truth in him. . . . Whoever is from God hears the words of God. The reason you do not hear them is that you are not from God" (John 8:44, 47–48).

Francis Moloney warns against interpreting the term "*hoi iudaeoi*" as referring to the entire Jewish people: "A critical reading of the Johannine Gospel makes it clear that 'the Jews' are those characters in the story who have made up their minds about Jesus. They are one side of a Christological debate."[17] Moloney notes that "the fact that the Johannine Christians were being ejected from the synagogue indicates that *many members of the Johannine community were also ethnically Jewish,* and committed to the religion of Israel."[18] In its original context, the dispute is a family quarrel that has become extremely heated.[19]

According to the passion narrative in John, Jewish officers cooperate with Roman soldiers in the arrest of Jesus (18:12) and take him to the Jewish authorities, Annas and Caiaphas, to be interrogated. As in the synoptic tradition, Pilate appears reluctant to condemn Jesus but does so at the urging of "the Jews" (19:6–16). The chief priests profess: "We have no king but the emperor" (19:15).

As in the case of the synoptic gospels, contemporary scholarship stresses the Jewish character of the fourth gospel. The Jewish scholar Adele Reinhartz comments: "The Fourth Gospel has an overall Jewish 'feel.' . . . Jesus and most of the other characters in the Gospel are Jews, and they participate fully in the Jewish world of early first-century Palestine."[20] Nonetheless, Reinhartz notes the problem that "the Gospel ascribes a villainous role to the Jews in its historical tale, associates them with the negative terms through the rhetoric of binary opposition in its Christological tale, and undermines Jewish covenantal identity in its cosmological tale."[21]

The First Letter of John provides the first explicit mention of the Antichrist:

Children, it is the last hour! As you have heard that antichrist is coming, so now many antichrists have come. From this we know that it is the last hour. . . . Who is the liar but the one who denies that Jesus is the Christ? This is the antichrist, the one who denies the Father and the Son. (1 John 2:18, 22)

In this context the antichrists are those who oppose the belief that Jesus is the Christ who has come in the flesh (1 John 4:2–3; 2 John 7); these are false teachers who oppose the Johannine community and who are to be shunned. The original use of the term *antichrist* comes out of a Christological dispute over the identity of Jesus and whether the Word had truly become flesh.[22] Antichrists are adversaries of God and of the Messiah (Christ). The term is not necessarily a title for a particular individual or a dreaded apocalyptic figure; it could simply mean "an anti-Christ" or opponent of Christ.[23] The term comes from the dissidents' denial that Jesus was the Anointed One or the "Christ."[24]

Acts of the Apostles

The death and resurrection of Jesus did not halt the cycle of controversy, for intense and sometimes deadly conflicts between followers of Jesus and other Jews continued afterward. According to the Acts of the Apostles, the deacon Stephen, a Greek-speaking Jew who has accepted the gospel, engages in heated polemics with representatives of the synagogue of Freedmen from Cyrene, Alexandria, Cilicia, and Asia (Acts 6:9–15). In response to the charges against him, Stephen recounts the history of ancient Israel, accenting the repeated rejection of God's representatives by Israelites and Jews. Stephen sums up their sinfulness:

> You stiff-necked people, uncircumcised in heart and ears, you are forever opposing the Holy Spirit, just as your ancestors used to do. Which of the prophets did your ancestors not persecute? They killed those who foretold the coming of the Righteous One, and now you have become his betrayers and murderers. You are the ones that received the law as ordained by angels, and yet you have not kept it. (Acts 7:51–53)

The crowd then stones Stephen to death, with Saul's approval (Acts 7:58–8:1). In its original context, this polemic comes in a dispute among Jews. For a Jew to recall the history of Jewish infidelity to other Jews is not anti-Jewish; it is a recapitulation of much of the Hebrew Bible with many points of contact with nonbiblical Jewish literature of the time.[25] Luke Timothy Johnson notes the central purpose of the speech: "Luke seeks to legitimate the messianic appropriation of Torah by showing how Torah itself demanded such an appropriation."[26] The speech inflames the crowd of listeners, who proceed to stone Stephen to death as the young Saul stands by approvingly (Acts 7:58–8:1).

Later in the narrative, Acts reports that "the Jews" approved of Herod Agrippa's decision to kill James, the brother of John, with the sword (Acts 12:2–3). Acts also narrates that after experiencing Christ on the road to Damascus, Paul proclaimed the message of Jesus Christ and also encountered difficulties with "the Jews." In Thessalonica, "the Jews became jealous, and with the help of some ruffians in the marketplaces they formed a mob and set the city in an uproar. While they were searching for Paul and Silas to bring them out to the assembly, they attacked Jason's house" (Acts 17:5). When Jews in Beroea proved more receptive to Paul and Silas, the Jews from Thessalonica came to stir up opposition to them (Acts 17:10–13). It is noteworthy that Paul regularly preaches in synagogues (Acts 13:5, 14; 14:1; 17:1, 10), and that when he speaks at the Areopagus in Athens, he appears as a Jewish philosopher.[27] Later in the narrative there are said to be "thousands of believers . . . among the Jews" (Acts 21:20; but Jewish opposition to Paul also continues as well, even to the point of violent attempts to kill him [Acts 21:27–31]).

Pauline Letters

Paul's letters include a number of statements that reflect conflicts with Jews, most notably in Thessalonica, the same place where the Acts of the Apostles also reports trouble:

> For you, brothers and sisters, became imitators of the churches of God in Christ Jesus that are in Judea, for you suffered the same things from your own compatriots

as they did from the Jews, who killed both the Lord Jesus and the prophets, and drove us out; they displease God and oppose everyone by hindering us from speaking to the Gentiles so that they may be saved. Thus they have constantly been filling up the measure of their sins; but God's wrath has overtaken them at last. (1 Thessalonians 2:14–16)

This passage, which appears in what is quite possibly the oldest surviving Christian text, resembles the Johannine usage of "the Jews" and Stephen's linkage of earlier Jewish persecution of the prophets to their involvement in the killing of Jesus. It is very harsh in its assessment of Jewish behavior past and present. It is, however, not characteristic of Paul's other writings and poses many puzzles.[28] Earl Richard contends: "The expression 'the Jews' is non-Pauline in its negative usage."[29] Full discussion of the difficult exegetical issues involved exceeds the limits of this essay; Richard and many other interpreters believe that this passage is an interpolation by a later Gentile Christian writing after the destruction of the Temple in 70 C.E.: "The author is post-Pauline and is writing from a Gentile-Christian perspective which one should characterize as anti-Jewish. The plight of the Jews, following the destruction of Jerusalem and later dispersal from Palestine, is seen as the result of divine retribution finally being meted out for centuries of hostility toward God and the whole of humanity."[30] Gerd Lüdemann, however, pointedly disagrees, arguing that this passage "on no account derives from a subsequent addition by an alien hand."[31] Lüdemann acknowledges that this passage contradicts Paul's hope for the salvation of all Israel in Romans 11:25–26, but he believes Paul changed his mind in the intervening years.

While Paul assumes that the Church comprises both Jews and Gentiles, he writes very critically about the lack of understanding of Jews who do not accept Jesus:

The letter kills, but the Spirit gives life. Now if the ministry of death, chiseled in letters on stone tablets, came in glory so that the people of Israel could not gaze at Moses' face because of the glory of his face, a glory now set aside, how much more will the ministry of the Spirit come in glory? . . . But their minds were hardened. Indeed, to this very day, when they hear the reading of the old covenant, that same veil is still there, since only in Christ is it set aside. Indeed, to this very day whenever Moses is read, a veil lies over their minds; but when one turns to the Lord, the veil is removed. (2 Corinthians 3:6–8, 14–16)

Jan Lambrecht comments on the meaning of this passage in its original context: "The old covenant is the ministration of death and condemnation; because of the absence of the Spirit it is only engraved on tablets of stone. No Jew who was not a Christian would speak in this way. It is a Jewish Christian who looks back on his non-Christian Jewish past."[32]

Writing to the Galatians, Paul interprets the Genesis account of Abraham, Sarah, Isaac, Hagar, and Ishmael allegorically as a basis for rejecting his opponents who insist on observance of the Mosaic Law. Paul urges the Galatians to follow the example of Abraham and drive out the slave woman and her son lest they share in the inheritance of the free son:

> Now this is an allegory: these two women are two covenants. One woman, in fact, is Hagar, from Mount Sinai, bearing children for slavery. Now Hagar is Mount Sinai in Arabia and corresponds to the present Jerusalem, for she is in slavery with her children. But the other woman corresponds to the Jerusalem above; she is free, and she is our mother. . . . Now you, my friends, are children of the promise, like Isaac. But just as at that time the child who was born according to the flesh persecuted the child who was born according to the Spirit, so it is now also. But what does the scripture say? Drive out the slave and her child; for the child of the slave will not share the inheritance with the child of the free woman. So then, friends, we are children, not of the slave but of the free woman. (Galatians 4:24–31)

While commentators have often understood the present Jerusalem to refer to Judaism and the heavenly Jerusalem to refer to Christianity, Frank J. Matera, following the lead of J. L. Martyn, argues persuasively that this is not the contrast Paul intends: "Paul talks about the children of two different apostolates: his circumcision-free apostolate and the circumcision-apostolate of the agitators. An important aspect of this approach is Martyn's insight that Paul is not referring to the religions of Judaism and Christianity in the Hagar-Sarah allegory but to Jewish Christians who insist upon the Law and Gentile Christians of a Pauline persuasion who do not. In other words, this passage reflects a struggle between two factions of early Christianity rather than opposition between Christianity and Judaism."[33] Paul is not calling for the expulsion of Jews or of Jewish Christians as such; his focus is specifically on his opponents in Galatia, the agitators who insist on observance of the full Mosaic Law in opposition to the agreement in Jerusalem (Galatians 2:3–10).[34]

Scholars disagree on whether Paul wrote 2 Thessalonians or whether it was written by a later follower after his death.[35] The letter warns of a coming "lawless one," described as "the son of destruction" (2:3; NRSV: "the one destined for destruction"; KJV: "son of perdition") who will play an important role in the events of the end-time. To Christians who are concerned about claims regarding the coming of Jesus, the letter urges "not to be quickly shaken in mind or alarmed, either by spirit or by word or by letter, as though from us, to the effect that the day of the Lord is already here" (2:2). This day will not happen until after the son of destruction has come and defiled the temple: "He opposes and exalts himself above every so-called god or object of worship, so that he takes his seat in the temple of God, declaring himself to be God." (2:4). In this context "the son of destruction" refers to a human being, not to Satan.[36] The author may be thinking of a false teacher in the threatened situation of Christians of the first century C.E., or possibly of an historical figure such as Antiochus IV, Pompey, or Caligula, who desecrated the Temple in Jerusalem.[37] The letter assumes a time of conflict and crisis, as Bonnie Thurston notes: "The writer of 2 Thessalonians knows that the mystery of lawlessness is active because evil has not yet reached its zenith."[38]

Book of Revelation

The Book of Revelation also reflects tensions between Jews and followers of Jesus, but this does not mean that it is anti-Jewish. The author was most likely Jewish, possibly from Judea.[39] The work assumes that followers of Jesus are within the community of Jews. Peder Borgen proposes "that John builds on traditions, thought-categories, and outlooks held by segments of Jewish people, and that he transforms them on the basis of belief in Jesus Christ. The book reflects a situation in which Christians understood themselves to be a distinct group within a Jewish context, and even thought themselves to be the true Jews."[40]

The prophet John sees a vision of one like the Son of Man (Revelation 1:13) and hears his message to the church in Smyrna: "I know your affliction and your poverty, even though you are rich. I know the slander on the part of those who say that they are Jews and are not, but are a synagogue of Satan" (Revelation 2:9). There has been much debate over the referent of the phrase "synagogue of Satan."[41] Adela Yarbro Collins comments on the original context in Smyrna: "The attack on the Jews in the same context (vs 9) is an indication that some Christians in Smyrna were probably accused before the Roman governor by Jews. According to Eusebius, Jewish citizens of Smyrna assisted the Roman authorities in convicting and executing some Christians in about 160, including the bishop, Polycarp. Thus the statement that the Jews of Smyrna *are a synagogue of Satan* is a remark born out of strife and controversy. It is not an expression of anti-Semitism. The title 'Jew' is respected; in fact, it is claimed for the followers of Christ."[42] Similarly, the church in Philadelphia is addressed: "I will make those of the synagogue of Satan who say that they are Jews and are not, but are lying—I will make them come and bow down before your feet, and they will learn that I have loved you" (Revelation 3:9). The message to Philadelphia also implies a situation in which Jews have opposed followers of Jesus. Collins comments: "As in the message to Smyrna, controversy is reflected here over who are the legitimate Jews. Members of the local synagogue probably had expelled the Christians when they refused to change their minds about Jesus."[43]

In the context of a Jewish Christian community threatened actually or potentially by the mighty Empire of Rome, the Book of Revelation renewed the ancient vision of a holy war fought by God and the angels against the forces of evil in the world.[44]

> Then I saw heaven opened, and there was a white horse! Its rider is called Faithful and True, and in righteousness he judges and makes war. . . . He is clothed in a robe

dipped in blood, and his name is called The Word of God. And the armies of heaven, wearing fine linen, white and pure, were following him on white horses. (Revelation 19:11, 13–14)

At the climax of the battle, the leaders of the evil armies are thrown alive into the lake of fire that burns with sulfur (Revelation 19:20). "All the rest were killed by the sword of the rider on the horse, the sword that came from his mouth, and all the birds were gorged with their flesh" (19:21). The Book of Revelation promises Christians in the late first century c.e. that their enemy, a mighty evil empire, will be destroyed and justice will at last be established; Christians who have been faithful through their trials will exult triumphantly in heaven (Revelation 18:1–19:8).

VARIETIES OF EXEGESIS IN THE LATER CHRISTIAN TRADITION

Generation after generation of Christians looked to the New Testament for guidance in their struggles against those with whom they disagreed, both those within the Christian community and without. A complete survey would require volumes; this discussion will briefly note some aspects of the history of interpretation of the New Testament in relation to Jews, Muslims, and other Christians viewed as heretical.

Relations with Jews

During the first centuries of the Common Era, there developed a complex, overlapping, and troubled network of relationships between Jews and Christians. For centuries, many believers considered themselves to be Jewish followers of Jesus. Recent studies have documented that Jewish-Christian practice was more widespread and long-lasting than had previously been thought.[45] For Jewish Christians or Christian Jews, there was no contradiction between being Jewish and following the path of Jesus: "they insisted that there was no need to choose between being Christians or Jews. Indeed, for them it was an altogether false choice."[46] However, the very existence of the Jewish Christian community posed a grave threat to the Jewish and the Christian elites. John Gager notes that according to the sociology of conflict, "the rule holds that the closer the relationship between two parties the greater the potential for conflict. In other words, whenever we encounter polemical language or the rhetoric of separation, we should look close to home for its source."[47] Jews who believed in Jesus claimed to be the true Christians and the true Jews; because of this claim, they posed a threat to Jews and Christians who sought to draw clear boundary lines between these communities.

There were, to be sure, numerous Jews who were not in any way followers of

Jesus; but increasingly Jewish scholars have recognized how important relations with Christians were for the formation of Rabbinic Judaism.[48] There were also Christians such as Marcion (d. c. 160) and the Gnostics who radically opposed Judaism, rejected the Hebrew Bible, and even denied that the God of Israel was the God of Jesus Christ.[49] However, most Christians refused to follow Marcion or the Gnostics and continued to read the Jewish scriptures, usually in the form of the Septuagint, as the First Testament of the Christian Bible. This set up a fierce, multisided debate over the interpretation of their Jewish heritage.

In the often angry arguments of these debates, early Christian writers produced anti-Jewish works, known collectively as *contra Judaeos* or *adversus Judaeos,* "Against the Jews." This tradition engaged in furious verbal polemics against Jews, long before there was physical violence. As we have seen, the writings in the New Testament are originally Jewish texts and reflect the intense debates among Jews in the first century c.e. During the succeeding centuries, Christians increasingly interpreted these texts in ways that impugned Judaism itself and all Jews who did not accept Jesus as Lord and Messiah. Alan Segal comments: "After Christianity separated from Judaism, the polemical passages in the New Testament were read in an unhistorical way, as testimony of hatred between two separate religions, when they should have been read as strife between two sects of the same religion."[50] An entire web of anti-Jewish presuppositions came increasingly to form the backdrop for traditional Christian theology and practice. Interpreting the New Testament conflicts of Jesus and the Pharisees in light of their own situations centuries later, Christians often viewed all Jews as hypocrites who fundamentally misinterpreted the Law of Moses. In the second century c.e., Justin Martyr (d. c. 165) debated with a Jew named Trypho. Continuing the style of argument of 2 Corinthians 3, Justin cited passages from the Hebrew Bible, taunting, "Aren't you acquainted with them, Trypho? You should be, for they are contained in your Scriptures, or rather not yours, but ours. For we believe and obey them, whereas you, though you read them, do not grasp their spirit."[51]

At the center of early Christian reproaches of Jews was the drama of Jesus's condemnation and death. In the late second century, Melito of Sardis (d. c. 190) composed the first Christian meditation *On Pascha* that has come down to us. Inspired by the gospels, especially Matthew and John, Melito ponders the guilt of the Jewish people for the death of Jesus in moving rhetorical phrases:

> But you cast the vote of opposition against your Lord,
> Whom the gentiles worshipped,
> At whom the uncircumcised marveled,
> Whom the foreigners glorified,
> Over whom even Pilate washed his hands;
> For you killed him at the great feast.
> Therefore the feast of unleavened bread is bitter for you. . . .

You killed the Lord in the middle of Jerusalem. . . .
Therefore, Israel,
You did not shudder at the presence of the Lord;
So you have trembled, embattled by foes.[52]

Later generations of Christians often saw virtually all Jews throughout the ages as rejecting God and God's messengers and as misunderstanding the covenant given through Moses. For centuries Christians interpreted the words of the crowd in Matthew 27:25 as testifying to the collective guilt of Jews for killing Christ and attempting to kill God.[53] Not long after Melito, Origen commented: "Therefore they [the Jews] not only became guilty of the blood of the prophets, but also filled up the measure of their fathers and became guilty of the blood of Christ. . . . Therefore the blood of Jesus came not only upon those who lived formerly but also upon all subsequent generations of Jews to the consummation."[54] The only way for Jews to escape guilt was to accept baptism and become Christian.

Eusebius of Caesarea (d. c. 340) interpreted the sufferings of the Jews during the Jewish revolt of 66–73 C.E. as "the penalty laid upon the Jews by divine justice for their crimes against Christ."[55] Similarly, Augustine interpreted the Jews' loss of an independent kingdom and dispersal among the nations as a punishment for killing Christ: "And if they had not sinned against Him, seduced by impious curiosity as if by magic arts, falling away into the worship of strange gods and idols, and at last putting to death the Christ, they would have remained in the same kingdom which, even if it did not grow in extent, would have grown in happiness."[56] Later in the fourth century, probably between 366 and 384, the unknown author referred to as Ambrosiaster linked the Son of Perdition of 2 Thessalonians 2:3 to the Jews. As Kevin Hughes notes, Ambrosiaster interprets the text of 2 Thessalonians to mean that the Son of Perdition will "either be born of the Jews or become a Jew, so that the Jews may believe in him."[57] In this reading, the Son of Perdition becomes a menacing Jewish figure who will lead astray some Christians and all Jews during the apocalyptic struggles of the end-time.

Following Paul's model in 2 Corinthians 3, Augustine believed that an obscuring veil covers the minds of Jews when they read the scriptures (*Against Faustus* 12.11); Jesus Christ unveils the mysteries for Christians through his death, but the Jews who killed Christ receive no benefit from this because they fail to believe (*City of God* 18.46).[58] Concerning policy toward Jews, Augustine cited Psalm 59:11: "Thou shalt not slay them, lest they should at last forget Thy Law; disperse them in Thy might."[59] Augustine insisted that Jews be allowed to live as unwilling witnesses to Christ: "it is for the sake of such testimony, with which, even against their will, they [the Jews] furnish us by having and preserving those books, that they themselves are scattered throughout all the nations."[60] By viewing the Jews as unwilling witnesses who must survive, Augustine's doctrine effectively protected them for centuries, albeit in subordinate positions in Christian societies.

John Chrysostom (d. 407) bitterly attacked Christians in fourth-century Antioch who attended synagogues and practiced Jewish rituals. Chrysostom understood the statement of the crowd in Matthew 27:25 to apply to the Jews of his own day, exclaiming pointedly to Christians who worshipped with Jews: "Is it not folly for those who worship the crucified to celebrate festivals with those who crucified him? This is not only stupid—it is sheer madness."[61] Chrysostom drew the conclusion that Jews could not share in salvation and that their sufferings were God's punishment: "You Jews did crucify him. But after he died on the cross, he then destroyed your city; it was then that he dispersed your people; it was then that he scattered your nation over the face of the earth."[62] Chrysostom cited Stephen's reproach to the Jews in Acts 7:51 as applying to the Jews of his day as well.[63] Robert Wilken comments on the rhetorical style of Chrysostom:

> John will cite a text from the New Testament to make his polemical point; then, acknowledging that Jews do not accept the authority of the New Testament, he immediately cites a passage from the Jewish prophets, ostensibly making a similar point. . . . The technique, however, is the same—exaggeration, insinuation, guilt by association. Chance phrases in the Bible are singled out because they merge easily with the rhetorical language.[64]

During the first millennium of Christianity, the violence directed against Jews was for the most part rhetorical. Jews were generally in inferior positions in Christian-ruled societies, but there were no widespread physical attacks against them. This situation changed in the eleventh century, after Europeans learned that in 1009 Muslims had destroyed the Church of the Holy Sepulchre in Jerusalem. In the wake of these reports, Jews in Europe were accused of urging the Fatimid caliph Al-Hakim bi-Amr Allah to destroy the sacred shrine of Christ's tomb. As a result, Rodolphus Glaber reports, in 1010 C.E. many Jews were expelled from their homes or killed, and some took their own lives.[65]

Conditions for European Jews worsened after Pope Urban II proclaimed the First Crusade against the Muslims who controlled the Holy Land. In the spring of 1096 some crusaders launched attacks on Jews in France and Germany, killing thousands of them, especially in the Rhineland. While the Jewish scholar Robert Chazan finds no evidence that Pope Urban intended the crusade to target the Jews, he notes the danger in the situation: "The notion of holy war against the enemies of Christendom could readily suggest that, of all the enemies of Christendom, none was more heinous and hence more properly an object of Christian wrath than the Jews. . . . To eleventh century Christians, the Muslims merely denied Jesus, while the Jews were responsible for his death."[66] Christians generally believed that God had abandoned the Jews; this was thought to be demonstrated by their weakness in the face of attacks. When crusaders attacked the defenseless Jews in 1096, this was taken as further proof of God's judgment. Even Christians who tried to protect the Jews from the crusaders interpreted the violence against Jews as God's abandonment of them.[67]

According to a Jewish recollection, one of the crusaders attacking Jews in Mainz reportedly exclaimed: "All this the Crucified has done for us, so that we might avenge his blood on the Jews."[68] Christopher Tyerman sees the popular, apocalyptic visionary preacher Peter the Hermit as most likely responsible for inciting the violence against Jews: "Part of the motive for the massacres of the Rhineland Jews identified in Jewish sources was a crude, vindictive and violent assertion of Christian supremacy and lust for vengeance for Christ Crucified; many of these pogroms were the work of contingents associated with Peter. That there was little or no such barbaric persecution of Jews by the armies recruited by Urban and his agents may point to a distinct difference of tone and content in Peter's preaching."[69]

For centuries, Christian celebrations of the death of Jesus during Holy Week led to attacks on the Jews.[70] Even in the twentieth century, children in Asturias in the northern part of Spain would chant: "Marrano Jews: you killed God, now we kill you, Thieving Jews: first you kill Christ and now you come to rob Christians."[71] Ritual attacks often led to physical attacks on Jews, but did not intend to destroy the Jews completely. David Nirenberg comments: "By alluding to and containing the original act of vengeance at the foundation of Christian-Jewish relations in the diaspora, Holy Week attacks flirted with but ultimately avoided the repetition of that violence in contemporary society."[72] Nonetheless, ritual accusations of Jews repeatedly led to physical attacks on them.

Relations with Muslims: Sacred Combat and Crusade

From the beginning, the relations of Christians and Muslims involved military combat. In the seventh century C.E., Christians in the Middle East experienced the onslaught of Arab Muslim armies on the warpath. Patriarch Sophronius (d. 638) of Jerusalem interpreted the Muslims' initial victories in the Holy Land as God's punishment of Christians for their sins.[73]

By the end of the seventh century, an anonymous writer known as Pseudo-Methodius had produced an apocalyptic interpretation of Muslims that would shape Christian attitudes for centuries.[74] Pseudo-Methodius wrote in Syriac in the late seventh century C.E. under the pseudonym of the revered fourth-century martyr who was bishop of Olympus in Lycia and who was killed in the Roman persecutions in 312 C.E. *The Apocalypse of Pseudo-Methodius* interprets the Arab Muslim triumphs as part of the ongoing drama of the four kingdoms described by Daniel, giving hope to Christians that in the end they will share in Christ's final triumph over their enemies. Pseudo-Methodius sees the "Ishmaelites" (i.e., the Arab Muslims) as preparing the way for the Son of Perdition. Their victories are not due to their righteousness or God's favor but rather to the sinfulness of Christians: "Similarly with these children of Ishmael: it was not because God loves them that he allowed them to enter the kingdom of the Christians, but because of the wickedness and sin which is performed at the hands of the Christians, the like of which has not been performed in any of the former generations."[75]

Much of Pseudo-Methodius's reflection turns on the application of 2 Thessalonians 2:3 to his situation: "This is the chastisement of which the Apostle spoke: 'The chastisement must come first, only then will that Man of Sin, the Son of Destruction, be revealed.'"[76] Pseudo-Methodius understands Jesus's parable of the wheat and the tares (Matthew 13:24–30) to explain that the sufferings of Christians must increase so that the faithful may be tested and known.[77] But after this suffering, "the king of the Greeks shall go out against them in great wrath," bringing destruction to the Ishmaelites and peace to Christians, a peace unprecedented in the history of the world.[78] There will, however, be more suffering when the king of the Greeks dies and the Son of Perdition appears and works the signs of deception foretold by Jesus (Matthew 24:24). The Son of Perdition will then take his seat in Jerusalem. "But at the Advent of our Lord from heaven he will be delivered over to 'the Gehenna of Fire' (Matthew 5:22) and to 'outer darkness,' where he will be amidst 'weeping and gnashing of teeth'" (Matthew 8:12).[79]

For Pseudo-Methodius, Muhammad is a forerunner of the Antichrist and the Son of Perdition; but the king of the Greeks, the Last Emperor (i.e., the Byzantine Emperor), brings hope for faithful Christians. Since the ultimate victory of Christ is assured, Pseudo-Methodius urgently encourages Christians to resist the Muslims and continue the struggle against them through all hardships. Pseudo-Methodius opposes any form of collaboration or acceptance of Muslim rule.[80] Bernard McGinn comments on the role of apocalyptic interpretations of difficult historical events:

> One of the characteristics of apocalyptic eschatology is its drive to find meaning in current events by seeing them in light of the scenario of the end. Such *a posteriori*, or after-the-fact, uses of apocalypticism are often reactions to major historical changes (like the conversion of the Empire or the rise of Islam) that do not fit into the received view of providential history. By making a place for such events in the story of the end, the final point that gives all history meaning, apocalyptic eschatology incorporates the unexpected into the divinely foreordained and gives it permanent significance.[81]

The Apocalypse of Pseudo-Methodius was translated into Greek and circulated widely for centuries, becoming the third most important apocalyptic text for medieval Christians, after the biblical books of Daniel and Revelation.[82] It was still being reprinted and distributed a millennium later in 1683, when the Ottoman army was besieging Vienna.[83]

Medieval Christians repeatedly interpreted Muhammad either as the Antichrist or as a forerunner of the Antichrist.[84] A long tradition in Latin Christianity reflected on the meaning of the Antichrist in relation to the Son of Perdition of 2 Thessalonians.[85] In calling for a new Crusade in 1213, Pope Innocent III condemned Muhammad as the Son of Perdition (2 Thessalonians 2:3); Innocent expected him to have a reign of 666 years, almost all of which had already passed.[86] Medieval Christians applied the term from the Book of Revelation "synagogues of Satan" to Muslims.[87] Apocalyptic imagery inspired Christians to fight against their Muslim adversaries for centuries, offering hope of eschatological vindication even in the most hopeless of earthly situations.

In the long struggle against Muslims in the Iberian Peninsula, James the Apostle, the son of Zebedee, became the heavenly patron in battle. Jesus had nicknamed James the "son of thunder" (Mark 3:17), apparently because he and his brother John wanted Jesus to call down thunder on those who rejected him (Luke 9:54). Even though Jesus sharply rebuked his fiery disciple for his temper (Luke 9:55), medieval Christians honored James for his ferocity, and he became the patron of Spain. According to legend, he miraculously intervened in the battle of Clavijo in 844, when Ramiro I of Asturias was leading Christians in battle against Muslims led by the Emir of Cordoba. James's heavenly assistance in battle earned him the new sobriquet "Matamoros," the Moor-slayer who kills the enemies of Christ. The church built in his honor at Compostela, where his remains were allegedly discovered, was one of the most important pilgrimage places of Europe.[88]

Decontextualized quotations from the Bible played an important role in the theology of holy war throughout the Middle Ages. Christopher Tyerman notes the usual practice of biblical interpretation at the time of the First Crusade: "As it had developed by the beginning of its second millennium in western Christendom, Christianity was only indirectly a scriptural faith. The foundation texts of the Old and New Testaments were mediated even to the educated through the prism of commentaries by the so-called Church Fathers."[89] Individual sayings were often taken out of their original context and applied to situations undreamed of by the biblical authors.

In particular, the challenge of applying the pacific teachings of Jesus to practical situations in a warlike world was acute. Even though medieval Christians honored the irenic ideals of Jesus as noble principles, they often applied them to private, personal relations while looking to the battles of the Hebrew Bible and the Book of Revelation for guidance in their public affairs.[90] Medieval Christians frequently imagined Jesus as a warrior in conflict with his adversaries and interpreted his harsh words as justification for their own attacks on opponents. The Christian imagination transformed the Prince of Peace into the Heroic Warrior of Sacred Combat. Wars were, after all, waged in order to establish a just peace. An early English poem, *The Dream of the Rood,* calls Jesus "the Warrior . . . the Mighty King,

Lord of Heavens" and "the Wielder of Triumphs."[91] Charlemagne appeared as the ideal Christian warrior, who asked the pope to pray that he might defeat his enemies by "the arms of Faith."[92] Ideals of chivalry combined monastic-style devotion to Christ with the warrior's courage in fighting for justice.[93]

At the center of the imagery of the First Crusade was Jesus's command to take up one's cross and follow him (Matthew 16:24). "The holy war [against Muslims] was perceived and possibly designed to revolve around Matthew 16:24."[94] For centuries the crusades took shape as a concrete way to accept this challenge. "This was the text referred to in the deal between the south-east German abbey of Göttweig and Wolfker of Kuffern, who had decided to join the march to Jerusalem in 1096 because 'he wanted to fulfill the Gospel command, who wishes to follow me.' "[95]

The sacred combat of the Book of Revelation was of particular importance in this process. Earthly enemies were repeatedly seen as the Son of Perdition, the Antichrist, or their accomplices. The bloody images of battle of the Book of Revelation shape the accounts of the sack of Jerusalem by the First Crusade in 1099. Raymond of Aguilers described the scene on the Temple Mount after the crusaders' victory: "it is sufficient to relate that in the Temple of Solomon and the portico crusaders rode in blood to the knees and bridles of their horses."[96] Tyerman notes: "Raymond was quoting Revelation 14:20: 'And the winepress was trodden without the city, and blood came out of the winepress, even unto the horse bridles.' It is hard to exaggerate the dependence of Raymond's contemporaries on the Scripture for imagery and language."[97]

Relations with Christian Heretics

Jesus's parable of the great dinner (Luke 14:16–24) played a major role in the treatment of Christian heretics. In the original tale, the host respects the free decision of the original guests; since they declined the invitation, they will not share in the feast. However, the later group that is to be found in the highways and byways is to be compelled to come to the feast. In one of the most influential interpretations in all of Christian history, Augustine cited the command of the master in Jesus's parable of the great dinner (Luke 14:23) to justify forcing heretics into unity, or at least conformity, with the Catholic Church.[98] Where the host in the parable respects the freedom of his original invitees, the later Christian tradition would draw the exact opposite conclusion and attempt to force dissenters to embrace orthodox Christian teaching and practice. During the controversy with the Donatists, Augustine interpreted the third invitation in the parable to go into the highways and hedges as applying to heretics and schismatics.[99] For Augustine, after the church became established as a power in society, it had the responsibility and duty to repress heresy and compel heretics to conform to Catholic belief and practice. This interpretation would later serve as the charter for the Catholic Inquisition.[100]

During the first millennium of Christianity, there was relatively little persecution of heresy. This too changed in the second millennium. In 1208, faced with the most widespread movement of Christian dissent in centuries, Pope Innocent III requested the king and nobility of France to attack the Cathars in the south of France.[101] While the king declined, many nobles accepted the challenge and slaughtered the inhabitants of Beziers, regardless of their religious conviction, in 1209. The Papal Inquisition was later established in 1233 to find the surviving Cathars. Crusades were called not only against external enemies but also against those who claimed to be within the Christian community.

In considering whether or not unbelievers should be compelled to believe, Thomas Aquinas (d. 1274) first notes that John Chrysostom interpreted Jesus's parable of the wheat and the weeds (Matthew 23:38) as teaching that heretics should not be slain; but Thomas counterbalances this ("sed contra") with Jesus's command in Luke 14:23 to "compel them to come in." Aquinas argues that those who never received the faith, such as "heathen and Jews," should not be compelled to the faith. However, he follows the precedent of Augustine on heretics and apostates and argues that "heretics and all apostates . . . should be submitted even to bodily compulsion, that they may fulfill what they have promised, and hold what they, at one time, received."[102] Later, Aquinas specifies that if the heretic is obstinate, "the Church no longer hoping for his conversion looks to the salvation of others, by excommunicating him and separating him from the Church, and furthermore delivers him to the secular tribunal to be exterminated thereby from the world by death."[103] The combined authority of Augustine and Aquinas in interpreting Luke 14:23 provided a theological justification for the Inquisition and persecution of heretics for centuries.

Medieval Popes applied the imagery of the Antichrist to their enemies, most notably to the Emperor Frederick II Hohenstaufen. Gregory IX (d. 1241) queried: "What other Antichrist should we await, when, as is evident in his works, he is already come in the person of Frederick?"[104] Once the principle of labeling an opponent an "Antichrist" was established, applications multiplied, including to the pope himself. Martin Luther (d. 1546) famously saw the pope as the Antichrist; since he also came to see Muhammad and Muslims as associated with the Antichrist, his followers developed a dual doctrine of both pope and Turk as Antichrists.[105] Such applications fueled repeated battles among Christians.

RESULTS OF EXEGESIS THROUGH HISTORICAL EXAMPLE: JEWS AND CHRISTIANS READING THE NEW TESTAMENT TOGETHER

The hermeneutical situation regarding the New Testament changed dramatically during the second half of the twentieth century. One factor lay in the atrocities of the Shoah (Holocaust). While the Nazi ideology and crimes were profoundly anti-Christian, many Christians and Jews recognized that centuries of Christian vilification of the Jews had tragically prepared the way for Nazi propaganda and atrocities.[106] Another major factor has been the awareness that the Jewish and Christian communities did not neatly divide into two religions during the first century C.E., as had often earlier been assumed. In this changed exegetical situation, descriptive and normative investigations intertwine. Jews and Christians in dialogue with each other have sought to understand New Testament texts.

Perhaps the most problematic passage of all is Matthew 27:25: "His blood be upon us and on our children." The Jewish scholar Steven L. Jacobs strongly criticizes this statement:

> From an historical perspective, Jews simply cannot affirm the accuracy of Matthew 27:25. A religious tradition that continues to assert the sanctity of the family as the basic unit and building block of society, and primacy of children to make that family whole, cannot abide a verse and scenario that not only degrades those Jews who were questionably present, but puts into their mouths a curse upon their own children, their children's children, and all generations to come. Even granting that there were those Jews possibly in league with the Romans and those duplicitous Jewish leaders interested in cozying up to their Roman oppressors, the announcement is itself so horrendous as to defy credibility, and must, therefore, be rejected as a true depiction of events.[107]

Jacobs demands that Christians recognize the complicity of this passage in preparing for the Shoah and drop the statement from the lectionary that is used in worship services.[108]

A number of Christian theologians have reflected on this challenge. Rosemary Radford Ruether makes a very harsh judgment on the Jewish Christian community that produced Matthew 27:25: "By the second decade of its mission it had come to believe that Judaism, represented by its dominant religious consciousness, was hopelessly apostate and represented a heritage of apostasy which merited its rejection."[109] David Tracy acknowledges the problem, proposing that "anti-Judaic statements of the New Testament bear *no* authoritative status for Christianity.... The heart of the New Testament message—the love who is God—should release the demythologizing power of its own prophetic meaning to rid the New Testament and Christianity once and for all of these statements."[110]

Clark Williamson, following Luke Timothy Johnson, interprets the statement as typical of the rhetoric of that age: "Realizing that this kind of slander was common parlance, that every body did it, relativizes our version of slander.... The problem with the New Testament is that it is too much like other literature from its time and place.... Without denying the intensity of the slander against the Jews that is found in parts of the New Testament, we should regard this calumny as typical of what passed for 'interreligious' discourse at the time and as reflecting animosities that occurred in the late first century."[111]

VIOLENCE IN THE NEW TESTAMENT   95

Daniel Harrington also recommends contextual interpretation: "Matthew 27:11–16 (and especially 27:25) is a major text in the history and present reality of Christian-Jewish relations. Teachers and preachers have a serious obligation to work through this text with care and objectivity. . . . Above all it is necessary to read Matt 27:25 ('His blood be upon us and upon our children') in its Matthean setting, not as applying to all Jews at all times or to just the small percentage of Jews in Jerusalem who involved themselves in Jesus' trial before Pilate. The Matthean setting involves both the time of Jesus and the time after A.D. 70, and it is rooted in an inner-Jewish quarrel."[112]

Raymond Brown notes a problem in the text, but doubts that contextualization really solves the difficulty: "One can benevolently reflect that the Matthean statement [27:25] was not applicable to the whole Jewish people of Jesus' time, for relatively few stood before Pilate, and also that it was an affirmation of present willingness to accept responsibility, not an invocation of future punishment or vengeance. . . . On the whole Matthew's attitude is generalizing and hostile, and we cannot disguise it."[113] Brown considers the proposal to drop this statement from the lectionary, but rejects it, reflecting on the underlying hermeneutical problem: "Sooner or later Christian believers must wrestle with the limitations imposed on the Scriptures by the circumstances in which they were written. They must be brought to see that some attitudes found in the Scriptures, however explicable in the times in which they originated, may be wrong attitudes if repeated today."[114]

Robert Daly notes that in traditional Christian settings it can be difficult to reject the doctrine of supersessionism, and he suggests that it is relatively easier to proclaim "that Jews are not the murderers of Jesus, however much some Christians of the past may have thought so. To claim that Jews are 'Christ-killers' or 'God-murderers' is itself a murderous lie."[115] Daly notes both the importance and the limitations of explaining the historical context. In the end, he suggests that only when Christian interpreters have gone through an inner conversion from supersessionism and "have learned to love the Jews" will Christian biblical interpretation be innocent.

In considering the problem posed by Matthew 27:25, the Pontifical Biblical Commission of the Catholic Church claims that the original context in Matthew not only expresses continuity with the Old Testament, implying the possibility of "fraternal bonds" between Jews and Christians, but also "reflects a situation of tension and even opposition between the two communities. . . . Since that situation [of tension] has radically changed, Matthew's polemic need no longer interfere with relations between Christians and Jews, and the aspect of continuity can and ought to prevail."[116]

John Dominic Crossan comments on Matthew 27:25 by way of Jesus's saying in Luke 23:34: "Father, forgive them; for they do not know what they are doing." Crossan notes that each saying is unique to its proper gospel and comments: "If some Christians take everything in the passion as actual, factual information, they must take both Matthew 27:25 and Luke 23:34 as historical data. But, because Jesus' prayer for forgiveness in Luke happened after the people's acceptance of responsibility in Matthew, it must surely have annulled it. Unless, of course, God refused Jesus' prayer. For Christians, like myself, who think that Matthew and Luke each created those specific verses out of their own theological backgrounds, there is a slightly different conclusion. Inspired Christian texts contain both virulent bitterness and serene forgiveness. It is necessary to know the difference and judge accordingly."[117]

Finally, as Jonathan Sacks insisted, the interpretive community chooses which texts to place in the foreground. In most of the recent Christian hermeneutical proposals, there is a stark recognition of how deeply harmful traditional Christian exegesis of Matthew 27:25 has been. Historical contextualization is important but by itself insufficient. The horizon of interpretation, including the entire network of interpretive presuppositions, must shift; to a significant degree this has begun to happen in Jewish-Christian dialogue over the last half-century. Problems certainly remain, but there is a wide and probably unprecedented degree of collaboration and Jewish-Christian dialogue in exploring the mixed heritage of violence in the texts of the New Testament.

NOTES

1. Unless otherwise noted, all scriptural quotations are taken from the New Revised Standard Version. Used by permission. For a range of interpretations of the teaching of Jesus on peace and violence, see Willard M. Swartley, ed., *The Love of Enemy and Nonretaliation in the New Testament* (Louisville: Westminster John Knox, 1992); Michel Desjardins, *Peace, Violence, and the New Testament* (Sheffield: Sheffield Academic, 1997).

2. Origen, *On First Principles*, trans. G. W. Butterworth (Gloucester: Peter Smith, 1973), 269–87; Augustine, *Teaching Christianity [De Doctrina Christiana]*, trans. Edmund Hill, ed. John E. Rotelle, Works of Saint Augustine (Hyde Park: New City, 1996), 175–80; Vatican Council II, *Dogmatic Constitution on Divine Revelation, Dei Verbum*, in *Vatican Council II: The Conciliar and Postconciliar Documents*, ed. Austin Flannery, rev. ed. (Northport: Costello, 2004), 756–58.

3. Friedrich Schleiermacher, *Hermeneutics: The Handwritten Manuscripts*, ed. Heinz Kimmerle, trans. James Duke and Jack Forstman (Missoula: Scholars, 1977), 115–17.

4. Jonathan Sacks, *The Dignity of Difference: How to Avoid the Clash of Civilizations*, rev. ed. (London: Continuum, 2003), 207–8.

5. William C. Wienrich, ed., *Revelation*, vol. 12 of *Ancient Christian Commentary on Scripture* (Downers Grove: InterVarsity, 2005), xx.

6. Donald Senior, *The Gospel of Matthew* (Nashville: Abingdon, 1997), 159.

7. Joseph A. Fitzmyer, *The Gospel according to Luke (X–XXIV)*, vol. 28a of *The Anchor Bible* (New York: Doubleday, 1985), 1053.

8. Ibid.

9. Ibid., 1057. Fitzmyer notes the similar situation in Genesis 19:3.

10. Daniel Boyarin, *Border Lines: The Partition of Judaeo-Christianity* (Philadelphia: University of Pennsylvania Press, 2004); Adam H. Becker and Annette Yoshiko Reed, eds., *The Ways That*

Never Parted: Jews and Christians in Late Antiquity and the Early Middle Ages (Minneapolis: Fortress, 2007).

11. Luke Timothy Johnson, "The New Testament's Anti-Jewish Slander and the Conventions of Ancient Polemic," *Journal of Biblical Literature* 108 (1989): 419–41.

12. Amy-Jill Levine, "Matthew, Mark, and Luke: Good News or Bad?," in *Jesus, Judaism, and Christian Anti-Judaism: Reading the New Testament after the Holocaust,* ed. Paula Fredriksen and Adele Reinhartz (Louisville: Westminster John Knox, 2002), 78.

13. John P, Meier, *Companions and Competitors,* vol. 3 of *A Marginal Jew: Rethinking the Historical Jesus* (New York: Doubleday, 2001), 339–40.

14. E. P. Sanders, "Jesus, Ancient Judaism, and Modern Christianity," in *Jesus, Judaism, and Christian Anti-Judaism: Reading the New Testament after the Holocaust,* ed. Paula Fredriksen and Adele Reinhartz (Louisville: Westminster John Knox, 2002), 54.

15. Raymond E. Brown, *An Introduction to the New Testament,* Anchor Bible Reference Library (1997; New York: Doubleday, 2007), 166.

16. Daniel J. Harrington, *The Gospel of Matthew,* Sacra Pagina (1991; Collegeville: Liturgical Press, 2007), 392.

17. Francis J. Moloney, *The Gospel of John,* Sacra Pagina (Collegeville: Liturgical Press, 1998), 10.

18. Ibid., 11.

19. John Ashton, *Understanding the Fourth Gospel* (Oxford: Oxford University Press, 1991), 151

20. Adele Reinhartz, "The Gospel of John: How 'the Jews' Became Part of the Plot," in Fredriksen and Reinhartz, *Jesus, Judaism, and Christian Anti-Judaism,* 102.

21. Ibid., 110.

22. Brown, *An Introduction to the New Testament,* 383.

23. Kenneth Grayston, *The Johannine Epistles,* New Century Bible Commentary (Grand Rapids, MI: Eerdmans, 1984), 76.

24. Ibid., 78.

25. Luke Timothy Johnson, *The Acts of the Apostles,* Sacra Pagina (Collegeville: Liturgical, 1992), 114–20; Joseph A. Fitzmyer, *The Acts of the Apostles,* vol. 31 of *The Anchor Bible* (New York: Doubleday, 1998), 364–86.

26. Johnson, *Acts,* 120.

27. Fitzmyer, *Acts,* 309.

28. Earl J. Richard, *First and Second Thessalonians,* Sacra Pagina (1995; Collegeville: Liturgical Press, 2007), 122.

29. Ibid., 125.

30. Ibid., 125. Brown offers arguments for and against Pauline authorship: *An Introduction to the New Testament,* 463.

31. Gerd Lüdemann, *The Unholy in Holy Scripture: The Dark Side of the Bible,* trans. John Bowden (Louisville: Westminster John Knox, 1997), 83. Karl P. Donfried also argues for the authenticity of the passage: "Paul and Judaism: 1 Thessalonians 2:13–16 as a Test Case," *Interpretation* 38 (1984): 242–53. Robert Jewett also reviews the literature and argues for Pauline authorship: *The Thessalonian Correspondence: Pauline Rhetoric and Millenarian Piety* (Philadelphia: Fortress, 1986), 36–46.

32. Jan Lambrecht, *Second Corinthians,* Sacra Pagina (Collegeville: Liturgical Press, 1999), 61.

33. Frank J. Matera, *Galatians,* rev. ed., Sacra Pagina (Collegeville: Liturgical Press, 2007), 173.

34. So also Brown, *An Introduction to the New Testament,* 473.

35. Ibid., 590–94. For a survey of views and a defense of Pauline authorship, see I. Howard Marshall, *1 and 2 Thessalonians,* New Century Bible Commentary (Grand Rapids, MI: Eerdmans, 1983), 25–45. For a deutero-Pauline interpretation, see Bonni Thurston, *Reading Colossians, Ephesians, and 2 Thessalonians: A Literary and Theological Commentary* (New York: Crossroad, 1995), 157–63.

36. Grayston, *The Johannine Epistles,* 188–90.

37. Thurston, *Reading Colossians, Ephesians, and 2 Thessalonians,* 178.

38. Ibid., 179.

39. Adela Yarbro Collins, "The Book of Revelation," in *The Continuum History of Apocalypticism,* ed. Bernard J. McGinn, John J. Collins, and Stephen J. Stein (New York: Continuum, 2003), 196.

40. Peder Borgen, "Polemic in the Book of Revelation," in *Anti-Semitism and Early Christianity: Issues of Polemic and Faith,* ed. Craig A. Evans and Donald A. Hagner (Minneapolis: Fortress, 1993), 200.

41. Ibid., 199–200.

42. Adela Yarbro Collins, *The Apocalypse* (Wilmington: Michael Glazier, 1979), 17. See also Wilfred J. Harrington, *Revelation,* rev. ed., Sacra Pagina (Collegeville: Liturgical, 2008), 59.

43. Collins, *The Apocalypse,* 28.

44. Adela Yarbro Collins, *Crisis and Catharsis: The Power of the Apocalypse* (Philadelphia: Westminster, 1984).

45. See Boyarin, *Border Lines,* and Becker and Reed, *The Ways That Never Parted.*

46. John G. Gager, "Did Jewish Christians See the Rise of Islam?," in Becker and Reed, *The Ways that Never Parted,* 370.

47. Ibid.

48. Israel Jacob Yuval, *Two Nations in Your Womb: Perceptions of Jews and Christians in Late Antiquity and the Middle Ages,* trans. Barbara Harshav and Jonathan Chipman (Berkeley: University of California Press, 2006).

49. W. N. C. Frend, *The Rise of Christianity* (Philadelphia: Fortress, 1984), 193–218.

50. Alan F. Segal, *Rebecca's Children: Judaism and Christianity in the Roman World* (Cambridge, MA: Harvard University Press, 1986), 142. See also William Nicholls, *Christian Antisemitism: A History of Hate* (Northvale: Jason Aronson, 1993), 170–87; Paula Fredriksen, *Augustine and the Jews: A Christian Defense of Jews and Judaism* (New York: Doubleday, 2008), xiv–xv.

51. Justin Martyr, *Dialogue with Trypho,* trans. Thomas B. Falls, revised by Thomas P. Halton, ed. Michael Slusser (Washington, DC: Catholic University of America Press, 2003), 44.

52. Melito of Sardis, *On Pascha With the Fragments of Melito and Other Material Related to the Quartodecimans,* trans. Alistair Stewart-Sykes (Crestwood: St Vladimir's Seminary, 2001), 62–63, 64.

53. For a survey of the Latin patristic authors, see Rainer Kampling, *Das Blut Christi und die Juden: Mt 27,25 bei den lateinischsprachigen christlichen Autoren bis zu Leo dem Grossen* (Münster: Aschendorff, 1984).

54. Quoted by Lüdemann, *The Unholy in Holy Scripture,* 98–99. See Origen, *In Matt. 27:22–26.*

55. Eusebius of Caesarea, *The History of the Church from Christ to Constantine,* trans. G. A. Williamson (Harmondsworth, UK: Penguin, 1965), 80.

56. Augustine, *The City of God against the Pagans,* ed. and trans. R. W. Dyson (Cambridge: Cambridge University Press, 1998), 86.

57. Kevin L. Hughes, *Constructing Antichrist: Paul, Biblical Commentary, and the Development of Doctrine in the Early Middle Ages* (Washington, DC: Catholic University of America Press, 2005), 43.

58. Fredriksen, *Augustine and the Jews,* 268.

59. Augustine, *City of God* 18:46; translation of Augustine's use of the Psalm by Dyson.

60. Augustine, *City of God* 18:46; p. 892; Fredriksen, *Augustine and the Jews,* 351–52.

61. John Chrysostom, *Discourses Against Judaizing Christians,* 1.5; quoted by Robert L. Wilken, *John Chrysostom and the Jews: Rhetoric and Reality in the Late 4th Century* (Berkeley: University of California Press, 1983), 125.

62. John Chrysostom, *Discourses Against Judaizing Christians,* 5.1; quoted in Wilken, *John Chrysostom and the Jews,* 126.

63. John Chrysostom, *Discourses Against Judaizing Christians,* 1.2; quoted in Wilken, *John Chrysostom and the Jews,* 124.

64. Wilken, *John Chrysostom and the Jews*, 124.

65. Rachel Fulton, *From Judgment to Passion: Devotion to Christ and the Virgin Mary, 800–1200* (New York: Columbia University Press, 2002), 65.

66. Robert Chazan, *In the Year 1096: The First Crusade and the Jews* (Philadelphia: Jewish Publication Society, 1996), 56.

67. Robert Chazan, *God, Humanity, and History: The Hebrew First Crusade Narratives* (Berkeley: University of California Press, 2000), 144–45. Thomas Aquinas shared the belief that the exile of the Jews was a divinely willed punishment for their guilt in the crucifixion of Jesus. See John Y. B. Hood, *Aquinas and the Jews* (Philadelphia: University of Pennsylvania Press, 1995), 77–111.

68. Christopher Tyerman, *God's War: A New History of the Crusades* (Cambridge, MA: Belknap Press of Harvard University Press, 2006), 104.

69. Ibid., 79.

70. David Nirenberg, *Communities of Violence: Persecution of Minorities in the Middle Ages* (Princeton: Princeton University Press, 1996), 200–30.

71. Ibid., 203.

72. Ibid., 218.

73. Quoted in F. E. Peters, *Jerusalem: the Holy City in the Eyes of Chroniclers, Visitors, Pilgrims, and Prophets from the Days of Abraham to the Beginnings of Modern Times* (Princeton: Princeton University Press, 1985), 175.

74. Text found in *The Seventh Century in the West-Syrian Chronicles,* trans. Andrew Palmer and Sebastian Brock (Liverpool: Liverpool University Press, 1993), 222–42; Paul Julius Alexander, *The Byzantine Apocalyptic Tradition,* ed. Dorothy de F. Abrahamse (Berkeley: University of California Press, 1985); F. J. Martinez, "Eastern Christian Apocalyptic in the Early Muslim Period: Pseudo-Methodius and Pseudo-Athanasius" (PhD diss., Catholic University of America, 1985), 58–246.

75. *Apocalypse of Pseudo-Methodius* 11.5 [section of the text itself], in *Seventh Century in the West-Syrian Chronicles,* 231 [page of the trans.].

76. *Apocalypse of Pseudo-Methodius* 11.17; *Seventh Century in the West-Syrian Chronicles,* 233. See also Alexander, *The Byzantine Apocalyptic Tradition,* 20–21.

77. *Apocalypse of Pseudo-Methodius* 13.4; *Seventh Century in the West-Syrian Chronicles,* 236.

78. *Apocalypse of Pseudo-Methodius* 13.11; *Seventh Century in the West-Syrian Chronicles,* 237.

79. *Apocalypse of Pseudo-Methodius,* 14.13; *Seventh Century in the West-Syrian Chronicles,* 242.

80. Bernard McGinn, *Visions of the End: Apocalyptic Traditions in the Middle Ages* (New York: Columbia University Press, 1979), 70.

81. Bernard McGinn, *Antichrist: Two Thousand Years of the Human Fascination with Evil* (San Francisco: HarperSanFrancisco, 1994), 88.

82. On the relation of the Greek translation to the Syriac original, see Alexander, *The Byzantine Apocalyptic Tradition,* 31–60.

83. McGinn, *Visions of the End,* 72.

84. Bernard McGinn, *Antichrist,* 85–86; Norman Daniel, *Islam and the West: The Making of an Image* (1960; Oxford: Oneworld, 2000), 210–12.

85. Cf. Kevin L. Hughes, *Constructing Antichrist.*

86. McGinn, *Antichrist,* 150.

87. Daniel, *Islam and the West,* 133–34.

88. Maryjane Dunn and Linda Kay Davidson, eds., *The Pilgrimage to Compostela in the Middle Ages* (New York: Routledge, 1996); Javier Garcia Turza, *El Camino de Santiago y la Sociedad Medieval* (Logroño: Ediciones Instituto de Estudios Riojanos, 2000).

89. Tyerman, *God's War,* 29.

90. Ibid., 30.

91. M. H. Abrams, ed., *The Norton Anthology of English Literature*, 5th ed. (New York: W. W. Norton, 1986), 1:23, 24.

92. Tyerman, *God's War*, 36.

93. Alan Baker, *The Knight* (Hoboken: John Wiley and Sons, 2003), 158–90.

94. Tyerman, *God's War*, 32.

95. Ibid.

96. Quoted by Tyerman, *God's War*, 31.

97. Ibid.

98. Augustine *Contra Gaud. Don.* 1.25, 28 [Corpus scriptorum ecclesiasticorum latinorum 53. 226–27]; cited by Fitzmyer, *Gospel of Luke X–XXIX*, 1057. See also F. A. Norwood, "'Compel Them to Come In': The History of Luke 14:23," *Religion in Life* 23 (1953–54): 516–27.

99. Norwood, "'Compel them to Come In,'" 517; Augustine, *Correction of the Donatists*, 6; Augustine, *Letter*, 93.2.5; Frend, *The Rise of Christianity*, 671–72.

100. Norwood, "'Compel them to Come In,'"519.

101. Malcolm Lambert, *The Cathars* (Malden, MA: Blackwell, 1998), 92–111.

102. Thomas Aquinas, *Summa Theologiae*, trans. Fathers of the English Dominican Province (New York: Benziger Brothers, 1947), 2–2.8; 2:1219. See also 2–2.11.3; 2:1226.

103. Ibid., 2–2.11.3; 2:1226.

104. Quoted in McGinn, *Antichrist*, 153.

105. McGinn, *Antichrist*, 206–13; Daniel, *Islam and the West*, 404–5.

106. Jules Isaac, *The Teaching of Contempt: Christian Roots of Anti-Semitism*, trans. Helen Weaver, biographical intro by Claire Huchet-Bishop (New York: Holt, Rinehart & Winston, 1964); Rosemary Radford Ruether, *Faith and Fratricide: The Theological Roots of Anti-Semitism* (New York: Seabury, 1974); Edward H. Flannery, *The Anguish of the Jews: Twenty-Three Centuries of Anti-Semitism* (New York: Macmillan, 1965); James Carroll, *Constantine's Sword: The Church and the Jews: A History* (Boston: Houghton Mifflin, 2001); David I. Kertzer, *The Popes against the Jews: The Vatican's Role in the Rise of Modern Anti-Semitism* (New York: Alfred A. Knopf, 2001).

107. Steven L. Jacobs, "Blood on Our Heads: A Jewish Response to Saint Matthew," in *A Shadow of Glory: Reading the New Testament after the Holocaust* (New York: Routledge, 2002), 62–63.

108. Ibid., 63, 65.

109. Ruether, *Faith and Fratricide*, 94.

110. David A. Tracy, "Religious Values after the Holocaust: A Catholic View," in *Jews and Christians after the Holocaust*, ed. Abraham J. Peck (Philadelphia: Fortress, 1982), 96–97.

111. Clark M. Williamson, *A Guest in the House of Israel: Post-Holocaust Church Theology* (Louisville: Westminster John Knox, 1993), 146, 148.

112. Harrington, *Gospel of Matthew*, 393.

113. Raymond E. Brown, *A Crucified Christ in Holy Week: Essays on the Four Gospel Passion Narratives* (Collegeville: Liturgical Press, 1986), 42.

114. Ibid., 16.

115. Robert J. Daly, "Removing Anti-Judaism from the Pulpit: Four Approaches," in *Removing Anti-Judaism from the Pulpit*, ed. Howard Clark Kee and Irvin J. Borowsky (Philadelphia: Continuum, 1996), 52.

116. Pontifical Biblical Commission, *The Jewish People and Their Sacred Scriptures in the Christian Bible*, 3.B.1. This document is available on the Vatican's website.

117. John Dominic Crossan, *Who Killed Jesus? Exposing the Roots of Anti-Semitism in the Gospel Story of the Death of Jesus* (San Francisco: HarperSanFrancisco, 1996), 158.

5

Finhās of Medina

Islam, "The Jews," and the
Construction of Religious Militancy

Michael A. Sells

Group names are inevitable. We cannot live without them. But we do not find it easy to live peacefully with them. A group name occupies an ambiguous zone between generalization and specification. Take the expression, which I invent for the purposes of illustration, "the Alberians carried out a crime against humanity." The group name designates a group and does not make any exceptions to the group designation. If found in a newspaper or history book, it might refer to a particular army or irregular militia unit that carried out a particular crime at a particular time and place, but which—for whatever valid or invalid reason—the author of the text associates with the people in whose name or under whose authority the subgroup committing the crime claims to operate. A group name, once used, sets into operation assumptions regarding authority, responsibility, and blame that can erupt suddenly and are controlled only with difficulty. And in divinely revealed or inspired discourse, recorded in sacred text, the questions surrounding such a group are particularly fraught.

Everything depends on establishing the frame of reference within which a given group is named. That frame will indicate that the reference is to some members of the named group at a particular time and place, all the people of the group at that time, all members of that group at all times, to mention only the largest sets of possibilities.

I take up here the group names in the Qur'an, qur'anic commentaries, and early Islamic historical accounts of the life of Muhammad that have been translated as "the Jews" or associated with Jews. As a test case, I examine the remarkable story of a Jewish elder from Medina named Finhās, whose words and actions were said to have led to several qur'anic revelations and to have played a dramatic role in the foundational events of Islam.

Early Islamic sources refer to him variously as Finhās bin ʿĀzurāʾ, Finhās al-Yahūdī, or simply as Finhās.[1] He was viewed as a *habr* (a religiously learned elder or teacher) from an important Jewish tribe in Medina who took part in disputations with the Prophet Muhammad as well as Muhammad's companion and the future first Caliph Abū Bakr. By "traditional sources," I mean reports *(akhbār)* that record the words and actions of the Prophet and his companions and that were passed down orally for several generations before they were written down and incorporated into the major genres of Islamic literature.

The Finhās-related reports are found in two interconnected genres: *sīra* and *tafsīr*. *Sīra* is sometimes translated as "biography" and in the early Islamic context refers to accounts of the life, actions, and battles of Muhammad. *Tafsīr* refers to compilations of word-by-word commentary on the Qurʾan. The two genres are symbiotic. Portions of the *sīra* were composed as attempts to explain passages of the Qurʾan; that is, the effort to explain passages of the Qurʾan at least to some extent appears to have been a part of a larger effort to record the life and deeds of the Prophet. The exegetical works, conversely, cited episodes of the Prophet's *sīra* in order to explain passages in the Qurʾan.[2]

Finhās the Yahūdī may or may not have lived, spoken, and acted as the sources examined below claim. There may have been more than one Finhās involved in disputations between Muhammad and Jews in Medina. Alternatively, one man named Finhās might have been involved in some disputes with Muhammad and his companions, and then later he may have been inserted into other incidents for which the names of the Jewish protagonists were unknown. It is possible to call into doubt the entire set of incidents and disputes involving a Medinan Jew by the name of Finhās. But however we judge the reliability or the veracity of the *akhbār* relating to Finhās, he emerges as a complicated and intriguing character and his words resound with theological, political, and social implications. In addition to playing a dramatic role in Muhammad's break with Jewish groups in Medina, the words of Finhās were said to have been either paraphrased or quoted verbatim within the Qurʾan, and to have been the occasion for divine rebukes and curses against Finhās and those Jews associated with him. Discussions of the Finhās episodes by classical Muslim scholars contribute as well to wider questions, not confined to Islam, concerning group names and collective responsibility within religious texts more widely.

A number of reports credit (or discredit) Finhās with responsibility for some of the "fighting words" in the Qurʾan. If all the reports involving Finhās are taken together, then this one Medinan Jewish elder would have played a central role in the sending down of the qurʾanic revelations found in eight passages of the Qurʾan: 3:75; 3:181; 4:153; 5:64; 6:91; 9:30; 17:90; and 45:14. I will focus on the two verses most frequently associated with Finhās within the *akhbār*. The first refers to a statement made by the Yahūd (a group name that, for reasons explained below, I do not translate) and the second to a statement made by an unspecified group.

> *And the Yahūd said God's hand is tied. Be their hands tied and be they cursed in what they said. Nay both his hands are stretched open. He spends forth as he pleases.* (Q 5:64, first part of verse)

> *God has heard the words of those who said God is poor and we are rich.* (Q 3:181, first part of verse)[3]

"GOD'S HAND IS TIED":
THE WRONGSAYER AND COLLECTIVE IDENTITY

There are useful words in English to designate those whose deeds incur divine wrath or punishment: "wrongdoers," "evildoers," "sinners," and "transgressors," for example. Some forms of transgression are verbal, however—purely verbal. I can find no specific word to indicate the kind of verbal transgression that earns the wrath of God, that is recorded in scripture, and that leads to a divine curse. "Blasphemer" might seem to fit, but the word *blasphemy* applies to statements that are egregiously transgressive. In the cases discussed here, however, the exact nature of the transgression has been a matter of debate and interpretation. I will refer to this type of ill-boding locution as a *wrongsaying*.

In this section, I take up the wrongsaying recorded in the first part of the long and complex verse Q 5:64: *God's hand is tied (yadu llāhi maghlūla)*. Others have translated *maghlūla* as "fettered," "chained," and "bound."

Muhammad's younger cousin, 'Abdullāh ibn 'Abbās, is among those who reported that it was Finhās who uttered these fateful words.[4] Other reports found in the *tafsīrs* attribute the offending remark to Finhās in conjunction with one or two others. The early exegete Muqātil (d. 150/767) states, for example, that the *Yahūd* who said "God's hand is tied" were "Ibn Sūriyā and Finhās, the two Yahūdīs, and 'Āzir bin abī 'Āzir."[5] Muqātil does not supply information on the names of the Prophet's companions who might have first reported the identity of the three wrongsayers or those who might have passed on that information to Muqātil. Muqātil's report was reproduced by later commentators such as Ibn al-Jawzī (d. 597/1200).[6]

Whether it was one individual or a few individuals who spoke wrong, the divine reaction was severe. *Be their hands tied and be they cursed in what they said* are the words proclaimed in the very next sentence of Q 5:64.[7] But who are the "they" who are cursed as a result of the words of Finhās alone or the words of Finhās and one or a few of his companions? The divine curse could apply only to those who spoke the offending words, Finhās and perhaps some of his companions; but, within the larger *sīra* narrative, it might be viewed as applying more widely to

Finhās's Qaynuqā' tribe, or to the Jews of Medina, to all the Jews of Muhammad's time, or even to all Jews ever after Finhās uttered his wrongsaying. The *tafsīr* and *sīra* works offer differing explicit and implicit takes on the scope of collective identity and collective responsibility.

Exegetes raise major questions regarding the hand-of-God-is-tied passage. What did "the Yahūd" (i.e., Finhās alone or with a few others, or another single individual or group from among the Jews in Medina) intend by the claim that God's hand is tied? What prompted him or them to make the claim? Was the Qur'an quoting the claim word for word or paraphrasing the gist of what was said? How were the hands of whoever uttered the claim then tied, or to be tied in the future, and would this binding take place in this world or the afterlife? Would it occur literally, as might be the case with those taken as prisoners of war who had fought in a losing cause, or was their binding of their hands a figure of speech for another kind of punishment? What was the curse? Was the curse to be identical to the divine call for the tying of the hands of the wrongsayers, or did it entail a punishment that might have included the tying of hands as well as other punishments? And, of course, who spoke wrongly in the first place?

The answer to the latter question may seem obvious. The qur'anic word *Yahūd* is rendered most often as "Jews." Arabic-speaking Jews have used the same word to refer to themselves. It also has a direct Hebrew equivalent. Thus, the phrase "the Yahūd" is rendered commonly into English as "the Jews." The gravity of language usage would seem to pull the meaning of the two locutions toward a universal condemnation: "the Jews" said God's hand is tied and, as a result, God decreed the chaining of their hands and cursed them. And, for those who read such qur'anic passages as universal condemnations of Jews and of Judaism, the identity of "the Jews" needs no explanation.

But, as the Finhās reports mentioned here suggest, early Muslim scholars did not assume or take for granted a generic interpretation of the word *Yahūd*. And some of the *akhbār* at the core of classical *sīra* and *tafsīr* literature work to dismantle generic interpretations regarding the identity of the Yahūd in the God's-hand-is-tied passage. By identifying a single person or a handful of individuals as the reference for the collective plural *al-Yahūd*, the Finhās *akhbār* narrow the reference, restrict the number, and specify the time and place of the Yahūd who are cited and rebuked.[8]

Early Christian polemics have raised similar issues regarding the New Testament. Who are "*hoi iudaioi*" denounced in the Gospel of John and other New Testament texts? Who are "*al-Yahūd*" denounced in several passages of the Qur'an? Both terms have been rendered as "the Jews," but is it all, many, some, a few, or even (as will be seen below) only one Jew that is being referenced by the definite collective plural? In other words, does the term translated as "the Jews" in these cases refer to certain Jews who acted in a particular way at a particular time, or to all Jews of the time, or, by extension, even to those of past and future times.

The qur'anic question regarding the Yahūd is tied into a wider set of qur'anic terms. The words al-Yahūd (universally translated as "the Jews") and al-nasāra (the Nazarenes, commonly translated as "the Christians") could indicate all Jews and all Christians or specific subgroups. The expression banū isrā'īl (Sons of Israel, Israelites) can refer to the ancient Israelite prophets and their followers, but at times seems to embrace Jewish contemporaries of Muhammad as well. The expression People of the Book (ahl al-kitāb) can refer to Yahūd, to Nasāra, or to both Yahūd and Nasāra at the same time. In addition, the Qur'an and early historical reports feature two common nouns, ahbār (sing., habr or hibr) and rabbāniyyūn, that designated elders or religious scholars; but neither the Qur'an nor the early historical reports provide a consistent confessional and social definition for these categories of elders.

Recurring shifts in person, tense, and context in the Qur'ān compound the questions surrounding individual and group identity. Who is speaking, who is being spoken to, and what is the time and place of the speech and of the events to which the speech makes reference? The qur'anic voice shifts its perspective continually. That perspective can encompass a cosmic vision in which the deity addresses all created beings; or the address can be made to all sentient beings, or jinn (creatures of smokeless fire) and humans together, or all believers (human and jinn), or all believing humans, or unbelievers, or Yahūd or Nasāra, whose status as believers or unbelievers is a matter of contestation within qur'anic interpretation. When presenting reproaches, the Qur'an continually moves between generalized terms and terms that explicitly rule out generalization. In some passages that criticize the Banū Isrā'īl for violating tradition and disobeying the words of Moses and other prophets, the Qur'an uses the collective, tribal name Banū Isrā'īl, but in others it specifically states that the criticism applies to "most of them," "many of them," "a number of them," "a group of them," or "a party of them."

Were the Banū Isrā'īl to be identified with the qur'anic Yahūd, who are usually understood to have been Jews living in Arabia at the time of Muhammad? The question is rendered more complicated by the status of pre-Islamic figures such as Moses, Aaron, Tālūt (who corresponds to the biblical Saul), David, Solomon, and the unnamed prophet who appears to correspond to the biblical judge Samuel, or those who remained faithful to them during times of crisis. Those figures clearly belonged to the Banū Isrā'īl in one sense, and some of them are explicitly mentioned as leaders of the Banū Isrā'īl. The Qur'an lauds those leaders, along with those of their followers who passed severe tests of faith, as positive role models for the people of Muhammad's time facing similar battles of their own. If the Banū Isrā'īl are to be equated with "the Jews," then it would seem that such figures and their devoted followers were also Jews. It is worth pointing out in this regard that post-

Second-Temple Judaism, Christianity, and Islam all claimed the positive legacy of the Israelites.

Given the problems discussed here in establishing the frame of reference for groups, I will avoid translating *al-Yahūd,* with the understanding that in the texts under consideration here, *al-Yahūd* is usually taken to refer to Jewish groups or individuals living in Arabia at the time of Muhammad.

The word *muslim* (one who submits) can take on different shades of meaning within the Qur'an. In some cases it appears to designate Muslims as a group marked off from other groups such as the Yahūd and the Nasāra. At other times it seems to designate those who submit to the will of God in a more general sense—a small-case sense of *muslim* as a general trait or category rather than as a distinct religious community contrasted to Jews and Christians. Thus, the Qur'an refers to Abraham as *muslim,* for example, and to the disciples of Jesus as *muslimūn.* The "muslim" character of such pre-Muhammad figures has engendered contrasting interpretations. Some evoke it in order to appropriate the Abrahamic legacy for Islam as opposed to Judaism or Christianity. Others evoke it to highlight the common legacy of all three traditions.[9]

With these general observations in mind, I turn to the discussion of Q 5:64 as it occurs in the work of two commentators, al-Zamakhsharī (d. 538/1144) and Ibn Kathīr (d. 774/1373), who represent widely divergent theological agendas and historical circumstances. *Tafsīr* has been called an "atomistic" genre of literature because of its reliance on interpretations of verses or even—as in the case of Q 5:64—parts of verses in isolation from the wider thematic and literary patterns of the larger qur'anic passage or chapter. Of special importance to this verse-by-verse method of interpretation were the *asbāb al-nuzūl,* "the occasions of revelation," that is, the specific historical incidents or situations that were said to have led to specific qur'anic words, verses, or passages being sent down to Muhammad. Whether the occasions of revelation that were adduced by early Muslim scholars to interpret the Qur'an and to illuminate the life of Muhammad were accurate, reliable, and appropriate as exegetical sources has generated vigorous debate among modern scholars. What seems clear, however, is that the occasion-of-revelation model provided a framework for the development of classical Muslim understanding of scripture and history.

The commentator Zamakhsharī, for example, was of the Mu'tazilite theological school, which opposed all anthropomorphic interpretations of the Qur'an. It is no surprise, then, that he was more concerned with possible interpretations of God's response to the hand-of-God-is-tied claim than he was with the wrongsaying to which God was responding. For Zamakhsharī, God's statement that his "two hands are stretched open" was liable to disastrous misinterpretation. Zamakhsharī insisted that God is beyond all spatial and anthropomorphic form, and that the deity's reference to his two hands be interpreted as a figure of speech indicative of his unlimited generosity and his power to dispense his bounty as he deems fit. In the course of his argument on behalf of the figurative meaning of *hand-is-tied* and *hands-are-stretched-open,* however, Zamakhsharī notes the identities of those who claimed God's hand was bound: "It is related that God stretched open *[basata]* [his bounty] to the Yahūd until they became the wealthiest of people. When they disobeyed God in regard to Muhammad and denied him, God cut off the flow of bounty that he used to stretch open to them. At that point, Finhās bin ʿĀzurāʾ said, *God's hand is tied.* The others assented to what he said and thus participated in it."[10]

Zamakhsharī does not give the source for the report attributing the wrongsaying to Finhās bin ʿĀzurāʾ. He cites the anonymous report as reinforcing his point that the stretching forth of hands means nothing more than the bestowal of bounty. But he is concerned over the manner in which the report specifies a single individual as speaking the words that were rebuked by God with a curse on "those" who said them, and over a reference to the Yahūd, a collective plural, as the speakers. He thus suggests that "the others" assented to the offending remark, but does not tell us if he is referring to Finhās's companions (widely assumed to have been from the Qaynuqāʿ tribe, but possibly including some individuals from other Medinan Jewish tribes), the entire Qaynuqāʿ tribe, or all the Yahūd of Medina or even of Arabia entire. The range of collective responsibility is tied to the question of assent, but Zamakhsharī does not indicate how "the others" assented or how they made known their assent. Did they verbally support Finhās on the spot? In that case, the assenters would be restricted to those who were with Finhās when he uttered his words.

The Andalusian commentator al-Qurtubī (d. 671/1272) explains in a somewhat different manner how the wrongsaying of Finhās could bring collective blame on a larger group. Qurtubī, like Zamakhsharī, states that "the others" assented, but then goes on to cite a principle for establishing assent: "And it is said that if a group says something and the others do not deny it, it is as if they all said it."[11] Such a principle of group responsibility raises further questions. Would it include not only those who were present with Finhās when he spoke wrong, but also those who might have heard about it later? And to whom did this principle of assent apply: the Yahud of Finhās's tribe, all the Yahūd of Medina, or all the Yahūd who might have heard of the dispute, including those in other areas of Arabia or even beyond?[12]

Even as they acknowledge and record the specifications reflected in their *akhbār* material, the commentators shape the manner in which the issue might be understood, thus allowing us not only to better understand the core semantic and theological problem, but also to see the particular agenda of specific thinkers as it worked to shape their response to that problem. By stating that the Yahūd were prosperous and then, because of their misbehavior, were punished with a cutting off of divine bounty, Zamakhsharī links a general (but still unspecified) Yahūd to the *God's-hand-is-tied* through his account of the conditions that elicited the wrongsaying. Thus, whether spoken by an individual or group, the offending words—Zamakhsharī implies—reflected the thought of the Yahūd, who had come into difficult circumstances. (As always, at some point, the identity of the Yahūd who came into economic difficulty remains in play, but at this point Zamakhsharī, by leaving out all specification, can be read as implying all the Yahūd of Muhammad's time or at least all of those in Medina.) As for the curse upon the wrongsayers, Zamakhsharī suggests that the wrongsayers were punished by having what they said of God turned back upon themselves. They said that God's hand was tied, and their hands were to be tied. That binding, Zamakhsharī says, could occur in this life with the binding of the hands of prisoners, or in the afterlife with the punishment of the chains of hell. Like his discussion of the motives for the wrongsaying, Zamakhsharī's speculation on the consequences of the wrongsaying widens the frame of reference.

Zamakhsharī's analysis takes the form of a double pyramid. He begins with a wide frame of reference, the Yahūd in general, who were prosperous and then, when God cut off his bestowal of bounty upon them, uttered the wrongsaying. He narrows the frame of reference down to Finhās bin ʿĀzurāʾ. Then he expands the reference by suggesting that "the others" assented, and then, in speculating on the meaning of the statement "*be their hands bound in what they said*," he refers again to the Yahūd in a general fashion.

A more dramatic double pyramid appears in the eighth/fourteenth-century *tafsīr* of Ibn Kathīr, who like Zamakhsharī, focuses on the interpretation of the *God's-hand-is-tied* and *his-two-hands-are-stretched-open* locutions as figures of speech. Ibn Kathīr begins at a level of sweeping generalization: "God has reported concerning the Yahūd—God's curses upon them until the day of resurrection— that they described God (may he be exalted far beyond what they said of him) as ungiving, just as they claimed that he was poor and they rich." Ibn Kathīr then cites traditions based on reports of earlier scholars (Mujāhid, ʿIkrima, Qatāda, al-Suddī, and al-Dahhāk) who stated that those who said *God's hand is tied* did so as a way of complaining that God was ungiving. Ibn Kathīr notes that the only other passage in the Qurʾan to use the word *maghlūla* (tied, chained, fettered), Q 17:29, declares, "*don't let your hand be tied to your neck*," in a context in which it is clear that the subject is the refusal to give generously.

So far, everything seems clear. The Yahūd ("God's curses upon them until the day of resurrection!" Ibn Kathīr interjects) are guilty of the wrongsaying. Then step-by-step, Ibn Kathīr switches from viewing the wrongsayers as "the Yahūd" in general to viewing them in a far more restricted fashion. Regarding the claim that God is ungiving, he writes: "And that is what *these* Yahūd *[hāʾulāʾi al-Yahūd]*— God's curse upon them—meant" (emphasis mine). No longer is he referring to the

Yahūd in a generic fashion, but *these* Yahūd, a specific subgroup of Yahūd. Ibn Kathīr then moves to an even more restrictive specification. " 'Ikrima said that the revelation was sent down concerning Finhās the Yahūdī, God's curse upon him. And he was the one who had earlier said *God is poor and we are rich,* for which statement Abū Bakr al-Siddīq struck him." (The Abū Bakr–Finhās incident is explored below.) From interpreting the wrongsayer(s) as the Yahūd generally and invoking curses (note the plural) upon the Yahūd until the day of resurrection, Ibn Kathīr has gone to interpreting the wrongsayer(s) as these Yahūd and cursing *these* Yahūd, and then to interpreting the wrongsayer(s) as Finhās and cursing *him.*

Ibn Kathīr then cites yet another tradition specifying a single person as the speaker of *God's hand is tied,* in this case Shās bin Qays. "Muhammad bin Ishāq related that Muhammad bin abī Muhammad related from Sa'īd or 'Ikrima that Ibn 'Abbās said: A man from among the Yahūd, said to be Shās bin Qays, said 'your lord is ungiving and does not spend forth' and so God sent down: *And the Yahūd said God's hand is tied. Be their hands tied and be they cursed in what they said. Nay both his hands are stretched open. He spends as he pleases.*" Note that this report, which came down through Ibn Ishāq but which was not included in Ibn Hishām's edition of the *Sīra,* suggests that Shās bin Qays did not actually say verbatim, "*God's hand is tied,*" but rather complained that God was not being generous to them, and that it was therefore God (as speaker within the Qur'an) and not the wrongsayer(s) who employed "*God's hand is tied*" as a figure of speech for divine refrain from giving. Had the wrongsayer(s) used the words given in the Shās bin Qays report, the references to God as ungiving *(bakhīl)* and refusing to spend forth *(lā yunfiqu)* would have been incendiary, given the context of the urgent demand, stipulated in the Pact of Medina, that each party spend forth *(yunfiqu)* as part of the war effort against the Quraysh.

Ibn Kathīr concludes by moving back out toward generalization, in this case couched not only in references to a curse upon al-Yahūd but also in a triumphal expression of contempt for the religious other and of an essentialist definition of the allegedly invariable (and invariably negative) character traits of al-Yahūd brought on as a result of the offending statement. "God refuted what they said of him and turned back upon them the foulness they aimed at him and the fabrication and slander they threw at him, saying, *Be their hands tied and be they cursed in what in what they said,* and that is what happened to them. Enormous is their parsimony and envy, and their cowardice and degradation constitutes an enormity." He proceeds to stitch together various passages from the Qur'an in a way that fits his negative views on the Yahūd—and, at this particular moment in his work, it seems safe to translate *al-Yahūd* as Jews, that is, as those who identified as Jews and were viewed as a distinct Jewish community by their Christian and Muslim neighbors at the time of Ibn Kathīr and all their predecessors back to the time of Muhammad, all of whom, Ibn Kathīr proclaims, are cursed by God to moral and social wretchedness to the end of history.

So here, within the work of one author, we find the following claims reported, one after another, with no effort to harmonize the clear conflict between generalization and specification:

> The wrongsayers were the Yahūd ("may God's curses follow them to the day of resurrection!").
>
> The wrongsayers were "these" Yahūd, a subgroup specified by a particular frame of reference.
>
> The wrongsayers were (was) Finhās the Yahūdī.
>
> The wrongsayers were (was) Shās bin Qays.
>
> The wrongsayers—whether an individual, subgroup, or all the Yahūd at the time of Muhammad—were representative of the Yahūd as a whole people and of the parsimony and envy that characterized them; and because of the parsimony and envy they expressed in the wrongsaying, all Jews were cursed to a condition of cowardice and degradation until the end of time.

Ibn Kathīr frames his discussion with vehemently anti-Jewish rhetoric. Yet he also included *akhbār* regarding Finhās the Yahūdī and Shās bin Qays that interfere with the generic condemnation of Jews he propounds.[13]

"GOD IS POOR": FINHĀS AND MUHAMMAD'S BREAK WITH THE YAHŪD

We now turn to Finhās not only in his role as the reputed author of words cited by God in the Qur'an and the provoker of some of God's rebukes or curses, but also as a key character within the *Sīra*, the account of Muhammad's mission, life, and battles, as told by Muhammad ibn Ishāq (d. c. 150/767), large parts of which are preserved in an edition by the later scholar Ibn Hishām (d. 218/833). (In what follows, references to the *Sīra* in uppercase indicate the specific work of Ibn Ishāq as it was edited by Ibn Hishām, in contrast to *sīra* in lowercase, which refers to the genre of literature more widely.) In the *Sīra*, Finhās is associated primarily with the fighting words *God is poor and we are rich*. Finhās's relationship to the *God-is-poor* wrongsaying is mentioned as well in the *tafsīr*s regarding Q 3:181.

The *Sīra* was compiled as a mixed genre. It outlined a sacred history spanning the period from Adam to Muhammad (which has been omitted from Ibn Hishām's edition), and included long sections of *tafsīr*-like commentary devoted to times of revelation, and then turned to *maghāzī*, detailed depictions of military expeditions, in this case, those ordered or commanded in person by the Prophet. The *maghāzī* genre took the form of a classical battle epic and was based in part on the epic accounts of the battles of the pre-Islamic Arabs *(Ayyām al-ʿArab)*. In the *Sīra*, Finhās marks not only the exegetical problem of locating the frame of reference for qurʾanic polemics in regard to the Yahūd or individuals or groups from among the Yahūd, but also an additional problem regarding the reason for Muhammad's break with the Jewish tribes of Medina and the circumstances under which that break occurred.

That mystery is not apparent in what has become an influential summary of Muhammad's break with three tribes of Yahūd in Medina. In the first summary version, each of the major battles against the Quraysh is associated with a pact violation by one of the three tribes of Medinan Yahūd and the subsequent punishment of the guilty tribe. The standard, mystery-poor summary was composed early on by al-Māwardī (d. 450/1058). According to al-Māwardī, when Muhammad came to Medina, he made a pact with the Yahūd for mutual support between Muslims and Yahūd in the war with the Quraysh. But the Yahūd violated the agreement. The Banū Qaynuqāʿ broke the pact first by supporting the Quraysh at the Battle of Badr. Muhammad moved against them, God gave him victory, and Muhammad expelled them from the city. Then the Banū al-Nadīr broke the treaty after the Battle of Uhud by plotting to assassinate Muhammad, but Muhammad moved against them, God gave him victory, and he expelled them from the city. Then the Banū Qurayzāʾ broke the treaty at the time of the Battle of the Trench by supporting the Quraysh. Muhammad moved against them, God gave him victory, and they were punished according to the judgment of one of Muhammad's warriors, Saʿd bin Muʿāz, and at the command of Muhammad. The adult males, some seven hundred in all, were offered a choice between accepting Islam or execution, and all with one exception chose execution, while the women and children were taken as slaves. The story is neat, clear, and symmetrical: three battles between Muhammad's followers and the Quraysh, followed by three campaigns by Muhammad's followers against Jewish tribes in Medina, each of which was provoked by a Jewish betrayal of the covenant.[14]

The modern historian Caesar E. Farah presents a similar narrative. Of the break with Finhās' tribe, the Qaynuqāʿ, Farah writes:

> The main Jewish tribes, the Qaynuqāʿ, Banū al-Nadīr, and Qurayzāʾ, though signatories of pacts with Muhammad, which had essentially granted protection to those who committed no crimes and provided for mutual assistance against aggression, chose not to abide by their commitment. Moreover, the Banu Qaynuqāʿ turned to ridiculing the Muslims and challenging their fighting abilities. Muhammad besieged them in their quarters for fifteen days following which they evacuated Medina for the borders of Syria. They had sided with Muhammad's enemies in open violation of the terms of the charter, and their protector Ibn ʿUbayy failed in convincing the Prophet to grant them protection.[15]

Ibn Isḥāq and other early historians, by contrast, not only fail to present such relatively straightforward accounts, they also bring forth historical reports that contradict such accounts and contradict one another; and in the process they expose profound enigmas regarding the circumstances leading up to each of the attacks on the Jewish tribes of Medina. I focus here on the dispute with the first of those tribes, the Banū Qaynuqāʿ, as it is portrayed in Ibn Isḥāq's *Sīra*, but note that the essential dilemma appears as well in the later account by al-Wāqidī (d. 207/822).

My aim is to neither defend nor challenge the historicity of these reports in Ibn Isḥāq or to establish what really happened between Muhammad and the three tribes of Yahūd in Medina in general and the Qaynuqāʿ in particular. Whatever the historicity of Ibn Isḥāq's account, it became a respected and influential source for early Islamic history.

Ibn Isḥāq's *Sīra* provides only the barest information on the cultural and religious identity of Finhās and the other Jews of Medina. They spoke Arabic fluently and participated fully in the various genres of oral discourse routinely performed among Arabs, from poetic eulogy and battle boast to conversational discourses regarding theology, tribal affairs, and political disputes. They possessed a Torah, but whether they had it in textual or oral form is unclear, and, if it was a text, its language, whether it was in Hebrew, Aramaic, or Arabic translation, is not specified. They kept the Sabbath and, according to one famous Hadith that would impact the development of Islamic law, their sacred texts mandated capital punishment for the crime of adultery, although three Jewish elders in Medina covered up or rationalized away the mandated punishment and refused to apply it.[16] Some names of Medinan Jews are standard Arab names, while some, like Finhās (Phineas), reflect names in the Hebrew Bible and Rabbinic texts. The reports do not inform us of the particular school or trend of Judaism represented by these Jewish groups in Medina, whether they or their ancestors were converts to Judaism, or (if not converts) when they might have migrated to Medina.

The *Sīra* quotes only one, quite laconic, report claiming (or seeming to imply) that the Banū Qaynuqāʿ broke the treaty with Muhammad. "ʿĀsim bin ʿUmar bin Qatāda related to me that the Qaynuqāʿ were the first of the Yahūd to break what was between them and the Messenger of God and they went to war during the period between [the battles of] Badr and Uhud."[17] But what was it that the Qaynuqāʿ did or were alleged to have done that violated the treaty or some other understanding between the Jews of Medina and Muhammad?

The other reports in the *Sīra* do not answer the question, but complicate it further; and none more so than those involving Finhās, who, during a dispute with Abū Bakr, utters the wrongsaying mentioned in Q 3:181: *God is poor but we are rich.* In this case, the tension between a plural noun and an individual reference is even more dramatic than in the case of Q 5:64. In Q 3:181, the Qurʾan begins with *God has heard the words of those who said.* Not only is the subject of "who said" in the plural, it is in an unspecified plural, not even confined to the Yahūd or a group or individual thereof. Yet most reports tie the verse to disputes with the Yahūd of Medina and many to the single figure of Finhās.[18]

This highly dramatic episode from the *Sīra*, which is also related in identical words in Tabarī's commentary, begins with Abū Bakr entering a site called *bayt al-midrās*, a Jewish center for study and worship, and confronting Finhās with some stark demands.[19] It records Finhās's vigorous argument made to rebut the statement of Abū Bakr. It then portrays an act of physical violence by Abū Bakr against Finhās, a subsequent complaint by Finhās to Muhammad regarding Abū Bakr's behavior, Muhammad's questioning of Abū Bakr, and a divine intervention that takes the form of a qur'anic revelation.

Abū Bakr al-Siddīq entered the house of *midrās*, where he found a large number of Yahūd gathered around a man of their own group, said to be Finhās. He was one of their religious scholars ['ulamā'] and elders [ahbār], and with him was another of their elders, said to have been Ashya'. Abū Bakr said:

"Woe to you, Finhās! Fear God and become Muslim [aslama; literally, "submit"]. By God, you know that Muhammad is God's messenger and has come with his truth. You find it [or him] writ within the Torah and the Gospel."

Then Finhās said to Abū Bakr:

"By God, Abū Bakr, we are not poor in relation to God. Rather he is poor in relation to us. We do not seek support in him, but he seeks support in us. We are rich in relation to him. He is not rich in relation to us. If he were self-sufficient regarding us, he would not have asked us for a loan, as your companion claims. He forbids you from taking interest but he gives it to us. If he were rich in relation to us he would not have granted us interest."

Abū Bakr became angry and struck Finhās hard in the face and said:

"By God, if it were not for the pact ['ahd] that was between us, I would have cut off your head."

Finhās went to God's Messenger and said:

"O Muhammad, look what your companion has done!"

The Messenger said to Abū Bakr:

"What drove you to do what you did?"

Abū Bakr said:

"O Messenger of God, the enemy of God said something grave [kabīr]. He claimed that God is poor in relation to them and that they are rich. When he said that I became angry over what he said and struck him in the face."

He [Finhās] denied it, stating:

"I did not say that."

Then God sent down a revelation regarding what Finhās had said, refuting him and vindicating Abū Bakr:

God has heard the words of those who said God is poor and we are rich. (Q 3:181)[20]

The first part of this vignette affirms that a pact was in place. Had the pact already been abrogated, Abū Bakr says, he would have killed Finhās. That pact, as it is enumerated in detail in Ibn Isḥāq, guarantees that Jews who are party to the pact are free to keep their religion and are not to be molested as long as they abide by the pact.[21]

The pact stipulated that all parties to it had to support one another and to spend on behalf of or contribute to *(anfaqa)* the war effort, both militarily and financially. The parties listed were the Muhājirūn (those Muslims who had emigrated [i.e., "made Hijra"] from Mecca to Medina with Muhammad), the Anṣār ("Helpers," the Arabs of Medina who had agreed to accept Islam and support Muhammad), and the Yahūd. No party was to be harmed as long as it abided by the agreement, and anyone who violated the agreement took responsibility on himself and his family alone for the violation. The pact would seem to protect the Yahūd from any religious pressure. "The Yahūd have their religion *(dīn)* and the Muslims theirs," reads one of its most famous clauses. Several scholars have pointed out that the actual text of the pact does not mention the Qaynuqāʿ tribe by name, but rather refers to various Jewish tribes in or near Medina insofar as they were allied with non-Jewish Arab tribes; thus some have argued that the text as it has come down does not include the Qaynuqāʿ. But in this vignette, as Abū Bakr vocally attests, the pact (or some similar pact) did apply to the Qaynuqāʿ.

If the pact was in place and if the Yahūd were guaranteed their religion and the Muslims guaranteed theirs, then Abū Bakr's initial actions in entering the Jewish study center and demanding that Finhās become Muslim may appear provocative. However one judges Finhās's response—as appropriate or inappropriate, politic or impolitic—it was Abū Bakr who entered the space, confronted Finhās in front of his students, and demanded that he "become *muslim*" and acknowledge that Muhammad's prophecy is affirmed in the Torah. Moreover, it was Abū Bakr who initiated a religious disputation by demanding that Finhās justify his refusal to teach that the Torah affirmed the prophecy of Muhammad.

Finhās responds with a confusingly elaborate argument. What would have led him to respond to Abū Bakr with an argument about God being rich or poor, asking for a loan, and offering interest? A second early version of the episode clarifies the rationale for his rejoinder by linking it to verse 2:245 of the Qur'an: *Who will grant to God a handsome loan* [qardan hasanan], *which God will double in your favor and make redound many times over? God closes and opens forth* [yabsut] *as he pleases and to him you all return.* This second version appears in the *tafsīrs* of Zamakhsharī, Baydāwī, and Rāzī. It includes a phrase, "*handsome loan*," that appears only one place in the Qur'an, Q 2:245, and thus evokes that particular qur'anic verse for those hearing or reading the account.

God's Messenger sent a missive with Abū Bakr al-Siddīq to the Yahūd of the Banu Qaynuqā', calling them to Islam and [calling them] to perform the prayer *[salāt]* and give the required alms *[zakāt]* and grant to God *a handsome loan.* (Q 2:245)

Finhās the Yahūdī replied:

"God must be poor if he is asking us for a loan."

Abū Bakr slapped him in the face and said:

"If it were not for the pact between us I would have cut off your head."

He [Finhās] complained to God's Messenger and denied what he said. At this point the revelation was revealed:

God has heard the words of those who said God is poor and we are rich. (Q 3:181)

In the same vein, they said:

God's hand is tied. (Q 5:64)[22]

The version presented by Tabarsī (on the authority of 'Ikrima, al-Suddī, Muqātil, and Ibn Ishāq) is similar to the version just quoted, but it also includes the story of Abū Bakr entering the study center and finding a group gathered around Finhās. In addition, Tabarsī has Abū Bakr promise the Yahūd in question that by accepting these demands they will secure themselves a place in heaven and compound their rewards.

The version found in al-Wāhidī's *Asbāb al-Nuzūl* (Occasions of Revelation) offers the more informal opening, without any reference to Muhammad's sending of Abū Bakr to deliver a message. On the other hand, Wāhidī offers a particularly detailed link between the demand for the *handsome loan* and the argument given by Finhās in response:

According to 'Ikrima, al-Suddī, Muqātil, and Muhammad bin Ishāq, one day Abū Bakr al-Siddīq entered the Jewish study center. There he found a ground of people gathered around one of their religious scholars, who was said to have been Finhās bin 'Āzurā', one of their religious scholars. Abū Bakr said to Finhās:

"Fear God and embrace Islam. By God, you know that Muhammad is the messenger of God who has come to you with the truth from God. You find it written in your Torah. So believe and affirm him, and grant to God *a handsome loan,* which will secure you entrance to paradise and compound your reward."

Finhās said:

"O Abū Bakr: you claim that our lord asks us to loan him from what we own, but a loan is requested only by a poor party from a rich party. If what you say is true, then God must be poor and we must be rich. If he were rich, he would not have asked us for a loan from what we own."

Abū Bakr became angry and struck Finhās with a heavy blow to the head, and said:

"By him in whose hand is my life, were it not for the pact between us I would have cut off your head."[23]

The immediate qur'anic context for the *handsome loan* appeal of Q 2:245 is an exhortation to fight in the way of God. The *handsome loan* verse is followed by the story (Q 2:246–53) of the unnamed prophet of the Banū Isrā'īl, whose role is similar to that of the judge Samuel in the Bible and who has been referred to by the name Samū'īl in some Muslim traditions. The prophet is preparing his people for battle. When they demand a king, God appoints Tālūt (Saul) as their leader. Tālūt first winnows his warriors by telling them that no one who drinks directly from a spring, rather than sipping the water from their hands, will be chosen for battle, and most of the warriors drink directly. Finally, Tālūt and his most faithful followers confront the powerful enemy Jālūt (Goliath). To those losing heart in the face of such a foe, the faithful state, *How often has an outnumbered group vanquished a larger foe by the will of God. God is with those who are steadfast.* In the ends, the small group prevails and Dā'ūd (David) slays Goliath.

The qur'anic voice then widens to a cosmic perspective with the famous throne verse proclaiming the majesty of God. But, then it moves back toward more immediate, practical affairs in an extended peroration, consisting largely of parables, that calls on believers to spend forth or contribute *(anfaqa)* on the path of God: one who spends forth is like a grain growing seven ears of corn, each with one hundred grains, or like a garden with a double harvest; the heart of one who spends only for show is like a hard rock on which rain falls but nothing grows; the heart of one who spends for the sake of God is like earth that blooms into lush vegetation. Verse after verse follows with pleas both solemn and urgent to spend forth on behalf of the poor and the ill-advantaged and the traveler, to spend forth in other acts of generosity, to spend forth fully, to spend forth night and day.[24]

Into this cascade of exhortations, there erupts a legal sanction: the qur'anic ban on interest-taking (Q 2:278–81), balanced with an assurance that those who renounce the interest due to them will be repaid handsomely in the final recounting. Finhās appears to allude to this qur'anic ban on interest-taking when he asks why God is asking "us" for a loan and even promising what can be viewed as a form of interest to those who grant it, despite the fact that interest is banned "for you." If the argument was indeed over Abū Bakr transmitting a demand to Finhās to provide a *handsome loan,* it appears that Finhās has found himself in a dilemma regarding the addressee of Q 2:245. Is that verse addressing all Muslims or all believers (in the more general sense that includes Jews who are part of the pact)? This issue of the addressee of qur'anic exhortations or commands relates in turn to Q 2:278–81, which prohibits loans-for-interest *(ribah),* a prohibition that Finhās apparently viewed as applying only to Muslims: the prohibition applied to "you" (Muslims) but not "us" (non-Muslims, including Finhās the Yahūdī and whoever else he viewed himself as speaking for).

The wider context of the *handsome loan* verse in sura 2 of the Qur'an, along with the lesson drawn from the story of Samuel, Saul, David, and Goliath, is an extended homily on *infāq*. I have translated the term as "spending forth" to distinguish it from "spending," which in English usage lacks the critical components of generosity and self-sacrifice, and from "contribution," which still seems to lack the sense of personally engaged giving evoked in this passage. The same theme of "spending forth" is evoked in the section of sura 3 that features the fighting words *God is poor and we are rich,* which center on questions of a battle, courage, loyalty, and willingness to spend forth in the cause of the struggle, with steadfastness in the face of a seemingly impossible and possibly fatal task. This section of sura 3 mentions the struggle at Badr—the only battle mentioned in the Qur'an—and includes passages believed to depict the Battle of Uhud, in which Muhammad was nearly killed, along with severe criticisms directed toward the People of the Book. The issue of "spending forth" is closely tied to concern over hypocrites (or, perhaps better, "waverers" or "those without firm loyalty," *munāfiqūn*), a word whose etymology (based, like *anfaqa,* on the n/f/q root) may suggest that one of its connotations relates to those who "make a show of spending forth" but do not follow through on it.

The second version of the Abū Bakr-versus-Finhās episode clarifies both Abū Bakr's initial action and Finhās's response. Rather than accost Finhās without apparent cause and confront him with harsh words and a demand that he convert, Abū Bakr instead arrives to deliver a written message from Muhammad calling for the giving of the *handsome loan.* Finhās's response can be diagrammed as follows: (A) You said God asks for a *handsome loan* and will repay in interest. (B1) Only a needy party would ask for a loan. (B2) Only a party that is well-off financially would be asked for a loan. (C) Therefore: (C1) either *God is poor and we are rich* or (C2) your claim that God asks us for a loan is false.

One of the descriptors of Allah in the Qur'an is *al-ghanī* (the wealthy, the abundant, the self-sufficient). That very epithet is evoked in Q 2:263 in a context that associates it, thematically at least, with earlier discussions of both *infāq* and the *handsome loan.* The word for "rich" in *God is poor and we are rich* is *aghniyā',* a plural form of *ghanī.* The verse, as it is reflected in Finhās's argument, could be rendered as *God is indeed indigent whereas we have more than we need.*

The commentator Fakhr al-Dīn al-Rāzī (d. 606/1209) suggests that the statement *We are rich and God is poor* can be read either as a form of mockery (*istihzā'*) or as a form of argumentation (*iltizām*) where the premises are drawn out to their logical conclusions in such a way as to demonstrate a flaw in the original argument.[25] Such argumentation can often be a form of mockery of the verbal opponent's position if not necessarily his person. In the case of the confrontation of Finhās and Abū Bakr, however, the most sensitive issue may have been what or who was being mocked beyond the reasonableness or appropriateness of the demands presented by Abū Bakr.

Still, although the context for Finhās's response is clarified in these reports, the dilemma is not resolved. Had the pact no longer been in place, then Abū Bakr's demand or Muhammad's letter would have been understandable. And had Abū Bakr urged Finhās to provide a *handsome loan,* it could be viewed as part of the efforts, ongoing throughout the first years of Islam, of Muhammad and his companions to prevail upon all the members of his coalition—the Muslims from Mecca, the Muslims of Medina, and the Jews of Medina—to provide what must have been onerous contributions to the war effort. On the other hand, by entering the Jewish space and demanding not only contributions to the common cause— goods and perhaps also fighters—but also, it seems, conversion to Islam, at a time when the pact remained in place, Abū Bakr instigates a disputation. The issues involved, as shown above, were complex and thorny. Ideally, the two parties could have negotiated the meaning of the letter and the various implications of it regarding the status of different groups within the pact and their obligations in the face of qur'anic injunction, with due attention to careful word choice and a careful regard for the sensitivities of the different parties. But the Quraysh were widening their alliances, bolstering their already significant military superiority over Muhammad's coalition, and preparing to attack Medina. The demand and the response were made in the urgency of the moment. Once it was underway, then Finhās's response to Abū Bakr's demand could well have been viewed as mocking the Qur'an and its divine author or else as mocking the messenger Muhammad. Abū Bakr appears to have taken it in one or the other or both of these ways. Zamakhsharī, for his part, states that whether it was viewed as mockery or as an "expression of contempt for the Qur'an," the wrongsaying was clearly the utterance of a hardened disbeliever.

Finally, two other reports in Ibn Ishāq indicate a similar ambiguity in the status of the pact at the time of polemical statements by members of Finhās's Qaynuqā' tribe. The following vignette appears twice in Ibn Ishāq's account: first in a section devoted to showing the occasions of revelation for qur'anic verses that are interpreted as referring to the events between the Battle of Badr and the Battle of the Trench or as reflecting Jewish elders' religious disputations with Muhammad; second in a historical narrative regarding the attack on the Qaynuqā'.

When God had dealt a blow to the Quraysh on the Day of Badr, God's Messenger convened some of the Yahūd at the market of the Qaynuqā'—immediately after he returned to Medina from Badr. He said:

"O you gathered here from among the Yahūd! Become Muslim (or submit, *aslamū*) before God deals you a blow like that he dealt to the Quraysh."

They responded:

"Muhammad. Don't deceive yourself. You killed some inexperienced Qurayshis who had never known battle. By God, if you fight us, you'll know that we are men, the likes of which you have not confronted before."[26]

Many disputations recounted in the *Sīra* are occasioned by the reluctance or refusal of Jewish elders in Medina to recognize Muhammad as the prophet announced in their own scriptures. Here again, the core ambiguity appears. The pact given in Ibn Ishāq states that Muslims and Yahūd each had their religion and that the Yahūd were required only to contribute to the common struggle. It did not prohibit Muhammad or his followers from calling the Yahūd to Islam, but the question was one of boundaries. When and how was it appropriate for one group to call the other to its religion? And if, as the *Sīra* suggests, it was appropriate for Muslims to call on Jews but not vice versa, then what were the protocols to be followed? Was it appropriate to put Jewish elders on the spot, in front of their students, to accept Islam and then to hold them to blame if in the course of the disputation they say something that could be viewed a dismissive? Indeed, if pushed to accept a different religion or forced to explain why he is not accepting it, a person may feel backed into saying something critical of it, unless that person is endowed with extraordinary presence of mind and tact. As in all the questions raised above, the core ambiguity resides in the status of the pact at the time of the incident. If the pact had been broken and dissolved, then Muhammad's demand that the Jewish elders recognize him as the prophet announced in their scriptures could be viewed as holding out an alternative to war. If the pact was still in place, how might such demands or even insistent urgings be consistent with allowing the Yahūd their own religion? Once they accepted Muhammad not just as a leader or as a prophet for others, but as the prophet announced in their own scriptures, would they then be able to maintain a religious law separate in any way from the one proclaimed in the Qur'an for Muslims? During a period of crisis, when positions were staked without the opportunity to deliberate or negotiate, the answers to such questions may not always have been clear to the protagonists.

Like the reply of Finhās to Abū Bakr, the reply of those Yahūd assembled at the Qaynuqā' market came in response to a call, and in the latter case, the call was accompanied by a threat. The response illustrated the bravado that could be expected in such circumstances. In Arabian society at the time, one could either accede to such a public demand or threat and be humiliated, or reject it and stand up for the fighting honor of one's group. The Qaynuqā' present at the market ridiculed the abilities not of the Muslims but of the Quraysh, though in the process they diminished the majesty of the victory over the Quraysh. And they warned Muslims not to test the mettle of the Qaynuqā' in battle.

The *Sīra* provides no example of pact violation by the Qaynuqā'. Nor does it cite any statement by Muhammad or any of his companions accusing them of breaking the pact. Ibn Ishāq reported that 'Āsim bin 'Umar bin Qatāda claimed that the Qaynuqā' were the first to break what was between them and Muhammad. The early transmitters and chroniclers would likely have assumed that 'Āsim bin 'Umar bin Qatāda's report was correct. If the companions who took part in the siege of the Qaynuqā' knew of a clear instance of the tribe's breaching of the Pact of Medina or any other understanding between them and Muhammad, it is hard to know why they would not have passed on that knowledge to their children and grandchildren and why early Muslim historians such as Ibn Ishāq would not have included it in their works. Perhaps the parties involved in the conflict—beyond Muhammad, whose own words are not reported on the issue of the breaking of the treaty by the Qaynuqā'—did not actually know what specific acts provoked it. The companions had every reason to remember why and how war would have broken out between the Qaynuqā' and Muhammad and every reason to recount the acts of treachery of the Qaynuqā' and Muhammad's announcement that the pact had been broken. Why would that information not have come down to Ibn Ishāq? Why would he not have mentioned it if it did come down to him? Is it possible that they knew that Muhammad had ordered the siege of the Qaynuqā' and that, because of their esteem and trust for Muhammad, they inferred that the Qaynuqā' must have broken the pact, even though they did not know what the act of pact-breaking was?

Ibn Ishāq's *Sīra* portrays a period marked by fears, suspicions, and rapidly changing political and military circumstances. Muhammad had just returned from the Battle of Badr. At Badr, his forces had defeated the more powerful Quraysh, but the Quraysh had assembled a wide coalition of their own and were about to bring the battle to Medina; and the Medina federation led by Muhammad was the weaker party. Heavy contributions—in both fighters and wealth—were demanded as part of the war effort. Spies operated on both sides. Some tribesmen switched allegiances. Others hedged their bets by contributing to one side, but saved enough wealth to allow them to survive if their side turned out to be the losers. The difference between tribe and religious community was as yet not fully understood. Rumors circulated about who might be losing heart and conniving with the enemy or considering such connivance. Nerves were raw. Tempers flared. Delicate religious issues were brought forth in situations of high tension. Words poured forth and could not be taken back. Covenants were evoked. Conflicting parties charged covenant-betrayal, lost face, and took offense. Early exegetical traditions—based on occasion-of-revelations reports—were woven into reports of the early battles in a manner that created a powerful epic narrative, but one filled with ambiguities and marked by contradictions between reports. And that epic narrative deepened rather than resolved the issues regarding religious identity within the Qur'an, particularly in regard to Christians and Jews.

The Qaynuqā' elders who were told *"aslamū!"* may have interpreted the command as a call to abandon their *dīn* and accept the *dīn* of Abu Bakr and other companions. Perhaps the original demand meant something more general, such as submiting (to the demands of the pact) and paying the required contribution. If that is the case, they may have thought they had already contributed their fair share.

Both Ibn Hishām and al-Wāqidi appear to have trouble understanding the reason for the war against the Qaynuqāʿ described in the account of Ibn Ishāq. They supplement Ibn Ishāq with a report that offers a vivid portrayal of an outbreak of violence between Muslims and Yahūd. It took place in the market of the Qaynuqāʿ when a Yahūdī goldsmith played a vicious joke on a bedouin woman who was selling her wares near the goldsmith's shop.

> ʿAbdullāh bin Jaʿfar bin al-Miswarī bin Makhrama recalled on the authority of Abū ʿAwn that: A bedouin woman [imra'atun min al-'arab] came along with her wares and sold them in the market of the Qaynuqāʿ. She sat at a goldsmith's shop there. Some men wanted her to show her face, but she refused. The goldsmith took a piece of her garment and tied it behind her. When she stood up, her private parts were exposed. The men burst out laughing. She screamed. A man from among the Muslims leapt at the goldsmith and killed him. [The goldsmith] was a Yahūdī, so the Yahūd attacked the Muslim and killed him. The family of the slain Muslim called out to the Muslims for support against some Yahūd ['alā Yahūdīn]. The Muslims became angry, and relations turned bad [waqa'a as-sharr] between them and the Qaynuqāʿ.[27]

The incident unfolded in a manner consistent with the Arabian tribal code of honor. Physical violence—or, as in the case of the goldsmith, violence against the honor of a woman—demands retribution. Retribution would often take the form of a killing. The retribution in turn demands retribution by the other side, usually another killing. The cycle of violence broadens as various allies of the initial parties are pulled in on one side or the other. Neither party to the conflict can refrain from retaliation: to do so is to lose face, and to lose face is to invite future attacks. Ultimately both sides (which have expanded from the initial protagonists to entire clans to larger tribal confederations) are decimated. It was such a tribal conflict that led the two major Arab tribes of Medina (the Aws and the Khazraj) and their respective allies among the Yahūd into war. That war culminated in the Battle of Buʿāth. And in the wake of that battle, a delegation of Aws and Khazraj tribesmen asked Muhammad to come to Medina and serve as a just and impartial leader for the city-state riven by conflict and suspicion.

In the story of the market melee, the protagonists are identified initially in nonreligious and nontribal terms, as a bedouin woman and a goldsmith. Then, after the conflict breaks out, the protagonists are identified as Yahūd and Muslim. Finally, by the end of the conflict, it is Muslims as a group versus a group referred to as (some) Yahūd.

By inserting the story of the market melee into the Sīra, Ibn Hishām and Wāqidī signal their dissatisfaction with the lack of a clear explanation for the break with the Qaynuqāʿ. The report that they inserted does show how violence broke out. However, it does not show any violation of the pact, but rather an outbreak of blood-feud tribal violence of the model that Islam was meant to replace.[28] And while Wāqidī attempts to offer a clearer narrative and explanatory framework for the conflict with the Qaynuqāʿ, in some cases his efforts succeed only in highlighting the enigma behind the conflict. To explain the reason for opening hostilities against the Qaynuqāʿ, Wāqidī adduces a report stating that on the eve of the attack against the Qaynuqāʿ, Muhammad received a revelation (Q 8:58) instructing him that if he suspected a group of being enemies, his suspicion was valid and that he should act accordingly: *"If you fear treachery on the part of any group, then throw it back upon them like-for-like."*[29] Wāqidī's recourse to Q 8:58 demonstrates that, for the early Muslim historians, the reasons for Muhammad's break with the first of the three Jewish tribes in Medina were not clear. Wāqidī uses the report concerning Q 8:58 as a *carte blanche* explanation: if the Prophet of Islam feared something amiss on the part of the Qaynuqāʿ, then treachery there must have been.[30] Thus, Wāqidī's text suggests that even Muhammad may have not noticed or known of any specific hostile act on the part of the Qaynuqāʿ, although his suspicions, of course, according the principle adduced from Q 8:58, would have been justified.[31]

Ibn Ishāq did not report that Muhammad expelled the Qaynuqāʿ after defeating them. That claim was added by Wāqidī and other authors. Neither Ibn Ishāq nor Wāqidi portrayed the Qaynuqāʿ as a moral foil to the early Muslims or branded them with the stigma of betrayal or cowardice. According to both authors, after the Qaynuqāʿ surrendered, ʿAbdullāh ibn ʿUbayy, their ally from the Khazraj tribe, intervened on their behalf assertively, at one point grabbing Muhammad by the fold of his robe. He urged Muhammad to turn the Qaynuqāʿ over to his custody, stating that three hundred of their warriors in armor and four hundred without armor had defended him at the Battle of Buʾāth. Muhammad finally said, "they're yours!"[32] According to Wāqidī, Muhammad had originally intended to execute the Qaynuqāʿ. He adds that Ibn ʿUbayy's insistent intervention led Muhammad's followers to strike him in the face in a manner that drew blood. When the Qaynuqāʿ saw what had been done to their protector, they told him that although they had been spared punishment, they would no longer stay in a town in which their ally had been dishonored. Despite Ibn ʿUbayy's protestations, they departed for exile in Syria, leaving behind most of their possessions. The Qaynuqāʿ, Wāqidī reported, were the most courageous of the Yahūd of Medina.[33]

JEWS, ISLAM, AND RELIGIOUS MILITANCY TODAY

By interrogating some of the Finhās reports as they appear within the *tafsīr* and *sīra* literature, I have sought to explore the tensions over the frames of reference involving groups within the Qur'an and its early interpretive tradition, in this case with reference to the Yahūd. I have not set out to make any claims about the position of the Qur'an or of Islamic teachings regarding Christians, Jews, or other named groups, but to explore that question through the dynamic of generalization and specification as it is brought out in the *sīra* and *tafsīr* reports.[34]

I define "religious militancy" as a form of interpretation that takes scriptural polemics and interpretive traditions and reads them as absolute condemnations of entire peoples and applies them directly to the conflicts of today. Militant interpretations of the qur'anic position and classical Muslim positions regarding Jews and Judaism can be composed by anti-Jewish Muslims or by anti-Islamic non-Muslims. Both read the Islamic foundational sources as calling on Muslims to view Jews with contempt or hatred and to view forms of respect toward them as a violation of God's command. My point is not to argue the opposite, namely that the Islamic sources call for respect and appreciation for Jews. What the sources teach regarding any group of people (and how the groups mentioned in the sources might be aligned with groups of the same name today) is a large and ongoing endeavor of exegesis and theology. My goal is simply at this point to illuminate the manner in which militant interpretations construct unequivocal, negative, monolithic divine judgments against named peoples in the contemporary world.

As an example of a militant position taken by an influential Muslim scholar, I quote here an undated sermon by Muhammad ibn Sālih al-'Uthaymīn (d. 2001), one of the most important Saudi religious scholars of the late twentieth century. The sermon is posted on Internet sites that identify with the Salafi movement as it is espoused by Saudi religious scholars. Of the break with the Qaynuqā', the sermon says:

> The Jews are the people who conspired against the Prophet and breached their treaty with him. When the prophet emigrated to Madeenah, there were three tribes of Jews with whom he concluded treaties of safety and security. However, due to their treachery and betrayal, they infringed on these.

> Therefore, after the Muslims returned to Madeenah after the victorious Battle of *Badr,* the Prophet expelled from Madeenah the Jews of the first of those tribes, *Banu Qaynuqa',* due to their violation of their treaty with him. Their women and offspring were evacuated safely, while the Muslims seized their property.

After summarizing the breaks with the other two tribes in a similar fashion, the sermon goes on to recount the later battle against the Yahūd of Khaybar in northern Arabia and then states, "These are just some of the examples of the treachery of the Jews against the Prophet." Al-'Uthaymīn then goes on to proclaim a sweeping, generic judgment against Jews as a people.[35]

Similar claims were made by Sayyid Muhammad Tantāwī, who would later become the head of al-Azhar University in Cairo, and a Lebanese writer, 'Afīf 'Abd al-Fattāh Tabbara, in the aftermath of the Arab defeat in the 1967 War with Israel. Tantāwī and Tabbara combined a conspiratorial view of Israel and of Jews more generally with their own anti-Jewish readings of the Qur'an, Hadith, *tafsīr,* and *sīra.* The same type of anti-Jewish hermeneutics marked the work of Sayyid Qutb, a leading figure of the Egyptian Brotherhood, who was executed by the Nasser regime in 1966. In a short tract titled "Our Struggle with the Jews," Qutb created a militant pastiche of the Qur'an, the *sīra,* and the Hadith and supplemented it with modern conspiracy theories to portray Jews—all and everywhere—as enemies of Islam. It is not clear when Qutb composed "Our Struggle with the Jews": the work appeared only after his death, in a collection of Qutb's essays, published in Saudi Arabia in 1970, that took its title from his anti-Jewish tract.[36]

The Saudi rendition of the Qur'an into English, produced under the sponsorship of 'Abdullāh Bin Bāz and titled *The Noble Qur'an in the English Language,* has been particularly influential in the propagation of such interpretations. *The Noble Qur'an in the English Language* interpolates the words *Jews* and *Christians* into dozens of qur'anic passages where they do not exist in the Arabic.[37] The method of the two translators, Taqiuddīn al-Hilālī and Muhsin Khān, becomes clear early on, in their rendition of the final verses of the Fātiha (the first chapter of the Qur'an). The verses include a prayer to be guided along the straight path, not the path of those at who have anger against them *(al-maghdūbi 'alayhim)* or those who have gone astray *(al-dālīn).* Using parentheses, Hilālī and Khān inserted the phrases "Like the Jews" and "Like the Christians," respectively, into the text. The same method is followed throughout the work. A straightforward rendition of Q 88:1–2, for example, would read: *"Has word come to you of the overcasting* [al-ghāshiya]? *Some faces on that day will be submissive* [khāshi'a]." Hilālī and Khān render these verses: *"Has there come to you narration of the overwhelming (i.e. the Day of Resurrection)? Some faces, that Day will be humiliated (in the Hell-fire, i.e. the faces of all disbelievers, Jews, and Christians)."* The qur'anic passage in question does go on to speak of those whose faces are submissive being burned in blazing fire. But the construction of globalized groups (all disbelievers, Jews, and Christians) is not a rendition of the Qur'an (which states nothing in this verse about disbelievers, Jews, or Christians), and it does not offer any interpretation that can fairly be said to be a summarized version of Al-Tabarī, al-Qurtubī, and Ibn Kathīr.[38]

The Arabic word *al-Yahūd* appears only eleven times in the traditional text of the Qur'an, and the word *al-nasāra* only fourteen times, yet the terms Jews and Christians appear hundreds of times within this rendition of the Qur'an.[39] The rendition thereby trains the eyes, ears, and minds of readers and Internet searchers, Muslim and non-Muslim alike, to perceive "Jews" and "Christians" as monolithic entities subject to divine rejection and opprobrium in a manner that systematically effaces the questions regarding group name, sliding reference, changing frames of reference, specification, and generalization that are discussed in this essay and that are richly explored within the classical *tafsīr*s, even that of the self-professedly and vehemently anti-Jewish commentator Ibn Kathīr. By contrast, the Hilālī and Khān rendition of the Qur'an eliminates exegetical possibilities that would put into doubt the extension of divine disfavor to all Jews and all Christians. It also extends qur'anic statements that are made in specific contexts about specific Jewish groups or individuals to Jews as an unchanging, monolithic, homogenous group (with exceptions made only for those who converted or who will convert to Islam and, according to the way the word *Yahūd* is used in Hilālī and Khān's work, would no longer be considered Jews).

Anti-Jewish interpretations of Islamic sources have been advanced by anti-Islamic interpreters as well. Examples of the latter can be found at various anti-Islamic websites as well as in Andrew Bostom's *The Legacy of Islamic Antisemitism: From Sacred Texts to Solemn History.*[40] The authors and editors of such works create their own pastiches of the Qur'an, Hadith, *tafsīr,* and *sīra,* take bits and pieces out of context, and string those pieces together to demonstrate that Islam is essentially anti-Jewish or even anti-Semitic.

Bostom introduces *The Legacy of Islamic Antisemitism* with a lengthy essay titled "A Survey of Its [Islamic Semitism's] Theological-Juridical Origins and Historical Manifestations."[41] In it, he reproduces pastiches by another author, Saul S. Friedman, which present a caricature of Islamic sources as relentlessly anti-Jewish as those offered up by al-'Uthaymīn, Tabbara, and Tantāwī.[42] In introducing the pastiches from Friedman, Bostom commends Friedman for weaving together an array of qur'anic motifs in a "very concise and logical presentation."

There follows a pastiche of anti-Jewish statements in the works of Ibn Kathīr, Tabarī, Zamakhsharī, and Baydāwī that leaves out the antiessentialist statements in such works.[43] The *sīra* and *maghāzī* literature is presented in a similar pastiche with the most anti-Jewish passages from various works along with the most graphic depictions of the execution of the Qurayzā'.[44] The volume holds out Tabbara, Tantāwī, and the virulently anti-Jewish writer Salāh 'Abd al-Fattāh al-Khālidī as exemplars of the position of modern Muslim scholarship, and reproduces large portions of their tracts depicting the evil nature of the Jews purportedly propounded by the Qur'an. Tabbara, Tantāwī, and Khālidī present a Qur'an as relentlessly Judeophobic as the one depicted by Saul Friedman.[45]

CONCLUSIONS

I have not discussed all reports involving Finhās the Yahūdī, but have focused on those that have been most frequently cited in the *tafsīr* and *sīra.* Those reports reflect the efforts of early Muslim scholars to engage the core issue of group names and divine judgment in the Qur'an. Over a period of centuries, scholars of differing political, theological, and personal viewpoints continued to cite those reports and to acknowledge that collective terms like "the Yahūd" and "those who said" cannot be taken at face value as referring to "the Jews" or "Jews" in a generic sense. The authors were very clearly neither pro-Jewish nor ecumenical in a modern sense. Many of them passed on strongly anti-Jewish claims or, as in the case of Ibn Kathīr, created their own pastiche-type anti-Jewish versions of qur'anic sources. Even in doing so, they reproduced reports, such as those involving Finhās, that challenge, in some ways radically, the notion of a generic qur'anic condemnation of Jews.

What holds true for interpretations of the Qur'an also holds true for interpretations of the life of Muhammad and the break with the Qaynuqā' tribe of Medina. In sharp contrast to what is found in the tracts of Tabbara, Tantāwī, Qutb, and Bostom noted above, the *sīra* literature as examined here offers no stark morality tale of Muslim virtue and Jewish villainy. It presents a tableau of heroism and triumph, but also tragedy, in which human beings, with complex and not always transparent motivations and allegiances, find themselves in a situation of crisis. Unlike the simplified "three betrayals by Jews, three attacks on Jews" version of the story, the *Sīra* of Ibn Ishāq refrains from removing the enigmas behind the conflict.

In addition to illuminating the workings of *tafsīr* and *sīra*, the Finhās reports help bring into focus wider issues in the study of Islam and of religions more broadly. Even if one rejects the occasions-of-revelation method on the grounds that it misrepresents the historical context for various qur'anic polemical statements, the *tafsīr* and *sīra* literature—composed by Muslim scholars with close attention to qur'anic grammar, syntax, and rhetoric—can serve as a reminder that group-name locution occurs within a given frame of reference; and even if the frame of reference is contested, nested within other frames, or perhaps unknown, the recognition that any utterance carries with it some frame of recognition is a vital corrective to unreflective essentializing of the group in question.

Apophatic writers (sometimes known as negative theologians) have exposed the tendency of names, when applied to a transcendent reality, to betray the transcendence of the deity they are being used to affirm. Those writers were concerned that habitual human understanding of names and naming leads ineluctably to a reification of the transcendent deity unless human discourse interrupts its tendency to reify that which is named as a delimited object. The problem with group names is different, but the need for constant reminders and interruptions is similar in both cases.

To use the pastiche method discussed above is not difficult. It requires only a perusal of the Jewish Bible, Christian Bible, or Qur'an. Every instance of divine wrath poured forth upon a particular group—infidels, Yahūd, Nasārā, Amelikites, Midianites, Edomites, Ishmaelites, Iudaios, Scribes, Pharisees, Babylon, Gog, and

Magog can be taken out of its context, likened to the other negative references, and woven into a terrifying vision in which God commands his followers to consider certain groups cursed, damned to eternal torment and to either subjugation or extermination on earth. We might wonder why in the three great Abrahamic scriptures, the Revealer did not make it clear how far the identity of such groups should be extended, how far the frame of reference should be widened, if at all. My suggestion here will not be theological, but semantic. To the extent that the revelation is to be understood by human beings, it will fall into the pattern of language conditioned by human interpretation. And the default interpretation, unless resisted, is the most general. In times of conflict, those who see themselves at war with a particular group can be led to create pastiches of terror, by dismembering the sacred texts of their own tradition or of the traditions of others, then stitching together selected pieces, without the historical, rhetorical, and theological tissues of the original. Group identity may be most genuinely affirmed when it is liberated from the abuse or careless use of the group name, which makes monsters of our religious selves as well as our religious others.[46]

NOTES

1. For a detailed discussion of the Jews of Medina in traditional Islamic literature, see Marco Schöller, *Exegetisches Denken und Prophetenbiographie: eine quellenkritische Analyse der Sira-Überlieferung zu Muhammads Konflikt mit den Juden* (Wiesbaden: Harrassowitz, 1998). For a study of qur'anic polemics regarding Christians and Jews in the interpretations of modern Muslim reformists, see Mun'im A. Sirry, "Reformist Muslim Approaches to the Polemics of the Qur'an Against Other Religions" (PhD dissertation, University of Chicago, 2012).

2. Unlike the Hadith genre, for which scholars had developed sophisticated criteria for judging both the reliability of the transmitters of *akhbār* and the modes of transmission, the biographical and exegetical works subjected the *akhbār* on which they relied to less rigorous scrutiny. Nevertheless, the early *sīra* and *tafsīr* exercised strong influence on later Muslim scholarly and popular circles.

3. All translations from the Arabic are my own unless otherwise noted. All translated qur'anic passages are placed in italic font. In translating Arabic texts, I have omitted the pious honorifics traditionally applied to God, Muhammad, and revered figures from the past. It suffices to note that in the texts translated, the deity is not mentioned by name or by epithet (such as "the messenger of God") without such honorifics. I have followed the modern style of not using large-case for pronouns interpreted as referring to the divine rather than human subject.

4. Majduddīn al-Fayrūzābādī, *Tanwīr al-Miqbās min Tafsīr Ibn ʿAbbās* (Beirut: Dār al-Kutub al-ʿIlmiyya, 2008), Q 5:64; also available at Altafsīr.com in Ibn ʿAbbās, *Tafsīr al-Qurʾān*. Plurals for singulars are common in other early Arabic contexts, from the most famous example of the deity referring to itself in the Qurʾan as "we" to reference to the beloved in love poetry as "they" in the third person or in the plural form of "you" in the second person, to the reference by the poet-lover to himself as "we." Because most of the commentators who explore the identity of the person(s) who made the statement do not raise the issue of grammaticality here or try to explain other usages of a third-person plural for a single in such a case, I rest here with pointing out that for them, it did not appear to be an issue worth exploring.

5. In this essay, the first date given is Islamic and the second is the Gregorian.

6. For the purposes of this study, I have consulted the *tafsīrs* of Muqātil (d. 150/767), al-Tabarī (d. 310/923), al-Wāhidī (d. 468/1075), al-Baghāwī (d. 516/1122), al-Zamakhsharī (d. 538/1144), al-Tabarsī (d. 548/1153), Ibn al-Jawzī (d. 597/1200), al-Rāzī (d. 606/1209), al-Qurtubī (d. 671/1272), al-Baydāwī (d. 688/1290), Abū Hayyān al-Gharnātī al-Andalusī (d. 754/1353), Ibn Kathīr (d. 774/1373), and al-Fayrūzābādī (d. 817/1414). In all future references, I refer to these *tafsīrs* by citing the author and the number of the Qur'an verse upon which he is commenting. I have utilized the online Arabic text of Altafsir.com. The works are: Muqātil ibn Sulaymān, *Tafsīr*; al-Tabarī, *Jāmi' al-Bayān fī Tafsīr al-Qur'ān*; al-Baghāwī, *Ma'ālim fī 'Ilm al-Tafsīr*; al-Zamakhsharī, *al-Kashshāf*; al-Wāhidī, *Asbāb al-Nuzūl*; al-Tabarsī, *Majma' al-Bayān fī Tafsīr al-Qur'ān*; Ibn al-Jawzī, *Zād al-Masīr fī 'Ilm al-Tafsīr*; al-Rāzī, *Mafātīh al-Ghayb*; al-Baydāwī, *Anwār al-Tanzīl wa Asrār al-Ta'wīl*; al-Qurtubī, *al-Jāmi' li Ahkām al-Qur'ān*; al-Gharnātī, *al-Bahr al-Muhīt*; Ibn Kathīr, *Tafsīr al-Qur'ān al-Karīm*; al-Fayrūzābādī, *Tafsīr al-Qur'ān*. After first use of a name beginning with "al," I use the informal version of the name without the "al": Tabarī, for al-Tabarī, for example. The relevant sections of these *tafsīrs* are based on reports that were passed on by scholars of the first century of Islam, including Ibn 'Abbās, 'Abdullāh bin Mas'ūd, 'Ubayy bin Ka'b, Zayd bin Thābit, and 'Abdullāh bin Zubayr. Students of Ibn 'Abbās included Mujāhid, 'Atā, and, of particular importance for our purposes here, 'Ikrima. Other early transmitters that appear in the reports regarding the Qaynuqā' and the fighting words discussed here are Zayd bin Aslam and al-Hasan al-Basrī.

7. I prefer the expression "spoke wrong" to "spoke wrongly" to emphasize the blameworthy nature of both the speaking and the content of what was spoken, in parallel to the popular English idiom "done wrong."

8. Given the way the divine curse relates to those who actually uttered the wrongsaying ("in what they said"), then by limiting the referential scope of al-Yahūd in qur'anic identification of the wrong-sayer(s), the reports also imply a limitation of the scope of the curse in the divine response as well.

9. For a recent perspective on this issue, see Fred M. Donner, *Muhammad and the Believers at the Origins of Islam* (Cambridge, MA: Belknap Press of Harvard University Press, 2010), 68–77.

10. The identical passage is found in al-Baydāwī's commentary, in regard to Q 5:64. Tabarī also shows a strong interest in the theological ramifications of the Qur'an's reference to God's two hands and devotes very little space to discussing the identity of the Yahūd who uttered the wrongsaying. He argues against the Mu'tazilite position by pointing out that while Arabic tradition supports the claim that the term *hand* can be used in connection with verbs or adjectives as a figure of speech for generosity, there is no precedent for using the dual *two hands* in such a figurative manner. Yet Tabarī follows the rules of the genre and devotes some time to recounting reports that attempt to identify the speaker or speakers of the claim that *God's hand is tied*. He cites two reports identifying the speaker as "Finhās the Yahūdī." He attributes one of the reports to an early Muslim scholar named Shibl and a second to 'Ikrima, a student of Ibn 'Abbās.

11. An earlier version of this position was articulated by Tabarsī, who wrote that "it was Finhās ibn 'Azūrā' who said God's hand is tied and the others did not contradict him and consented in what he said, and thus he made them participants in his statement."

12. Finhās's position as an authority figure might also bear on the question of assent. In a few instances, not related to the Q 5:64 wrongsaying, Finhās is called the chief *(sayyid, ra's)* of the Qaynuqā'. See Schöller, *Exegetisches Denken und Prophetenbiographie*, 235. Zamakhsharī and Qurtubī apparently did not view Finhās as exercising such authority or else did not view his position as, in itself, a cause for holding all members of the tribe responsible for the wrongsaying.

13. Early reports were not unanimous in interpreting the statement *God's hand is bound* to be a claim that God is ungenerous or ungiving. Tabarī cites a report by Hasan of Basra interpreting the sentence to mean that "God has clenched his hand out of punishment toward us." Whether the "us" refers to the group of Yahūd associated with the statement or Yahūd in general is not stated. As for what the punishment might be for the object of complaint against those saying *God's hand is tied*,

Ibn al-Jawzī offers two possibilities: that it refers to God's ceasing to bestow blessings and bounty upon the Yahūd—a possibility already mentioned in reports cited above—or to the destruction of Jerusalem's Temple at the hands of the Nebukhadnezzar. "After the Nasārā helped Bakhtnasar [Nebu-khadnezzar] the Zoroastrian destroy the temple, the Yahūd said: 'If God had been in a proper way [saḥīḥ], he would have protected us from him, but his hand was tied.'" Ibn al-Jawzī at first quotes the report without citing a source. He then states that Qatāda had also passed on such a report. The anach-ronistic reference to the Nasārā playing a role in an event that happened centuries before the birth of Christianity raises a number of questions that cannot be pursued in this essay. One possible line of inquiry would be to pursue a conflation of the destruction of the First and Second Temples and a further conflation of those events with the battle for Jerusalem that occurred just prior to Islam, as such conflations were used in anti-Jewish Christian polemics. In regard to Ibn Kathīr's preservation of the Finhās reports that narrow the frame of reference for Q 5:64 in a manner that complicates, at the very least, the generalized condemnation of Jews he elsewhere works to construct, it appears that what Walid Saleh has called the genealogical nature of Sunnī tafsīr is operative. Two aspects of the genealogical principle, as formulated by Saleh, appear particularly relevant to the analysis here. Saleh writes that in regard to the commentary tradition "there was never one meaning for any one verse; even if one commentary gives only one meaning, there was always a multitude of meanings," and that "nothing, once picked up, could be jettisoned." Walid Saleh, The Formation of the Classical Tafsīr Tradition: The Qur'ān Commentary of al-Thaʿlabī (d. 427/1035) (Leiden: Brill, 2004), 20.

14. I have summarized the account from Schöller's German translation of Māwardī's text, leaving out mention of ʿAbdullāh ibn Ubayy's intervention on behalf of the Qaynuqāʿ. See Marco Schöller, Exegetisches Denken und Prophetenbiographie, translation of ʿAlī bin Muhammad al-Māwardī al-Shāfiʿī, Al-Hāwī al-Kabīr, ed. ʿAlī M. Maʿawwad and ʿĀdil A. ʿAbd al-Mawjūr (Beirut: Dār al-Kutub al-ʿIlmiyya, 1994–96), 14:350. Schöller aptly calls this standard summary the "orthodox" version, using the quotation marks to indicate that it became widely viewed as the correct version. Schöller's study also draws attention to the symmetrical three-betrayals-three-wars pattern in the orthodox version of the first five years of Islam. Cf. Muhammad ibn ʿUmar al-Wāqidī, Kitāb al-maghāzī, ed. Marsden Jones (London: Oxford University Press, 1966) and The Life of Muhammad: al-Wāqidī's Kitāb al-Maghāzī, ed. Rizwi Faizer, trans. Rizwi Faizer, Amal Ismail, and AbdulKader Tayob, with an introduction by Rizwi Faizer and Andrew Rippin (New York: Routledge, 2011); and Michael Lecker, "Wāqidī's Account on the Status of the Jews of Medina: A Study of a Combined Report," Journal of Near Eastern Studies 54 (1995): 15–32, reprinted in Uri Rubin, ed., The Life of Muhammad (Aldershot, UK: Ashgate Variorum, 1998), 23–40.

15. Caesar E. Farah, Islam (Hauppauge, NY: Barrons, 2000), 50–52.

16. ʿAbd al-Mālik ibn Hishām and Muhammad ibn Ishāq, Ibn Ishāq, Al-Sīra al-Nabawiyya (Riyadh: Maktabat al-ʿUbaykān, 1998): 2:159–61; Sīrat al-Nabī [The Sīra of the Prophet] (Beirut: Dār Rayhānī, 1965); The Hadith, transmitted by Abū Hurayra, became one of the central supports for the institution of capital punishment by stoning as the punishment for convicted adulterers in the major branches of Sunni and Shiʿite law, despite the qurʾanic texts specifying noncapital forms of punishment for the offense.

17. Al-Sīra al-Nabawiyya 2:339. Cf. A. Guillaume, The Life of Muhammad: A Translation of Ibn Ishāq's Sīrat Rasūl Allāh (Oxford: Oxford University Press, 1955), 361. Guillaume translates the Arabic mā baynahum wa bayna rasūl allāh, which literally means "what was between them and the Mes-senger of God," as "agreement": "The B. Qaynuqāʿ were the first of the Jews to break their agreement with the apostle." His translation is not unreasonable. The question remains whether or not the agreement or understanding mentioned by Ibn Qatāda was the pact of Medina presented earlier on in the sīra.

18. An exception to the narratives discussed here is provided by Rāzī in his commentary on Q 3:181. Rāzī takes an unusually strong stand against interpreting the plural "those who said" as a refer-

ence to a single individual such as Finhās, stating that it is flat out impermissible to interpret the plural noun as referring to a single individual in this case.

19. The term does not appear in the Qur'an. For the possible meanings of *bayt al-midrās* and *kanīsa*, another term applied to Jewish sites in Medina at the time of Muhammad, see Schöller, *Exegetisches Denken und Prophetenbiographie*, 210–11.

20. *Al-Sīra al-Nabawiyya* 2:154–55; *Sīrat al-Nabī*, 303; Guillaume, *The Life of Muhammad*, 263. Cf. Tabarī's *tafsīr*, in the section on Q 3:181. There Tabarī offers the following *isnād* for the report: from Abū Karīb, from Yūnis bin Bakīr, from Ibn Ishāq, from Muhammad bin abī Muhammad, a client of Zayd bin Thābit, from 'Ikrima, from Ibn 'Abbās.

21. The Arabic *dīn* could be interpreted as financial obligation. Were we to adopt such an interpretation, the exploration of the Finhās episodes would need to be adjusted accordingly, an endeavor that would exceed the boundaries of this essay. The literature on the Agreement of Medina is large. It includes R. Stephen Humphreys, "The Constitution of Medina," in *Islamic History: A Framework for Inquiry* (Princeton: Princeton University Press, 1991), 92–98; Uri Rubin, "The Constitution of Medina: Some Notes," *Studia Islamica* 62 (1985): 5–23; Akira Goto, "The Constitution of Medina," *Orient/ Tokyo* 18 (1982): 1–16; R. B. Serjeant, "The *Sunnah Jami'ah*, Pacts with the Yathrib Jews, and the *Tahrim* of Yathrib: Analysis and Translation of the Documents Comprised in the So-Called 'Constitution of Medina,'" *BSOAS* 51 (1978): 1–42; Moshe Gil, "The Constitution of Medina: A Reconsideration," *Israel Oriental Studies* 4 (1974): 44–65; R. B. Serjeant, "The Constitution of Medina," *Islamic Quarterly* 8 (1964): 3–16; W. Montgomery Watt, *Muhammad at Medina* (Oxford: Oxford University Press, 1956), 221–60; A. J. Wensinck, *Muhammad and the Jews of Medina* [*Mohammed en de Joden te Medina* (1908)] (Freiburg: K. Schwarz, 1975), 57–71; Leone Caetani, *Annali dell'Islam* 1 (Milan: U. Hoepli, 1905), 391–408; Julius Wellhausen, "Muhammad's Constitution of Medina" [German original is in *Skizzen und Vorarbeiten* 4 (1889): 67–8], translated in Wensinck, *Muhammad and the Jews*, 128–38; Fred M. Donner, "From Believers to Muslims: Confessional Self-Identity in the Early Islamic Community," *Al-Abhāth* 50–51 (2002–03): 9–53; Michael Lecker, "Wāqidī's Account on the Status of the Jews of Medina: A Study of a Combined Report," in *The Life of Muhammad*, ed. Uri Rubin (Ashgate: Brookfield, VT, 1998), 23–40; Reuven Firestone, *Jihād: The Origin of Holy War in Islam* (New York: Oxford University Press, 1999), 117–24.

22. Muqātil gives the same version of the dialogue between Abū Bakr and Finhās, but does not mention Abū Bakr striking Finhās. Zamakhsharī precedes his portrayal of the drama between Abū Bakr and Finhās with Mu'tazilite arguments to the effect that God's "hearing" of what was said was a figure of speech for taking seriously what the wrongsayer(s) said and that preparing a proper punishment and "writing it down" was a figure of speech for not forgetting it.

23. On Wāhidī's account, see also Mahmoud M. Ayoub, *The Qur'an and Its Interpreters* (Albany: SUNY Press, 1992), 2:392–94.

24. See Irfan A. Khan, *Reflections on the Qur'ān: Understanding Sūrahs Al-Fātihah and Al-Baqarah* (Markfield: Islamic Foundation, 2005), 691–714, for an extended discussion of *infāq*, or spending, in the passages just mentioned.

25. The commentators Tabarī, Rāzī, Qurtubī, and Ibn Kathīr also related the response of Finhās (or, in the case of a tradition transmitted by Hasan of Basra, another Jewish elder of the Banu Qaynuqā' by the name of Huyyay bin Akhtab) to Abū Bakr's call on Finhās both to convert and to grant God a *goodly loan*. Tabarī also cites a version of the story sourced to Suddī that puts it into the clear context of Q 3:181, though in Suddī's version, Finhās is a member of the Banū Marthad rather than the Banū Qaynuqā'. In commenting on Q 3:181, al-Rāzī states, "Finhās the Yahūdī from the Banū Marthad said it. Abū Bakr confronted him and spoke to him, saying: 'O Finhās, Fear God and believe and give voluntary alms [as opposed to the *zakāt* required of Muslims] and grant to God a *goodly loan*,' Finhās replied: 'O Abū Bakr: you claim that our lord is poor and asks us for a loan. A loan is something the needful asks from the nonneedy. If what you said were true, then God would be in need.'" The report

of Ibn 'Abbās transmitted in Fayrūzābādī reads, "Then Allah mentioned the Jews—Finhās Ibn 'Azūrā' and his companions when they said: 'O Muhammad! Allah is poor: He is asking us to give Him a loan'—saying, *We heard the saying of those*—Finhās Ibn 'Azurā' and his fellows—*who said,* when asked for contributions to the war, *Allah is poor:* He needs us to give Him a loan, *and we are rich* and we do not need a loan from Him." Wāqidī's *Maghāzī* mentions Finhās only once, in an excursus on the occasions of qur'anic revelation associated with the period of the Battle of Uhud. In the course of that excursus, Wāqidī links Finhās to both Q 3:181 and Q 2:245, stating that Finhās uttered the wrongsaying of 3:181 in response to the *goodly loan* verse of Q 2:245, and then reemphasizes the link by stating that "Finhās the Yahūdī said: '*God is poor and we are rich* for He seeks a loan from us.'" *Kitāb al-Maghāzī*, ed. Marsden Jones (London: Oxford University Press, 1966), 1:328; and Faizer, *The Life of Muhammad*, 159.

26. *Al-Sīra al-Nabawiyya* 2:148 and 2:339; *Sīrat al-Nabī*, 296–97, 398; Guillaume, *The Life of Muhammad*, 260, 363.

27. *Al-Sīra al-Nabawiyya* 2:339–40; *Sīrat al-Nabī*, 98–99. In Guillaume's translation, this report is relegated to an appendix with other material added by Ibn Hishām. Guillaume, *The Life of Muhammad*, 751. For al-Wāqidī's version, see Al-Wāqidī, *Kitāb al-Maghāzī*, 1:176–80; Faizer, *The Life of Muhammad*, 88.

28. Elsewhere, the *Sīra* shows Muhammad taking extraordinary measures to avoid being drawn into tribal patterns of retaliation. The best-known example occurred when members of the Khazraj tribe circulated rumors that Muhammad's wife 'Ā'isha had committed adultery, and members of the Aws tribe told Muhammad they would kill those in the Khazraj who committed the slander. Muhammad refrained from defending her in such an immediate fashion, and when, after an agonizing period, a revelation came vindicating her, 'Ā'isha refused her parents' demands to thank Muhammad, responding that Muhammad had done nothing to save her and that her thanks went only to God. In the case of 'Ā'isha, had Muhammad defended her personally or had 'Ā'isha thanked Muhammad for her vindication, he would have been drawn into the role of a tribal champion, a role that would have been incompatible with his role as the prophet and leader of an Islam that aimed to replace the traditional code of conflict. In the case of the Qaynuqā' market melee, if, as the story's placement in the *Sīra* suggests, Muhammad ordered an attack on the Qaynuqā' because of the crime, retaliation, and retaliation for the retaliation that occurred between some Muslims and some Yahūd in the Qaynuqā' market, his behavior would seem to contrast with the behavior he showed in the wake of the slander against 'Ā'isha.

29. Al-Wāqidī, *Kitāb al-Maghāzī*, 177; and Faizer, *The Life of Muhammad*, 88. See also Schöller, *Exegetisches Denken und Prophetenbiographie*, 246–47. For a discussion of how Wāqidī reshaped Ibn Ishāq's *Sīra* in a manner that makes the case subsequently taken up in the standard version, namely that the Qaynuqā' were exiled shortly after they surrendered, see Rizwi S. Faizer, "Muhammad and the Medinan Jews: A Comparison of the Texts of Ibn Ishāq's *Kitāb Sīrat Rasūl Allāh* with al-Wāqidī's *Kitāb al-Maghāzī*," *IJMES* 28, no. 4 (1996): 463–89.

30. Barakat Ahmad has noted that the entirety of sura 8 of the Qur'an is usually viewed as addressing events that occurred well after the Qaynuqā' incident. Barakat Ahmad, *Muhammad and the Jews: A Reexamination* (New Delhi: Vikas, 1979), 60–61. The *Sīra* appeals to similar international interventions to elucidate Muhammad's decisions to order attacks on the Banū Nadīr and the Qurayzā'. News comes down from heaven *(khabar min al-samā')* to Muhammad telling him that a group of the Banū Nadīr is plotting his assassination. In the case of the Qurayzā', Muhammad ordered the attack only after the angel Gabriel made a majestic appearance to him as he was preparing to demobilize his soldiers after the third and final battle, the Battle of the Trench. Gabriel instructed him that the fight was not over, an appearance that led to Muhammad ordering the attack on the Qurayzā'. *Al-Sīra al-Nabawiyya* 3:143; 3:189–90; Guillaume, *The Life of Muhammad*, 437, 461.

31. Wellhausen and Wensinck resolved the enigma regarding the Qaynuqā' in a different fashion

from the three-betrayals, three-attacks theory. For both, Muhammad found the three Jewish tribes to be in his way and attacked them. "It was Muhammad who committed the perfidy. He gladly used every change to punish the Jews, and contrived to create reasons if there were none," wrote Wellhausen. Julius Wellhausen, "The Constitution of Medina," in Wensinck, *Muhammad and the Jews,* 137. Wensinck's position appears to replace perfidy with a ruthless *realpolitik* as a guide for Muhammad's policy in Medina: "The Jews as a body had adopted an unfriendly attitude to the Prophet. From the religious point of view they became inconvenient; and from the political angle, as a powerful foreign body within the newly converted town, they were a great danger. When Muhammad felt his position strengthened by the battle of Badr, he must soon have determined on expelling his enemies. The Kaynukāʿ, as they lived in the city itself, were the first he wished to be rid of. Regarded in this light, his attack on the Kaynukāʿ (in all probability as early as Shawwāl 2/April 624) is sufficiently explained." A. J. Wensinck, "Kaynukāʿ, Banū," in *Encyclopedia of Islam,* 2nd ed.

32. Al-Sīra al-Nabawiyya 2:341–41; Guillaume, *The Life of Muhammad,* 363.

33. A high compliment, given that the two other tribes were shown behaving with similar dignity after their defeat, and that the Qurayzāʾ in particular, faced with a choice of accepting Islam or being killed, chose to die rather than to betray tradition. On the portrayal of the Qurayza's demeanor in the face of execution and for an argument for viewing the episode in literary rather than historical terms, see W. N. Arafat, "New Light on the Story of the Banū Qurayza' and the Jews of Medina," *Journal of the Royal Asiatic Society* 2 (1976): 100–107; and Barakat Ahmad, *Muhammad and the Jews,* 67–94.

34. My goal here is to examine the interpretation of qur'anic verses regarding the Yahūd rather than to trace the history of Jewish beliefs, practices, and divisions in general or in Arabia at the time of Muhammad. For a study of the history of Arabian Jewry, see Gordon Newby, *A History of the Jews of Arabia from Ancient Times to Their Eclipse under Islam* (Columbia: University of South Carolina Press, 1988). As for a Jewish text or tradition that might offer a parallel to the God's-hand-is-tied reference in Q 5:64, Lamentations 2:3 provides one possible link. Among a series of images, metaphors, and similes demonstrating the divine wrath, God is said to have withdrawn or held back his right hand from aiding Israel against its enemies. A text known as *3Enoch* or *Sefer Hekhalot* includes a reference to the right hand of the deity being held back, but where, when, and by whom the texts found in 3Enoch were composed remains unclear, and the passage on the right hand of God, 3Enoch 4:8a, may have been composed at a different time than the main narrative that precedes it. I find particularly intriguing the passage of the Rabbinic text *Lamentations Rabba* 2.3 that was pointed out by David Halperin in his discussion of Q 5:64. In *Lamentations Rabba* 2.3, the holding back of God's right hand is interpreted as a gesture of sympathy for the captivity of the Israelites, whose hands have been tied behind their backs by their enemies. See David Halperin, *Faces of the Chariot: Early Jewish Responses to Ezekiel's Vision* (Tübingen: J. C. B. Mohr, 1988), 467–69; and Newby, *A History of the Jews of Arabia,* 58–96. Newby argues that the Jews in Arabia at the time of Muhammad would have included Rabbinic groups with the mystical tendencies depicted in the *Hekhalot* literature. For the regional conflicts between Jews, Christians, and the forces of Zoroastrian Persia at the time of Muhammad, see Robert Hoyland, "Sebeos, the Jews, and the Rise of Islam," in *Medieval and Modern Perspectives on Muslim-Jewish Relations,* ed. Robert L. Netter (Amsterdam: Harwood, 1998), 89–102. For the possibility of placing qur'anic polemics within the wider exegetical debates of the late antique Middle East, see John C. Reeves, ed., *Bible and Qur'ān: Essays in Scriptural Intertextuality* (Leiden: Brill, 2004); and Gabriel Said Reynolds, *The Qur'ān and Its Biblical Subtext* (New York: Routledge, 2010). For an effort to periodize the various images of the Banū Isrāʾīl early Islamic literature, see Uri Rubin, *Between Bible and Qur'ān: The Children of Israel and the Islamic Self Image* (Princeton, NJ: Darwin Press, 1999).

35. Muhammad al-ʿUthaymeen, "The Jews and their Treachery," trans. Nasim Chowdhury, ed. Al-Manaar Publishing House, distributed by www.al-minbar.com and www.islamicawakening.com,

FINHĀS OF MEDINA   133

among other web sites. Another example of such interpretation can be found in 'Abdullah al-Tall, *Al-Khatar al-Yahūdiyya al-'ālamiyya 'alā al-islām wa al-masīhiyya* [The global Jewish threat to Islam and Christianity] (Cairo: Dār al-Qalam, 1964), 38–52 (chapter on *al-yahūd wa al-islām* [The Jews and Islam]), 53–68 (chapter on *al-qur'ān wa al-yahūd* [The Qur'an and the Jews]).

36. Sayyid Qutb, *Ma'ārikatunā ma'a al-Yahūd* [Our struggle with the Jews], in *Ma'ārikatunā ma'a al-Yahūd*, ed. Zayn al-Dīn al-Rakkābī (Jidda, Saudi Arabia: al-Dār al-Sa'ūdiyya, n.d.). A translation of the tract can be found in Ronald L. Nettler, *Past Trials and Present Tribulations: A Muslim Fundamentalist's View of the Jews* (Oxford: Pergamon Press, 1987), 72–89. For close study of Tantāwī's and Tabbara's texts as specific examples of modern constructions of qur'anic teachings regarding Jews, see Suha Taji-Farouki, "A Contemporary Construction of the Jews in the Qur'an: A Review of Muhammad Sayyid Tantāwī's *Banū Isrā'īl fī al-Qur'ān wa al-Sunna* and 'Afīf 'Abd al-Fattāh Tabbara's *Al-Yahūd fī al-Qur'ān*," in *Muslim-Jewish Encounters: Intellectual Traditions and Modern Politics*, trans. Ronald L. Nettler and Suha Taji-Farouki (Amsterdam: Harwood, 1998), 15–38.

37. Dr. Muhammad Taqi al-Dīn Al-Hilālī and Dr. Muhammad Muhsin Khān, *Translation of the Meanings of the Noble Qur'an in the English Language* (1985; Riyadh: Maktabat al-Salam, 1995). The official online edition can be found at the website for the King Fahd Complex for Printing the Holy Qur'an, www.qurancomplex.org. The languages button at the top right of the website allows the user to access an English page. The Hilālī and Khān translation is accessible through the "Translations" menu on the left of the website. *The Translation of the Meanings of the Noble Qur'an* appears as the first option. As of April 2, 2010, the second option, "New Translations," leads to a page announcing the complete translation of the Qur'an into German and Chinese and partial translations into Russian and Gypsy. Only the Hilālī and Khān English version is available online at King Fahd Complex site however. The online King Fahd Complex version includes a noticeable change from earlier printed versions and from other online versions. The phrases "such as the Christians" and "such as the Jews," which had gained negative publicity, have been omitted from the Fātiha. All the other interpolations of Hilālī and Khān remain as before, however. As of April 2, 2010, online versions with the "such as the Christians" and "such as the Jews" interpolations to the Fātiha could be found at www.iium.edu .my/deed/quran/nobelquran/index_t.html and www.tanzeem.org/resources/quranonline/English/ Noble/Default.html. In Q 60:13, the two translators again emend the text to include a specific reference to Jews: "O you who believe. Take not as friends the people who have incurred the Wrath of Allah (i.e. the Jews)."

38. For a more detailed discussion of the rendition of Hilālī and Khān, the intellectual and political climate in which it took shape, and its international influence, see Michael A. Sells, "War as Worship, Worship as War," *Religion and Culture Forum,* December 2006, http://divinity.uchicago.edu/ martycenter/publications/webforum/122006/commentary.shtml.

39. See Gerhard Böwering, "Reconstructing the Qur'an," in *The Qur'an in Its Historical Context*, ed. Gabriel Said Reynolds (New York: Routledge, 2008), 70–87, with special reference to pp. 81–82. The Qur'an also refers in one instance to the "People of the Gospel."

40. Andrew Bostom, ed., *The Legacy of Islamic Anti-Semitism: From Sacred Texts to Solemn History* (Amherst, NY: Prometheus Books, 2008).

41. Ibid., 41–208.

42. Ibid., 40–41, as quoted selectively by Bostom from Saul S. Friedman, "The Myth of Islamic Toleration," in *Without Future: The Plight of Syrian Jewry* (New York: Praeger, 1989).

43. Haggai Ben-Shammai, "Jew Hatred in the Islamic Tradition and the Koranic Exegesis," in Bostom, *The Legacy of Islamic Anti-Semitism,* 221–28.

44. "Anti-Jewish Motifs in the Sira," in Bostom, *The Legacy of Islamic Anti-Semitism,* 263–314.

45. "Extracts from Muhammad Sayyid Tantāwī, *The Children of Israel in the Qur'an and the Sunna*," in Bostom, *The Legacy of Islamic Anti-Semitism,* 391–402; 'Afīf 'Abd al-Fattāh Tabbara, "Extracts from *The Jews in the Qur'an*," in Bostom, *The Legacy of Islamic Anti-Semitism,* 403–428;

"Extracts from Salāh 'Abd al-Fattāh al-Khālidī, *Qur'anic Truths regarding the Palestinian Issue*," in Bostom, *The Legacy of Islamic Anti-Semitism*, 429–54.

46. The questions addressed in this essay informed my spring 2011 seminar on "Readings in the Qur'an, Tafsir, and Sira" at the University of Chicago, and have been sharpened by contributions from all of those who participated in that seminar. I offer special thanks to Reaz Khan and Francesca Chubb-Confer for their editorial comments on earlier drafts of this essay, to Françoise Meltzer for her response to a draft of this essay, and to Raphael Descalu for his help with the Hebrew text of *Lamentations Rabba* 2.3.

6

The Baha'i Tradition

The Return of Joseph and the Peaceable Imagination

Todd Lawson

In the Baha'i tradition, nonviolence is not a principle derived primarily through exegesis but one given through revelation, to use the Baha'i technical term for its primary scripture. There can be no dispute or discussion on this point by either a follower of the Baha'i faith or those who study and understand this relatively recent religion. What may be a source of discussion is the question of how in the context of the history of religion and religions and especially the history of the Baha'i faith this came to be. Here I will first offer a brief discussion of the role and status of violence in the Baha'i tradition, based on a comparatively limited selection of the most influential and characteristic statements from the vast library of Baha'i writings. The chapter will then examine some possible religious, historical, and social conditions in which these doctrines were articulated.

Baha'i teachings are unambiguous: the purpose of religion is the promotion of harmony and unity among human beings.[1] The founder of the Baha'i faith, Mirza Husayn 'Ali Nuri (1817–92), who is most widely known as *Baha'u'llah* (the glory of God), has written that if religion becomes the cause of disharmony then it is better that there be no religion at all.[2] Baha'i teachings condemn violence as something to be avoided at all costs. The Baha'i tradition is perhaps too young to have generated much in the way of exegesis as normally understood. However, exegesis is relevant in the sense that Baha'i writings may be thought of, in some ways, as an interpretation of Islamic scripture. (Here scripture would include both the Qur'an and the Hadith corpus.) Baha'u'llah was of course a son of Shi'i Islamic culture. A careful reading of the authoritative literature of the Baha'i faith leaves little doubt that its adherents are proud to acknowledge their tradition's Shi'i roots.[3]

The "grammar and syntax" of the piety and religious practice of both traditions have much in common. However, with regard to specific points of doctrine there are dramatic and unbridgeable differences. In some instances, these differences have been made clear through a distinctive literary "event" I have elsewhere called "interpretation as revelation."[4] It is clear that one of the two most important works of Baha'u'llah, the *Kitāb-i Iqān*, is primarily a work of exegesis.[5] It was written to explain how the messianic claims of Sayyid 'Ali Muhammad Shirazi (1819–50), better known as the Bab (Arabic for "gate" or "door"),[6] may be understood in the light of certain qur'anic verses and Hadith or *Akhbār,* holy traditions or statements traced to the Prophet or, in this case, one of the other thirteen pure ones (Persian: *chehardeh ma'sūmāt*),[7] namely the Prophet's daughter Fatima, his son-in-law 'Ali ibn Abi Talib, and the remaining eleven Imams acknowledged by Ithna 'ashariyya or Twelver Shi'ism.[8] Composed around 1862, the book is relatively early in the corpus of Baha'u'llah's writings.[9] In this early major work the problem of violence is mentioned chiefly with regard to the violent response of humankind to all the prophets and messengers of God, including the Bab. In several passages, the author suggests that all previous prophets were considered by their immediate audiences, or at least a segment of them and sometimes an overwhelming majority, to be seditious or heretical. Such concerns are particularly poignant in the case of Shi'ism and its expectation of the last day, the Day of Resurrection, *yawm al-qiyāma.* Traditionally, this "Day" is viewed as the time when the heretofore hidden Imam would appear with his faithful companions to "fill the earth with justice as it is now filled with tyranny."[10] The hero of this event, the returned twelfth Imam, is known by numerous epithets, among which the most common and perhaps most emblematic of a certain robust theme of Shi'i eschatology is "the one who arises with the sword," *al-qā'im bi al-sayf.*[11]

Baha'u'llah argues in the *Book of Certitude* that this divinely guided hero had indeed arisen and that his message had indeed been proclaimed. But the vast majority of those who have been in the peculiarly Shi'i sacramental state of messianic expectation and hope (namely *intizār*) these eleven or so centuries (that is, the Shi'a themselves) had failed to recognize him because they misinterpreted all of those traditions and qur'anic verses they had traditionally studied, memorized, and commented on in the hope of preparing themselves for his glad advent (*zuhūr*).[12] Thus, the same violent response to all previous divinely sanctioned prophets and messengers had also greeted the Bab, culminating in his execution, in 1850, in Tabriz. Baha'u'llah writes:

> Why is it that the advent of every true manifestation of God *[mazhar-i ilāhī]* has been accompanied by such strife and tumult, by such tyranny and upheaval? This notwithstanding the fact that all the prophets of God, whenever made manifest unto the people of the world, have invariably foretold the coming of yet another prophet after them, and have established such signs as would herald the advent of the future dispensation. To this the records of all sacred books bear witness. Why then is it

that despite the expectation of men in their quest of the manifestations of holiness, and in spite of the signs recorded in the sacred books, such acts of violence, of oppression and cruelty, should have been perpetrated in every age and cycle against all the prophets and chosen ones of God? Even as He has revealed: "As oft as an Apostle cometh unto you with that which your souls desire not, you swell with pride, accusing some of being impostors and slaying others (Qur'an 2:87)." (*Book of Certitude*, 12–13/10)[13]

An arguable subtext is that such persecution is indeed the most compelling credential for the claims of such prophets. Though this is not an exclusively Shi'i attitude (the Qur'an itself is replete with examples of the persecuted chosen one),[14] it is an orientation or theme taken to its most developed extent in Twelver Shi'ism. With regard to the specific expectation that the Qá'im would arise with an actual sword and defeat all of the enemies of God in an apocalyptic battle, the *Book of Certitude* suggests that such a sword is best understood as a metonymic allusion to the sovereignty (*saltānat*) of the Qá'im, a sovereignty with which all divine messengers have been endowed and which "is inherently exercised by the Qá'im whether or not He appear in the world clothed in the majesty of earthly dominion" (*Book of Certitude*, 107/80). Such sovereignty, also known to the wider Shi'i tradition by the cognate and near synonym *walāya* (Persian: *valāyat/vilāyat*), is expressed (namely wielded), according to Baha'u'llah in this same work, through the revelation or words of the one divinely chosen. This divine word has the power to both separate—like a sword—and unite, as a word unites otherwise disparate and perhaps even otherwise uncongenial sounds and letters into a unit of meaning. In the following quotation, Baha'u'llah expands on this distinctive feature of Baha'i hermeneutics. Note also the reference in this passage to reunion and unification, fragrance and garment (*qamīs*), at the end of this passage. These "josephian" metaphors play a key role in signaling the "return of Joseph" and will be discussed further in the second part this chapter.

The following is an evidence of the sovereignty exercised by Muhammad, the Daystar of Truth. Have you not heard how with one single verse He sundered light from darkness, the righteous from the ungodly, and the believing from the infidel? All the signs and allusions concerning the Day of Judgment, which you have heard, such as the raising of the dead, the Day of Reckoning, the Last Judgment, and others, have been made manifest through the revelation of that verse. These revealed words were a blessing to the righteous who on hearing them exclaimed: "O God our Lord, we have heard, and obeyed." They were a curse to the people of iniquity who, on hearing them affirmed: "We have heard and rebelled." Those words, *sharp as the sword of God,* have separated the faithful from the infidel, and severed father from son. You have surely seen how they that have confessed their faith in him and they that rejected him have warred against each other, and sought one another's property. How many fathers have turned away from their sons; how many lovers have shunned their beloved! So mercilessly trenchant was *this wondrous sword [īn sayf-i badī']* of God that it cleft asunder every relationship! On the other hand, consider the welding power of His Word. Observe, how those in whose midst the Satan of self had for years sown the seeds of malice and hate became so fused and blended through their allegiance to this *wondrous and transcendent Revelation [īn amr badī' manī']* that it seemed as if they had sprung from the same loins.[15] Such is the binding force of the Word of God, which unites the hearts of them that have renounced all else but Him, who have believed in His signs, and quaffed from the Hand of glory the Kawthar of God's holy grace.[16] Furthermore, how numerous are those peoples of divers beliefs, of conflicting creeds, and opposing temperaments, who, through the *reviving fragrance* of the Divine springtime, blowing from the Ridván of God, have been arrayed with the new robe *[qamīs-i jadīd]* of divine Unity, and have drunk from the cup of His singleness![17] (*Book of Certitude*, 111–112/84–85, italics added)

Thus, the Awaited Imam *(al-imām al-muntazar)*, the Master of the Age *(sāhib al-zamān)*, the One who arises by Divine right *(al-qā'im bi 'l-haqq)*, had been murdered through an act of violence by the very people who should have welcomed him with open hearts. The condemnation of such violent opposition to God's messengers may be thought a major theme of this book. Its source, Baha'u'llah says here, is selfishness, jealousy, egotism, and vested interest. Though never stated explicitly, the conclusion is certainly difficult to avoid coming to that the author thought it was also caused by an appalling, painful, and pathological lack of imagination. The exegeses performed in the *Iqān* offer imaginative and poetic ways of understanding various predictions about the return *(raj'a)* of the hidden or twelfth Imam, interpretations that are largely symbolic and metaphorical. As the answer to those who argue, for example, that the Imam (here associated with the Son of Man's return in clouds of heaven in Matthew 24:29–31) is expected to return "in the clouds" and have wrongly imagined them to be clouds of the meteorological variety, Baha'u'llah explains that in reality the word *cloud* must be understood quite differently:

And now regarding His words, that the Son of man shall "come in the clouds of heaven." By the term "clouds" is meant those things that are contrary to the ways and desires of men. Even as God has revealed in the verse already quoted: "As oft as an Apostle cometh unto you with that which your souls desire not, ye swell with pride, accusing some of being impostors and slaying others. [Qur'an 2:8])" These "clouds" signify, in one sense, the annulment of laws, the abrogation of former dispensations, the repeal of rituals and customs current amongst men, the exalting of the illiterate faithful above the learned opposers of the faith. In another sense, they mean the appearance of that immortal Beauty in the image of mortal man, with such human limitations as eating and drinking, poverty and riches, glory and abasement, sleeping and waking, and such other things as cast doubt in the minds of men, and cause them to turn away. All such veils are symbolically referred to as "clouds." (*Book of Certitude*, 71–72/55)

Viewing such exegetical virtuosity in the context of the subsequent, fully articulated Baha'i ethos, it seems hard to avoid the conclusion that, according to that
ethos, violence may indeed be thought to stem from a general poverty of imagination.[18] The Baha'i faith and teachings would eventually develop a new rhetoric, or
what has been referred to as a distinctive "expressive style":[19] distinctive, that is,
with regard to the major concerns and guiding ethos of its parent religion, Twelver
Shi'ism. Baha'u'llah wrote the above words not in Iran but in Baghdad, where he
had been exiled as a result of a general government crackdown on the Babis. It has
been suggested that Baghdad, as a much more cosmopolitan milieu than the comparatively xenophobic Tehran, provided an apt and congenial setting for the first
formulation of Baha'i universalism (as distinct from Babi parochialism).[20]

Baha'u'llah himself and his growing entourage came to be known and in fact to
identify themselves as Babis until around 1868 when the adjective "Baha'i" started
to be used more categorically. Even now though, the implication, at least to the
uninitiated, is that we are speaking of Baha'i "Babism" as distinct from Azali
"Babism."[21] Explanations of the transition from Babi to Baha'i identities and orientations are spoken of in terms of "progressive revelation," a cardinal and distinctive Baha'i teaching that explains both history and religion in one gesture by as-
serting that all prophets have been sent by the same God from time to time in
order to promote and carry forward an "ever-advancing civilization."[22] Thus "civilization" as such is a distinct and explicit religious value in the Baha'i teachings.
And, it may be thought to represent a particular "exegesis" of basic qur'anic pronouncements on the "sacramental value" of community (umma), social justice,
and a searching contemplation of the cosmos, the self, and the holy books. Such
Islamic beliefs are, in the Baha'i faith, universalized beyond their formative Arabo-
islamicate matrix, and beyond their evolution or development in the more far-flung
realms of later islamicate civilization.[23]

Civilization, accordingly, in order to be true to itself must be peaceful. Thus,
violence is completely outlawed in the Baha'i faith and the idea and law of "religiously sanctioned warfare" (cf. jihād) is, in conversation with and distinct from
the Islamic tradition, completely, irrevocably, and unambiguously abrogated.[24]
The time line of this abolition is also not open to dispute. It was first unambiguously and publicly identified with the religion of Baha'u'llah in 1863 in Baghdad,
even though it appears to have been part of the noetic substance of a revelatory experience a year or so earlier.[25] While the spirit of this abolition is certainly prominent in Baha'u'llah's Most Holy Book, composed in Ottoman Palestine, in 1873, it is
in a later composition that religiously sanctioned warfare is again specifically outlawed in no uncertain terms.[26]

In a brief work composed toward the end of his life, known as the Tablet of
Glad-Tidings (Lawh al-bishārat), Baha'u'llah listed the major principles of his new
religion.[27] The fifteen distinct laws or verities may be thought a precursor to the

later, perhaps more widely circulated, "Twelve Principles of the Baha'i Faith."[28] At this earlier stage, they are, in this order:

(1) the abolition of religiously mandated warfare;

(2) lifting the ban on associating with followers of other religions;

(3) the promotion of a universal language;

(4) the obligation to support any "king" who arises to protect the beleaguered new religion;

(5a) enjoining obedience to the laws of the country in which any of his followers reside;

(5b) enjoining the inhabitants of the world to aid his persecuted followers so that the "light of unity and concord may shine forth and shed its radiance upon the world";

(5c) the hope that all weapons of war be converted "into instruments of reconstruction and that strife and conflict may be removed from the midst of men";

(6) the principle of the Lesser Peace;[29]

(7) people are permitted to wear whatever clothing they wish and to cut their hair anyway they wish as long as they do not allow themselves to become "playthings of the ignorant";

(8) the abolition of celibacy and monasticism of all kinds so that "monks and priests" may live in the world and enter into wedlock to "bring forth one who will make mention of God";

(9) one must seek forgiveness from God alone; confession to fellow creatures is prohibited (when followed by a prayer for forgiveness);

(10) the prohibition of the destruction of books;

(11) permission to study arts and sciences that are beneficial;

(12) the obligation to acquire a trade or profession—work and trade are regarded as a form of worship.

The first principle or "good news" is expressed as follows:

O People of the World! The first Glad-Tidings *[bishāra]* which the Mother Book has, in this Most Great Revelation, imparted unto all the peoples of the world is that the law of *jihād* has been blotted out from the Book *[ya ahl-i ard bishārat-i avval kih az umm al-kitāb dar īn zuhūr-i a'zam bi-jāmi'-i ahl-i 'alam 'ināyat shud mahv-i hukm-i jihād ast az kitāb].* Glorified be the All-Merciful, the Lord of grace abounding, through Whom the door of heavenly bounty has been flung open in the face of all that are in heaven and on earth.[30]

The explicit mention here of the familiar, frequently vexing, originally qur'anic term *jihād* indicates that there is no ambiguity about this law. *Jihād* is neither explained nor interpreted; it is simply abolished. This bold proclamation should be seen as one of the chief means whereby the founder of the Baha'i faith sought to distinguish his religion from traditional Islam. It may be, as is certainly the case with the tenth principle (against the destruction of books), that the first audience here was the Babis themselves, there having been serious and prolonged disagreement, since the execution of the Bab, about precisely such matters as religiously mandated violence and other distinctively and traditionally unexceptionable topics found mentioned in the writings of the Bab.[31] But it is also obvious from the text that these "glad tidings" are addressed to humanity in general. Furthermore, according to recent scholarship, the tablet itself was first sent specifically to the leaders of thought and state in Britain and Russia, probably as the result of a contemporary event that called into question the Baha'i attitude toward violence.[32] By this time, Baha'u'llah had successfully created a peaceable, law-abiding community out of the rather roiling welter of Babi disarray, in which there had been, for example, obvious and dramatic controversy over the role and status (if any) of *jihād* in what we saw referred to above in the quotation from the *Book of Certitude* as the "new Revelation *[amr-i badī']*."[33] To the extent that this was achieved, the resulting community ultimately came to be known as Baha'i.

THE RETURN OF JOSEPH

The Baha'i era is held to have begun on the evening of May 22, 1844/1260 (that is, at onset of the Twelver Millennium) in Shiraz. This is when the young merchant, Sayyid 'Ali Muhammad (known to history as the Bab), began the composition of a highly unique commentary, itself cast in the form of the Qur'an complete with separate suras (with titles), *āyas,* the number and place of revelation indicated, and, in the oldest manuscripts, marginal indications where prostration should occur. The medium was the message: a new revelation had happened.[34] This unusual Qur'an commentary *(tafsīr),* presented as a "new" Qur'an—or more accurately the "original" uncorrupted Qur'an, which until now had been in the keeping of the hidden Imam—was restricted to one qur'anic chapter, the sura of Joseph.[35] Later Baha'i readers see this as an allusion to and prophecy of Baha'u'llah's advent *(zuhūr),* a return of the True Joseph.[36]

Without delving into great detail, I would like simply now to emphasize that, of all the qur'anic prophets and messengers, Joseph is distinguished by his moral and physical beauty, a major component of which is his willingness to forgive his faithless brothers their evil betrayal. In an act of world-changing tolerance, wisdom, and forbearance, he summons the hitherto scattered forces of his holy lineage to become the salvation and preservation of Israel and, from the point of view of Islam, the prophecy—or, perhaps better stated, God's very connection with the world. In Arabic, such tolerance, wisdom, and forbearance are combined in the word *hilm.* *Hilm* is a frequent word in the Qur'an, where it appears in the divine attribute *al-halīm,* indicating God as the *par excellence* model and source of long-suffering, patience, control of anger, tolerance, slowness to punish, gentleness, and wisdom.[37] Its meaning and moral scope is exemplified in numerous instances in pre-Islamic Arabic poetry, the stories of the Prophets, and in the overall literary and poetic heritage of islamicate culture.

In line with the qur'anic logic of prophecy, all prophets are endowed with this and every other noble moral virtue, but some are more exemplary of this or that virtue than others.[38] Of the many examples of this virtue that have been celebrated and admired in Islam, whether Sunni, Shi'i, or Sufi of whatever specific iteration, or even at the "nonaligned" level of the folktale, none is more characteristic, compelling, or universally admired than the way in which the prophet Joseph, son of Jacob, exemplified this all-important religious virtue in his dealings with those who betrayed him. According to the qur'anic telling of his life in the sura of Joseph, his betrayers are his brothers, the wife of the powerful Egyptian into whose household he had been sold as a slave, her husband the powerful Egyptian himself, and the fellow prisoner who broke his jailhouse promise.[39] Certainly many other prophets (and indeed other heroic or powerful figures in Islam or Islamic history, including the controversial Mu'awiya) exemplify this distinctively Islamic virtue.[40] But Joseph is arguably the prime example. Without raising the problematic question of causality, I suggest that the Baha'i elimination of violence, vengeance, religiously mandated violence, and indeed hatred is a reflection of the image of Joseph and its centrality in its own particular ethos and history. This unites the various streams of influence and discourse flowing from the Qur'an, its exegesis, and its contemplation within both Sunni and more particularly Shi'i contexts. It also unites the whole range of islamicate moralia and pedagogy *(adab/akhlāq),* poetry (mystical and profane), specific tonalities of Twelver Shi'i piety, and eschatology that, by the time of the genesis and rise of the Baha'i faith, had become seamlessly joined to the greater mystical and spiritual tradition of Islam.

The word *bishāra,* "glad tiding," from the title of the tablet summarized above, is not qur'anic. But the basic root idea is frequent in the form of *bashīr,* "bearer of good tidings."[41] As such, it often occurs with a companion term, warner *(nadhīr),* as one half of the prophetic office, as it were. Muhammad is described as such in Q 2:119, 5:19, 7:188, 11:2, 34:28, 35:24, 41:4.[42] The remaining instance of *bashīr* occurs in the famous scene in the sura of Joseph (12:96) when after long years languishing in painful and blinding separation from his beloved son, Jacob miraculously detects—and at great distance—the presence of Joseph from the scent of his famous, spiritually charged shirt *(qamīs).* The joy of such a perception is indescribable, and this is probably why the Qur'an presents it in such a striking scene. If it were a film, it would function as a dramatic cutaway. Joseph's brothers are crossing "the border" separating Egypt and Canaan. The scene shifts instantly to the aged Jacob, languishing a great distance from this border (presumably in the family pasturage in north Canaan) and sensitized through his deep abiding and prophetic love, who immediately senses through the extraordinary shirt *(qamīs)* which the brothers are bringing to him that his beloved and heretofore bitterly lamented son Joseph lives:

> And as soon as the caravan [with which Jacob's sons were traveling] was on its way *[falamma fasalat al-'īr]*, their father said [to the people around him]: "Behold, were it not that you might consider me a dotard, [I would say that] I truly feel the breath of Joseph [in the air]!" (Q 12:94)

In the previous verse, the previously hidden and now manifest Joseph had instructed his brothers to take this shirt back to their home and to lay it on the eyes of their blinded-by-grief father so that his sight would be renewed:

> "Go with this my shirt, and cast it over the face of my father: he will come to see (clearly). Then return (here) to me together with all your family." (Q 12:93)

The Qur'an continues:

> Then, when the bearer of good news *[bashīr]* came and placed the shirt on to Jacob's face, his eyesight returned and he said, "Did I not tell you that I have knowledge from God that you do not have." (Q 12:96)

It is of some interest to note that another form of the same root *B-SH-R* occurs early in the this story at Q 12:19, precisely when Joseph is discovered in the well by the traveling caravan that would then purchase him from his perfidious brothers and remove him to Egypt, thus beginning the crushing separation from Jacob:

> Some travelers came by. They sent someone to draw water and he let down his bucket. "Good news *[bushrā]!*" he exclaimed. "Here is a boy!" They hid him like a piece of merchandise—God was well aware of what they did.[43]

The prophetic career of Joseph had long been of special interest and importance to the Ithna 'ashari Shi'a for a number of reasons. In the Shi'i understanding of the qur'anic account, Joseph is distinguished as an embodiment of the mystery and confluence of divine selection, occultation, and pious dissimulation *(walāya, ghayba,* and *taqiyya)*, three very important Shi'i religious "sacramental" categories. In addition, the entire story may be characterized as "an apocalypse of reunion,"[44] emblematic of the important and distinctive Shi'i doctrine of "return" *(raj'a)* in which this eschaton is typologically prefigured in the qur'anic reuniting of Joseph with his family.[45] There are several other interesting features of the twelfth sura that were taken to the bosom of Shi'ism; but it may be the figure of Joseph as a peacemaker—benevolent, patient, chaste, pious, and wise—that captured the imagination of the founders of the Baha'i tradition.[46] Joseph orders no war. On the contrary, he forgives those who betrayed him. In this particular context, it is difficult to avoid the thought that it is through the powerful example of Joseph that the Shi'i community may be able to find the strength and courage to forgive the Sunni community (and, of course, vice versa). Such "iron in the soul" appears to be something highly important to the Baha'i tradition.[47]

Joseph also qualifies as an example and type of the *Verus Propheta*, or ruling prophet (on the ancient model of Melchizedek), in which both spiritual and worldly/political authority are clearly vested and perfectly combined, as in the Shi'i ideal of the Imam.[48] The continuation of such veneration in the Baha'i faith may be thought a logical development from both the Shi'i and the Sufi traditions, a veneration that begins in earnest with the Bab's remarkable *tafsīr* on Q 12 and continues through the many allusions and references to the Joseph story scattered throughout the writings of Baha'u'llah.[49] For example, in the *Most Holy Book (Kitāb Aqdas)*, written in 1873 by Baha'u'llah, after he had been further exiled from Iran through Baghdad to Istanbul, Edirne, and finally 'Akka in what was then Ottoman Palestine, we find the following characteristic reference to the story of Joseph in which the "josephian" metaphors of beauty, scent, garment, blindness, heartbreak healed, and family reunited are clearly combined with the idea of divine messenger and "administrative or legislative wisdom." Note also the qur'anic diction of this passage, beginning with the characteristic imperative "Say" *(qul):*

> Say: From My laws the sweet-smelling savor of My garment *[qamīsī]* can be smelled, and by their aid the standards of Victory will be planted upon the highest peaks. The Tongue of My power has, from the heaven of My omnipotent glory, addressed to My creation these words: "Observe My commandments, for the love of My beauty *[hubban li-jamālī]*." Happy is the lover that has inhaled the divine fragrance of his Best-Beloved from these words, laden with the perfume of a grace which no tongue can describe. By My life! He who has drunk the choice wine of fairness from the hands of My bountiful favor will circle around My commandments that shine above the Dayspring of My creation.
>
> Think not that We have revealed unto you a mere code of laws. On the contrary, We have unsealed the choice Wine *[al-rahiq al-makhtūm]* with the fingers of might and power. To this bears witness that which the Pen of Revelation has revealed. Meditate upon this, O men of insight! (*Most Holy Book*, para. 4, 20–21/3–4)

THE TABLET OF THE TRUE SEEKER

The question of "religiously mandated combat" *(jihād)*—or more precisely the "religiously motivated warrior" *(mujāhid)*, "one who struggles in holy combat"— had arisen much earlier, in the same *Book of Certitude* excerpted above. Again, writing in Baghdad in the wake of several severely violent clashes between the followers of the Bab and the forces of the Shah, Baha'u'llah, in what seems to be a parenthesis to his general plan to elucidate the divine truth of the Bab's mission, defines this "warrior" in a lengthy passage now known in the Baha'i community as the "Tablet of the True Seeker." What follows is a brief examination and explication of a few key passages containing the theme of "combat" and those josephian metaphors indicated above. The tablet *(lawh)* opens as follows:

> But, O my brother, when a true seeker *(mujāhid)* determines to take the step of search in the path leading to the knowledge of the Ancient of Days, he must, before all else, cleanse and purify his heart, which is the seat of the revelation of the inner mysteries of God, from the obscuring dust of all acquired knowledge, and the allusions of the embodiments of satanic fancy. (*Book of Certitude*, 192/148–49)[50]

Although a thorough analysis of the entire tablet is not possible here, suffice it to mention that neither here nor anywhere in the rest of the *Book of Certitude* (or anywhere else in the Baha'i writings) is there any suggestion that those engaged in the pursuit of truth and the quest for divine nearness in this the Day of Resurrection (*yawm al-qiyāma:* the fulfillment of the Shi'i eschaton) are expected to bear actual arms and engage in anything resembling armed or military activity. On the contrary, the remainder of the "Tablet of the True Seeker" is concerned with inculcating spiritual, moral, and ethical standards reminiscent of the preaching of the earliest Sufi masters such as Muhasibi (d. 857), Junayd (d. 910), Hallaj (d. 922), and al-Makki (d. 996), which is consolidated in the work of Ghazali (d. 1111). The tablet also echoes themes and insights developed in the later Islamic spiritual and mystical traditions by such luminaries as Ibn 'Arabi (d. 1240), Rūmi (d. 1273), and Shabistari (d. 1340), to name only three of the numerous religious virtuosi whose own mystical and spiritual struggle, including literary composition, contributed to the culture from which the Baha'i faith emerged, a culture whose study is necessary for a proper understanding of Baha'i teachings.[51] In the "Tablet of the True Seeker," any explicit Shi'i references are confined—in addition to the quoting of specifically Shi'i Hadith mentioned earlier—to the general if not generic sense of expectation and fulfillment, a sense not out of place within Sunni Islam after all.[52] As the passages excerpted here show, the central, pervasive metaphors of scent, messenger, separation and distance, and knowledge and reunion represent a typological reiteration of the story of Joseph in the Qur'an. Here is a Joseph who, through the exemplification of forbearance, tolerance, and long-suffering, transforms the earlier betrayal of his brothers into a spiritual event that, devoid of violence and bitterness, serves to cause the reunion and healing of the fractured family, a family which in Baha'i thought is emblematic of humanity.

In the excerpts below, the reader experienced with Islamic mystical works will see much that is familiar. Yet the combination of the idea of "holy struggle" *(jihād)* with the josephian imagery and metaphors of beauty, lover and beloved (Jacob and Joseph, Zulaykha and Joseph), attainment of spiritual knowledge, scent and perfume as an emblem of or metaphor for spiritual knowledge, and the related elements of the qur'anic narrative seems to set the tone of the Baha'i ethos in an original and creative way. The tablet continues:

> He must purge his breast, which is the sanctuary of the abiding love of the Beloved, of every defilement, and sanctify his soul from all that pertains to water and clay, from all shadowy and ephemeral attachments. He must so cleanse his heart that no remnant of either love or hate may linger therein, lest that love blindly incline him to error, or that hate repel him away from the truth. Even as you see in this Day how most of the people, because of such love and hate, are bereft of the immortal Face, have strayed far from the embodiments of the divine mysteries, and, shepherdless, are roaming through the wilderness of oblivion and error. That seeker must, at all times, put his trust in God, must renounce the peoples of the earth, must detach himself from the world of dust, and cleave unto Him Who is the Lord of Lords. He must never seek to exalt himself above any one, must wash away from the tablet of his heart every trace of pride and vain-glory, must cling unto patience and resignation, observe silence and refrain from idle talk. For the tongue is a smoldering fire, and excess of speech a deadly poison. Material fire consumes the body, whereas the fire of the tongue devours both heart and soul. The force of the former lasts but for a time, while the effects of the latter endures a century.

The next passage offers again explicit reference to a *jihād* restricted to the spiritual or existential realm:

> These are among the attributes of the exalted *['ālin]*, and constitute the hall-mark of the spiritually-minded *[rūhāniyīn]*. They have already been mentioned in connection with the requirements of the wayfarers *[sharā'it-i mujāhidīn wa mashy-i sālikīn]* that tread the path of the pursuit of the knowledge of certitude *[dar manāhij-i 'ilm al-yaqīn]*. When the detached wayfarer *[sālik-i farīgh]* and sincere seeker *[tālib-i sādiq]* has fulfilled these essential conditions *[ba'd az tahaqquq īn maqamāt]*, then and only then can he be called a true seeker *[laf' mujāhid dar barih-yi 'ū sādiq mi'ayad]*. Whenever he has fulfilled the conditions implied in the verse: "Those who make efforts for Us *[al-ladhīna jāhadū fīna]*," (Qur'an 29:69) he shall enjoy the blessings conferred by the words: "In Our Ways shall We assuredly guide him." (Q 29:69)

In the following paragraph we see a return to those traditional moral, ethical virtues and themes associated with Sufism. This is a prelude to the dramatic reference to precisely the "messenger of joy" *(bashīr)*, translated here as "Mystic Herald," who brings the glad tidings of the "return" of Joseph (something of an apocalyptic reversal, since it is in reality the family, led by Jacob, who "returns" to him). That the adjective *apocalyptic* is appropriate is borne out by mention of, among other allusions, the qur'anic image of the Trumpet Blast, immediately followed by reference to the new creation or new life that results from this spiritual event/experience:

> Only when the lamp of search *[sirāj-i talab]*, of earnest striving *[mujāhada]*, of longing desire, of passionate devotion, of fervid love, of rapture, and ecstasy *[dhawq,*

shawq, 'ishq, walah, jadhb, hubb] is kindled within the seeker's heart *[dar qalb rawshan shud]*, and the breeze of His loving-kindness is wafted upon his soul, will the darkness of error be dispelled, the mists of doubts and misgivings be dissipated, and the lights of knowledge and certitude envelop his being. At that hour will the Mystic Herald, bearing the joyful tidings of the Spirit, shine forth from the City of God resplendent as the morn *[dar ān hin bashīr-i ma'navī bi-bishārat-i rūhānī az madīnah-yi ilāhī chun subh-i sādiq tali' shavad]*, and, through the trumpet-blast of knowledge, will awaken the heart, the soul, and the spirit from the slumber of heedlessness *[wa qalb wa nafs wa rūh ra bi-sūr ma'rifat az nawm-i ghaflat bīdar namayad]*. Then will the manifold favors and outpouring grace of the holy and everlasting Spirit *[rūh al-quds-i samadānī]* confer such new life *[hāyat-i tazah-yi jadīd]* upon the seeker that he will find himself endowed with a new eye *[chishm-i jadīd]*, a new ear *[gūsh-i badī']*, a new heart, and a new mind *[qalb wa fu'ād-i tazah]*. He will contemplate the manifest signs of the universe, and will penetrate the hidden mysteries of the soul. Gazing with the eye of God, he will perceive within every atom a door that leads him to the stations of absolute certitude. He will discover in all things the mysteries of divine revelation, and the evidences of an everlasting manifestation.

Joseph and his story are present again in the following direct continuation of the preceding excerpt, especially in speaking of detecting the "fragrance of God" from a great distance and also in the reference to perfume, breath, and fragrance in other contexts:

I swear by God! Were he that treads the path of guidance *[sālik-i sabīl-i hudā]* and seeks to scale the heights of righteousness *[tālib-i ma'ārij-i taqi]* to attain unto this glorious and exalted station *[bih īn maqām-i buland-i a'lā wāsil gardad]*, he would inhale, at a distance of a thousand leagues, the fragrance of God *[rā'ihāh-yi haqq rā az farasangha-yi ba'idih istinshāq namāyad]*, and would perceive the resplendent morn of a divine guidance rising above the day spring of all things *[wa subh-i nūrānī-yi hidāyat rā az mashriq-i kull-i shay' idrāk kunad]*. Each and every thing, however small, would be to him a revelation, leading him to his Beloved, the Object of his quest. So great shall be the discernment of this seeker that he will discriminate between truth and falsehood, even as he doth distinguish the sun from shadow. If in the uttermost corners of the East the sweet savors of God be wafted, he will assuredly recognize and inhale their fragrance, even though he be dwelling in the uttermost ends of the West *[mathalan agar nasīm-i haqq az mashriq-i ibdā' wazad wa 'ū dar maghrib-i ikhtirā' bāshad al-battah istishmām kunad]*. . . . When the channel of the human soul is cleansed of all worldly and impeding attachments, it will unfailingly perceive the breath of the Beloved across immeasurable distances, and will, led by its perfume, attain and enter the City of Certitude. . . . With both his inner and outer ear, he will hear from its dust the hymns of glory and praise ascending unto the Lord of Lords, and with his inner eye will he discover the mysteries of "return" and "revival" *[wa asrār-i rujū' wa iyāb rā bi-chashm-i sirr mulāhazah farmayad]*. . . . The attainment unto this City quenches thirst without water, and kindles the love of God without fire. Within every blade of grass are enshrined the mysteries of an inscrutable Wisdom, and upon every rose-bush a myriad nightingales pour out, in blissful rapture, their melody. Its wondrous tulips unfold the mystery of the undying Fire in the Burning Bush *[nār-i mūsawī]*, and its sweet savors of holiness breathe the perfume of the Messianic Spirit *[wa az nafahāt-i qudsiyyah-ash nafkhah-yi rūh al-qudus-i 'isawī bāhir]*. It bestows wealth without gold, and confers immortality without death. In each one of its leaves ineffable delights are treasured, and within every chamber unnumbered mysteries lie hidden.

The tablet concludes with a reiteration of the nature of *jihād* in using the by now familiar words *religiously motivated warrior (mujāhid)* and *struggle (juhd)*. The agony of separation (cf. Jacob's separation from Joseph) is conjured here as well:

> They that valiantly labor in quest of God *[wa mujaāidin fi Allāh]*, will, when once they have renounced all else but Him, be so attached and wedded to that City, that a moment's separation from it would to them be unthinkable. . . . Once in about a thousand years shall this City be renewed and readorned *[dar ra's-i hizār sanah aw azyad aw aqall tajdīd shavad wa tazyīn yābad]*.
>
> Wherefore, O my friend, it behooves us to exert the highest endeavour to attain that City *[bāyad juhdi numūd tā bih ān madīnah wāsil shawīm]*, and by the grace of God and His loving-kindness, rend asunder the "veils of glory" *[kashf-i subūhat-i jalāl]*; so that with inflexible steadfastness, we may sacrifice our drooping souls in the path of the new beloved *[dar rāh-i mahbūb-i tāzah]*. . . . That City is none other than the Word of God revealed in every age and dispensation *[ān madīnah kutub-i ilahiyyah ast dar har 'ahdī]*. In the days of Moses it was the Pentateuch; in the days of Jesus, the Gospel; in the days of Muhammad, the Messenger of God, the Qur'án; in this day, the Bayan; and in the Dispensation of Him Whom God will make manifest, His own Book *[dar 'ahd-i man yab'athuhu allāh kitāb-i 'ū]*—the Book unto which all the Books of former Dispensations must needs be referred *[kih rujū'-i kull-i kutub bih ān ast]*, . . . Upon detached souls [those Books] bestow the gift of Unity. (*Book of Certitude*, 192–200/148–54)

CONCLUSION

Islam, beginning with the Qur'an, divides history into two main eras. The one is characterized by savagery, barbarity, brutality, ignorance, and violence and is designated by the Arabic word *jahl*. The other, characterized by the Arabic word *islām*, comes to stand for everything opposite to *jahl*. *Jahl* is personified in the Qur'an by, among others, the pre-Islamic Arabs whose way of life was characterized by pride in bravery, vengeance, tempestuous anger, and a fatalistic disdain for consequence. *Islam* is personified in the lives of the prophets and messengers sent, since the beginning of time, to every community (Q 10:47). Since, according to the *Oxford English Dictionary*, violence has its root meaning in impetuosity and vehemence, there may be some truth to the idea that Islam itself arose in response to such human failings in addition to the more theologically abstract ideas of "polytheism" *(shirk)* and "ingratitude and faithlessness" *(kufr),* as these were seen to characterize the pre-Islamic era known as the Time of Ignorance, *jāhiliyya.* But *jahl,* from a linguistic point of view, is not merely the opposite of knowledge and the act of knowing *('ilm),* but rather the opposite of *hilm,* the rich, multisemic Arabic word introduced earlier that means patience, forbearance (bordering on forgiveness), and a complete absence of flaring anger and violence. Further, it emerges that *hilm* is, in some ways, synonymous with *islām.*[53] It is therefore perhaps natural that the Baha'i teachings, as a distinct development-cum-interpretation of islamicate moral, spiritual, and social values and practices, outlaw not only *jihād* as such, but violence of any kind. This appears to be nonnegotiable. The one exception is in the case of aggression when it is not merely permissible but obligatory to rise up against it. This would seem also to posit a type of violence—whether physical or spiritual in force—that is necessary when combating aggression.

One of the striking results of the Safavid "venture" (1501–1722), when Shi'ism for the first time in centuries became consolidated as the official religion of a distinct polity, was the transposition of Twelver Shi'ism from the "key of Arabic" to the "key of Persian." Joseph had always loomed especially important in persianate Islam,[54] whether as a symbol of divine kingship (and therefore "civilization as such") or as an example of the kind of moral and ethical restraint and wisdom in governance—indicated in the term *hilm*—that lends a particlar élan to his holy heroism. As such, he is an exemplar for kings and shahs, sufi shaykhs, their disciples, *and* the common "average" Muslim, who, as this tradition so wisely observes, is assaulted by the same passions as the king. The *halīm* is, in the final analysis, the civilized man whose soul is formed by the energies and expectations of the last divine revelation: a true Muslim. As such, he is the polar opposite of the *jāhil,* the savage, uncivilized inhabitant of a brutal world, unregenerated by and ungrateful for revelation, the word of God.[55]

It was during the nineteenth century, perhaps with the photographed horrors of the American Civil War, that the glory associated with military might and achievement began to diminish, a process that seems to have ended in the abject brutality and carnage of World War I, the Great War. The Baha'i teachings are therefore very much in harmony with what might be thought a particular *Zeitgeist:* the world was becoming smaller, a new globalization was on the horizon. Baha'u'llah saw this, as is clear from his many writings on the oneness of humanity, the oneness of the world, and the oneness of religion and God. It is also clear that these freshly articulated ideas had a history, especially in Islam, the parent religion and culture of the first three central figures of the Baha'i faith: the Bab, Baha'u'llah, and 'Abdu'l-Baha. I have argued elsewhere that to some extent Baha'i irenics may be seen as a response to, in the first place, the violent and brutal animosity that had split and aggravated anew the unity of the post-Muhammadan Muslim world.[56] With the rise in the later medieval and premodern periods of the three mutually exclusive islamicate imperial protonations, the Ottoman, the Mughal, and the Safavid, such disunity and estrangement became reified, certainly politicized, and frequently dramatized. Figuring thereby a distinctive islamicate modernity, these new alignments and rivalries sought, through what might be thought more purely religious emblems, to mobilize loyalties and enmities. The late Henry Corbin's designation of Twelver Shi'ism as a *"religion d'amour par excellence"* accurately captures one arc of Shi'i piety, namely the central and defining attitude and relationship of allegiance to charismatic absolute authority *(walāya)*.[57] The other arc, one that may complete the circle of Twelver Shi'i religious dynamism, has been characterized as "sacred hatred."[58] The operative technical term is *tabarra,* a companion concept for *tawalla* (from W-L-Y, which is also the basis for the word *walāya*) built on the root verb *bari'a* (from B-R-'A):

> For the imams, *bara'a* [or *tabarrī*] is the indispensable complement to, and opposite of, *walāya* [or *tawallī*]. If we translate *walāya* [or *tawallī*] by "faithful, tender love" of the Imam, then *bara'a* [or *tabarrī*] would be "wild, implacable hatred" of the Enemy of the Imam. . . . According to the imams, one cannot fully love the Imam and his Cause without simultaneously hating the Enemy opposed to him and to his Cause since the time of creation; the "believer" who is faithful to the imams should pledge Love and Obedience to the Master who initiates him into the divine Sciences, and Hatred and Disobedience to him who stands for the opposite of this Initiation. If the world is the way it is, invaded by evil and darkness that will only increase until the triumphal return of the Mahdī, it is because the Masters of Injustice and the mass majority *['amma]* that follows them are dominant, condemning the Sages and the chosen minority *[khassa]* that follows them to isolation and suffering. . . . [T]he imams have forbidden their faithful to show their Hatred or their Disobedience in the form of revolt or open insurrection; *bara'a* should thus remain interiorized (just as is the case for *walāya,* because of the danger of death for the person who professes it) until the return of the hidden imam, even if on the outside obedience to the unjust is forced; this is one of the facets of the Battle that has forever opposed the initiated and the counter initiated; *sabb al-sahāba* [insulting or even damning members of the early community seen as enemies of the Shi'a] is one way of upholding it.[59]

History of Religions, including the anthropology of religion and other related disciplines, tells us that what we refer to as religion or religions includes a vast number of "systems" for affirming identity, making sense of the world, and pursuing happiness (for lack of a better term). It also tells us that because it is a human activity the contents of one may be found in all. The particularity of the phenomenon exists not in the utter novelty of its constituent forms and orientations, its rituals and doctrines. Rather, the distinctiveness of this or that tradition resides in the degree and particular way in which it emphasizes and prioritizes an otherwise commonly held element in a creative or distinctive manner. Frequently, the difference between traditions is subtle, at least at the borders. Perhaps it is a bit like the light spectrum or a rainbow. It is not always easy to pinpoint precisely where violet becomes blue, but we know it does, as it were, after the fact. And once the two become distinct, they can never be assimilated again.

It may well be that the founders of the Baha'i religion were expressing a general cultural exhaustion with such powerful spiritual incongruities, non sequiturs, and contradictions as are implied in such formulae as "sacred hatred." The first audience of the earliest Baha'i kerygma was, after all, Islam itself, an Islam that was not only patently suffering as a result of its own internally generated challenges but that had relatively recently fallen prey to a rather full catalogue of ills as a result of imperial and colonial interests from beyond the abode of Islam.[60] The gospel of harmony, peace, and nonviolence that so has characterized the Baha'i message from its beginning until today was certainly first heard by Muslims for whom the tragedy of the first Fitnah, the apparently irreparable breaking of the unity of the *umma,* was not really a thing of the past but an ever-present heartbreak, embarrassment, and shame drawing attention to the all-too human failings of egoism, jealousy, envy, betrayal, and greed. That this message came later to be addressed to and taken to heart by a wider "constituency" beyond the traditional historical, religious, and cultural borders of the Dar al-Islam simultaneously celebrates and laments a common humanity. It also casts a warm light on the inexhaustible spiritual resources of Islam, the parent religion of the Baha'i faith.

NOTES

1. The new book by Fred Donner, *Muhammad and the Believers: At the Origins of Islam* (Cambridge, MA: Belknap Press of Harvard University Press, 2010) argues that this was in fact the driving purpose of the original preaching of Muhammad.

2. Continuing this theme of nonviolence, Baha'u'llah's son and successor, *Abdu'l-Baha',* the title by which Abbas Effendi (1844–1921) is most widely known, has left numerous, emphatic pronouncements, such as the following:

> True religion is based upon love and agreement. Bahā'u'llāh has said, "If religion and faith are the causes of enmity and sedition, it is far better to be nonreligious, and the absence of religion would be preferable; for we desire religion to be the cause of amity and fellowship. If enmity and hatred exist, irreligion is preferable." Therefore, the removal of this dissension has been specialized in Bahā'u'llāh, for religion is the divine remedy for human antagonism and discord. But when we make the remedy the cause of the disease, it would be better to do without the remedy. (Bosch Baha'i School, *The Promulgation of Universal Peace* [Santa Cruz, CA: Bosch Baha'i School, (1983)], 231)

3. In his history of the first 100 years of the Baha'i Faith, first published in 1944, Shoghi Effendi Rabbani (d. 1957), the first and only Guardian of the Baha'i faith *(walī amr Allāh),* wrote: "I shall seek

to represent and correlate, in however cursory a manner, those momentous happenings which have insensibly, relentlessly, and under the very eyes of successive generations, perverse, indifferent or hostile, transformed a heterodox and seemingly negligible offshoot of the Shaykhí school of the Ithná-'Asharíyyah sect of Shí'ah Islám into a world religion ... whose adherents are recruited from the diversified races and chief religions of mankind" Shoghi Effendi [Rabbānī], *God Passes By* (Wilmette, IL: Bahá'í Publishing Trust, 1970), xii. Hereafter cited parenthetically in the text.

4. Todd Lawson, "Interpretation as Revelation: The Qur'an Commentary of Sayyid 'Ali Muhammad Shirazi, the Bab," in *Approaches to the History of the Interpretation of the Qur'an*, ed. A. Rippin (Oxford: Oxford University Press, 1988), 223–53. On the question of genre in Baha'i scripture, see Franklin Lewis, "Scripture as Literature: Sifting through the Layers of the Text," *Baha'i Studies Review* 7 (1997): 125–46.

5. Christopher Buck, *Symbol And Secret: Qur'an Commentary in Baha'u'llah's* Kitáb-i íqán (Los Angeles: Kalimát Press, 1995).

6. The standard scholarly discussion of the rise of the Babi religion is Abbas Amanat, *Resurrection and Renewal: The Making of the Babi Movement in Iran* (Ithaca: Cornell University Press, 1989).

7. With the passive construction of the participle comes the idea that these Fourteen are not pure by their own efforts; it emphasizes, rather, that they are protected from sin and error by God.

8. By the ninth century C.E. (third century A.H.), various interpretations of Islam had come to be known by the designations Sunni and Shi'i. Within Shi'ism there were further subdivisions based on the number of post-Muhammadan religious authorities, namely Imams, who were recognized. The group most pertinent to the study of the rise and development of the beliefs and practices of the Baha'i faith, the Imami or Ja'fari Shi'is, are also known as the "Twelvers" (Arabic: *Ithna-'ashariyya*). Two other Shi'i groups are frequently, if erroneously, designated "Fivers" (Zaydiyya) and "Seveners" (Isma'iliyya) by analogy. Of these latter two numerical designations, the first is not found in the medieval literature. See Heinz Halm, "Sab'iyya," in *Encyclopedia of Islam, 2nd Edition*, ed. C.E. Bosworth, E. van Donzel, W.P. Heinrichs, and G. Lecomte (Leiden: Brill, 1986–c. 2000), 8:683. Herafter cited as *EI2*.

9. Sholeh Quinn and Stephen Lambden, "Ketab-e Iqan," in *Encyclopedia Iranica*, ed. Ihsan Yarshater (London: Routledge & Kegan Paul, 1985–c. 2000), www.iranicaonline.org. Hereafter cited as *EIr*.

10. Moojan Momen, *An Introduction to Shi'i Islam: The History and Doctrines of Twelver Shi'ism* (Oxford: George Ronald, 1985), 45, 165–70; W. Madelung, "Ka'im Al Muhammad," in *EI2* 4:456–57.

11. I am unaware of any explicit commentary on this epithet by Baha'u'llah. It is possible that such a commentary would employ the familiar (at least in Baha'i writings) figure, or a variation thereon, of "the sword of good character" found throughout his writings.

12. There are, of course, no such things as sacraments in Islam, whether Shi'i or Sunni. I use the word here as an analogy—surely imperfect, as all good analogies are—for structures, doctrines, and institutions in Islam that function *somewhat like sacraments*, which according to Augustine of Hippo are "visible signs of an invisible reality." In Islamic sources a number of phenomena could thus qualify, from the ubiquitous and mightily charged "with the grandeur of God" *ayat* or divine signs, to the more complex, less automatic phenomena and functions such as the community *(umma)*, history, and revelation. It may be that what I am thinking of as sacraments also corresponds, however obliquely, to those "doors" described and analyzed in John Renard, *Seven Doors to Islam: Spirituality and the Religious Life of Muslims* (Berkeley: University of California Press, 1996).

13. When quoting Baha'i scripture, the first page number is to the English translation and the second to the original language, either Arabic, Persian, or a combination of these two. In this instance the reference is to Baha'u'llah, *The Kitab-i-Iqan: The Book of Certitude Revealed by Baha'u'llah*, trans. Shoghi Effendi (1931; Wilmette: Baha'i Publishing Trust, 1970). The Persian original is Baha'u'llah, *Kitab-i mustatab-i iqan* (Cairo: Faraj'u'llah Zaki, 1934), reprinted in 1980 C.E./136 B.E. (Baha'i Era) by Bahá'í-Verlag, National Spiritual Assembly of the Baha'is of Germany. Hereafter cited parentheti-

cally in the text. In some instances with regard to both this work and others quoted below, slight adjustments have been made to the "official" translation, including capitalization and the use of more archaic diction to conform to the editorial style of this volume. All extended citations are allowed in view of Baha'i community's liberal usage of foundational texts.

14. See Michael Zwettler, "Mantic Manifesto: The Sūra of the Poets and the Qur'anic Foundations of Prophetic Authority," in *Poetry and Prophecy: The Beginnings of a Literary Tradition,* ed. James L. Kugel (Ithaca: Cornell University Press, 1990), 75–119.

15. *az yek sulb zāhir shudeh:* a clear, if mildly ironic, allusion to the day of *alast* tradition based on Q 7:172.

16. This sentence is in quotation marks in the original. I do not know the source. It is perhaps a Hadith. The comments in 'Abd al-Hamid Ishraq-khavari (*Qamūs,* 3:1294–95) do not suggest a source. *Kawthar* (abundance) is generally identified as either a pool or river in Paradise.

17. Though it is not precisely clear which (if any) verse is being specified, in a brief exegetical article dedicated to this very sentence (*Qamūs,* 1:363–65) the author suggests the possibility of Q 7:158: "O humankind! I am sent unto you all, as the Messenger of Allah, to Whom belongs the dominion of the heavens and the earth" (*Qamūs,* 1:364; thanks to Dr. Mina Yazdani for this reference). Other suggestions include Q 54:1 and 13:31 (Buck, *Symbol and Secret,* 210). The point may be independent of which specific verse is referred to and may be seen as descriptive of the virtues of the divine word in general. By its very nature, it divides the world into those who believe and those who reject. And, by its very nature, it unites those who believe. This is a standard Shi'i orientation, though, as we see below, many of the more divisive and convulsive energies of such an orientation are neutralized in such distinctive Baha'i scriptural passages as the Tablet of the True Seeker (see below), where the drama of the traditional Shi'i apocalypse is transferred to the realm of spiritual search and enlightenment, both individual and communal.

18. A fine study of these literary and hermeneutical issues as they may pertain to the *Book of Certitude* is, in addition to the article by Lewis ("Scripture as Literature"), the groundbreaking work of Christopher Buck, *Symbol and Secret.*

19. Alessandro Bausani, "Some Aspects of the Baha'i Expressive Style," *World Order* 13 (1978–79): 36–43.

20. Todd Lawson, "Globalization and the *Hidden Words,*" in *Baha'i and Globalisation,* ed. Margit Warburg, Annika Hvithamar, and Morten Warmind (Aarhus: Aarhus University Press, 2005), 35–36.

21. On the division of the Babis into Azalis and Baha'is, see Adib Taherzadeh, *The Revelation of Baha'u'llah* (Oxford: George Ronald, 1977), 2:161–70.

22. "All men have been created to carry forward an ever-advancing civilization." Baha'u'llah, *Gleanings from the Writings of Baha'u'llah* (Wilmette, IL: Bahá'í Publishing Trust, 1969), 215. Baha'u'llah, *Muntakhabati az athar-i Hadrat-i Baha'u'llah* (Hofheim-Langenhain: Bahá'í-Verlag, 1984), 140: *jami'az hara'yi islah-i 'alam khalq shudah and.*

23. Though the order and even substance of these principles can appear differently, one such list is: (1) unity of God; (2) unity of religion; (3) unity of humanity; (4) equality of men and women; (5) elimination of all forms of prejudice; (6) world peace; (7) harmony of science and religion; (8) independent investigation of truth; (9) universal compulsory education; (10) universal auxiliary language; (11) civil obedience and noninvolvement in partisan politics; (12) elimination of extremes of wealth and poverty.

24. Such a position should not be mistaken for pacifism. See, e.g., below, the quotation from 'Abdu'l-Baha'.

25. [*The Tablet of Ridván/Lawh-i Ridvan =*] Baha'u'llah, *Gleanings, #XIV.* On the announcement of the abolition of *jihād* in this work, see Stephen Lambden, "Some Notes on Baha'u'llah's Gradually Evolving Claims of the Adrianople/Edirne Period," *Baha'i Studies Bulletin* 3, no. 1 (June 1984): 4–67.

For commentary, analysis, and further publication and translation details, see Juan Cole, *Modernity and the Millenium: The Genesis of the Baha'i Faith in the Nineteenth Century Middle East* (New York: Columbia University Press, 1998), 115–16.

26. Baha'u'llah, *The Kitáb-i Aqdas: The Most Holy Book* (Mona Vale, NSW: Bahá'í Publications Australia, 1993), para. 159, 76–77/159: "It has been forbidden to you to carry arms unless essential" *(harrama 'alaykum hamal al-at al-harb illa hin al-darūra)*. Hereafter cited parenthetically in the text.

27. Recent scholarship has illumined the composition and publication of this work far beyond what was hitherto known. See Christopher Buck and Y. A. Ioannesyan, "Baha'u'llah's Bisharat (Glad-Tidings): A Proclamation to Scholars and Statesmen," *Baha'i Studies Review* 16 (2010): 3–28.

28. For example, those discussed in Moojan Momen, "Learning from History," *Journal of Bahá'í Studies* 2, no. 2 (1990): 55–68.

29. Literally, *al-sulh al-akbar*. This distinctive Baha'i term is the companion idea to The Most Great Peace *(al-sulh al-a'zam)*, which is the second stage of a process begun with the revelation of Baha'u'llah. For details on this, see Michael Karlberg, *Beyond the Culture of Contest: From Adversarialism to Mutualism in an Age of Interdependence* (Oxford: George Ronald, 2004).

30. For the debate on the problem of whether the Bab invoked the law of *jihād*, see the series of articles and responses by Muhammad Afnan and William S. Hatcher, "Western Islamic Scholarship and Bahá'í Origins," *Religion* 15 (1985): 29–51; Muhammad Afnan and William S. Hatcher, "Note on MacEoin's 'Bahá'í Fundamentalism," *Religion* 16 (1986): 187–92; Denis MacEoin, "Baha'i Fundamentalism and the Academic Study of the Babi Movement," *Religion* 16 (1986): 57–84; idem, "Afnan, Hatcher and an Old Bone," *Religion* 16 (1986): 193–95.

31. One of these was the command to destroy all other books but his. See Amanat, *Resurrection and Renewal*. This may provide an interesting variation on the distinctive Islamic "contexts for revelation" *(asbāb al-nuzūl)* tradition. In this case, the Babi confusion would be the context for the proclamation of a more general and universal message. We may also see here a distinctive variation on what is, as far as I know, the characteristic Twelver Shi'i hermeneutic mode ascribed to certain passages of the Qur'an that might otherwise call into question the "sinlessness" *('isma)* of the Prophet Muhammad (e.g., the passage in which he is upbraided by God for spurning a needy petitioner—"he frowned"; cf. Q 80:4–10). The operative technical formula in the *tafsīr* literature is: *iyyaki a'ni wa'sma'i ya jara* [Even though I appear to be addressing you directly, this message is really for the one who is standing within earshot]. On this formula, see Todd Lawson, "Akhbari Shi'i Approaches to Tafsir," in *The Koran: Critical Concepts in Islamic Studies,* vol. 4, *Translation and Exegesis,* ed. Colin Turner (London: RoutledgeCurzon, 2004), 163–97.

32. Buck and Ioannesyan, "Baha'u'llah's *Bisharat* (Glad-Tidings), esp. 13–14.

33. But this does not mean that his exhortations are for Babis only. In subsequent writings, the same message is addressed explicitly to the peoples of the world, to the kings and rulers, to humanity as a whole.

34. The writing of this commentary is in response to a question from his guest, the young Shaykhi Mulla Husayn. For details, see Amanat, *Resurrection and Renewal,* and Lawson, "Interpretation as Revelation: The Qur'an Commentary of Sayyid 'Ali Muhammad Shirazi, the Bab," in *Approaches to the History of the Interpretation of the Qur'an,* ed. A. Rippin (Oxford: Oxford University Press, 1988), 223–53.

35. Todd Lawson, *Gnostic Apocalypse and Islam: Qur'an, Exegesis, Messianisn and The Literary Beginnings of the Babi Movement* (New York: Routledge, 2011).

36. Muhammad-Husayni, Nasrata Allah, *Yūsuf-i Baha'* (Dundas: Mu'assasah-yi Ma'arif-i Baha'i bi-Lisan-i Farsi, 1991).

37. Charles Pellat, *hilm,* in *EI*2 3:390–92.

38. This is exemplified in the Qur'an and the Tales of the Prophets literature and is also the subject

of the most popular work by Ibn 'Arabi, the *Fusūs al-hikam.* A modern scholarly discussion of this distinctive islamicate religious orientation is Michael Zwettler's pioneering study of typological figuration in the Qur'an, "Mantic Manifesto." In brief, each prophet is spiritually present in every other prophet, but depending upon the specific details of this or that prophet's mission, various virtues will be emphasized while various others will be deemphasized.

39. Joseph as model of *hilm* has not been noticed in the excellent studies of either the qur'anic story or the post-qur'anic treatment in countless poems, tales, religious performances, and institutions. A valuable summary of this material is John Renard, "Reprise: Joseph of the Seven Doors," in *Seven Doors to Islam,* 259–72.

40. "[Mu'awiya's] was a style that involved indirect rule through the *ashraf,* supplemented by his own personal touch with delegations *[wufūd]* and, not least, by his *'ilm* [q.v.], 'the patient and tireless cunning in the manipulation of men through knowledge of their interests and passions' . . . which in his case included 'the prudent mildness by which he disarmed and shamed the opposition, slowness to anger, and the most absolute self-command.' . . . In one of those semiapocryphal stories with which Arabic literature is so rich, Mu'awiya is quoted as having said, 'If there were but a single hair between myself and my people, it would never be severed. . . . I would let it go slack if ever they tugged it, and I would tug it myself if ever they slackened it.'" Martin Hinds, "Mu'awiya I ibn Abi Sufyan," in *EI2* 7:263–68.

41. B-SH-R is a frequent qur'anic root. It is in the form *bashar* "(mortal and fallible) man" thirty-seven times. In a nearly equal number of passages, however, it is connected with a rather interesting semantic reversal from the somewhat gloomy connotations of *bashar,* namely "human as weak," in numerous words for joy and glad tidings; in addiiton to *bashīr,* they are: *bushr* (three times), *bushrā* (fifteen times), *bashshāra* (thirty-three times), *istabshāra* (eight times), *abshara* (one time).

42. *Nadhīr* is said to be the opposite of *bashīr* in A. J. Wensinck, "Nadhir," in *First Encyclopedia of Islam, 1913–1936,* eds. M. Houtsma, A. J. Wensinck, E. Levi-Provencal, H. A. R. Gibb, and W. Heffening (Leiden: Brill, 1993), 6:806. Wensinck does not comment on the interesting juxtaposition of these two opposites as descriptive of the office of prophet, though he does remark that *nadhīr* is held by some to be a synonym for *rasūl,* "messenger." There is no article in *EI2* for *bashīr.*

43. The irony expressed by this specific lexical juxtaposition has, as far as I know, not been explored. On the distinctive circular structure of sura 12, see Mustansir Mir, "The Qur'anic story of Joseph: Plot, Themes, and Characters," *Muslim World* 76 (1986): 1–15. Further discussion of the distinctive spiritual function of the qur'anic Joseph is in Todd Lawson, "Typological Figuration and the Meaning of 'Spiritual' in the Qur'an: Joseph and His Story," *Journal of the American Oriental Society,* forthcoming.

44. Lawson, "Typological Figuration and the Meaning of 'Spiritual.'"

45. Cf. the comparison made between this family reunion and the birds attaining the presence of the Simurgh in 'Attar's famous poem, in Todd Lawson, *Gnostic Apocalypse and Islam.* The idea of the "apocalypse of reunion" was raised some years ago in Todd Lawson, "Reading Reading Itself: The Surat Yusuf in Shi'i Mystical Scriptural Exegesis," *Occasional Papers in Shaykhi, Babi and Baha'i Studies* 1, no. 7 (November 1997), www.h-net.org/~bahai/bhpapers/vol1/nahl1.htm.

46. Joseph's popularity may also be connected to his functioning as an emblem of "irenic relief" in an otherwise polemic-saturated milieu within Shi'ism.

47. *Iron in the Soul* is the title of a book by Kenneth Cragg that examines the role and model of Joseph, especially for the value it might have for coming to peaceful terms in the Palestinian/Israeli conflict: *The Iron in the Soul: Joseph and the Undoing of Violence* (London: Melisende, 2009). For example, in a recent message to the beleaguered Baha'i community of Iran, the Universal House of Justice counseled the Baha'is as follows: "The proper response to oppression is neither to succumb in resignation nor to take on the characteristics of the oppressor. The victim of oppression can tran-

scend it through an inner strength that shields the soul from bitterness and hatred and which sustains consistent, principled action." Quoted in Michael Karlberg, "Constructive Resilience: The Bahá'í Response to Oppression," *Peace & Change* 35, no. 2 (April 2010): 222–57, quote at 234.

48. Cf. Henry Corbin, *Temple and Contemplation*, trans. Philip Sherrard and Liadain Sherrard (London: Kegan Paul International, 1986), 331–33.

49. A complete study of the Joseph motif throughout the Baha'i writings (including those of the Bab, 'Abdu'l-Baha, Shoghi Effendi, and even the messages and decisions of the Universal House of Justice) would, I am certain, confirm the general argument of this chapter.

50. *Ay barādar-i man shakhs-i mujāhid kih irādih namūd qadam-i talab wa sulūk dar sabīl-i ma'rifat-i sultān-i qidam gudhārad bāyad dar badāyat-i amr qalb ra kih mahall-i zuhūr wa burūz-i tajalli-yi asrār-i ghaybi-yi ilāhī ast az jamī'-i ghubārāt-i tirih-yi 'ulūm-i iktisābī wa ishārat-i mazāhir-i shaytānī pāk wa munazzah farmāyad.* (*Book of Certitude*, 148–49)

51. "[The Baha'is] must strive to obtain, from sources that are authoritative and unbiased, a sound knowledge of the history and tenets of Islam—the source and background of their Faith—and approach reverently and with a mind purged from preconceived ideas the study of the Qur'án." Shoghi Effendi, *Guidance for Today and Tomorrow* (London: Baha'i Publishing Trust, 1973), 226.

52. One exception is the reference to "rending the veils of glory" *(kashf subūhāt al-jalāl)* toward the end of the tablet. On this metaphor, which may also be translated "be aware of delusions of grandeur," see Todd Lawson, "The Bab's Epistle on the Spiritual Journey towards God: Provisional Translation, Commentary and Preliminary Edition of the Arabic Text of the Risalatus'suluk," in *The Baha'i Faith and the World Religions*, ed. Moojan Momen (Oxford: George Ronald, 2005), 231–47, esp. 239 and the notes. On the importance of the Mahdī to Sunni Islam, see Wilferd Madelung, "al-Mahdī," in *EI2* 5:1230–39.

53. Toshihiko Izutsu, *God and Man in the Koran* (Tokyo: Keio Institute of Cultural and Linguistic Studies, 1964), 198–229. See the rich discussion of *hilm* in Pellat, q.v. *EI2* 3:390–92, who accepts Iztusu's analysis. See also a similar conclusion in Mohammed Arkoun, "Violence," in *Encyclopedia of the Qur'an*, 5:432–33.

54. Annemarie Schimmel, *A Two-Colored Brocade: The Imagery of Persian Poetry* (Chapel Hill: University of North Carolina Press, 1992), 64.

55. Quoted in Pellat, *hilm*.

56. Lawson, "Globalization and the *Hidden Words*."

57. Henry Corbin, *En Islam iranien, aspects spirituels et philosophiques* (Paris: Gallimard, 1971–72), 1:301: "La piété et la spiritualité shî'ite culminant ainsi dans cette *walâyat* vouée à l'Imâm, comme Forme théophanique sous laquelle l'*Absconditum* se révèle à l'homme, et sous laquelle le Dieu caché devient objet d'amour (cette Forme en étant le *mahbūbiya*). Et c'est pourquoi tout amour de Dieu, du fait qu'il postule un Dieu qui soit objet d'amour, est *walâyat* de l'Imâm."

58. Mohammed Ali Amir-Moezzi, *The Divine Guide in Early Shi'ism: The Sources of Esotericism in Islam*, trans. David Streight (Albany: SUNY Press, 1994), 87–88. See also the same author's "Notes à propos de la *walaya* imamite (aspects de l'imamologie duodécimaine, X)," *Journal of the American Oriental Society* 122, no. 4 (2002): 722–41.

59. Amir-Moezzi, *The Divine Guide in Early Shi'ism*, 88. Such a piety is far from Baha'i teachings and may indeed provide the foil against which these teachings began to be distinguished for their universality.

60. See Juan Cole, *Modernity and the Millennium: The Genesis of the Baha'i Faith in the Nineteenth-Century Middle East* (New York: Columbia University Press, 1998). Although the notion of modernity at work here is largely external to the Islam world, the book is important for the thoroughness with which it tracks possible external or non-Islamic factors in the rise of the Baha'i Faith. This is done to such a degree that it may be thought to ignore quite robust and distinctive native islamicate resources, most notably the pervasive and powerful *wahdat dar kathrat* variety of an especially

persianate Islamic "mystical" discourse, especially because this fell heir to the *wahdat al-wujūd* "theosophy" of the exponents, preachers, and teachers of the vision of Ibn al-'Arabi (d. 1240). The thorough examination of the relationship between Baha'i scriptures and the *wahdat al-wujūd* and/ or *shuhūd* "schools" remains an especially interesting project for understanding the formation of doctrine and religious identity in the modern period. We know, for example, that there are striking similarities between the thought of the highly influential "*shuhūdī*" 'Ala al-Dawla Simnani (d. 1336) and Shaykh Ahmad al-Ahsa'i (d. 1823), whose "Shaykhi movement" (mentioned in note 3) was the precursor of the Babi-Baha'i religions. (See Josepf Van Ess, " 'Ala' al-Dawla Semnani," in *EIr* 1:774–77, following Hermann Landolt, "Der Briefwechsel zwischen Kashani und Simnani über *wahdat al-wujūd*," *Der Islam* 50 [1973]: 29–81, esp. 62–63.)

7

Justifiable Force and Holy War in Zoroastrianism

Jamsheed K. Choksy

PRELIMINARY OBSERVATIONS

There are numerous past and present scholarly debates over interpretations of theological, ritual, and philological issues in the Zoroastrian Avesta, or scriptures, and its *Zand*, or priestly commentaries. However, unlike for example the raging discussions over the Muslim pillar of faith known as *jihād*, scholars of the ancient Iranian religion named Zoroastrianism, after its founder Zarathushtra, have rarely broached the issues of just and unjust violence and of holy and sacrilegious war. Combat when examined both by the faith's practitioners and by scholars is largely understood in terms of theodicy and eschatology linked to the human condition.

Many individuals who inquire into the workings of faith while aware of Zoroastrianism's fabled status in the history of religions actually know few specifics; and the same holds for most general readers. Therefore, broader details of Zoroastrianism's history, beliefs, and practices need to be discussed since those are relevant to this inquiry into religion, violence, and the interpretation of sacred texts.

HISTORICAL CONTEXTS

Each Zoroastrian customarily refers to himself or herself as a Mazda-worshipper (Avestan: *Mazda-Yasna,* Middle Persian: *Māzdēsn,* Gujarati: *Mazda-Yasnī*) because the religion's creator deity or god is Ahura Mazda. Designations such as Zoroastrian (Middle Persian: *Zarduxshtīg,* New Persian: *Zardoshti,* Gujarati: *Zarathushtri*) and Magian (Arabic: *Majūs*) are based on the faith's founder, Zarathushtra, and the male clergy or magi. Zoroastrianism's basic doctrines are traced back to a devotional poet named Zarathushtra, who much later was called Zoroaster by the classical Greeks. Zarathushtra's time and place of ministry are uncertain. Most likely, he lived sometime between the eighteenth and sixteenth centuries B.C.E., during the late Bronze Age. Most probably, he preached somewhere in Central Asia. His words gradually drew followers and, around 1500 B.C.E., after the Proto-Iranians began migrating to the land that gained its name—namely Iran—from them, Zarathushtra's hagiography was modified to depict him as the prophet of ancient Iran and a major religious founder.

From among the newly resettled Iranian tribes, first the Medes (673–550 B.C.E.) and then the Achaemenid clan of the Persians (550–331 B.C.E.) founded empires that at their zenith extended from Egypt and Turkey to the Indus River Valley. After the reign of Darayavahush or Darius I (522–486 B.C.E.), Zoroastrianism was clearly the official faith of Iran, although other religions were freely practiced as well. Conflict between Iranians and Greeks eventually resulted in the Greco-Macedonian conquest, led by Alexander in 334–31 B.C.E., and the Seleucid kingdom (312–238 B.C.E.), both cast by the magi as evil, confused periods. Iranian rule and Zoroastrianism as the official religion were reestablished in the region from the Euphrates River to western Central Asia under the Parthian Kingdom (247 B.C.E.– 224 C.E.) and then the Sasanian (224–651 C.E.) Empire.

Arab Muslims conquered Iran in the seventh century C.E., and Zoroastrianism gradually became a minority faith through conversion to Islam between that time and the thirteenth century C.E. In the tenth century C.E., a few Zoroastrians emigrated from Iran to the Indian subcontinent to freely practice their own religion. Their descendants are called Persians or Parsis (Sanskrit: *Pārsika,* Gujarati: *Pārsi*) by other Indians. Although a very small minority in demographic terms, Parsi Zoroastrians spread throughout the Indian subcontinent in the centuries after, contributing to culture, politics, and economy. They also survived in Iran, again in small numbers.[1] Since the eighteenth century C.E. onward, Zoroastrians have migrated to other countries as well and now form a worldwide community of approximately 120,000–200,000 individuals.[2]

TERMS, TEXTS, AND COMBAT THEOLOGY

Zoroastrian scripture postulates a universal battle at both the spiritual and the corporeal levels between two eternal principles: *asha* (Avestan) or order (Old Persian: *arta,* Middle Persian: *ardā,* New Persian: *ord,* Gujarati: *asha*), which is equated to righteousness, truth, good, right, and holy; and *drug* (Avestan) or confusion (Old Persian: *drauga,* Middle Persian: *drō, druj,* New Persian: *doruq,* Gujarati: *drug*), which is equated to evil, lying, bad, wrong, and the profane. War or *ardīg* (Middle Persian) is considered an appropriate means of striving, struggling, and fighting (Middle Persian: *kōxshishnīg, kōshishnīg*) against all forms of evil during the period, known as the time of the long dominion (Middle Persian: *zamān ī dagrand-xwadāy*), when order and confusion are in a state of intermingle-ment (Middle Persian: *gumezishn*) within corporeal creations. Indeed, the term for holy war, *ardīg*, derives from *arta*, and refers to the correct way or religious path. These ideas are central not only to the Avesta (Middle Persian: *Abestāg*) or Praise scriptures, including its core texts called the Gāthās, or Devotional Poems, attributed by the faith's tradition to the prophet Zarathushtra himself, but also to Middle Persian or Pahlavi, New Persian or Farsi, and Gujarati commentaries written by magi or priests and lay devotees alike.

Zoroastrians believe that all evil must be battled so that it can be defeated and rendered separate (Middle Persian: *wizārishn*) from good, resulting in an escha-tological refreshening or renovation (Avestan: *frashō-kereti*, Middle Persian: *fra-shagird*) when absolute order will be reestablished. So a righteous warrior, fighting on behalf of a religiously just cause or country, is termed a holy warrior or *ardīgkar* (Middle Persian: *artēshtār*, New Persian: *arteshdār*). Another Avestan term, *ras-man* (Middle Persian: *razm*), also came to denote warfare and battle in the techni-cal sense rather than with religious overtones.[3]

Zoroastrians regard the corporeal or material world not just as an arena in which humans combat evil but as the trap into which *Angra Mainyu* or the Angry (or Evil) Spirit (Middle Persian: *Ahreman*, New Persian: *Ahriman*) or the devil was lured by Ahura Mazda or the Wise Lord (Old Persian: *Ahuramazda*, Middle Persian and New Persian: *Ohrmazd*) or god at the beginning of time. Once trapped in matter, Angra Mainyu ostensibly is gradually vanquished via good thoughts, good words, and good deeds by divine beings and devotees acting in unison to fight all manifestations of evil. So a divinely ordained combat against everything that is considered bad and harmful became the faith's and each practitioner's raison d'être.[4] A Middle Persian exegetical text by a ninth century C.E. *herbed* (theologian), the *Doubt Dispelling Exposition* (*Shkand Gumānīg Wizār* 4:63–80), allegorically described this belief by comparing Ahura Mazda to a wise gardener who protects his garden, which is paradise (Old Persian: *paradayadā*, Muddle Persian and New Persian: *pardis*), by luring "the disruptive creature who seeks to ruin it" into a trap. Within the battlefield of the trap, "the strength and power of the evil creature are neutralized and it is vanquished . . . during the time estab-lished for the battle."[5]

The reward of heaven, after death, is offered to the souls of believers who have upheld order and combated evil during their lifetime.[6] Moreover, Zoroastrian exegesis posits that at the end of time, Ahura Mazda will descend to earth with the other heavenly spirits, and a final spiritual savior will separate the righteous human souls from the evil ones. Each sinner, having already suffered in hell after death, will be purified of his or her transgressions and impurities by means of an ordeal involving molten metal. Immortality of body and soul then will be granted to all humans. Ahura Mazda, the beneficent immortals, and other divine beings will end the universal struggle between good and evil by annihilating all demons and demonesses. Angra Mainyu will be forced to scuttle back into hell. Finally, hell will be sealed shut with molten metal, safeguarding the spiritual and material worlds from evil forever, or so Zoroastrians believe. Once the separation of evil from good has been accomplished, Ahura Mazda will renovate the universe in the religious year 12,000, at the end of time.

Religious history supposedly will end with the termination of the cosmic battle. Eternity will recommence in absolute perfection, and humanity will begin dwelling in happiness upon a refurbished earth according to eschatological doctrine expounded by medieval magi or Zoroastrian priests in the *Book of Primal Creation* (*Bundahishn* 34:1–32) and the *Commentary on the Hymn to Vohu Manah* (*Zand ī Wahman Yasht* 9:1–23).[7] So the entire Zoroastrian religious ethos is structured around a holy war, fought on the spiritual and material fronts in the domains both otherworldly and of this world, a struggle thought to last from cosmogony to eschaton.

TEXTUAL BASES OF APPROPRIATE FORCE AND HOLY WAR

According to the Gāthās preserved in the Avesta, Zarathushtra spoke of an ethical and moral dualism between *asha* and *drug,* associating the former with god or Ahura Mazda and the latter with the devil or Angra Mainyu. Followers of Zarathushtra were required to "differentiate between the just and the unjust" (*Ushtauuaitī Gāthā, Kamnamaēzā Hāitī, Yasna* 46:15). Zarathushtra, the devotional poet turned prophet, is said to have commented: "O Ahura Mazda, you know about the many disruptive deeds by which each evil person seeks fame, . . . ravages the pastures, and wields a weapon against the followers of order" (*Ahunauuaitī Gāthā, Xvaētumaitī Hāitī, Yasna* 32:6, 10). Such individuals were said to have "missed the veracity of the straight way . . . and strayed from the path of order" (*Vohuxshathrā Gāthā, Vohuxshathrā Hāitī, Yasna* 51:13). Zarathushtra wished to know from god, for his followers and himself, "when the disparate hordes confront each other . . . to whom will you grant victory?" (*Ushtauuaitī Gāthā, Tat thwā-peresā Hāitī, Yasna* 44:15). "I seek strong power for myself, through good thought, with the increase of which we may defeat confusion" (*Ahunauuaitī Gāthā, Tā-vē-uruuātā Hāitī, Yasna* 31:4), he is said to have stated. Confident in the correctness of his views after the revelation from Ahura Mazda, Zarathushtra predicted: "Destruction will come to confusion" (*Ahunauuaitī Gāthā, At-tā-vaxshiiā Hāitī, Yasna* 30:10), because "the evil mob fears us, for we the strong ones smite those weaker evil ones according to the strictness of your law, O Mazda" (*Ahunauuaitī Gāthā, Yā-shiiaothanā Hāitī, Yasna* 34:8). He urged his deity to "place a mighty sword upon the evil ones, to bring appropriate recompense to them, O Mazda" (*Ushtauuaitī*

Gāthā, Tat-thwā-peresā Hāitī, Yasna 44:14) and enjoined his congregation to "strike sharply at cruelty" (*Spentāmainiiu Gāthā, Yezidhā Hāitī, Yasna* 48:7).[8]

The magi interpreted Zarathushtra's message to mean that persons who fight, morally and tangibly, for order will reach their "promised prize" in the paradisiacal "house of song" or heaven as stated in the Gāthās (*Vohuxshathrā Gāthā, Vohuxshathrā Hāitī, Yasna* 51:15). On the other hand, those who spread confusion and harm will, upon death, be condemned by their own actions to be "guests in the spiritual house of deceit," according to Zarathushtra's sarcastic words (*Spentāmainiiu Gāthā, At-māiiauuā Hāitī, Yasna* 49:11).[9] So the stage was set for a universal battle or holy war between the followers of order and confusion within the religion's worldview. It was and still is viewed by devotees as a holy struggle involving all Zoroastrians against the manifestations of evil, including followers of other faiths, atheists, agnostics, and especially anyone who threatens society.

By medieval times, the magi began to suggest through their textual discourses that humans had entered into a covenant with their god, Ahura Mazda, to specifically function as the deity's troops in the vital struggle against Angra Mainyu's confused, destructive hordes. According to the cosmogonical myth that those priests canonized in the *Bundahishn:* "Ahura Mazda deliberated with the perceptions and immortal souls of humans . . . saying 'incarnate you can battle with evil and vanquish it and I consent to resurrect you perfect and immortal at the end.' . . . The immortal souls of humans agreed to enter the material world to become perfect and eternal in their final bodies" (*Bundahishn* 3:23–24).[10] Owing to belief in this agreement between god and humans, the life purpose of every Zoroastrian was postulated by the magi as being the fixed one of combating *drug* in all its manifestations (religious, social, and political), utilizing all appropriate means, including violence if and when necessary. The central notion is that good actions by people in the corporeal state can ensure the eventual triumph of order over confusion, of righteousness over evil, on the spiritual level forever.

A UNIVERSAL HOLY WAR

Belief, praxis, and texts were conjoined in Zoroastrianism by the faith's prophet, priests, and theologians to propose that the raison d'être of human life is a collective holy war, in addition to each person's individual struggle. In that cosmic conflict, the use of physical force is regarded as both necessary and justified as a means of countering the unholy and unjustified violence of the devil and his spiritual and corporeal minions.

As a result, Zarathushtra is credited by historians of religion with having laid the framework for belief in eschatology within his combat theology through passages such as these four:

I ask you, O Ahura Mazda, . . . how things will turn out when the final reckoning takes place. (*Ahunauuaitī Gāthā, Tā-vē-uruuātā Hāitī, Yasna* 31:14)

When the final judgment comes for these sins, then the power shall be presented through good thought to you, O Ahura Mazda, to command those who shall deliver confusion into the hands of order. May we be those persons who will refresh existence, O Ahura Mazda and other lords, through the bringing of transformation and order. . . . Then destruction will come down upon confusion's distention. The swiftest [i.e., the believers] shall be harnessed to gain good renown up to the good abode of good thought of Ahura Mazda and of order. (*Ahunauuaitī Gāthā, At-tā-vaxshiiā Hāitī, Yasna* 30:8–10)

Joy instead of sorrow will come to the persons who sought order. But to a long period of gloom, foul food, and the word "woe," to such an existence your views will lead you, deceitful ones, through your own actions. (*Ahunauuaitī Gāthā, Tā-vē-uruuātā Hāitī, Yasna* 31:20)

O Ahura Mazda, whoever, man or woman, grants me those things that you know are the best for existence—namely, reward for truth and power through good thought—and whom I shall inspire to glorify ones such as you, I will cross over the Bridge of the Compiler [the bridge to heaven] with all of them. (*Ushtauuaitī Gāthā, Kamnamaēzā Hāitī, Yasna* 46:10)

Zarathushtra's ideas of god and devil, angels and demons, and righteous and unrighteous humans in opposition are thought to have spread, eventually, to other religions such as postexilic Judaism, Christianity, and Islam, laying the seeds of combat theodicy in those faiths too.[11] But, though influenced by the social flux of his time (involving a gradual decline of Central Asian Bronze Age settlements, a resurgence of nomadism, violence against settled people, and southwesterly relocations onto the vast plateau those people would come to call Iran), Zarathushtra's vision was not one of punishment meted out by god for human transgression. Rather, like god and the devil, all persons are said in the faith's ancient and medieval texts to have a choice between order and confusion, between following the path of righteousness and wandering the alleys of wickedness. Those choices supposedly determine all conditions, including retributions in life and afterlife (*Ahunauuaitī Gāthā, At-tā-vaxshiiā Hāitī, Yasna* 30:1–6).[12]

As discussed previously, magi built upon Zarathushtra's basic ideas during Antiquity and the Middle Ages, producing complete, written apocalyptical and eschatological schemes. In Zoroastrian belief, signs that the end of the world is approaching include a steady increase in evil and suffering, especially warfare and death. In response, three consecutive saviors will "wield the triumphant mace" to smash the faith's enemies and other miscreants, according to an Avestan Devotional Poem whose ideas predate Achaemenian times but whose canonization probably dates to the third century B.C.E. (*Zamyād Yasht* 19:92).[13] The final confrontation between order and confusion, represented in medieval texts as an apocalyptic battle between good and evil, supposedly will involve the deity and devotees, including resurrected mythic heroes who will "smite the triumphant mace upon the heads" of demons, demonesses, and hoary villains (*Ayādgār ī Jā-māspīg* 6:6; *Bundahishn* 33:29–34:32; *Wizīdagīhā ī Zādspram* 35:34–47; and *Zand ī Wahman Yasht* 4:3–68, 9:1–23).[14] So as in life, even at the very end, god and the celestial horde will fight side by side with humans to ensure the final victory of good over evil. Despite the centuries since these ideas developed, a time period during which Zoroastrianism has been reduced to a minority faith around the world, Zoroastrians still believe in this combat eschatology, even more so now that they find themselves a dwindling presence among the world's religions, for they cling to the notion that all will be made right in the end.

MYTHS AND LEGENDS OF LAWFUL FORCE

The theme of combat between good and evil was incorporated into Devotional Poems *(Yashts)* to beneficent spirits said to have been created by Ahura Mazda (in fact, these celestial beings had been assimilated into early Zoroastrianism from previous Iranian religiosity and made subordinate to Ahura Mazda).[15] So, the female worship-worthy spirit (Avestan: *yazata*) Aredvi Sura Anahita (later called Ardwisur Anahid) was portrayed in the Avesta as "charging her chariot" to "overcome the opposition of all demonic and mortal enemies," in addition to granting mythic heroes such as Haoshyangha (later called Hoshang) and Yima Xshaeta (later called Jamshed)—who had allied themselves with *asha*—the ability to "smite two-thirds of the demons and villains" and "wrest goods, revenue, flocks, and herds from evil ones" (*Ardwīsūr Yasht* 5:11, 13, 22, 26). In keeping with the notion that the armies of persons allied with *drug*—such as the legendary archenemy Azi Dahaka (later called Azdahag)—should not be assisted in battle, when beseeched by foes of Zoroastrians this female spirit "did not grant boons" (*Ardwīsūr Yasht* 5:31). Rather, it was written, she assisted Zoroastrians by smiting adversaries "with one hundred blows for every fifty [the enemies deliver], with one thousand blows for every hundred blows [the enemies deliver]" (*Ardwīsūr Yasht* 5:54).[16] Eventually, Anahita would come to be regarded as the spirit of kingship, depicted on Sasanian silver coinage (Middle Persian: *drahm*) bestowing diadems that symbolized legitimate rule upon worthy monarchs.[17]

The male worship-worthy spirit Mithra (later called Mihr), who oversees covenants, contracts, and social order on behalf of Ahura Mazda, was depicted in a *Yasht* from late Achaemenian times as "the expert warrior who bears spears with sharp tips and long shafts" and as "the far-shooting archer with swift arrows" because he was a "caretaker who protects Ahura Mazda's creatures" (*Mihr Yasht* 10:102–103). Mithra supposedly functioned as the patron of Ahura Mazda's mortal rulers and armies "as they descend[ed] upon the battlefield against the bloodthirsty enemy troops" (*Mihr Yasht* 10:8). He is believed to give Zoroastrian warriors "the ability to rout lawless hostile enemies" when he himself "takes his stand in battle" by their side to "mash the evil regiments . . . and lop heads off the evil men" (Mihr Yasht 10:11, 36–37). This beneficent spirit also is thought to serve as the foremost, ever watchful scout "who has ten thousand spies" working on the behalf of Zoroastrians who uphold order (Mihr Yasht 10:60, 82). Associated with Mithra was said to be the spirit of victory, named Verethraghna (later Wahram and Behram), who flies in front of the covenant-enforcing Mithra's celestial chariot "cutting everyone bad to pieces all at once, mixing together the bones, hair, brains, and blood of covenant-breakers on the ground" after "killing them with a single blow" (*Mihr Yasht* 10:72; *Wahrām Yasht* 14:15). Essentially, humans who engage in thoughts, words, and deeds regarded as evil by the faith are seen as having violated the primordial covenant between their immortal souls and god by choosing to side with the devil. They are condemned as contract-breakers (Avestan: *mithrō-drukhsh*) who are worthy of death because "they wreck society" (*Mihr Yasht* 10:2).[18] As the passages cited demonstrate, physical force when exercised by the human and spiritual followers of Ahura Mazda against those persons regarded as evildoers is not regarded in Zoroastrian written sources as inappropriate or unjust and especially is not equated to violence.

So like good humans, god's heavenly legions too can resort to force to quash evil. All those individual attacks, and even collective warfare, are condoned by scripture and exegesis as necessary for corporeal and spiritual well-being. Moreover, although Zoroastrian scriptural sources provide justification for seemingly violent acts by good people and beneficent spirits, those actions are not regarded as divine wrath or vengeance. Additionally, while the deployment of force against evil is regarded as a necessary part of the divine plan, its negative effect is not viewed as created by god. Rather, violence is seen as produced by the devil for oppression and subjugation of heaven and earth. Those persons who choose evil are believed, as stated in Magian exegesis, to have set into motion the conditions that result in violence boomeranging back to themselves through the correct actions of the faithful. Exegesis reassures Zoroastrians that the purpose of all actions by good spirits and humans is ultimately "to repel and ward-off whatever damage may come to God from an adversary [the devil] who could harm Him; this is the entire purpose for the act of creation" (*Shkand Gumānīg Wizār* 8:1–134).[19]

Indeed, in Zoroastrian theogony, Ahura Mazda did not create Angra Mainyu; both were and are eternally existing spirits, and Ahura Mazda chose order whereas Angra Mainyu chose confusion:

> These two spirits, who are the original twins, revealed their distinction in a vision. They are the better one and the worse one in thought, word, and deed. Between these two the judicious discern appropriately, not so the confused. When these two spirits

come together, from the beginning they create existence and nonexistence. So, at the end, there will be the worst existence for followers of confusion but the best dwelling place for followers of order. Of these two spirits, the confused one chooses to do the worst things while the holiest spirit who is clothed in the hardest stones chooses order as do those persons who satisfy Ahura Mazda through good deeds. The demons cannot discern appropriately between these two spirits for, as they deliberate, confusion comes upon them resulting in their choosing the worst thought. Then they scurry together with wrath to afflict mortal existence. (*Ahunauuaitī Gāthā, At-tā-vaxshiiā Hāitī, Yasna* 30:4–6)[20]

Hence, through his appropriate choice of order (or *asha*), one of the primeval spirits became the Wise Lord or Ahura Mazda, presented as the "holiest" one. The other primeval spirit, who chose poorly, created an affiliation with confusion (or *drug*) and so became the Angry Spirit or Angra Mainyu, presented as the "confused" one. As a result, the authors of medieval Zoroastrian texts claim that Ahura Mazda is the source of everything good, including peace, welfare, health, happiness, and life, whereas Angra Mainyu is the origin of everything bad, including war, harm, sickness, sadness, and death.[21] This distinction is the logic underlying Zoroastrian notions of how and why fighting words and martial deeds can and do have good outcomes when performed for the correct reasons by the right individuals. It also underlies why Zarathushtra's combat theology came to influence other religions whose followers were seeking explanations to the trials and tribulations of human conditions.

The theme of battling opponents in Zoroastrianism became a central part of the Iranian national epic as well. That text is a mixture of myth and history, heroism and romance. It represents the epic on a grand scale, was initially composed under the Middle Persian title *Book of Lords (Xwadāy nāmag)* during the Sasanian era, and was finalized in New Persian verse as the *Book of Kings (Shāh nāme)* during the eleventh century C.E. Tracing the history of Zoroastrian Iran from the first mythological rulers to the defeat of the last Sasanian king of kings by the Arabs in the middle of the seventh century C.E., it proved an ideal bridge between religious and secular thought. Among its literary subcycles are ones on the prophet Zarathushtra and his royal patron king *(kavi)* Vishtaspa (later Goshtasp), Alexander (rendered as Eskandar or Sekandar), and the east Iranian Saka or Scythian tribal hero Rostam. Rostam in particular epitomizes the epic: he is depicted battling villains, male and female ghouls, and monsters, bringing kings to power, defending the kingdom repeatedly, and, in one tragic episode (supposedly predetermined by bad destiny playing upon the hero's hubris), failing to recognize his own son Sohrab and consequently slaying that youth after one-on-one combat (*Shāh nāme* 6, 8, 9, 14).[22] The unifying theme of this epic is the concept of kingship bestowed by god, sacral kingship that upholds social and moral order and stresses honor, freedom, and patriotism while opposing all forms of disorder, even by clout and war when necessary.[23] Indeed, defending Zoroastrianism using all means available became a central part of ancient or pre-Islamic Iranian identity through the tales codified in the *Xwadāy nāmag* and the *Shāh nāme*. Rostam, like Vishtaspa, was cast as a model protector of faith and state who battles valiantly for the welfare of Zoroastrians as their "illustrious warrior" and proffers advice for the benefit of "kings and nobles," while following his religiously prescribed duties to the end because he believes in "god . . . and judgment day" and commits his soul to Ahura Mazda (referred to by the Zoroastrian New Persian term *yazad* or divinity, which derives from Avestan *yazata*) at the moment of death (*Shāh nāme* 6:10, 8:7, 14:16).[24]

DOCUMENTARY CLAIMS OF NECESSARY MARTIAL DEEDS

The notions of force and warfare as aspects of statecraft necessary to protect faith and country would become clearly enshrined in religious theology and societal practice during the Sasanian period. Magi linked faith and nation through injunctions such as "religion and state were born from one womb, joined together never to be separated" (*Tōsar nāmag* 8), and "essentially, royalty is religion and religion is royalty" (*Dēnkard* 3:58).[25]

Yet the practice of allegedly unavoidable, religiously necessary martial deeds by Zoroastrian rulers dates back at least to Darius I. That Achaemenid king of kings justified both his ascension to power and his military suppression of rivals with a specific phrase: "The Lie became great" (*Behistun inscription* 1:10). He was referring to the demonic personification of evil, *drauga,* to explain why it was essential that he take the throne: to ensure god's will and divinely sanctioned order prevailed. He went on to claim through a monumental Old Persian rock inscription that "I am king by the will of Ahura Mazda," "Ahura Mazda granted me the kingdom," and "my army defeated that rebellious army completely by the will of Ahura Mazda . . . when we fought the battle" (*Behistun inscription* 1:11–12, 94–96; also 2:34–37, 40–42). So he would command his troops: "Go forth, vanquish that army that does not ally itself with me!" (*Behistun inscription* 3:14–15; also 2:20–21, 83–84). Those who allegedly opposed Ahura Mazda by resisting Darius I's sovereignty were meted out brutal recompense to serve as warnings to others: "I cut off his nose, ears, and tongue, and blinded one eye; he was kept bound at my palace gate so all the people could see him; then I impaled him" (*Behistun inscription* 3:32; also 3:33).[26] Particularly vexing opponents, including a magus named Gaumata who had seized the throne, were depicted as either dead under his foot (as in the case of Gaumata) or bound by their necks and hands in his presence. As captives suffer, Darius triumphantly faces his god, represented in winged disk, who proffers the king a diadem of sovereignty in a victory scene that accompanies the inscription.

Darius would go on to write that Ahura Mazda aided him: "Because I was not malevolent, I was not a follower of the Lie, I was not a doer of wrong . . . I conducted myself according to Order. I did no wrong to either the weak or the powerful. I rewarded appropriately whoever cooperated with my dynasty. I disciplined appropriately whoever did injury. . . . Do not befriend anyone who is a follower of the Lie, rather discipline them appropriately" (*Behistun inscription* 4:61–69).[27] So violence, warfare, even torture would be legitimized as justice and appropriate recompense rather than tyranny and excessive punishment, and came to be seen as mechanisms necessary for maintaining *asha/arta* and countering *drug/drauga* in the world.

His son and successor, Khshayarsha or Xerxes I (r. 486–65 B.C.E.), continued the use of war to enforce socioreligious authority: "When I became king there was among the lands one in rebellion. Then Ahura Mazda bore me aid. By the will of Ahura Mazda I smote that land and put it back in its place" (*Persepolis inscription* H 28–35).[28] Many centuries later, Ardeshir I (r. 224–40 C.E.), who founded the Sasanian dynasty, is reported to have equated rebellion to heresy against the crown and religion. So Ardeshir "dispatched his army against the rebels in Kerman, commanding that their fortress be demolished" (*Kār nāmag ī Ardeshīr Pāpakān* 13:18–19).[29]

Yet even before Darius and Xerxes, and long before Ardeshir, the Achaemenid dynasty's founder Kurush or Cyrus II (r. 550–30 B.C.E.) claimed on a clay cylinder that he sent troops to capture Babylon and oust its allegedly tyrannical ruler Nabonidus so that stability would be reestablished there according to the will of god (in this instance Ahura Mazda among the Zoroastrians, Marduk among the Babylonians, and Yahweh among the Jews). Cyrus's endeavor apparently proved both swift and successful, for not only did his forces enter Babylon "as a friend" to "reestablish its seat of government," but they were also able to prevent "anyone from terrorizing the country," which allowed the "people [to walk] around in peace." The reconstruction teams he deployed brought "relief to dilapidated houses" and "put an end to other complaints," royal propaganda stated. Cyrus's intervention set free not only the local population but also Jews who had been held captive there. His conquest was acclaimed by Babylonian and Israelite priests as divinely ordained, according to the surviving textual records such as Deutero-Isaiah (45:1).[30] His actions were considered a success because they supposedly excised a clear and present danger, rebuilt a failing administration, mitigated internal conflict, ensured health and welfare, reintegrated people and resources while respecting and working within the mores of the society that was being stabilized and reconstructed, and, above all, "endeavored to treat the conquered people justly." So even Marduk and Yahweh, although not part of Zoroastrian belief, "declared Cyrus ruler of all the world" and "the Lord's anointed one" (*Cyrus Cylinder; Isaiah* 45:1).[31]

Because martial endeavors were considered essential in safeguarding religion, country, and people, military instruction was emphasized for princes and courtiers. So Darius I claimed: "I am trained to use both hands and feet. As a rider, I am a good rider. As an archer, I am a good archer both on foot and on horseback. As a lancer, I am a good lancer both on foot and on horseback. Ahura Mazda bestowed physical dexterity upon me. . . . What has been done by me, I have done with the skill that Ahura Mazda bestowed upon me" (*Naqsh-e Rostam inscription* B 40–49).[32] A Middle Persian text captures the essence of Sasanian-era education, which combined secular and sectarian education with military instruction. A page boy is said to have stated to his monarch, Khusro I (r. 531–79 C.E.):

> Thanks to god's grace . . . I was placed in school and was steadfastly zealous in studies. I memorized completely the *Yasht*s, *Hādōkht, Yasna,* and *Vidēvdād* scriptures like a theologian and studied their interpretation passage by passage. My scribal skill is such that I am well versed in fine literature and calligraphy, seek knowledge, and am capable of rhetoric. My prowess in riding and archery is such that the opponent is fortunate if he can escape my arrow while riding. My prowess in throwing the spear is such that unfortunate is the rider who seeks combat with me on horseback using spear and sword. (*Khusrō ud Rēdag* 4–12)[33]

A textual contrast occurs with regard to Alexander's conquest of the Achaemenian Empire. In secular Iranian traditions, the cause of the empire's fall was explained as Alexander, as the half brother of Darius III, returning to claim territory that was rightfully his. However, in Magian tradition Alexander was derided as "hate-filled" (Middle Persian: *gizistag*), which allegedly lead to him "extinguishing many holy fires, killing magi, and burning the *Avesta*" (*Bundahishn* 33:14; *Denkard* 4:16).[34] Essentially, the magi were reacting both to the end of an empire that they viewed as having been established by Ahura Mazda and to the advent of Greek religious beliefs and rites onto the Iranian plateau.

HISTORICAL VOICES ABOUT OTHER SPECIFIC CONFLICTS

Religious tenets carried over to historical campaigns because the idea of order versus confusion, good against evil, and lawful force countering unlawful violence could be applied to warfare arising from political situations, even if only as the casus belli. According to the Greek historian Herodotus (ca. 484–30 B.C.E.), Xerxes I had a divinely inspired dream that supposedly foretold success in battles against the Greeks (*History* 7:12–15). Later, when a storm washed away bridges his troops were to cross, he commanded that the Hellespont be "scourged with three hundred lashes, and a pair of fetters be thrown into the sea" while admonishing the water as "bitter," adding "you did him [Xerxes] wrong when he had done you none" (*History* 7:35).[35] Essentially Xerxes drew upon his beliefs that the Hellespont, as a creation of Ahura Mazda, should have cooperated with his cause as the Zoroastrian god's chosen ruler. Because it seemingly had not, Xerxes regarded it as having sided with his enemy the Greeks and therefore as having earned vigorous retribution. Again, physical force directed even at an inanimate object was justified in terms of good versus evil.

The Sasanian dynasty was founded in 224 C.E. when Ardeshir the satrap of Persis (Persia) successfully rebelled against his Parthian overlord king Ardawan (Artabanus) V. The new monarch presented his ascent to power as good vanquishing evil. Part of the imperial propaganda to legitimize his seizing the throne included monumental rock carvings in which Ardeshir, on horseback, was presented with the diadem of sovereignty by an anthropomorphic rendition of Ahura Mazda, also astride a horse. In those reliefs, such as at Naqsh-e Rostam, the king's horse stomps upon the dead body of Ardawan while god's horse stomps upon the defeated devil or Angra Mainyu as Ardeshir gestures in reverence to his patron divinity. So the defeated foe was equated with the personification of evil. Similarly, Ardeshir II's (r. 379–83 C.E.) advent to kingship after defeating opponents in battle was also depicted on a rock relief, at the site of Taq-e Bostan, where an anthropomorphized Ahura Mazda and the king stand upon an enemy's corpse while the *yazata* Mithra protects the king's back.[36]

In yet another instance, the Sasanian king of kings Shapur I (r. 240–72 C.E.) inscribed his reasons for going to war against the Romans, including a claim that untruths had been spoken by his opponents. He implied that the Romans were allied with *drug* and Angra Mainyu: "Caesar lied again and attacked Armenia, so we attacked the Roman Empire" (*Naqsh-e Rostam inscription* 4). War as a means of establishing Zoroastrianism was also mentioned by Shapur I in the same inscription: "We have sought and seized many lands with divine aid so that in every land we would establish many holy Wahram fires, confer benefits upon many magi, and expand the worship of god" (*Naqsh-e Rostam inscription* 17). Since Shapur I had defeated the Roman leaders Gordian III, Philip the Arab, and Valerian (*Naqsh-e Rostam inscription* 3–4, 9–11), those victories were depicted on monumental rock reliefs imbued with religious symbolism.[37] So at the site of Bishapur, the Sasanian king's triumphal relief depicts Gordian dead, Philip kneeling, and Valerian held captive as angels bring victory wreaths to Shapur.

Attempts at protecting Zoroastrianism were one factor that resulted in particular battles. When Armenian rulers, who had been Zoroastrian, allied religiously and politically with Byzantium against Iran and adopted Christianity in the early fourth century C.E., the Sasanian king of kings Shapur II (r. 309–79 C.E.) conducted military campaigns in a futile effort to have them reconvert to Zoroastrianism and re-ally with his empire.[38] Another case of violence being couched in terms of good versus evil, this time directed at Zoroastrians, is found in Muslim accounts of the fall of the Sasanian Empire from the ninth century C.E. When Arab Muslim troops invaded Iranian territory during the seventh century C.E. and laid siege to the Sasanian capital city of Ctesiphon, "Iranians who saw Muslims crossing the Tigris River cried out, 'devils have come.' They then said to each other, 'By god, we are not waging war against mortals. Rather, we are fighting none other than evil spirits.' So they fled . . . believing Satan has arrived."[39]

By the ninth century C.E., the defeat of the Sasanians and the conversion of most Zoroastrians to Islam had been rationalized by incorporating those events into eschatology. A premonition of unsuccessful resistance against violence by Arab Muslims upon Iranian Zoroastrians was even attributed to the prophet Zarathushtra: "Ahura Mazda said, 'The seventh age, of alloyed iron, entails evil rule by disheveled demons descended from the clan of Kheshm' " (*Zand ī Wahman Yasht* 1:6, also 3:29).[40] The term *Kheshm,* usually the name for the Zoroastrian demon of wrath, was employed in this passage as a pun on Hashim, the founder of the prophet Muhammad's clan. So, in these instances, the textual tradition put forward an interpretation that the subjugation of Zoroastrians was unjust and violent, and identified Arab Muslims with the devil's evil corporeal hordes.

The breakdown in cooperation between Muslim authorities and lay Zoroastrians may have been one factor provoking the rebellions that tore apart society in Khorasan during the eighth century C.E. Particular note should be paid, in this respect, to uprisings by two heterodox Zoroastrians: Bihafrid-e Mahfravardin (from 747–49 C.E.) and Sinbad (in 754–55 C.E.). Both movements reveal a degree of commonality between plebeian Muslim and Zoroastrian religio-political notions.[41] Perhaps it was this very syncretism that alienated the magi who allied themselves with Muslim authorities and had their own ecclesiastical authority reinstated once the revolts were quashed. So those acts of violence and warfare failed because the Zoroastrian priesthood viewed them as terrorism against both friend and foe rather than as justifiable attacks against foes alone.

On the other hand, in 1465 C.E., Parsi Zoroastrians fought unsuccessfully alongside Hindus against Muslim troops of the Muzaffarid sultan Mahmud I Begath (r. 1458–1511 C.E.) to defend the city of Sanjan. According to one tale, after the Hindu troops fled "Zoroastrians alone stayed to resist . . . arrows rained down everywhere. . . . [B]lood spurted from their bodies like from fountains . . . yet none turned their faces" (*Qessa-e Sanjān* 285, 291, 298). Their resistance bought time to facilitate the magi transferring a holy fire to the safety of a hillside cave, at the nearby locale of Bahrot, for the next twelve years: "Those of the noble faith fled there. . . . [T]he Iran Shah fire was borne by them up there . . . so their pure faith could survive" (*Qessa-e Sanjān* 353, 355, 362).[42]

Centuries later, Parsi Zoroastrians, as citizens of colonial India, volunteered for service in the armed forces of the British Empire in World War I. One publication, commemorating Parsi servicemen in that war, even referred to it as "the great war between the forces of the Good Spirit [Ahura Mazda] versus the Evil one [Angra Mainyu], of humanity versus the devil."[43] Parsi Zoroastrian men and women enlisted in the British Army during World War II as well. They served against Japanese forces in Burma and Southeast Asia, fighting for the Allied cause which they believed to be both good and just. Similarly, others served as physicians in the British forces.[44] The concept of assisting communities and nations that provide safety for followers of the faith continues to the present day, as evidenced by Parsis in modern India serving with that country's armed forces at all levels, including as generals, and assisting in development of that country's nuclear weapons program as engineers and physicists. Others residing in postindependence Pakistan do so too.[45]

ZOROASTRIAN TEXTS AND MODERN SCHOLARS

There are a few exceptions to the scholarly silence on texts and traditions dealing with violence and warfare. The most notable theologically and ritually vexed issue relating to inappropriate, and therefore unjust, violence surrounds the question of whether Zarathushtra condemned the legendary Yima Xshaeta for conducting sacrifices that were brutal and needlessly vicious toward the animals offered up in worship. That worship service (or *Yasna*) involved the preparation of a symbolic elixir of immortality known as *haoma* (the Vedic soma). Originally, among the proto-Iranians to whom Zarathushtra preached, the *Yasna* also included a flesh offering. One way, suggest some contemporary scholars, that Zarathushtra seems to have distinguished his nascent tradition from the commonly practiced one of his times was by condemning any sacrifices that were not humane.[46]

Indeed, the pertinent scriptural passages do speak of violence against harmless animals as reflecting a daevic or demonic cult that Zarathushtra's chosen divinity, Ahura Mazda, did not approve of. The distinction, it appears, was between necessary sacrifice and unnecessary suffering. So while Zarathushtra did not prohibit ritual sacrifice of animals, he may have advocated limits to the number of cattle, sheep, and goats offered to heaven, while insisting that the creature's end be swift and calm. Indeed, in attested Zoroastrian praxis, it is usually a small mammal such as a goat or sheep that is ritually sacrificed. Even that custom fell into disuse, largely because Zoroastrians felt the killings were unnecessary by the early twentieth century.

Another ancient Iranian document whose interpretation has been challenged recently is not a religious text but an inscription claiming that actions were based on Zoroastrian doctrine: the Behistun inscription of Darius I. As discussed previously, Darius claimed that his takeover of the Achaemenian Empire was necessary to prevent evil-inspired chaos, and that his brutal suppression of challenges to the legitimacy of his authority also were necessary because those revolts went against the need to reestablish and maintain *arta* (or order). Yet all the extant accounts of the events leading to his gaining power, including that of Herodotus, appear to be based on the royal palace's version, which Darius eventually had inscribed in Old Persian, Elamite, and Babylonian at Behistun. There is no independent corroboration of those events, let alone of the protagonists' motives. All who opposed his power were deemed irreligious and war against them became holy, according to Darius's explanation. Although Darius's version has long been accepted as canonical, recently the possibility has been suggested that the monarch at least shaped the narrative along Zoroastrian lines and at most concocted much of it to justify his usurpation of the throne.[47]

IMPLICATIONS FOR THE FAITH'S FOLLOWERS

In Zoroastrianism, physical force and warfare essentially became a socioreligious notion, theoretically, although not always successfully, directed at protecting Zoroastrianism and its adherents against political and sectarian domination. Fighting words served as guidelines and parameters for human action against evil. Less often in the history of Zoroastrian societies has war been utilized ideologically and practically as a means of spreading the faith. Zoroastrians usually have viewed themselves not as proselytizers combating infidels but as allies of god defending righteous order while doing as little harm as possible and working with, rather than against, established regimes. So when utilized by devotees of the faith, forceful actions were not regarded as violence but as essential and lawful tasks done in accordance with god's will. Yet when directed against the faithful, similar acts were labeled as violence instigated by and unlawfully conducted on behalf of the devil.

This situation is especially so at present when, as religious minorities in Iran, India, Pakistan, and now Western nations such as the United States and England, adherents of Zoroastrianism attempt to maintain a low religious profile so as not to attract proselytization and persecution from members of other sects. They support their governments and fellow citizens, believing that they cannot "turn the other cheek . . . [that] active opposition to evil is a religious duty . . . [and that] allowing evil to flourish when one can stop it is to take the side of Ahriman and is therefore opposing the good."[48] They feel compelled by their religion's scriptures and exegeses to act as model yet vigilant citizens and never as terrorists. Ultimately, Zoroastrians in the present, like their ancestors, see themselves as holy warriors working for order in the corporeal world, with violence and war being justifiable actions when necessary to purge and purify society.

NOTES

1. For an overview of Zoroastrians, their beliefs, practices, and history, see Jamsheed K. Choksy, "Zoroastrianism," in *Encyclopedia of Religion*, 2nd ed., ed. Lindsay Jones (New York: Macmillan, 2005), 14:9988–10008.

2. Roshan Rivetna, "The Zarathushti World: A Demographic Picture," *FEZANA Journal* 17, no. 4 (2004): 22–83.

3. On these technical terms, see further Christian Bartholomae, *Altiranisches Wörterbuch* (1904; Berlin: Walter de Gruyter, 1979), 229–38, 778–81, 1008, 1513–14; Roland G. Kent, *Old Persian: Grammar, Texts, Lexicon*, 2nd ed. (1953; New Haven: American Oriental Society, 1982), 171, 192; Henrik S. Nyberg, *A Manual of Pahlavi* (Wiesbaden: Otto Harrassowitz, 1974), 2:30, 77, 86, 119, 169, 211, 228; and David N. MacKenzie, *A Concise Pahlavi Dictionary*, 2nd ed. (London: Oxford University Press, 1986), 11, 27, 33, 38, 52, 71, 92, 98.

4. A detailed description is provided in Jamsheed K. Choksy, *Purity and Pollution in Zoroastrianism: Triumph over Evil* (Austin: University of Texas Press, 1989), 128–30.

5. Jamaspji M. Jamasp-Asana and Edward W. West, ed., *Shikand-Gumanik Vijar* (Bombay: Government Central Book Depot, 1887), 200–202.

6. Mary Boyce, *Zoroastrians: The Religious Beliefs and Practices* (London: Routledge and Kegan Paul, 1979), 27–29; and Choksy, *Purity and Pollution in Zoroastrianism*, 130–31.

7. Tahmuras D. Anklesaria, ed., *The Bundahishn* (Bombay: British India Press, 1908), 220–28; and Behramgore T. Anklesaria, ed., *Zand-i Vohuman Yasn and Two Pahlavi Fragments* (Bombay: K. L. Bhargava, 1957), 73–82.

8. Karl F. Geldner, ed., *Avesta: The Sacred Books of the Parsis*, 3 vols. (1886–95; Delhi: Parimal Publications, 1982), 1:108, 110, 116, 117, 125, 132, 164, 170, 182.

9. Ibid., 1:175, 183.

10. Anklesaria, *The Bundahishn*, 38–39.

11. See Jamsheed K. Choksy, "Iranian Apocalypticism and Eschatology: Grappling with Change," *Journal of the K. R. Cama Oriental Institute* 70 (2010): 9–40, for full references to scholarly views on this matter. See also Philippe Gignoux, "L'apocalyptique iranienne est-elle vraiment la source d'autres apocalypses?," *Acta Antiqua Academiae Scientiarum Hungaricae* 31 (1985–88): 67–78; and idem, "Nouveaux regards sur l'apocalyptique iranienne," *Comptes rendus de l'Académie des inscriptions et belles-lettres* (1986): 334–46.

12. Geldner, *Avesta*, 1:105–107.

13. Ibid., 2:242.

14. Jivanji J. Modi, ed., *Jamaspi: Pahlavi, Pazend, and Persian Texts* (Bombay: Education Society, 1903), 75; Anklesaria, *The Bundahishn*, 218–27; Behramgore T. Anklesaria, ed., *Vichitakiha-i Zatsparam* (Bombay: Parsi Panchayat, 1964), 1:158; Anklesaria, *Zand-i Vohuman Yasn*, 17–38, 73–81.

15. Details of the Yashts are provided by Jamsheed K. Choksy and Firoze M. Kotwal, "Praise and Piety: Niyāyishns and Yashts in the History of Zoroastrian Praxis," *Bulletin of the School of Oriental and African Studies* 68 (2005): 215–52.

16. Geldner, *Avesta*, 2:84–87, 90.

17. Jamsheed K. Choksy, "Sacral Kingship in Sasanian Iran," *Bulletin of the Asia Institute*, new series, 2 (1988): 35–52; and idem, "A Sasanian Monarch, His Queen, Crown Prince, and Deities: The Coinage of Wahram II," *American Journal of Numismatics*, second series, 1 (1989): 117–35.

18. Geldner, *Avesta*, 2:125, 127, 133, 138, 140, 142, 147, 208–209.

19. Jamasp-Asana and West, *Shikand-Gumanik Vijar*, 50–63.

20. Geldner, *Avesta*, 1:106–107.

21. Choksy, *Purity and Pollution in Zoroastrianism*, 2–7, provides further details.

22. R. Reuben Levy, ed. and trans., *The Epic of Kings: Shah-Nama* (London: Routledge and Kegan Paul), 47–80, 99–151, 194–217.

23. See further Choksy, "Sacral Kingship in Sasanian Iran," 36–40.

24. Levy, *Epic of Kings*, 61, 108, 205, 217.

25. *The Letter of Tansar,* trans. Mary Boyce (Rome: Istituto Italiano per il Medio ed Estremo Oriente, 1968), 33–34; Dhanjishah M. Madan, ed., *The Complete Text of the Pahlavi Dinkard,* 2 vols. (Bombay: Society for the Promotion of Researches into the Zoroastrian Religion, 1911), 1:47.

26. Kent, *Old Persian,* 117–18, 121–22, 125.

27. Ibid., 129. On the issue of religiously sanctioned torture, see also Bruce Lincoln, *Religion, Empire, and Torture* (Chicago: University of Chicago Press, 2007), 17–49.

28. Kent, *Old Persian,* 151.

29. Edalji K. Antia, ed., *Karnamak-i Artakhshir Papakan* (Bombay: Fort Printing Press, 1900), 40.

30. See also Lisbeth S. Fried, "Cyrus the Messiah? The Historical Background to Isaiah 45:1," *Harvard Theological Review* 94, no. 4 (2002): 373–79.

31. James B. Pritchard, ed., *Ancient Near Eastern Texts Relating to the Old Testament* (1969; Princeton: Princeton University Press, 1992), 315–16; *New Oxford Annotated Bible with the Apocryphal and Deuterocanonical Books,* New Revised Standard Version, 3rd ed. (New York: Oxford University Press, 2001), 1040.

32. Kent, *Old Persian,* 139.

33. Jamshedji M. Unvala, *The Pahlavi Text "King Husrav and His Boy"* (Paris: Paul Geuthner, 1921), 12–15.

34. Anklesaria, *The Bundahishn,* 274–77; Madan, *Complete Text of the Pahlavi Dinkard,* 1:412. On the descriptions of Alexander in Zoroastrian documents, see further Robert C. Zaehner, *The Dawn and Twilight of Zoroastrianism* (London: Weidenfeld and Nicolson, 1961; reprint New York: Phoenix Press, 2002), 175–76; and Mary Boyce, *A History of Zoroastrianism* (Leiden: Brill, 1991), 3:14–17.

35. Herodotus, *History,* ed. Alfred D. Godley, Loeb Classical Library 117–20 (1920–25; Cambridge, MA: Harvard University Press, 1981), 3:324–27, 347–49.

36. Jamsheed K. Choksy, "Zoroastrianism," in *Encyclopedia of Religion and War* (New York: Routledge, 2004), 470–76.

37. Michael Back, ed., *Die sassanidischen Staatsinschriften,* Acta Iranica 18 (Leiden: Brill, 1978), 289–314, 328–30.

38. Richard N. Frye, *The History of Ancient Iran* (Munich: C. H. Beck, 1984), 309–12.

39. Ahmad b. Yahya al-Balādhurī, *Futūh al-buldān,* ed. Michael J. de Goeje (Leiden: Brill, 1866), 263; Abu Ja'far Muhammad b. Jarīr al-Tabarī et al., ed., *Ta'rīkh al-rusul wa 'l-mulūk,* ed. de Goeje and others, 15 vols. (Leiden: Brill, 1879–1901), series 1, 2440–41. On these passages, see further Jamsheed K. Choksy, *Conflict and Cooperation: Zoroastrian Subalterns and Muslim Elites in Medieval Iranian Society* (New York: Columbia University Press, 1997), 57, 158–59.

40. Anklesaria, *Zand-i Vohuman Yasn,* 3, 16.

41. See Richard N. Frye, *The Golden Age of Persia: Arabs in the East* (1975; London: Weidenfeld and Nicolson, 1988), 128–29, 134–35, 140, where additional references are provided.

42. Alan Williams, ed., *The Zoroastrian Myth of Migration from Iran and Settlement in the Indian Diaspora: Text, Translation and Analysis of the 16th Century Qesse-ye Sanjan 'The Story of Sanjan'* (Leiden: Brill, 2009), 285, 291, 298, 353, 355, 362.

43. John R. Hinnells, "War and Medicine in Zoroastrianism," in *Zoroastrian and Parsi Studies: Selected Works of John R. Hinnells* (Aldershot: Ashgate, 2000), 288–89, 294, n. 56.

44. Ibid., 278, 289.

45. Ibid., 289–91; Jamsheed K. Choksy, "Parsis," in *Encyclopedia of Religion,* 10:6997–7001.

46. This debate about textual interpretation can be seen in the writings of two leading researchers

on Zoroastrianism in the twentieth century: Zaehner, *Dawn and Twilight of Zoroastrianism,* 84–90, who advocates the notion that Zarathushtra opposed animal sacrifice; and Mary Boyce, *A History of Zoroastrianism,* 2nd ed. (Leiden: Brill, 1989), 1:214–16, who, because Zoroastrians did continue to make animal sacrifices into premodern times, rejects any suggestion of Zarathushtra having condemned animal sacrifice.

47. Darius's manipulation of fact and faith to suit his own political ambitions has been discussed most plausibly by Richard N. Frye, "Darius the Liar and Shapur the Heritor," in *The Spirit of Wisdom: Essays in Memory of Ahmad Tafazzoli,* ed. Touraj Daryaee and Mahmoud Omidsalar (Costa Mesa: Mazda Publishers, 2004), 77–82.

48. Hinnells, "War and Medicine," 294–95, 300.

8

The Failure of Allegory

Notes on Textual Violence and the Bhagavad Gita

Laurie L. Patton

In late November 1992, I visited the Gandhi Memorial in bustling Delhi. Eight days later I traveled to the remote city of Nanded, in the Indian state of Maharashtra, for ethnographic research. At the Gandhi memorial, the Gita was regularly cited by tour guides and was even part of a makeshift display on the techniques of nonviolence that Gandhi used. The verses displayed were from the second half of the second chapter of the Gita, verses about attaining inner peace and self control, which Gandhi (d. 1948) felt were the core of the Gita's message. Later that week in Nanded, the same verses were quoted by a Hindu businessman who was about to go on a *yatra,* or pilgrimage, to protest the mosque that had been built over the Ram temple several centuries earlier in the northern city of Ayodhya. "Gandhi went to jail, and so will I," he said after finishing his Gita recitation. The next week, members of that pilgrimage of protest broke through police ranks and violently destroyed the mosque, sparking riots all over India. In a word, Gandhi's allegorical interpretation of the text, and his related teaching that the Gita's essential teaching was nonviolent, had failed. His Gita interpretation did not serve as a reminder to the Hindu businessman that, for Gandhi, collective restraint was more important than collective violence.

How could this Hindu text be cited in such radically different ways in the same week? Such diversity of interpretation is scarcely new; in the same century, an activist caught with two copies of the Gita on his person in colonial Bengal was immediately arrested as a threat to the state. Later that same century, American students in my classroom know vaguely that the Gita is related to nonviolence, but are frequently not even aware that its setting is that of war. I will discuss the

Gita's particularly diverse legacy later on. But such diversity does, I believe, take on a particular patina in the current Hindu worlds, which are both postcolonial and global, as well as steeped in a legacy of debates about whether to be violent or nonviolent. In such a world, allegorical interpretations such as Gandhi's usually have a particular aim in addressing a particular historical moment.

Here, however, I will argue that no matter how temporarily effective they are as nonviolent strategies, such allegories, if understood as the final meaning of a text, tend to fail. They fail because no allegory can make sense of the plurality of meanings in a single sacred text. Relatedly, thinking through my cognitive dissonance in 1992, this chapter is an attempt to make a new sense, or perhaps create a new sensibility, in the interpretation of sacred texts with explicitly violent content in Hinduism. The sensibility would move beyond allegory into an ethical interpretive dynamism around the question of necessary force.

The issue of violent content in texts is of concern in any religious tradition, and has been addressed by feminists (most famously Phyllis Trible)[1] as well as recent theorists of conflict and religion (including Scott Appleby, David Smock, and Marc Gopin).[2] Many of the concerns about violence and the sacred have to do with the justification of contemporary violence through recourse to a violent passage in a sacred text. But there is another focus that some scholars have, particularly in the case of the Gita and other early Indian texts: the denial of violence in the sacred text through the interpretive strategies of allegorization or spiritualization of explicitly violent passages. In early India, this concern tends to focus on questions of sacrificial violence, but it is relevant in any number of interpretive situations, as Jan Houben, in particular, argues.[3]

How might we study such patterns? As a beginning of an answer, I have elsewhere suggested ways in which we might read violent narratives from early India *as narratives,* in addition to understanding them solely as philological or philosophical "examples" of the *ahimsa,* or noninjury, principle or as contradictions to such a principle through valorization of injury *(himsa).*[4] This approach to violent narratives would allow for a complex and subtle understanding of how violence is understood not just on its own, but *within* the construction of the narratives. Such an analysis would include how narratives of violence deal with such issues as emplotment, character, empathy, and performance, just to name a few. In addition, as Val Daniels and Gyan Pandey have written in very different ways, an interpreter would attend to the unspoken residue, the lacunae, in narratives of violence where trauma cannot be spoken.[5] Then we read the "violence" of the Mahabharata or the sacrificial deaths in the Brahmanas as something far more human, as episodes in the history of a particular character or a particular social dilemma, episodes with deep literary structure. I hope more work like this can be done so that such earlier Indian texts can be understood with their full literary complexity and subtlety in play.

There is one text that has indeed been subject to an intense and complex treatment like the one I describe above—the Bhagavad Gita. It is a text explicitly about war in that, on the eve of a great battle to win back his patrimony, the Pandava brother Arjuna questions the validity of going into battle against the Kauravas, who are his cousins, uncles, and teachers. His charioteer, Krishna, exhorts him to fight, to engage in the *dharmic,* or moral, action of a warrior without clinging to the fruits such actions may or may not bring. He teaches Arjuna a series of lessons about the nature of yoga, or self-discipline in action; the nature of renunciation, or nonaction; and the material nature of the universe (the three qualities of *sattva,* or truth; *rajas,* or passion; and *tamas,* or heavy darkness). Later, at Arjuna's request, Krishna reveals himself as God. Arjuna sees the wisdom of Krishna's teachings, particularly about action without clinging, and resolves to fight.

The Gita is a colonial text par excellence in that, in the early twentieth century, it was heralded as the equivalent to the Bible in the Western world, and in that it has been translated more than any other work and now has a global circulation in English. In addition, the approaches to the text have indeed swung in both violent and nonviolent directions in the twenty-first century: Yes, say some, such as G. B. Tilak, the text is a justification of violence and should be used and understood as such. No, say others, such as Besant, Judge, and Gandhi, the text is not about physical violence but spiritual warfare between the two aspects of the self.

The history of this interpretation of the Gita has been well documented, and it is not my purpose to rehearse that history in detail here. Rather, I would like to look at one particular approach—the strategy of allegory. Allegory can be defined loosely as any nonliteral interpretation, and in that sense almost all interpretations of the Gita are allegorical in nature. However, allegory can also be defined more strictly as an extended metaphorical approach that involves the use of figures and symbols "standing for" particular qualities, or even lessons. In the case of the Gita, we frequently encounter such approaches, including the spiritualization of a violent text to create another meaning. After reviewing these strategies, I argue that they inevitably fail to create a sense of coherent alternative meaning to the text because of the inherent plurality of its teachings. I then suggest an alternative hermeneutic that moves away from Indian philosophical approaches and is grounded instead in Indian aesthetic theory.

THE PLURALISM OF THE GITA:
NONLITERAL AND ALLEGORICAL APPROACHES

The pluralism of interpretive approaches to the Gita has had a long and illustrious history. While space prevents a long discourse on the various meanings that commentators have seen in the Gita,[6] it is worth going into some detail here. The varying emphases of the Gita—especially on the three themes of *karma* (action), *jñana* (knowledge), and *bhakti* (devotion)—make it extremely challenging for there to be a single "secret" or "single message" of the Gita that a commentator can unlock. In its pluralism of paths, *bhakti marga* (the path of devotion), *jñana marga* (the path of knowledge), and *karma marga* (the path of action) all compete for the commentators' attention. Indeed, one Indian commentator, T. G. Mainkar, in his comparative study of commentators has written that "no single commentator has been absolutely faithful to the Gita."[7] Many smaller commentaries probably existed and were read before the ninth century, such as those of Vrittikara and Bodhayana. According to most scholarly assessments, these commentators seemed to have emphasized the pluralism of the text and not privileged one aspect of its teachings over another. Such a situation makes nonliteral, or even fully allegorical, interpretations (to be defined and discussed below) an intriguing challenge.

However, the best-known commentators do privilege a singular meaning to the text, and attempt to subordinate certain verses to other verses. As we shall see below, this approach necessarily entails nonliteral interpretations, since not all verses can be taken at face value. Thus, commentators' exegesis of explicitly violent passages, where Arjuna exhorts Krishna to fight, differ accordingly to the perceived "singular meaning" of the text.

Some Nonliteral Examples

Perhaps the most famous commentary is that of the philosopher Shankara, born in the late eighth century.[8] Even those who disagree with Shankara still tend to see him as the standard.[9] His work on the Gita was one of the cornerstones of his Advaita, or "nondual," philosophy, which understood all phenomena in the world as subordinate to the one, universal animating principle of Brahman. He argued that the main point of the great dialogue between Arjuna and Krishna was *jñana marga,* or the path of knowledge, and the giving up of action. He focused particularly on 4.33:

> Son of Pritha,
> all action
> is fully contained
> in knowledge:
> the sacrifice of knowledge
> is better than
> the sacrifice of worldly things;
> Scorcher of the Enemy.[10]

What knowledge was so precious and all-encompassing for this philosopher? Shankara saw the true object of all of our knowledge as Brahman, the eternal force animating the world. For Shankara, even the attributes of Krishna, so beautifully discussed and explained in chapters 10 and 11, are illusory compared with the single, all-consuming reality of Brahman and the identification of the single *Atman,* or self, with the energy of Brahman that unified all things.

Through the teachings of the Gita, the individual soul can realize liberation only through its abandonment of *avidya,* or ignorance, and its identification and unification with the real self, or Brahman. All else is cognitive illusion, or *maya.* Shankara's interpretation spawned a school of strict nondualist interpreters, some of whom were invited to the Mughal court of Akbar (r. 1560–1606) to share their views.

Shankara's view was such that any verses that did not engage with questions of knowledge as such would be subordinated to other verses that did. We see this explicitly in what some might call a "violent" passage, where Krishna exhorts Arjuna to fight. Krishna has just explained the immutability of the self *(atman)* and has further commented that, if Arjuna dies, he goes to heaven, and if he does not die, he attains glory here on earth. Krishna goes on:

> If you are killed,
> you shall reach heaven;
> or if you triumph,
> you shall enjoy the earth;
> so stand up,
> Son of Kunti,
> firm in your resolve
> to fight!
> When you have made
> pleasure and pain the same—
> also gain and loss,
> and victory and defeat,
> then join yourself
> to battle;
> and in this way,
> you will not cause harm.
>
> (2.37–38)

Shankara dubs this discussion *"laukika nyaya,"* or worldly advice that leads to, but does not directly engage, the larger teaching of Brahman. Indeed, he sees Krishna's words as "incidental" *(prasangika)* to the real teaching about the self that should be the main meaning of the Gita. Krishna uses this worldly teaching to dispel Arjuna's grief and illusion. The exhortation to battle here is a device to help Arjuna get over his despair and be open to the path of knowledge.

Other Gita commentators disagreed with Shankara's view of God and the universe, and felt that God's qualities should be understood as real. A school of philosophy sprang up in sharp disagreement with Shankara's idea that all except Brahman is illusory. These were called Vishishtadvaita philosophers, or "qualified nondualist" thinkers. Although such thinkers emerge as early as the tenth century, the best-known was Ramanuja,[11] who lived about two centuries later than Shankara. He argued that the Gita's teachings were exactly the opposite of what Shankara had supposed, and that the path of devotion rather than of knowledge was most important. In Ramanuja's view, Shankara's focus on the doctrine of nondualism and the path of knowledge did not allow for the path of devotion and the ways in which a supreme deity, such as Vishnu, could be understood as part of reality.

For Ramanuja, *bhakti yoga,* or the path of devotion, was the real force behind the teachings of the Gita, particularly chapters 12 and 18. Ramanuja focused on chapter 12 as the major contribution of the Gita, where God's attributes in all of their splendors are put forward. Krishna shows his "true form" to Arjuna, and this manifestation is a kind of transformative reality for Arjuna. Ramanuja particularly saw the later chapters of the Gita as crucial to this central meaning:

> Son of Bharata,
> go, with your whole being,
> to that One alone,
> and from that grace,
> you will reach
> the eternal
> dwelling place.
> (18.32)

Ramanuja's school of thought did in fact thrive through other commentarial writers until the seventeenth century.

Ramanuja too shows the ways in which *atman* is real, but also acknowledges that Krishna is real and devotion to Krishna a legitimate, indeed supreme, path. For Ramanuja, Krishna's exhortation to Arjuna in verses 2.37–38, discussed above, is not a way of dispelling fear, as Shankara argues, but a way of arguing that the *atman* is real. (Shankara would agree with Ramanuja of course on the point that the *atman* is real, but he did not choose these particular verses to illustrate it.) In commenting on this verse, Ramanuja mentions the idea of a sacrificial victim earning a better, more beautiful body by being killed. Thus the sacrifice is not *himsa,* or violence, but rather like a physician using a thorn to further his larger goal of healing. So, too, Ramanuja argues, is the reality of *atman,* which is such that the self who is injured will still continue on a path of liberation even if it is injured or injures others in this war. Arjuna's violence will move beyond the literal in that it is like a cosmic physician's violence, not the violence of human upon human.

Yet a third school of philosophy, Dvaita (dual), also found a crucial text in the Gita. Its main proponent, Shri Madhva,[12] was born in the late twelfth century. Madhva argued that one should maintain a strict dualism, or distinction, between

God and the world. This distinction made it possible to argue that both the path
of knowledge and the path of devotion were central to the Gita, and that one should
not be put above the other. The relationship between the Lord and the created
world is not one of absolute reality and pure illusion, but rather more like the
relationship between a man who does not need a stick to walk, but uses one play-
fully anyway. Following this idea, one of the central verses for this school was this
verse from chapter 9:

> Borne up by my own
> material nature,
> again and again
> I send out,
> by the power
> of material nature,
> this whole collection of beings
> which is, in itself, powerless.
>
> (9.8)

Like Ramanuja's school, Madhva's commentators regularly looked to the Gita as
a central text throughout the seventeenth century. In their view, when commenting
on verses 2.37–38 and others like them, the *himsa*, or violence necessary for Arjuna,
is part of the reality of the world, the stick that one must use to walk.

Allegorical Approaches

Finally, the Kashmiri Shaivite school of mystical interpretation develops what
might be called a fully allegorical approach to the Gita. The larger frame of the
approach is to make a kind of rapprochement between the paths of knowledge,
action, and devotion, or *jñana, karma,* and *bhakti.* For Abhinavagupta, the great
Kashmiri poet, philosopher, and mystical thinker of the early eleventh century,
jñana is flanked by *karma,* also called *vijñana.*[13] Actions are modified and transformed by knowledge, so that they are eventually no longer necessary. As Abhinavagupta put it, "actions flee before knowledge of Brahman like gazelles in the
jungle when the lion roars." Abhinavagupta found a verse from chapter 6 particularly apt in this regard:

> The follower
> of Yoga
> who resorts to Me
> as one who abides
> in all beings,
> abiding in oneness
> existing in all ways,
> that one dwells in Me.
>
> (6.31)

Even as God remains nondual, its opposite, *maya* (illusion), is not negative, as Shankara implied, but is also the free play of consciousness.

More importantly, he understands the entire Kaurava and Pandava war as the battle between ignorance and knowledge, and the related dualism of body and spirit, passion and equanimity. The Kauravas stand for ignorance and the Pandavas stand for knowledge. Arjuna's battle is thus to be read as a battle for knowledge, resulting in the free play of consciousness mentioned above. Thus, every verse, including 2.37–38, is interpreted in light of this extended metaphor. One must have energy to engage in this larger spiritual process whereby ignorance is eliminated.[14]

THE GITA IN ENCOUNTER WITH THE WEST: THE BLOSSOMING OF ALLEGORY

The Singular Message

We know that Muslim rulers of India knew of the Mahabharata, and by extension the Gita, as an important text from as early as the tenth century, and that it remained somewhat in courtly consciousness throughout Mughal rule. However, the British colonial environment and the rise of the East India Company provided a whole new stage for the emergence of the Gita as a transcultural text.[15] In 1782, a merchant in the company, Charles Wilkins, received permission from Warren Hastings to continue to study Sanskrit in the Hindu city of Varanasi, and in 1785 the Gita made its first appearance in the European context.[16] Hastings felt that advocacy for Hindu learning could help business, and it "was part of a system he had for reconciling the people of England to the natives of Hindustan."[17] Already, with this view in mind, we can see a colonial context for understanding a single "transcendent" meaning for the Gita.

Later, in the 1820s the Hindu reformer Rammohun Roy had used the Gita, and its precepts of selfless action, to argue against *sati,* the practice of widow immolation, in Bengal. In Roy's view, *sati* was a rite performed with a view toward the reward of heaven, and the Gita, a text much more authoritative than the legal texts that many pandits relied on to justify the practice, would teach against the idea of action with regard for the fruits.[18] In using the Gita to argue against *sati* as a form of violence that subordinated means to ends, Rammohun Roy laid the groundwork in colonial discourse for the idea that the text contains an essential moral teaching.

With one or two exceptions such as that of Rammohun Roy, for the next century, debate about the Gita was conducted almost entirely in the West and on Western terms, particularly concerning its relationship to Christian teaching and doctrine. Here too we see the continuing focus on a single meaning to the text. Herder began to introduce the idea of India as the source of all wisdom. August Wilhelm von

Schlegel took on the mantle of the first European Professor of Sanskrit in 1818, and in 1825 published a translation of the Gita into Latin. A year later, Wilhelm von Humboldt published a German lecture on the Gita, in which he was attracted to the idea of *dharma,* or sacred duty, as analogous to the philosophical idea of the categorical imperative of Immanuel Kant, a kind of innate moral sensibility in the midst of devotion to Krishna. The Gita contained a Hindu version of the single, and singular, categorical imperative.

Humboldt's view of the Gita as "the deepest and most elevated [text] the world has to offer" was shared by the Transcendentalists in America.[19] For Emerson (who seemed to understand it mistakenly as a Buddhist text), it comprised the "essence of human intuition, and the first of books."[20] He read Wilkins's translation in 1845, and was inspired by the French philosopher Cousin's attempt to place it in the context of world philosophy. The Gita may well have inspired Emerson's concept of the "Oversoul." Thoreau's reading of the Gita was slightly later than Emerson, and focused on the difference between "Occidental" and "Eastern" thought, an unfortunate dichotomy that, while perhaps useful in Thoreau's time, is singularly unhelpful in today's complex intellectual landscape. Thoreau focused on the Western need for the practice of detachment, what I have rendered in this translation as "nonclinging."

The conversation about the Gita between missionaries, administrators, and Indians in India, while slow to start, also became focused on its singular meaning.[21] Many felt that the Gita had uses in India, and that a discovery of its meaning would help the larger colonial project. The well-known English Sanskritist Ralph T. H. Griffith had "painful feelings" about what he and other writers interpreted erroneously as the Gita's indifference to the world.[22] Griffith saw in the discipline of yoga a great deal of insight into the ebb and flow of desire and the human attempts to eradicate desire. But ultimately, he felt that the correspondence between the Gita and Christian teaching was best used as a way of helping Hindus to convert. At the same time, for the German translator Eugene Burnouf, the Gita was the very essence of brahminical philosophy and a "sure-footed entry into the knowledge of India."[23]

At this point, until the great Krishna renaissance of the 1880s the Gita was now able to be compared with other texts and have some of its origins speculated upon. Many European Indologists, such as the well-known Max Mueller, felt that the Gita should be understood as lesser literature than the prestigious Vedas, which provided "the" key to all Indian and indeed all Indo-European civilization.[24]

But perhaps the writer who did the most to promote the Gita as a wisdom text and place it squarely into the center of later theosophical thinking was Sir Edwin Arnold. His "Song Celestial," a versified, paraphrased rendering of the Gita from Sir John Davies's translation, reflected Arnold's liberal Christian understanding.[25] In his view, the great Eastern traditions were not sufficient without Christianity, but could nonetheless stand in their own right as works of spiritual depth. While scholars such as Mueller understood the Gita as a lesser moment in Indological history, the liberal theologians best represented by Arnold understood it as timeless transcendental philosophy.

From Singular Message to Allegory

In the 1880s, with printing presses in industrial cities producing translations in German, French, English, and Latin, the Gita was as accessible to the average European as it was to the average Hindu, if not more so. But by the 1890s, a great change occurred. The Gita emerged in India as a national symbol, newly accessible beyond the pandits, or Hindu religious experts. It had become the main text of a newly literate class. The agents for this change were the Indian National Congress and the Theosophists. And in the midst of this conversation, allegorical understandings of the Gita blossomed fully. In intellectual centers in India, particularly Bengal and Maharashtra, there emerged two major intellectual currents that placed the Gita at the forefront: the idea of India as a motherland and the central idea behind the Krishna renaissance that Krishna was an *avatar,* or incarnation, of Vishnu who came to earth to reestablish the law of *dharma,* or righteous conduct, in the land. And the British policies of government made it clear that the colonizers were not acting according to *dharma.*

Bankim Chandra Chatterji (1836–94) was the great inspiration for the nationalist movement, whereby the concept of the goddess as Mother India was fully developed.[26] He composed an unfinished commentary on the Gita, and understood it as the defining text of the Hindu religion. The Gita stood in marked contrast to the earlier Vedas, and any other revealed composition controlled by a religious elite. In addition, the Hindu god Krishna was the ideal man who exemplified human virtues, a god who was both earthly wise and eternal. Bankim Chandra's writings were the beginning of India's spiritual answer to the West; the Gita could be part of India's answer to technological domination and missionizing zeal of colonialism. It could be read as an allegory that asserted the ancient wisdom of India in the face of contemporary oppression.

The Theosophists continued to develop this idea of the Gita as "essential Hinduism," proof of India's spiritual superiority to the West and therefore its need for independence. Theosophists began to arrive in India by 1879, and actively began to produce translations by Indians such as Subba Rao and M. M. Chatterjee.[27] One theosophical thinker, William Judge, produced a translation in 1890 in which he firmly stated that the text of the Gita was read by Theosophists all over the world.[28]

In what was to become a dominant interpretation for many, the theosophical tradition of interpretation understood the Gita as an allegory for the spiritual struggle of humanity. The leader of the Theosophists, Annie Besant, understood Arjuna as a model for the "mind unfolding"; she saw his opposing family, the

Kauravas, as the lower desires of man, the passion against which we all battle. The Gita was "the universal philosophy" of humankind.[29] Indeed, for the Theosophists, its universality necessitated its allegorization.

Intriguingly, the Theosophists joined hands during this period with Bal Gangadhar Tilak (1856–1920), a journalist from the Western Indian state of Maharashtra. Tilak refused service in the Indian government and turned to a life of writing about the value of Indian culture and the necessity of violent resistance to an oppressive British rule. Together, Besant and Tilak formed the All-India Home Rule League. While Tilak was incarcerated in Burma, he continued to study Sanskrit and wrote his commentary on the Gita, *Gitarahasya*. In Tilak's view, Arjuna must perform the *dharma* of his *varna*, or station in life, which is to fight. Arjuna is initially an unenlightened warrior who might fight, but would do so for the wrong reasons. Arjuna is only the instrument for his opponent's becoming a victim of their own *karma*. So, too, must resisters to the colonial regime function in the same way in relation to the British.[30] Here, too, the interpretation is allegorical and in many ways follows in the footsteps of Bankim Chatterji: the Gita can be read as an allegory for the just war that historical circumstances call on Indians to fight, as well as for the just warrior.

A social reformer better-known to the West, Swami Vivekananda (1863–1902), also gave lectures on the Gita to Western audiences as his fame grew as a "translator" of Hinduism in America and Europe. When he spoke to these audiences, Vivekananda compared Jesus to Krishna as emanations of the universal deity. When he spoke to Indian audiences, he was more allegorical, emphasizing a reading of Krishna and Arjuna as "men of action" who could stand as embodiments of the energy and insight needed to reform Hindu society and resist British oppression. In his discussion of the historicity of the Gita, Vivekananda is explicitly allegorical about the role of the "inner battle" that the text must represent:

> Now to the third point, bearing on the subject of the Kurukshetra War, no special evidence in support of it can be adduced. But there is no doubt that there was a war fought between the Kurus and the Panchâlas. Another thing: how could there be so much discussion about Jnâna, Bhakti, and Yoga on the battle-field, where the huge army stood in battle array ready to fight, just waiting for the last signal? And was any shorthand writer present there to note down every word spoken between Krishna and Arjuna, in the din and turmoil of the battle-field? According to some, this Kurukshetra War is only an allegory. When we sum up its esoteric significance, it means the war which is constantly going on within man between the tendencies of good and evil. This meaning, too, may not be irrational.[31]

History, then, is immaterial given the Gita's larger allegorical meaning. In a later passage, Vivekananda goes on to acknowledge the validity of historical research, even though it cannot help with the acquisition of *dharma,* or moral righteousness: "One thing should be especially remembered here, that there is no connection between these historical researches and our real aim, which is the knowledge that leads to the acquirement of Dharma. Even if the historicity of the whole thing is proved to be absolutely false today, it will not in the least be any loss to us. Then what is the use of so much historical research, you may ask. It has its use, because we have to get at the truth; it will not do for us to remain bound by wrong ideas born of ignorance."[32] Vivekananda thus opens the way for an interpretive tradition that sees the Gita as an allegory, but that allows also for the possibility of historical research on the Mahabharata war. However, Vivekananda is quick to remark that the spiritual significance of historical research is immaterial to those who seek truth. As he puts it, even if everything were to be proven a fabrication, the text would be no less important.

This dynamic of history vs. allegory was the major one for M. K. Gandhi, arguably the most important interpreter of the Gita in the twentieth century. Gandhi was introduced to the text via the West, more specifically, and not surprisingly, the Theosophical Society in London. Gandhi did not see himself as a textual interpreter, but a man of moral action whose goal was to take the Gita's principles to heart. He called the Gita his "spiritual dictionary," and used it to give political and spiritual advice as well as perfect the state of his own soul.

In 1925, Gandhi published an article in which he summarized his view of the Gita. In his view, the Mahabharata epic should not be read as a historical text, but rather as a large allegorical teaching in which forces of good and evil battle against each other. Gandhi also understood the events of the Gita as a pyrrhic victory, an object lesson about when the cost of the war is too great.[33] The Gita's centrality in this hopelessly violent epic means all the more that the Gita is a teaching about nonviolence, not violence. With Aurobindo,[34] Gandhi too resisted Tilak's more militaristic (but no less allegorical) interpretation that the right *dharma* was to fight the British with force.[35]

For Gandhi, this nonviolent essence of the Gita was contained in the last twenty stanzas of the second chapter, which describe a person who has achieved control over his inner self. Cold and hot, desire and hatred, even gold and dung are the same to that equanimous person. He or she exists in a heightened state of mental balance, and does not cling to anything. For Gandhi, the rest of the Gita was a commentary on this passage, which was in his view "the essence of dharma."[36] Yet even more importantly, Gandhi argued that, while other sacred scriptures might also teach this view, the Gita contained a method by which this truth force could be achieved.

Such a person could embody *satyagraha,* the force of truth, and act so nonviolently in the world. For Gandhi, renunciation, or *sannyasa,* was far more a key to the Gita than knowledge or devotion. The person who has achieved the most self-control is also the person who is most devoted and has the most knowledge. Selflessness and renunciation are intrinsically connected with nonviolence, or the renunciation of violence. How could such a text clearly about war and violence be understood as nonviolent? The work of the poet and the nature of the poetry are in the answer. The poetry of the Gita changed the meaning of sacrifice, so that it means not an offering into a fire but the service of others. Thus, as Ramana Murthi notes, "even if the literal meaning of the text could reconcile violence with selflessness, his own experience of living out its teaching led him to conclude that perfect renunciation is impossible without perfect observance of *ahimsa* in every shape and form."[37] The oneness of humanity dictated the principle of *ahimsa*.[38] Gandhi's statement on the Gita's violence goes as follows:

> I do not believe that the Gita teaches violence for doing good. It is pre-eminently a description of the duel that goes on in our own hearts. The divine author has used an historical incident for including the lesson of doing one's own duty even at the peril of one's life. It inculcates performance of duty irrespective of the consequences; for, we mortals, limited by our physical frames, are incapable of controlling actions save our own. I do not agree that the Gita advocates and teaches violence in any part of it. See the concluding discourse at the end of Chapter Two. Although that chapter lends itself to a violent interpretation, the concluding verses seem to me to preclude any such interpretation. The fact is that a literal interpretation of the Gita lands one in a sea of contradictions. "The letter killeth, the spirit giveth life."[39]

As Ramana Murthi puts it, Gandhi and Gandhians argue that, if it is difficult to reconcile the spirit of certain Gita verses with nonviolence, it is even more difficult to see it in the entire frame of violence. Instead of teaching the rules of warfare, it teaches how a perfect man is to be known.[40]

Many scholars have recently discussed Gandhi's approach to the Gita. Ramana Murthi is the first to focus on the centrality of the Gita to Gandhi's political technique. Agarwal has shown the ways in which Gandhi's Gita interpretation focused on social action, particularly *lokasamgraha*, or the holding together of the world. J. T. F. Jordens has focused on the methods by which Gandhi differed from traditional pandits, making the self-control of chapter 2 the basis of the meaning of the texts. Robinson focuses on the images of the Hindu tradition such a view of the Gita espouses.

Most importantly for our purposes, almost all of these scholars describe, but do not necessarily emphasize, Gandhi's struggle with the question of a *singular* meaning to the text. Let us turn to that central passage again: Following Vivekananda and the Theosophists, Gandhi moves away even more strongly than his predecessors from a literal interpretation of the Gita. The Gita must represent a duel in our own hearts. What is more, a literal interpretation "lands us in sea of contradictions," because of the two possible meanings present in chapter 2, one part of which advocates violence and the other of which advocates transcendence and self-control. Gandhi's use of the Gita for personal reflection as well as moral and political guidance reflects the social uses of the Gita during this late colonial period. From the establishment of the Gita Press in the early twentieth century in Gorakpur, the Gita became a staple in many different walks of life. For example, during one period of resistance to colonial rule, anyone with more than one copy of the Gita in his possession was considered a terrorist against the state. And in another quite opposite vein, in 1927, the Gita Press began producing "Gita Diaries" in which the verses of the text were divided over the whole year, and daily meditation on its wisdom was possible.

Note, then, that in contrast to Vivekananda, for Gandhi the idea of the Gita as a vehicle—an allegory for the struggle of the soul—*precludes* historical meaning altogether. There can only be one meaning, and that must be the meaning that creates the most "consistent" message in the text. And for Gandhi, the nonviolent meaning replaces the violent meaning.

BEYOND ALLEGORY: TOWARD A DYNAMIC INTERPRETATION OF THE EXHORTATION TO FIGHT

Gandhi's allegorical interpretation was clearly geared for a particular political moment, one that involved the intertwining of Western and Indian ideologies. The British would understand his motives and the Indians would understand his version of *satyagraha*. And perhaps it is no surprise that allegory worked in his case. As Gordon Teskey and Lidia Yuknavitch have shown, in the history of the Western tradition allegory can be integrally bound up with ideology, and even violence in its own right, insofar as it wrests a singular meaning out of a text that has multiple ones.[41] Teskey also notes how allegory has been used in Western modernity for didactic purposes, and even explicitly political ones.

In addition, as Sayre Greenfield argues, allegory is always untidy in that there is a residue (if not a large reservoir) of meaning that cannot be taken up by an allegorical interpretation.[42] In the case of an allegorical interpretation of violent texts such as Gandhi's, then, one might say that one does interpretive violence to the textual violence, in that one wrests nonviolent meanings out of a text. But even nonviolent allegory will fail because it cannot fully account for the entirety of the text.

But there is also an Indian source for the singularity of allegorical moves. This debate about a singular interpretation of the Gita, and its related question about violence, also mirrors the question of *siddham*, or final meaning, in philosophical discourse. The scholastic use of *iti siddham* in philosophical and scientific commentaries generally means "thus it is proven" or "thus it is established." In its earlier usages, the term can mean "accomplished, fulfilled, effected, gained, acquired," or "one who has attained his object, successful," or even "one who has attained the highest object, thoroughly skilled or versed in." According to the grammarian Panini, it can mean "valid" (as a rule in grammar), and in philosophical usages, it means "admitted to be true or right, established, settled, proved."

In commentaries on authoritative texts like the Gita, the phrase usually occurs after a long debate with an imagined opponent, called a *purvapakshin,* who raises a series of objections to the philosophical position being put forward, each of which are refuted in turn. Thus every commentary proceeds as a staged conversation between the *purvapakshin,* who upholds the contrary question, and the *siddhantin,* the upholder of the final word or established opinion. As Gary Tubb puts it, "sometimes the *siddhanta* is stated first, only to be attacked by the *purvpakshin* and defended in the ensuing debate. In longer arguments the *siddhanta* may be confronted with a series of questions."[43] At times there are even several *purvapakshins* at once, who represent several different positions.[44] And there is a set of Sanskrit dialogical conventions (such as the words *nanu* and *atha* for the objector and responder) that signal who is speaking in each part of the debate.

While many commentators in English might not explicitly use this Sanskritic convention, its shadow is still present. There is still a strong sense in the twentieth-century debate about the Gita's violence that there can be only one meaning to the text, that there must be a *siddhanta.* Even taking together those who have debated the question of violence in the Gita—thinkers such as Tilak, Aurobindo, Gandhi, Bhave, and Radhakrishnan—there is still an understanding of a single meaning. While there may be a multiplicity of voices debating multiple ideas about the text, each thinker argues for a particular position about *the* overall significance of the text. Even those who criticize Gandhi's view of the text as "nonviolent" write about his denial of the violent aspects, thus implying that the *real meaning* of the text is a justification of violence.[45] As mentioned above, this perspective is present even in scholarly approaches to texts with violent content, where the only hermeneutical possibilities must be that the violence is denied or justified.

Violence and the denial thereof seem to swing on an exegetical pendulum. Violence and nonviolence cannot be held together in the same approach. And it leaves the exegete with a commitment to nonviolence only two options: either reject the text with explicitly violent content or allegorize it away into a deeper meaning of the struggle of the soul.

In what follows I would like to suggest that there is a third approach to Indian texts with clearly violent content such as the Gita: hold both the violent and the nonviolent meanings together in a single, tension-filled interpretation that does not argue for one "real" meaning over the other. This exegetic approach is culled not from Indian philosophy, with the idea of an established, resolved meaning at the end of a debate. Rather, it derives from the basics of Indian aesthetics, in which what is compared and what is comparand are held together in tension with each other.

I have written elsewhere that, even in the earliest poetics, there is a dynamic aspect to early Indian theories of simile and metaphor.[46] As Edwin Gerow states beautifully, "It may well be the Veda, understood as Veda, as self existent utterance (mantra) . . . that created *kavya* by serving as its model.[47] The *rishi*s are also *kavi* poets. And as such, they show "self conscious organization of language whose delineation and rationalization constitute the matter of later poetic traditions." By definition, Gerow concludes, the first poetics is implicit in the first poetry.[48] To take a simple and well-known example, many Vedic interpreters have pointed out that the Vedic poets clearly understood that fire, *agni,* meant both the physical element and a divine agent. The same is true of substances such as Soma, the hallucinogenic plant that provided inspiration to the poets.

These are important observations, but as Gerow also acknowledges, this does not make a full-blown poetics. We do know, however, that a general theory of comparison existed before either of these writers, poet or theorist, composed their works.[49] There are terms that suggest links with poetics in Yaska's *Nirukta.* Yaska (*Nirukta* 3.13) discusses an idea about *upama* or simile, which is attributed to Gargya: *upamāyad atat tat sadrśam,* "Not that, but like that." The grammarian Panini (*Asthadhyayi* 2.1.55.6; 2.3.72; 3.1.10) also uses the four elements of comparison: the subject of comparison *(upameya* or *upamita);* the thing with which it is compared *(upamana);* the property of similarity *(samanya,* or *samanadharma);* and the grammatical indicator of comparison *(samanyavacana* or *dyotaka).*[50]

Gerow sees in these basic ideas not a full-blown poetics, but a general rhetorical and exegetical status that these terms could have had in both poetry and *shastra* (legal texts). Yaska and Panini are concerned with the semantic properties of language here. Yaska is focused on whether the subject of comparison *(upameya)* is greater or less than its comparand *(upamana).* Panini needs these terms to explain grammatical constructions that create similarities, such as compounds, suffixes, and so on. In both cases, however, there is a sense of simultaneity of meaning and the necessity of focusing on *both* meanings in the comparison, whether explicit or implied. And many suggest that comparison can take place at the level of the word, the sentence, or even the chapter.

Before moving to a small case study of Gita verses, it is worth noting that much of contemporary metaphor theory also proffers a definition of metaphor that focuses on holding together the tension between elements in the comparison and reducing the meaning of neither. One thinks of Max Black and Paul Ricoeur in this regard, but there are many others.[51] And of course, the Western philosophical and literary interpretive tradition is of great use in a number of different textual traditions, not just Western ones. However, it is important to look at theories roughly contemporary to the Gita because such theories suggest *how a tradition might have interpreted itself.* Certainly, Panini and Bharata would have known some form of the Mahabharata epic, and probably some form of the Bhagavad Gita, and are far closer to the immediate cultural significance of the text than we are.

What if we applied these techniques to the exegetical process of texts like the Gita? We might apply them to particular words denoting violence, and we might

THE FAILURE OF ALLEGORY   193

also apply them more generally to the possibility of two different interpretations at once. And in each case, the act of interpretation would neither deny violence nor glorify it. Rather, the interpretive act that saw the work as violent would at one and the same time remember that the exhortation could also be an exhortation to an inner spiritual battle. Conversely, the interpretation of the Gita as describing an inner spiritual battle would also remember that the verse could also be a simple exhortation to violence, even if dharmically committed.

Let us conduct this experiment with a verse from the last twenty verses of the Gita, the ones that Gandhi was insistent contained the meaning of the Gita. We conduct this with the early Indian aesthetic admonition to keep the *upamana* (the subject, in this case, violent content) and the *upameya* (the comparand, in this case, the nonviolent meaning) both in mind. Turning again to 2.37, this verse seems very much like an exhortation to violence. Indeed, Gandhi himself admits that this verse and the verses around it are easily lent to a violent interpretation when he argues that the later verses of chapter 2, focusing on equanimity and self-control, cancel the violent aspects of these earlier verses out. But, a reader like Gandhi could, in this situation, understand even this verse as a spiritual battle, in which the question of being killed by someone else is more important than that of the harm done to one's person, and in which one remains resolved to fight *because one is fighting nonviolently*. This interpretation is indeed essentially Gandhi's reading of this verse and verses like these.

However, in the dynamic reading style inspired by basic Indian poetics I suggest above, one would be constantly aware of the *other* tendency even as one chose a particular interpretation. Thus, one would be resolved to fight violently, but would be aware that in that violence there is the shadow of equanimity, of being firm in resolve not to harm even if one has chosen to harm. The next choice in the fight might well be the one that does not lash out against another person. And, conversely, if one took the idea of being "firm in resolve to fight" to mean "to fight nonviolently," one would be forever aware that one's capacity for violence was just at the edge of one's resolve, waiting to erupt if one was not vigilant.

So, too, could one conduct one's reading in the same way for explicitly nonviolent verses, the ones that Gandhi admired so deeply, such as 2.64:

> One not joined
> to passion and hatred,
> always moving
> in the spheres of the senses
> by the senses,
> the one who thus
> restrains the Self,
> and who governs the Self,
> attains peace.

This verse is explicitly about self-control, and could be an argument for the Gita really being about nonviolence, about canceling out the violence, as Gandhi thought.

However, in a dynamic reading, one could say that the violence remains quite close to the surface in the first two lines, always ready to fall into passion and hatred. In addition, one can read it as an exhortation to dharmic violence, in which the fight that Arjuna conducts is a real fight, but one that is self-controlled and disciplined, as any warrior should be. Indeed, in the midst of actual war such inner peace would be most essential for the warrior. And yet, in reading it this way, one might also remember that the result of such self-control could lead to the cessation of violence altogether in certain circumstances.

Read in this way, one can engage many possible meanings of the Gita within the clear boundaries of the verse. However, a reader would not be obsessed with the "real" meaning, nor would she be trapped by the literal meaning or the spiritual meaning, or any other possible meaning in between. In fact, in this mode of reading one works with the assumption that violent interpretations can still imply nonviolent possibilities, and that nonviolent possibilities can imply violent ones.

CONCLUDING THOUGHTS: TAKING ADVANTAGE
OF THE SPACE BETWEEN DELHI AND NANDED

We return, then, to the larger question of textual violence and explicitly violent passages. I have argued several points: (1) the Gita interpretive tradition is radically plural, and has had a variety of opinions about its "essential" meaning, whether it be *karma, bhakti,* or *brahman;* (2) there has been a tendency for each author to assign a single meaning to the text in debates and subordinate some verses to other verses, resulting in a nonliteral interpretation; (3) the nineteenth- and twentieth-century debates about violent passages of the Gita and the overall nature of the text tended to focus on an extended nonliteral meaning, and developed frequently into full-blown allegorization; (4) the possibility of moving beyond allegory and interpreting violent passages in a dynamic, aesthetic way has been underutilized; and (5) using such an aesthetic approach actually results in a way of reading that does not reduce violence to nonviolence or nonviolence to violence.

In addition to these points, I would end by remarking that both those in charge of the Gandhi Memorial and the Nanded businessman whose words and actions began this article have something in common. They understood the Gita as a complex text with a simple meaning. But my argument here is that there are real benefits to making the Gita understood as a complex text with a complex meaning. If the Gita is in part an invitation to deliberation, then interpreting textual violence becomes part of the thought process of public debate, not simply a "sacred slogan" to call upon in any case. To create such complexity in the public sphere puts questions of violence and nonviolence on a very different footing indeed. This approach moves us beyond simple, or even complex, allegory. Gandhi may have needed the allegory to accomplish what he did. But perhaps we now need a new hermeneutic to address India's radically different situation sixty years after independence.

This question of admitting complexity in a text depicting war like the Gita is especially difficult when it comes to postcolonial religion such as Hinduism. First, like all postcolonial religions, Hinduism is caught up with the doubleness of what it means to be defined by a colonial power as well as by members of its own religious elite. Second, even self-definition has not always emerged from a position of political strength; it has also resulted from a position of reactivity or a defensive posture that "Hindu texts are as good as or even better than" the colonizing religion. Third, in the postcolonial contemporary world, Hindu texts are still confronted with a problem of representation, in that they are not the "given" religion of a twenty-first century globalizing culture, but rather the "marked" tradition that needs to be explained because of its exoticism or strangeness.

Given this explanatory burden, when Hindu texts contain violent passages (to no more or less degree than any other religion), it is more likely that they will be understood as intrinsically violent, or at the very least as "primitive" because of that violence. Even if one admits the clear ethic of nonviolence that is part of the Indic intellectual traditions of Brahmanical, Buddhist, and Jain traditions, the interpretive challenge is no less difficult. In these cases, episodes of violence tend to be understood as "contradictions" to a "peaceful" tradition rather than as simply part of the complexity of any religious tradition, which inevitably will contain both nonviolent and violent passages.

In other words, in the globalizing but still Western discourse, Hinduism remains "marked" as a religion that must explain itself, and as one whose violent passages cannot be accepted simply as part of its complex identity (as such passages frequently are in Judaism and Christianity) but rather will be frequently indexed to its identity as an "exotic" and "primitive" tradition. A nonallegorical dynamic approach to texts like the Gita in the public sphere would go a long way to closing this exegetical gap. And perhaps the twenty-first century exegetes, versions of the attendants at the Gandhi Memorial as well as the business citizens of Nanded, would participate in that public sphere in entirely new ways.

NOTES

1. Phyllis Trible, *Texts of Terror: Literary Feminist Readings of Biblical Narratives* (Chicago: Fortress Press, 1984).

2. R. Scott Appleby, *The Ambivalence of the Sacred: Religion, Violence, and Reconciliation* (Lanham, MD: Rowan and Littlefield, 2000); Marc Gopin, *Between Eden and Armageddon: The Future of World Religions, Violence, and Peacemaking* (New York: Oxford University Press, 2000); idem, *Holy War, Holy Peace: How Religion Can Bring Peace to the Middle East* (New York: Oxford University

Press, 2002); idem, *To Make the Earth Whole: The Art of Citizen Diplomacy in an Age of Religious Militancy* (Lanham, MD: Rowan and Littlefield, 2009); David Smock, *Interreligious Dialogue and Peacebuilding* (Washington: United States Institute of Peace Press, 2002).

3. Jan Houben and Karel R. Van Kooij, eds., *Violence Denied: Violence, Non Violence, and the Rationalization of Violence in South Asian Cultural History* (Leiden: Brill, 1999).

4. Laurie Patton, "Telling Stories about Harm: An Overview of Himsa in Early Indian Narratives," in *Religion and Violence in South Asia: Theory and Practice* (New York: Routledge, 2007), 10–38.

5. Val Daniel, *Fluid Signs: Being a Person the Tamil Way* (Berkeley: University of California Press, 1987), 151–52; Gyanendra Pandey, *Remembering Partition: Violence, Nationalism, and History in India* (Cambridge: Cambridge University Press, 2001), 177–182; idem, "In Defense of the Fragment: Writing about Hindu-Muslim Riots in India Today," in *Subaltern Studies Reader, 1986–1995,* ed. Ranajit Guha (Minneapolis: University of Minneapolis Press, 1997), 1–33.

6. For general works in this area, see T. G. Mainkar, *A Comparative Study of the Commentaries on the Bhagavadgita* (Delhi: Motilal Banarsidass, 1969); Robert Minor, *Bhagavadgita: An Exegetical Commentary* (Delhi: Motilal Banarsidass, 1982); Arvind Sharma, *The Hindu Gita: Ancient and Classical Interpretations of the Bhagavadgita* (London: Duckworth, 1986). *Bhagavad Gita: Bhashya and Tatparyanirnaya,* trans. and notes Nagesh D. Sonde (Bombay: Vasantik Prakashan, 1995); Vasudeva Laxman Shastri Panshikar, ed., *Sankaracarya Bhagavadgitabhasya,*Vrajajivan Pracya Bharati Granthamala Series 64 (Delhi: Caukhamba Samskrta Pratisthana, 1992). This includes Shankara's main commentary on the Bhagavad Gita and also the following commentaries: Sankarabhashya with Anandagiri, Nilakanthi, Bhasyotkarshadipika of Dhanapati, Sridhari, Gitarthasangraha of Abhinavagupta, and Gudharthadipika of Madhusudana with Gudharthatatvaloka of Sridharmadattasarma (Bachchasarma).

7. Mainkar, *A Comparative Study of the Commentaries,* 65.

8. Kashinath and V. G. Apte, eds. *Srimadbhagavadgita: Anandagiri-kritatikasamvalita-Shankarabhashya-samaveta* (Bombay: Anandrashrama Press, 1936). One English translation to consult is Alladi Mahadeva Sastry, *The Bhagavadgita: With the Commentary of Shri Shankaracarya* (Madras: V. Ramaswamy Sastrulu and Sons, 1961). See the discussion in Winand Callewaert and Shilanand Hemraj, *Bhagavadgitanuvada: A Study in Transcultural Translation* (Ranchi: Satya Bharata Publications, 1982), 89ff.

9. The most famous of these disagreements is that of Bhaskara, a possible near contemporary of Shankara. His argues that Shankara's views do not acknowledge that Brahman's energies, *shakti,* consist of a real world in itself, and are real modifications of Brahman. See Krishnamurti Sarma, "Bhaskara—A Forgotten Commentator on the Gita," *Indian Historical Quarterly* 9 (September 1933): 663–77; also V. Raghavan, "Bhaskara's Gitabhashya," *Wiener Zeitschrift für die Kunde Süd- und Ostasiens, und Archiv für indische philosophie* 12–13 (1968–69): 281–94. See also discussion in Minor, *Bhagavadgita: An Exegetical Commentary,* xvii.

10. All citations are from my recent translation, *The Bhagavad Gita* (Harmondsworth, UK: Penguin, 2008).

11. For an English translation, see J. A. B. Van Buitenen, *Ramanuja on the Bhagavadgita: A Condensed Reading of the Gitabhashya with Copious Notes and Introduction* (Delhi: Motilal Banarsidass, 1968). Also see *The Gitabhashya of Ramanuja,* trans. M. R. Sampatkumaran (Madras: Prof. M. Rangacharya Memorial Trust: M. C. Krishnan, Vidya Press, 1969). See discussion in Callewaert and Hemraj, *Bhagavadgitanuvada,* 90ff.

12. Madhva, *Gitabhashyam,* 1st ed. (Bengaluru: Purnaprajnavidyapitham, 1981). Another important Gita commentator from South India worthy of mention is Vedantadeshika, for whom space does not permit a detailed analysis here.

13. Abhinavagupta, *Gitarthasangraha,* trans. with an introductory study by Arvind Sharma (Leiden: Brill, 1983). Also see *Abhinavagupta's Commentary on the Bhagavad Gita: Gitarthasangraha,* trans. from Sanskrit with introduction and notes by Boris Marjanovlc (Varanasi: Indica Books, 2002).

14. Despite all of these high-level arguments about the relative importance of action, knowledge, and devotion, the Gita did not remain confined to the Sanskrit elite tradition. The tradition of writing about the Gita in Marathi began in the fifteenth century, and traditions in Bengali, Tamil, Kannada, Punjabi, Telugu, and other regional languages are probably also several centuries old.

15. Among the many helpful general works on this topic, see Eric J. Sharpe, *The Universal Gita* (London: Open Court, 1985); Robert Minor, ed., *Modern Indian Interpreters of the Bhagavadgita* (New York: SUNY Press, 1986); P. M.Thomas, *Twentieth-Century Interpretations of the BHAGAVADGITA: Tilak, Gandhi and Aurobindo* (Bangalore: Christian Institute for the Study of Religion and Society, 1987).

16. Hastings's investment in the translation was strong, and he saw in it "a performance of great originality, of a sublimity of conception, reasoning and diction almost unequaled." Cited in Sharpe, *The Universal Gita,* 8. See Charles Wilkins, *The Bhagavad Geeta* (Bombay: Subodha Prashka Press, 1885), 19ff., for a longer portrait and discussion of Hastings's patronage of Wilkins, as well as Sharpe, *The Universal Gita,* 3–11.

17. Ibid., 8. Also see Mersey, *The Viceroys and Governors General of India* (London: Murray Press, 1949), 18ff.

18. See Rammohun Roy, *Translation of Several Principal Books, Passages, and Texts of the Veda, and of Some Controversial Works on Brahminical Theology,* 2nd ed. (London: Parbury, Allen, 1832), 215ff. Also cited in Sharpe, *The Universal Gita,* 12.

19. Rudolf Haym, *Wilhelm von Humboldt: Lebensbild und Charakteristik* (Berlin: R. Gaertner, 1856), 580ff. Also see Marianne Cowen, *Humanist without Portfolio* (New York: Wayne State University Press, 1963).

20. Cited in Christy, *The Orient and American Transcendentalism,* 23, and Sharpe, *The Universal Gita,* 24. See also Brookes Atkinson, ed., *The Selected Writings of Ralph Waldo Emerson* (New York: Modern Library, 1950) for Emerson's firsthand responses to the Gita.

21. In 1849, there was a publication of a Sanskrit, Canarese, and English Gita, but even during the mid-nineteenth century the Gita was not yet a truly popular text.

22. See J. Garrett, ed., *The Bhagavat-Geeta, or dialogues of Krishna and Arjoon; in eighteen lectures. Sanscrit, Canarese, and English: in parallel columns* (Bangalore: Wesleyan Mission Press, 1849). See also R. D. Griffith, "An Essay on the *Bhagavat Geeta,*" in Garrett, *The Bhagavat-Geeta,* xxxvii–lvii. See discussion in Sharpe, *Universal Gita,* 35.

23. Emil-Louis Burnouf, *La Bhagavadgita ou le chant du bienheureux: poème indien* (Paris: Duprat, 1861). The Gita was also gaining ground in other parts of Europe; Abbe Paraud's French translation appeared in 1847 before Burnouf's Gita appeared in 1861. It was preceded by a Sanskrit grammar in 1859 and followed by a dictionary in 1863.

24. Under Mueller's chief editorship of the Sacred Books of the East series, however, there emerged an edition of the Gita edited by Kashinak Tribak Telang; see K. T. Telang, *The Bhagavadgita* in the *Sacred Books of the East Series,* vol. 8. (Oxford: Oxford University Press, 1882). Telang's thought was that the Gita, along with the Upanishads, made up the pre-Buddhist matrix in which Buddhism flourished. This view reflected the general opinion that the Gita was originally some sort of Upanishad that was inserted into the Mahabharata epic.

25. Edwin Arnold, *The Song Celestial* (Boston: Roberts Brothers, 1885).

26. See Ajit Ray, "Bankim Chandra Chatterji's New Hinduism and the *Bhagavad Gita,*" in Minor, *Modern Indian Interpreters,* 11–34.

27. Subba Rao, *The Bhagavadgita: Translation and Commentaries in English According to Shri Madhvacarya's Bhashya* (Madras: Minerva Press, 1905).

28. William Judge, *The Bhagavad-Gita: The Book of Devotion,* 4th ed. (Los Angeles: Theosophy Co., 1928), xvii. Also see the discussion in Sharpe, *The Universal Gita,* 103–7.

29. Annie Besant, *Hints on the Study of the Bhagavad Gita* (Benares: Theosophical Publishing Society, 1906), 1–12.

30. B. G. Tilak, *Gitarahasya*, trans. B. S. Sukthanker (Bombay: Bombay Vaibhav Press, 1935). See also Robert Stevenson, "Tilak and the *Bhagavagita*'s Doctrine of Karma Yoga," in Minor, *Modern Indian Interpreters*, 44–61; and Pratap Agarwal, *The Social Role of the Gita* (Delhi: Motilal Banarsidass, 1983), 89–137.

31. Swami Vivekananda, *The Complete Works of Swami Vivekananda* (Calcutta: Advaita Ashrama, 1951), 1:446–80; also see Harold French, "Swami Vivekananda's Use of the *Bhagavadgita*," in Minor, *Modern Indian Interpreters,* 131–47.

32. French, "Swami Vivekananda's Use of the *Bhagavadgita.*"

33. Satyagraha, leaflet no. 18, in *Collected Works of Mahatma Gandhi* (Amehdabad: Navajivan, n.d.), 15:288; see also "Discourses on the Gita" (*Collected Works*, 32:94), "The Gita According to Gandhi" (*Collected Works*, 41:90), and "Letters on the Gita" (*Collected Works*, 49:111). The best-known work is perhaps Gandhi, *Gita: The Mother,* ed. Jag Pravesh Chander, 4th ed. (Lahore: India Publishing Works, 1946).

34. Another journalist, Aurobindo Ghose (1872–1950), also began with an extreme version of resistance to British rule. After a year in prison for conspiracy charges, Aurobindo underwent a spiritual transformation and moved to Pondicherry to start an *ashram*, or spiritual retreat, and teach a new, holistic form of Yoga called "Integral Yoga." In this stage of his life, he wrote *Essays on the Gita*, in which he taught the opposite of Tilak's more militant argument. For Aurobindo, the Gita did not simply teach *dharma* with the good of the nation at heart. Rather, the Gita taught devotion *(bhakti)* and knowledge *(jñana)* as a form of practical discipline, or practical Yoga. The three steps of action, devotion, and knowledge form a unified synthesis against which any single verse must be interpreted. See Sri Aurobindo, *Essays on the Gita, XIII* in *Birth Centenary Library* (Pondicherry: Sri Aurobindo Ashram, 1970). See Minor, "Sri Aurobindo as a Gita Yogin," in Minor, *Modern Indian Interpreters*, 61–88; and Agarwal, *The Social Role of the Gita,* 137–87.

35. Mahadev Desai, *The Gospel of Selfless Action or the Gita According to Gandhi* (Ahmedabad: Navajivan Publishing House, 1946). See discussions in Agarwal, *The Social Role of the Gita,* 187–260; J. T. F. Jordens, "Gandhi and the *Bhagavadgita*," in Minor, *Modern Indian Interpreters,* 88–110; and Sharpe, *The Universal Gita,* 103–23.

36. M. K. Gandhi, *The Teaching of the Bhagavad Gita* (1925; Mumbai: n.p. 1971), 9.

37. Ibid., 133–34.

38. Catherine A. Robinson, *Interpretation of the Bhagavad Gita and Images of the Hindu Tradition: The Song of the Lord* (New York: Routledge, 2005), 63.

39. Gandhi, *Teaching of the Bhagavad Gita,* 129.

40. V. Ramana Murthi, *Non-Violence in Politics: A Study of Gandhian Techniques and Thinking* (Delhi: Frank Bros., 1958), 139–42.

41. Gordon Teskey, *Allegory and Violence* (Ithaca: Cornell University Press, 1996), xi–xii; Lidia Yuknavitch, *Allegories of Violence: Tracing the Writings of War in Late Twentieth-Century Fiction* (New York: Routledge, 2001).

42. Sayre Greenfield, *The Ends of Allegory* (Cranbury: Associated University Presses, 1998), 66–85.

43. Gary Tubb and Emery Robert Boose, *Scholastic Sanskrit: A Handbook* (New York: Tibet House and Columbia University Press, 2007), 240–41.

44. Ibid., 199, 219, 220.

45. For an intriguing recent departure from this debate, see Rochona Majumdar and Dipesh Chakravarty, "Gandhi's Gita and Politics as Such," *Modern Intellectual History 7* (2010): 335–53. The Gita, in Gandhi's hand, became a talismanic device that allowed the *satyagrahi* his or her involvement in political action while providing protection from the necessary and unavoidable venality of politics and its propensity to violence.

46. Laurie Patton, "Reading Rishis Across Difference: Notes on the Study of Metaphor in Early India," *Journal of Hindu Studies* 1, no. 2 (2008): 46–79.

47. Edwin Gerow, *Indian Poetics* (Wiesbaden: Harrasowitz, 1977), 21.

48. Also see Louis Renou, *Etudes védiques et paninéennes* (Paris: Publications de L'Institut de Civilisation Indien, 1955), 1:26–27; 9:15–16; Jan Gonda, *Vedic Literature* (Leiden: Otto Harrasowitz, 1975), 71, 74.

49. E.g., "Bhamaha (fl. c. 680) . . . [was] a Buddhist writer whose *Kavyalamkara* systematically discusses poetic embellishments. His work lays stress on subject-matter and form (ornateness) to the neglect of the 'soul' of poetry. He is regarded as one of the chief founders of the alamkara school." Benjamin Walker, "Poetics," in *Hindu World* (New York: Prager, 1968), 2:220. See Gerow, *Indian Poetics.*

50. Gerow, *Indian Poetics,* 221–22.

51. Paul Ricoeur, *The Rule of Metaphor: The Creation of Meaning in Language,* trans. Robert Czerny with Kathleen McLaughlin and John Costello (New York: Routledge, 2003); Max Black, "How Metaphors Work: A Reply to Donald Davidson," in *On Metaphor,* ed. Sheldon Sacks (Chicago: University of Chicago Press, 1979), 18–92.

9

Words as Weapons

Theory and Practice of a Righteous War
(Dharam Yudh) in Sikh Texts

Pashaura Singh

The last two decades of the twentieth century witnessed a popular representation of Sikhs in the Indian media as bloodthirsty avengers rather than as bloodied victims. The principal reason for this stereotype was the rise of Sikh nationalism in the early 1980s. Akali Dal (army of the immortal), the main political party of the Sikhs in the Punjab, was demanding increased autonomy for all the states of India. During that period, relations with the Indian government became increasingly strained as a result. In an apparent attempt to sow dissension in the ranks of the Akali Dal, the Congress government encouraged the rise of a charismatic young militant named Sant Jarnail Singh Bhindranwale (1947–84), a "homespun village preacher who called for repentance and action in defense of the faith."[1] But this strategy backfired in the spring of 1984, when a group of armed radicals led by Bhindranwale decided to provoke a confrontation with the government by occupying the Akal Takhat (throne of the immortal) building inside the Golden Temple complex in Amritsar. The government responded by sending in the army. The assault that followed—code-named "Operation Blue Star"—resulted in the deaths of many Sikhs, including Bhindranwale, as well as the destruction of the Akal Takhat and severe damage to the Golden Temple itself. A few months later, on October 31, 1984, Prime Minister Indira Gandhi was assassinated by her own Sikh bodyguards. For several days unchecked Hindu mobs in Delhi and elsewhere killed thousands of Sikhs. As a consequence of these events, 1984 became a turning point in the history of modern Sikhism, precipitating an identity crisis within the Sikh Panth (community) and perpetuating "the image of a bearded, turban-wearing Sikh male with sword as a negative icon symbolizing religious violence and separatism."² The following decade saw the Sikh religious rebellion marked by bloody encounters between militant Sikhs and the armed forces of the secular state of India.³

Recent research has made us aware of two divergent views on the place of religious violence in the Sikh tradition. The first view is based on the framework of the "early pacifism versus later militancy" discourse that has dominated in the popular writings on Sikhism. It draws attention to the apparent contradiction between the *interior* devotion of early Nanak-panth (followers of Guru Nanak's path) and the militant signature of the Khalsa tradition. For instance, Khushwant Singh's history of the Sikhs contains a chapter titled "From the Pacifist Sikh to the Militant Khalsa."⁴ Following the Orientalist paradigm, such works ignore the contextual depth and misrepresent the process of evolution by focusing too much on the apparent contradiction between religion and politics in the Sikh tradition. The second view has emerged more recently in the writings of Balbinder Singh Bhogal and Navdeep Mandair, who claim that canonical sources reveal a more startling view of warfare as a phenomenon that is profoundly excessive to any rationalization.⁵ In particular, the central theme of the three goddess compositions in the Dasam Granth is focused on unrelentingly gruesome battles against demons, with the poet delighting in sketching images of shining swords and other weapons flashing as warriors wield them against their enemies, the sounds of swords and arrows whizzing through the air, the shrieks and cries of warriors, and gaping wounds, severed body parts, and flowing rivers of blood. However, the killing of demons that occurs in these battles is auspicious, even to be celebrated, for it represents a triumph of the forces of good and allows good people to live well.⁶ Navdeep Mandair points out the savage excesses of the goddess *(Chandi/Durga)* who delights in conflict and carnage, expressing a horrid pleasure when she laughs mightily amid the bloody wreckage of battle. For him, it is the gleeful accent of this onslaught that renders it excessive, a violence that exceeds the measures that are strictly necessary to restore order and righteousness *(dharam)*, and that are therefore regulated by the capricious tempo of divine play *(lila)*.⁷ Accordingly, Sikh religious violence must be understood by taking into account its profoundly gratuitous nature, an intensity that is not irrational but incommensurate with a rationale. These are the two extreme positions based upon doctrinal readings of textual sources.

The present study offers a measured assessment of canonical sources and follows a genealogical mode of reading by employing multiple voices to relativize all the voices so that no single voice becomes dominant. It will examine the connection, both actual and perceived, between Sikh sacred sources and the justification of violent acts as divinely mandated. Recently, Dorn and Gucciardi have pointed out that Sikhs have yet to "build a theory for the justified use of armed forces and for military ethics more generally."[8] A key reason for the lack of a formal tradition of just war theorizing in Sikhism is that, as the world's youngest major religion, Sikhism has had to address the various doctrinal, philosophical, and cultural dilemmas and divergent approaches in a more compact time frame and within a context of persistent political turmoil. While many other world religions have had many centuries, even millennia, to work through various theological and ethical issues, Sikhism has only just begun to make its impact in both the scholarly field and the world of comparative religion and ethics.

The first and foremost category of canonical collection for addressing the issue of warfare is the Adi Granth, the sacred scripture of the Sikhs. It includes the works of the first five Sikh Gurus and the ninth, plus material by four bards (Satta, Balvand, Sundar, and Mardana), eleven Bhatts (court poets who composed and recited panegyrics in praise of the Gurus), and fifteen Bhagats (devotees of the Sant, Sufi, and Bhakti traditions, including the medieval poets Kabir, Namdev, Ravidas, and Shaikh Farid), a total of thirty-six contributors stretching historically from twelfth century to the seventeenth. It is normally referred to as the Guru Granth Sahib (Honorable Scripture Guru), and carries the same status and authority as the ten personal Gurus from Guru Nanak (1469–1539) through Guru Gobind Singh (1666–1708). Thus it provides the authoritative Sikh response to the issues related to the nature of conflict and its resolution, the place of violence and nonviolence in the tradition, and the idea of a just war when the very survival of *dharam* (righteousness) is at stake under the peril of tyranny. It should, however, be emphasized that each generation will have its own view of that authoritative understanding based on its particular interpretation of the text.

The second sacred collection, the Dasam Granth (Book of the Tenth Guru), is attributed to the tenth Guru, Gobind Singh. Its standard version offers four major types of compositions: devotional texts, autobiographical works, miscellaneous writings, and a collection of mythical narratives and popular anecdotes.

A third category of sacred literature consists of works by Bhai (Brother) Gurdas (c. 1558–1637) and Bhai Nand Lal Goya (1633–1715). Along with the sacred compositions of the Gurus, their works are approved in the official manual of the *Sikh Rahit Maryada* (Sikh Code of Conduct) for singing in the *gurdwara* (Guru's Door), the Sikh place of worship.

Three distinct genres make up the last category of Sikh literature. The *janam-sakhis* (birth narratives) are hagiographical accounts of Guru Nanak's life dating from the seventeenth century but based on earlier oral traditions. The *rahit-namas* (manuals of code of conduct) provide rare insight into the evolution of the Khalsa code in the course of the eighteenth and nineteenth centuries. And the *gur-bilas* (splendor of the Guru) literature of the eighteenth and nineteenth centuries praises the mighty deeds of the two great warrior Gurus, Hargobind and Gobind Singh in particular.

THE ADI GRANTH

In the context of early Indian narratives, it is assumed that "violence is always a problem in any literary representation—an event that resists narrativization even as it might be justified and incorporated into the text."[9] In the Adi Granth, however, "violence" is represented as an integral part of the human situation. The Punjabi term used for "violence" within specific poetic genres of the Adi Granth is *hansu* or *hinsa,* referring to "the infliction of injury" in the situation of conflict. Employing the metaphor of a burning river for human existence, Guru Nanak proclaims: "Violence, attachment, avarice, and wrath are the four rivers of fire. Falling into these, people get burnt, O Nanak; they can be saved only through the grace of loving devotion at the Master's feet."[10] In his spiritual vision, both good and evil exist in the divine plan. While appreciating the beauty and wonder of goodness in the world in the seventeenth stanza of his *Japu* (Recitation), Guru Nanak simultaneously admits the existence of evil and violence in the straightforward language of the following stanza: "Countless the fools, the thieves, the swindlers; countless those who rule by force. Countless are the cutthroats and violent murderers; countless those who live evil lives."[11] Again, violence is divinely sanctioned: "When it pleases You, some wield swords cutting off heads [of their enemies] as they move."[12] In the *Maru* hymn, Akal Purakh ("Timeless One," God) is represented as both violent and benevolent: "He himself kills and rejuvenates."[13] Not surprisingly, love and violence, pains and pleasures, good and evil, matter and spirit are intrinsic to the human condition.

During his invasions to secure northern India in the 1520s, the first Mughal emperor, Babur (1483–1530), achieved his final victory over Ibrahim Lodhi in 1526 on the field of Panipat. Most instructively, Guru Nanak commented upon the violence inflicted on innocent people in his four hymns, collectively known as *Babarvani* (Utterances concerning Babur).[14] In fact, these hymns provide an eyewitness account of Babur's invasion of India and throw considerable light on the devastation caused by his army. In *Asa Astapadi,* for instance, Guru Nanak offers the rationale that violent acts are divinely mandated because "those whom the Creator would destroy—He first strips them of virtue."[15] Nevertheless, he was pained to see the suffering of the innocent who had little to do with politics and war:

> You spared Khurasan but
>   yet spread fear in Hindustan.
> Creator, you did this, but to avoid the blame
>   you sent the Mughal as the messenger of death.
> Receiving such chastisement, the people cry out in agony
>   and yet no anguish touches you. (1)
> Creator, you belong to all.
> If the mighty destroy only one another,
>   one is not grieved. (1) (Refrain).

But if a mighty lion falls upon a herd of cattle,
  then the master is answerable.
The wretched dogs [Lodhis] have spoiled the priceless jewels;
  when they are dead no one will regard them.
You alone unite and you alone divide;
  thus is your glory manifested. (2)
If anyone assumes an exalted name
  and indulges always in whatever his mind desires;
He becomes as a worm in the sight of the Master,
  regardless of how much corn he pecks up.
Die (to self) and you shall truly live.
  Remember the Name, Nanak, and you shall receive a portion. (3)[16]

Evidently, the actual context of this hymn is the battlefield when Babur's army invaded India. Here, the principal theme is related to the question of why the weak and innocent should suffer unmerited torment at the hands of the strong, and in this respect this hymn has obvious affinities with the Book of Job. God is called into account, just as Job summons him. Guru Nanak makes it quite explicit that it was the Creator who sent Babur as the messenger of death to destroy the Lodhi Sultanate. With a firm belief in Akal Purakh's omnipotence, he provides a rationale for the normalization of violence as follows: "You alone unite and you alone divide; thus is your glory manifested." He thus stresses the absolute nature of divine will, order, and command *(hukam),* which is ultimately beyond human comprehension. A similar response appears in certain other *Babar-vani* verses: "To whom should we complain when the Creator himself acts and causes others to act? To whom should one go to lament when You yourself dispense suffering and happiness through your will?"[17] Here, Guru Nanak is looking at the violent historical events from a mystical perspective. Nevertheless, he underscores the point that if any mighty person attacks "the weak and unarmed" person, then it is a violation of an ethical norm of warfare.[18]

It should, however, be emphasized that Guru Nanak's response to war and suffering is not limited to his personal anguish. He is responding to an actual life situation with his profound inner experience. In tune with Akal Purakh, he reflects on the situation at hand from various perspectives. In this context, J.S. Grewal argues that there is a moral dimension which restrains Guru Nanak from an outright condemnation of either the conqueror or the conquered.[19] Balbinder Bhogal, on the other hand, underlines Guru Nanak's "powerlessness" and "blunt tone of abject resignation" in response to the devastation caused by Babur's army.[20] This was certainly not the case. A careful examination of the four hymns of the *Babur-vani* reveals a powerful critique of both the invaders and the rulers. For instance, Guru Nanak describes the Lodhis as "wretched dogs" for their moral failure to protect their sovereignty and the innocent (*ratan,* "jewels") people. They had acted in a manner contrary to the divine intention and were responsible for the ultimate overthrow of their dynasty. In the *Tilang* hymn, on the other hand, Guru Nanak refers to Babur's army as the "marriage-party of evil" *(pap ki janj),*[21] and thus charges them for their moral failure to forcibly demand a "dowry" *(dan)* from the suffering people.

Elsewhere, Guru Nanak holds the general public responsible for bringing about this retribution because they did not heed Akal Purakh. Indeed, the greater part of human suffering is caused by those people who freely choose to act against the divine will. In the case of the rape of women, for instance, Guru Nanak makes the following observation:

> The wealth and sensual beauty which intoxicated them
>> became their enemies.
> The messengers (of Death), under orders to persecute,
>> strip them of their honour and carry them off.
> Glory or punishment, either (one) we gather,
>> as God in his purpose declares.
> Had they paused to think in time,
>> then would they have received the punishment?
> But the rulers paid no heed,
>> passing their time instead in revelry;
> Now that Babur's authority has been established
>> the princes starve.[22]

Clearly, all the violence involved in war and rape was not wholly undeserved. It was caused by the senseless pursuit of worldly pleasures and by the rulers and the ruled alike not heeding Akal Purakh. Some other verses present a terrible portrait of women being raped by soldiers who do not bother to discriminate between the Hindus and Muslims who were in their path: "Some lost their five times of prayer, some the time of *puja.*"[23] Thus, Guru Nanak was deeply anguished over the horrible situation of women. He employed the Punjabi phrase "stripping of one's honor" to describe the rape of women by the Mughal army. In fact, rape is regarded as a violation of women's honor in the Punjabi culture. It amounts to the loss of family honor, which in turn becomes the loss of one's social standing in the community. The notion of family honor is intimately linked with the status of women in Punjabi society. For all his sympathy with the suffering people, however, Guru Nanak was fully cognizant of the situation of the poor women. Their agony, in fact, reminded him of a religious truth that "God's justice cannot be ignored, that the divine order *[hukam]* cannot be defied, that unrighteousness will be punished."[24] Those who have committed unpardonable crimes will certainly receive punishment in the future. Here we have a rationale for the normalization of violence from a moral dimension, a process that stresses both free-will and retributive themes. Nevertheless, these themes cohere into the higher purpose of divine will, order, and command *(hukam)*.

Guru Nanak thus admits the enormity of violence caused by Babur's army as part of Mughal invasions of India, but he renders it small from the perspective of a larger metaphysics. The *Janam-sakhi* narratives suggest that Guru Nanak witnessed the sacking of Saidpur by the Mughal armies, and they contain the story of his meeting with Babur. The invading emperor is told: "If you desire mercy [from God], release the prisoners." Babur then clothed the captives and set them free.[25] Finally, Guru Nanak made a proclamation that "they [Mughals] have come in seventy-eight and will go in ninety-seven and another disciple of a warrior will arise."[26] The usual exegesis of this statement refers to Babur's entry into India in *sambat* 1578 (1521–22 C.E.) and to Humayun's departure in *sambat* 1597 (1540 C.E.). The "disciple of a warrior" *(marad ka chela)* is said to refer to Sher Shah Sur, who defeated Humayun in 1540 C.E. and established his own rule.[27] Although this event followed Guru Nanak's death in 1539 C.E. (which is why W. H. McLeod regards the Guru's statement in the *Tilang* hymn as "an enigmatic" line),[28] it may be understood in the context of his prophetic statement.

In order to understand the dynamics of religious violence, we need to understand the human actors who participate in warfare or sporadic acts of violence from time to time. One must comprehend the motivation of those warriors who fight in the battlefield, resulting in the shedding of blood in violent encounters. They may be inspired by the religious ideals of their faith. One may die fighting for "heroic values," and his death may be constructed as the ideal of a martyrdom. Let us examine the Sikh understanding of a "true hero" in the Adi Granth. The notion of the "hero" who fights for righteousness and for a "heroic death" may be traced back to the works of Guru Nanak and his successors. There are a number of references to the lifestyle of "true heroes" *(sura, sur, vir,* or *surbir)* in the text that may point out how one lived heroically. In his *Ramakali* hymn, for instance, Guru Nanak addressed a Nath yogi *(audhu)* about his understanding of a "true hero":

> O *audhu,* one can become a [true] hero *[sur]* throughout the four ages
>> If one contemplates the divine Word *[shabad].*
> Thus one must contemplate the sacred utterances of the Guru
>> With deep devotion.[29]

Similarly, the third Guru, Amar Das (1479–1574), defined the "true hero" *(sura variamu)* as the one "who overcomes within [oneself] the enemy of self-centeredness."[30] The fifth Guru, Arjun (1563–1606), concurred with his predecessors: "The one who destroys [duality] is the [true] hero."[31] Again, he asserts that "one who eradicates his own evil is a brave warrior."[32] Evidently, a true hero is defined in spiritual terms by the Gurus as the one who participates in the battle that is fought within oneself against the five evil impulses of lust, anger, covetousness, attachment, and pride.

The use and imagery of weapons—the tools of *hinsa*—in the Adi Granth offer a rationale for violence in its own right. The rhetoric of weaponry can provide us with a window into the reality of "how instruments of harm were understood within the complex web of social relationships that necessitated them."[33] Since the reign of Guru Amar Das, for instance, the court poets (Bhatts) eulogized the Gurus as the "warriors of the Word" *(shabad sur)*, as kings whose rule is eternal, and as warriors of truth, wielding the power of humility and fighting the battles of righteousness *(dharam)*:

> Wearing the armor of absorption [*smadhi*] [in the divine Name],
>   [The third Guru] has mounted [the horse] of wisdom.
> Holding the bow of righteousness [*dharam*],
>   He has released [the arrows of] devotion and morality in the fight.
> He has wielded the lance of fear of the Fearless One;
>   He has thrust the spear of the Guru's Word into the mind.
> Thus equipped, he has cut down the five demons of lust, wrath,
>   greed, attachment, and egoistic pride.
> The noble King Amar Das, son of Tej Bhan,
>   has been exalted King of kings by the blessings of [Guru] Nanak.
> The bard Salh proclaims,
>   Verily, you have overthrown this hoard by waging such a battle.[34]

Wielding weapons here symbolizes the cultivation of ethical virtues in the internal struggle against worldly temptations. In the Adi Granth the sword is variously visualized as the Word, Name, Guru, God *(prabhu kirpan)*, and Wisdom, but also as the loving devotion: "The Loving devotion *[bhagati]* of God is the sword *[kharag]* and armor of the True Guru with which the tormentor death is slain and subdued."[35] Indeed, the sword of Wisdom *(gian kharag)* is meant to slay duality, the false self, and its desires and delusions. It is in this sense that the scriptural words have the power to act as weapons in the battle whether it is fought within the self or with the external enemies who are a threat to the faith.

The following verses by Guru Nanak were the most popular scriptural passages of those that served as the inspiration for Bhindranwale and his followers:

> If you want to play the game of love
>   Step into my lane with your head on the palm of your hand.
> Place your feet on this path
>   And give your head without any fear or grumbling.[36]

> He alone truly lives in whose heart dwells the Lord.
>   O Nanak, no one else is truly alive.

> If one lives in ignominy by losing one's self-respect *[pati]*,
> All that one eats [for survival] is illegitimate *[haram].*[37]

For Guru Nanak, to place one's "head on the palm" symbolizes the sacrifice of one's egoistic self. Thus, loving devotion in the Sikh tradition is a matter of life and death where to love ultimately means to sacrifice one's life. This motif of love and violence may be seen in the tradition of the "Cherished Five" *(panj piare)* who offered their "heads" at the call of Guru Gobind Singh when he inaugurated the institution of the Khalsa (Pure) on Baisakhi Day of 1699. An enormously popular tradition involving the ultimate sacrifice of one's head is lionized in the narrative of the eighteenth-century martyr Baba Dip Singh, who became an icon for Bhindranwale.[38]

Further, in Guru Nanak's view the notion of honor and self-respect *(pati)* is highly prized. For him, a heroic death must be based upon the true "honor" obtained before the divine court of Akal Purakh: "Blessed is the death of heroic men if their dying is approved of [by the immortal Lord]. Only those men may be called heroes who obtain true honor before the divine Court."[39] They who practice the discipline of meditation on the divine Name *(nam simaran)* during their lifetime receive true honor at the final moment of death. In fact, there are two levels of violence/death, one false and one true. Forgetting the divine Name is the only violence/death: "If I repeat the Name I live; if I forget it, I die. Repeating the Name of the True One is hard, but if one hungers for it and partakes of it all sadness goes."[40] Forgetting the divine Name produces spiritual death; only those who "remember" the divine Name are truly alive. There is no violence apart from the separation from Akal Purakh, and those who forget the divine Name have to suffer the pain of physical death repeatedly.

A new reading of Guru Nanak's verses on self-respect and honor emerged in the historical context of the Punjab crisis of the 1980s among the Sikh militants to justify their resolve to fight in the struggle for greater autonomy. For instance, Bhindranwale ended his speech of April 13, 1983, with the following exhortation: "Yes, stay peaceful everywhere and put on the train [of death] anyone who dishonors Satguru Granth Sahib or a daughter or a sister."[41] This twin concern with the honor of the sacred text and the Sikh women as part of the legitimization of armed resistance indicates that there was no real distinction between the private matters of Sikh men and women and the public matters of the relationship between the Sikhs and the Indian state. Thus, violence by militant groups was seen to be legitimate when the honor of Sikh women was harmed by police or army personnel, or by members of other communities. The honor of Sikh women reflected the social standing of the Sikh community as a whole in Bhindranwale's worldview. Any breach of this collective honor by outside society was the primary cause of a righteous war *(dharam yudh)* against the Indian state.

THE WORKS OF BHAI GURDAS

The second major source is linked with the name of Bhai Gurdas, whom Guru Arjun chose to act as his amanuensis during the final recording of the Adi Granth text in 1604. From his earliest days he was closely associated with four Sikh Gurus, serving successively Guru Amar Das, Guru Ram Das, Guru Arjun, and Guru Hargobind. He personally witnessed the peaceful days of Emperor Akbar's reign (r. 1556–1605), Guru Arjun's martyrdom in the beginning of Emperor Jahangir's reign (r. 1605–27), Guru Hargobind's reaction to this major event, and his armed conflict with Mughal authorities in the reign of Emperor Shah Jahan (r. 1627–58). In this context, J. S. Grewal adroitly remarks that Bhai Gurdas "lived in a phase of Sikh history that was marked by a critical transition."[42] In his works, therefore, one can find the source material for the early history of the Panth.

Guru Arjun's execution in Mughal custody in 1606 empowered the Sikhs to stand for the ideals of truth, justice, and fearlessness more boldly. A radical reshaping of the Sikh Panth took place after his martyrdom. His son and successor, Guru Hargobind (1595–1644), signaled the formal process of empowering the Sikh Panth for defense purposes when he traditionally donned two swords symbolizing the spiritual *(piri)* as well as the temporal *(miri)* investiture. He also built the Akal Takhat (Throne of the Timeless One) facing the Harimandir (the present-day "Golden Temple" in Amritsar), which represented the newly assumed role of temporal authority. Under his direct leadership the Sikh Panth took up arms to protect itself from Mughal hostility. From the Sikh perspective this new development was not taken at the cost of abandoning the original spiritual base. Rather, it was meant to achieve a balance between temporal and spiritual concerns. Thus, Guru Arjun's martyrdom became the watershed in Sikh history, contributing to the growth of Sikh community self-consciousness, separatism, and militancy. Indeed, it became the single most decisive factor for the crystallization of the Sikh Panth.

In the context of the present discussion, Bhai Gurdas makes it quite explicit that Guru Hargobind's way of life was indeed different from that of his predecessors. Note the following famous stanza:

> The earlier Gurus sat peacefully in the "place of worship" *[dharamsal]*;
>> This one roams the land.
> Emperors visited their homes with reverence;
>> This one they cast into gaol.
> No rest for his followers, ever active;
>> Their restless Master has fear of none.
> The earlier Gurus sat graciously blessing;
>> This one goes hunting with dogs.
> They composed the *bani* [inspired utterance] for listening and singing;
>> This one neither composes [the *bani*] nor sings.

They had servants who harbored no malice;
This one encourages scoundrels.
Yet none of these changes conceals the truth;
The Sikhs are still drawn as bees to the lotus.
The truth stands firm, eternal, and changeless;
And pride still lies subdued.[43]

Here, Bhai Gurdas provides us with the firm evidence of the change that took place under Guru Hargobind. In the first six lines of the stanza, he poses the problem he sees in the contemporary discussion among the Sikhs, and then provides his own answer in the remaining two. As a loyal disciple of the Guru, he defends the new martial response as "hedging the orchard of the Sikh faith with the hardy and thorny *kikar* tree."[44] It should, however, be emphasized that Guru Hargobind, who fought to resist the oppression of Mughal authorities, instructed his followers that even when one is fighting in battle, one should do so without any feeling of enmity toward one's foe. His contemporary Maubad Zulifkar Ardastani (c. 1615–70), in the Persian text *Dabistan-i-Mazahib* (School of Religions), recorded on the basis of his personal knowledge: "It comes to my mind that sword-striking of the Guru was also by way of teaching, for they call the teacher a *Guru* (or that *Guru* means a teacher), and not by way of anger because it is a condemned thing."[45]

After four skirmishes with Mughal troops, Guru Hargobind withdrew from Amritsar to the Shivalik hills—beyond the jurisdiction of the Mughal state—and Kiratpur became the new center of the mainline Sikh tradition. Relations with the Mughal authorities eased under the seventh and eighth Gurus, Har Rai (r. 1630–61) and Harkrishan (r. 1655–64), although the Gurus held court to adjudicate on temporal issues within the Panth and kept a regular force of Sikh horsemen. But the increasing strength of the Sikh movement during the period of the ninth Guru, Tegh Bahadur (1621–75), once again attracted Mughal attention in the 1670s. Guru Tegh Bahadur encouraged his followers to be fearless in their pursuit of a just society: "He who holds none in fear, nor is afraid of anyone, is acknowledged as a man of true wisdom."[46] In so doing, he posed a direct challenge to Emperor Aurangzeb (r. 1658–1707), who had imposed Islamic laws and taxes and ordered the replacement of Hindu temples with mosques. Guru Tegh Bahadur was summoned to Delhi, and when he refused to embrace Islam he was publicly executed on November 11, 1675. If the martyrdom of Guru Arjun had helped to bring the Sikh Panth together, this second martyrdom helped to make human rights and freedom of conscience central to its identity.

THE DASAM GRANTH

From the perspective of this study, the Dasam Granth is the principal source for understanding the idea of a just war *(dharam yudh)* based upon Guru Gobind

Singh's reflections on his experience of warfare against both the Mughal authorities and the local Hindu hill chiefs. For him, Akal Purakh is supremely just, exalting the devout followers and punishing the wicked. In the everlasting cosmic struggle between the forces of good and evil, Akal Purakh intervenes in human history to restore the balance in favor of those who wage war on behalf of the good. From time to time particular individuals are chosen to act as agents of God in the struggle against the evil forces. Defining his mission in his autobiographical *Bachitar Natak* (Wondrous Drama), the Guru firmly believed that he was such an agent of God: "For this purpose I was born in this world. The divine Guru *[gurdev]* has sent me to uphold righteousness *[dharam]*, to extend the true faith everywhere, and to destroy the evil and sinful."[47]

Guru Gobind Singh identifies Akal Purakh with the Divine Sword in the celebrated canto of *Bachitar Natak:*

> Thee I invoke, All-conquering Sword,
>   Destroyer of evil, Ornament of the brave.
> Powerful your arm and radiant your glory,
>   Your splendor as dazzling as the brightness of the sun.
> Joy of the devout and Scourge of the wicked,
>   Vanquisher of sin, I seek your protection.
> Hail to the world's Creator and Sustainer,
>   My invincible Protector the Sword.[48]

Similarly, the "divinity" is addressed as "all-steel" *(sarb loh)* or as the "revered sword" *(sri bhagauti)*, a mode of expression that reveals "a dark and turbulent presence which is only ever encountered through the convulsive events of battle and love, birth and death."[49] In his celebrated *Jap Sahib* (Master Recitation), Guru Gobind Singh proclaims: "I bow to you, the one who wields weapons that soar and fly. I bow before you, Knower of all, Mother of all the earth" (v. 52).[50] Thus, the divine Being is a great warrior who wields weapons of all kinds. But before he uses those weapons, he has the perfect knowledge of what is right and what is wrong. And, during the battle he does not fight savagely with anger but with the nurturing presence of the mother whose aim is to reform her children who have gone astray.

Following the earlier *miri-piri* tradition of Guru Hargobind, Guru Gobind Singh assumed characteristics of the spiritual leader and of a ruler who had specific responsibilities to protect righteousness *(dharam)*.[51] Not surprisingly, waging battle was part of the dharmic responsibility of the Guru. The majority of the narrative of his life is devoted to detailed descriptions of a series of battles. Indeed, Guru Gobind Singh was an able spiritual and political leader who maintained a court at Anandpur and led an army in many battles throughout his life, some of which are described in the *Bachitar Natak* section of the *Dasam Granth*.[52] On the Baisakhi Day of 1699, he established his army in the Order of the Khalsa (Pure), which would retain "its commitment by steadfastly refusing the temptation to seek concealment in times of danger."[53] Thus, in transforming Sikhs into a self-governing warrior group, the tenth Guru set in motion a profound change in the political and cultural fabric of the Mughal province of Punjab.[54] Most instructively, his army was never to wage war for power, for gain, or for personal rancor. As McLeod says, "The Khalsa was resolutely to uphold justice and to oppose only that which is evil."[55]

Let us now closely look at the text of *Zafarnama* (Letter of Victory) from the perspective of restorative justice.[56] The *Zafarnama* is the letter that Guru Gobind Singh addressed to Aurangzeb in response to his personal message. It contains certain references to the promises made by the Mughal officials before the evacuation of Anandpur by Guru Gobind Singh, who had resisted them for a considerable length of time. These promises were not kept, and the Guru was obliged to fight the battle of Chamkaur, in which he was overwhelmed by a disproportionately large number of Mughal troops. Although he himself escaped unscathed, he lost two of his sons and many followers in the battle. Again, there is a reference to the written and verbal messages from Aurangzeb, probably asking the Guru to present himself before the emperor. Guru Gobind Singh wrote the *Zafarnama* in the Persian language from Dina Kangar in the southern Punjab in February 1705 when he heard the news of the execution of his other two sons at Sarhind. In response to the written and verbal messages from Aurangzeb, Guru Gobind Singh was prepared to meet with him at his camp in the Deccan in South India where the emperor was engaged in quelling disturbances. Unfortunately, Aurangzeb died while the Guru was on his way to the South, and thus the actual meeting between the two never took place.

The text of the *Zafarnama* nevertheless shows forth Guru Gobind Singh's "reputation for reconciliation."[57] In the first place, the Guru begins with the invocation to the Supreme Being who is merciful particularly to those who follow the way of truth and trust. Those who serve the "One beyond Time" *(Akal)* and the "Source of all Goodness" *(Yazdan)* are protected by him against all enemies. The fact that Guru Gobind Singh had been protected by the Lord was ample proof of the justness of his cause: "Not even a single hair of mine was touched, nor my body suffered. For, God, the Destroyer of my enemies, himself pulled me out to safety."[58] The Guru reminds Aurangzeb of divine justice as follows: "When you and I will, both, repair to the Court of God, you will bear witness to what you did unto me."[59] Here, Guru Gobind Singh is using the Islamic notion of judgment to expose the injustice of the emperor who followed the law and traditions of Islam in every detail. He further warns Aurangzeb that his rule is one of painful oppression: "Shed not recklessly the blood of another with your sword, lest the Sword on High falls upon your neck."[60] The sword that is invoked here is Akal Purakh made manifest. Indeed, it is the God of justice visibly present as a sword wielded in defense of truth and righteousness. In the face of divine justice, tyrannies collapse because they run against the grain of human community.[61]

Secondly, the *Zafarnama* is essentially a homily on keeping one's word. It is no wonder that Guru Gobind Singh upbraids Aurangzeb for breaking the oath he took on the Qur'an. This refers to the treachery of his generals during the siege of Anandpur when, after promising safe conduct to the Guru's forces for leaving the city, they attacked and looted the Guru's property.[62] It was a clear violation of solemn "treaty and agreements" reached during warfare.[63] The following verses are particularly noteworthy:

> He who puts faith in your oath on the Qur'an,
>   comes to ruin in the end.
> The people who honor their faith and are true to their religion
>   do not break their promises in the here and hereafter.
> A man ought to adhere to his pledge.
>   He must not say one thing but practice another.[64]

These verses emphasize the importance of adhering to a promise once it has been made. They explicitly state how the officials of Aurangzeb had forced an unjust war on the Guru and had broken their oaths on the Qur'an. Here, the Guru is challenging the emperor on moral grounds. He is simply aghast at the emperor's sense of strange justice.[65] In this context, J. S. Grewal has aptly described the *Zafarnama* as "the epistle of moral victory."[66]

Thirdly, Guru Gobind Singh advocates the doctrine that one must first try all the peaceful means of negotiation in the pursuit of justice. Only when all those methods of redress have failed is it legitimate to draw the sword in defense of righteousness. The following celebrated verse of the *Zafarnama* makes this point explicitly:

> When all other methods have been explored
>   and all other means have been tried,
>
> Then may the sword be drawn from the scabbard,
>   then may the sword be used.[67]

Interestingly, Guru Gobind Singh is adapting here the Persian-writing Shaykh Sa'di's (d. 1292, of Shiraz, Iran) eighth admonition *(pand)* of his *Gulistan* ("Rose Garden") to appeal to Aurangzeb, who would undoubtedly be familiar with the text: "When the hand is foiled at every turn it is then permitted to take the sword in hand."[68] In line with Sa'di's understanding, the Guru justifies the use of force in defense of justice when all other alternatives fail. In this context, W. H. McLeod makes an important observation: "None of this should suggest that the Panth exists only to breathe fire or wield naked swords."[69] The use of force is certainly allowed in the Sikh doctrine, but it is authorized only in defense of justice and only as a last resort. Moreover, in the face of tyranny, justice can be defended and maintained only through sacrifices. The *Zafarnama* further stresses that no sacrifice is too great for the sake of truth and justice: "It does not matter if my four sons have been killed; the Khalsa is still there at my back."[70]

Fourthly, Guru Gobind Singh is extending an invitation to Aurangzeb to come to the village of Kangar in the southern Punjab. In spite of his terrible losses, the Guru shows his willingness to enter into dialogue with the emperor. Note the following verses:

> If only you were gracious enough to come to the village of Kangar,
>   we could, then, see each other face to face.
> On the way, there will be no danger to your life,
>   For, the whole tribe of Brars accepts my command.
> Come to me that we may converse with each other,
>   And I may utter some "kind" words to you.[71]

Here, one can see how Guru Gobind Singh is prepared to "encounter" the emperor and see him "face to face." He wants to keep the channels of communication open with Aurangzeb. He promises protection to the emperor on his journey in the area where the "whole tribe of Brars" is under his direct influence. Since the Guru has been quite blunt and forthright in his letter, he promises to use "kind words" in their personal conversation. Now all these features are most significant in the process of reconciliation, and they are an integral part of the restorative approach.

Finally, Guru Gobind Singh praises Aurangzeb and characterizes him with qualities that, according to some Sikh scholars, are not really vouched by the other parts of the *Zafarnama*.[72] They maintain that this part of the text is apparently "slipshod," and that it "hardly squares" with other statements. This is simply not the case. We need to closely look at the following verses:

> O Aurangzeb, king of kings, fortunate are you,
>   An expert swordsman and a horseman too.
> O one of brilliant conscience and handsome body,
>   You grant riches and lands in charity.
> You are the king of kings, ornament of the thrones of the world:
>   Ruler of the age, *but far from Islamic faith [din]!*[73]

Here, Guru Gobind Singh is trying to consider Aurangzeb as a person in new ways. He is focusing on his good qualities from a human perspective. He does not want to give offense to him with his ironic rebukes only. He is rather trying to convince the emperor that he can no longer claim any legitimacy for his imperial sway, since he has departed from the principles of Islamic faith *(din)*. The Guru is trying to appeal to Aurangzeb's "brilliant conscience" *(raushan zamir)* to see what his officials had done to him. In fact, the Guru had made a perfect case before the emperor in the *Zafarnama* and won his immediate attention to redress his grievances. It is the restorative perspective that lends basic unity to the whole text of the *Zafarnama*.

According to a contemporary news item in the *Akhbarat-i-Darbar-i-Mu'alla* (Jaipur), Aurangzeb ordered Guru Gobind Singh to present himself before the emperor after receiving his letter.[74] He dictated a royal decree (*hasbul-hukam,* "as commanded") to the secretary Inayatullah Khan, which was collected within the latter's *Ahkam-i Alamgiri,* referring to the petition received from the tenth Guru: "In these times of great victory the world-ruling order has been issued that a note be dispatched to his ministerial highness to the effect that Gobind, the *ra'is* [leader] of the *Nanak-parastan* [devotees of Nanak], had sent a petition *[arz dasht]* along with a representative to this sky-glorious court, expressing a desire to kiss the imperial threshold *[astan bus]* and make a plea for issuance of an order in his favor."[75] Although this entry is written from the imperial perspective, it nevertheless provides the hard evidence of how Aurangzeb dispatched the imperial order in response to Guru Gobind Singh's letter. Further, the emperor deputed Muhammad Beg (a *gurzbardar*) and Shaykh Yar Muhammad (a *mansabdar*) to approach Guru Gobind Singh through Mun'im Khan, the governor of Lahore, and use all diplomacy in persuading him to go to the emperor.[76] The imperial order stressed that if Guru Gobind Singh was to march through the territory of Sarhind, his safety was to be guaranteed, and if he needed money for his travel, that was to be supplied from the properties seized from the Guru himself.[77]

The earliest Sikh tradition in *Parchian Sewadas* (c. 1708–09 C.E.) provides a narrative background to the writing of the *Zafarnama* as follows:

> [The Guru] then commanded the Khalsa, "Go, battle the Turks and slay them." The Khalsa replied, "O true king, the Turks are very wicked. They are accompanied by a million horsemen. We will nevertheless obey your command." [The Guru] then said, "This is good. Let us proceed this way: a letter will be written to the [emperor of the] Turks [which] will kill him. When he reads this letter he will die." The Khalsa said, "O true king, you are the doer of all things: that which pleases you comes to pass." The Guru Baba then wrote this letter and addressed it to Aurangzeb. He titled it the *Zafarnama,* the Epistle of Victory.[78]

Similarly, the *Gurbilas* literature claims that after reading the *Zafarnama* Aurangzeb felt remorse for what he had done to the Guru. He wanted to see him immediately, but he soon died of mental distress while reading the words of the *Zafarnama,* which acted as a powerful weapon. In particular, Santokh Singh's *Gur-pratap Suraj Granth* (1843) describes the narrative of conversation of the Guru when he heard the news of Aurangzeb's death from the Sikhs who had delivered the letter to the emperor: "The Guru was delighted by their reply and said, 'Even your tongue holds the sword. At whichever place your word is uttered, it will have as immediate an effect as a weapon.'"[79]

The *Zafarnama* is far more realistic in illuminating how the violence was experienced by the Khalsa in the battle against the Mughal authorities and how it was normalized in Sikh narratives with the moral victory of Guru Gobind Singh over the deceptive framework of Aurangzeb, who ultimately died by the powerful weapon of the words of the Guru. This discourse enjoyed popularity in premodern times and greatly appealed to the followers of Bhindranwale who were fighting in the "righteous war" *(dharam yudh)* against the discriminatory policies of the Indian state under Prime Minister Indira Gandhi, assassinated by her own Sikh bodyguards after ordering a bloody assault on the Golden Temple in 1984.

THE *RAHIT-NAMAS* (MANUALS OF CODE OF CONDUCT)

The final textual source in our discussion relates to a new genre of literature known as *Rahit-namas*, or "manuals of code of conduct." The word *rahit* itself was used by Guru Nanak in his works, where it stands for the code of conduct that the early Sikhs were expected to follow in their lives. At the inauguration of the Khalsa order in 1699, however, a formal Rahit was promulgated, and since then it has acquired the paramount position in the life of the Panth. All who chose to join the order of the Khalsa through the *amrit* ceremony (i.e., "initiation rite of the nectar of immortality"), involving sweetened water stirred with a double-edged sword and sanctified by the recitation of five liturgical prayers by the "Cherished Five" *(panj piare)*, were understood to have been "reborn" in the house of the Guru and thus to have assumed a new identity. For the Khalsa the dominant ethical duty is the quest for justice: "The Khalsa was created to fight injustice, and fighting injustice is still its calling."[80]

The *Rahit-namas* provide a rare insight into the evolving nature of the Khalsa code in the eighteenth and nineteenth centuries. In fact, the Rahit grew considerably during the eighteenth century in response to Mughal campaigns and later to the Afghan menace, and it produced injunctions that were clearly aimed at protecting the Khalsa from enemies who were seen to be Muslims. In this context, we need to closely examine W. H. McLeod's work on six *Rahit-namas* of the eighteenth century that provide us with an understanding of early Sikh views on warfare.[81] These are the *Tanakhah-nama* attributed to Bhai Nand Lal, the *Sakhi Rahit Ki*, the *Chaupa Singh Rahit-nama*, the *Prahilad Rai Rahit-nama*, and the *Daya Singh Rahit-nama*. Of these texts, the *Tanakhah-nama* is the oldest document written during the period of Guru Gobind Singh, and its earliest extant manuscript is dated 1716 C.E. The following relevant extract from it throws considerable light on the ideology concerning warfare:

He is a Khalsa who in fighting never turns his back. He is a Khalsa who slays Muslims [turk]. He is a Khalsa who triumphs over the five [evil impulses]. He is a Khalsa who avoids another's woman. He is a Khalsa who fights face to face. He is a Khalsa who destroys the oppressor. He is a Khalsa who carries weapons.[82]

McLeod has translated the word *turk* as "Muslims" because of its sense of religious identity in North Indian usage. However, any Sikh who will read this translation will be stunned. This is certainly not the contextual meaning of the original passage. It is directly against the teachings of the Sikh Gurus to kill anyone because of one's religious affiliation. In fact, the word *turk* in the *Rahit-namas* and early Sikh literature refers to an "invader" or an "oppressor." In almost all cases, *turk* or *turkara* refers to the Mughal rulers of the day or to Afghan invaders, although neither of these groups were of Turkic ethnic origin. They were perceived to be oppressors and hence it was the fundamental duty of the Khalsa to "slay oppressors."

In the *Chaupa Singh Rahit-nama* (1740–65 C.E.), we find certain rules pertaining to weapons and warfare and the Khalsa reverence for the swords and other weapons in several passages. There are also certain references to ideas of legitimization: "The right to rule is won and sustained by the sword. Arms should only be used, however, when there is good cause for doing so."[83] Assuming the knowledge of his audience, Chaupa Singh did not elaborate on what such "good cause" might be for limiting the use of deadly force under particular circumstances. From the historical context, however, we can speculate that resistance against the oppression of the Mughals was the legitimate reason for going to war. Further, Chaupa Singh provided some brief comments on rules for the battlefield: "A Singh should never turn his back in battle. Always aid a wounded, disabled or exhausted Sikh on the battlefield. Always have slain Sikhs cremated on the battlefield if possible."[84]

The *Rahit-nama* of Bhai Desa Singh offers the following injunctions regarding warfare:

> In battle the Singh should roar [like a lion]. Fighting them face to face he defeats Muslims [malechhan].
> In battle let [the Khalsa] never be defeated. He should forget sleep, [remaining ever alert] to fight the Muslim [turk]. Let him with determination do the deeds of a Kshatriya, crying "Kill! Kill!" [as he fights] in the battle.
> Fear not, for many are fearlessly fighting. Sustain the spirit [which declares]: "I shall kill the enemy!" Those [Khalsa] who die in the course of a battle shall certainly go to paradise.
> He who defeats the enemy in battles will find his glory resounding the whole world over. Stand firm, therefore, in the fiercest of conflicts. Never turn and flee from the field of battle.[85]

Again, we find here few more details about warfare. The original texts have two words *malechh* (barbarians) and *turk* (invaders) that refer to Mughals but have been translated as "Muslims." They reflect an extremely negative view of Mughal rule, and by implication of Muslims in general. The Khalsa was exhorted to fight in much the same way that a Kshatriya was so ordained in the Hindu legal texts *(Dharma Sutras)*.

The Khalsa spent most of its first century fighting the armies of Mughals and Afghan invaders. Finally, in 1799, Ranjit Singh (1780–1839) succeeded in unifying the Punjab, taking control of Lahore, and declaring himself Maharaja. For the next four decades, the Sikh community enjoyed more settled political conditions, and with territorial expansion as far as Peshawar in the west, people of different cultural and religious backgrounds were attracted into the fold of Sikhism. The appearance of the Golden Temple today owes a great deal to the generous patronage of the Maharaja, who himself was a Khalsa Sikh. Indeed, the rule of Maharaja Ranjit Singh was marked by religious diversity within the Sikh Panth. After his death in 1839, his successors could not withstand the pressure exerted by the advancing British forces. After two Anglo-Sikh wars, in 1846 and 1849, the Sikh kingdom was annexed to the British Empire. With the loss of the Punjab's independence, the Sikhs were no longer the masters of their own kingdom.

FIVE VARIETIES OF EXEGESIS

During the late nineteenth and early twentieth centuries, the elite group of the Singh Sabha (Society of Singhs) movement remodeled the Rahit according to the rationalist principles that were prevalent among the educated within India. The most significant question for the present discussion is raised by Khushwant Singh: How do we explain the transition "from the pacifist Sikh to the militant Khalsa"?[86] There are various answers to this question. In colonial India the statutory law required the British to maintain "the separation of secular and religious matters, neutrality in the treatment of religious communities and the withdrawal from involvement in religious institutions."[87] In the case of the Sikhs, however, they even sidestepped the law to pamper and control them through the direct management of the Golden Temple and deployed their insidious system of control by including the Sikhs among the "martial races" to serve their own military purposes. Not surprisingly, one theory of exegesis bestowed credit for Sikh militancy on the British rulers who picked up the militant Khalsa version out of several Sikh identities available in the nineteenth century.[88] The same identity became the focus of the Singh Sabha leaders for their reforming activities.

The second theory of exegesis appeared in Gokul Chand Narang's influential work *Transformation of Sikhism,* which provides a Punjabi Hindu (particularly Arya Samajist) perspective on Sikh militancy:[89] "The sword which carved the Khalsa's way to glory was, undoubtedly, forged by Govind, but the steel had been provided by Nanak, who had obtained it, as it were, by smelting the Hindu ore, and burning out the dross of indifference and superstition of the masses and the hypocrisy and pharisaism of the priests."[90] The book presents the earlier, premodern Sanatan interpretation of Sikhism explicitly and argues that the Khalsa should exist as a voluntary association for the defense of the Indian nation within the larger Panth that includes both Hindus and Sikhs who venerate the teachings of Guru Nanak.

A third and dominant theory of exegesis on the issue of why a tradition built on Guru Nanak's *interior* discipline of "meditation on the divine Name" *(nam-simaran)* should have become a militant community and proclaimed its identity by means of prominently displayed *exterior* symbols comes from the Singh Sabha scholars. It stresses the point that the militarizing of the Panth by the sixth Guru, Hargobind, and the subsequent creation of the Khalsa by the tenth Guru were strictly in accord with Guru Nanak's own intention. In fact, the classic statement of this claim may be seen in the stirring words of Joseph D. Cunningham's *History of the Sikhs,* first published in 1849: "It was reserved for *Nanak* to perceive the true principles of reform, and to lay those broad foundations which enable his successor *Gobind* to fire the minds of his countrymen with a new nationality, and to give practical effect to the doctrine that the lowest is equal with the highest, in race as in creed, in political rights as in religious hopes."[91] That is, Guru Nanak's egalitarian teachings provided the basis for the institution of the Khalsa to fight for equality, justice, and human rights. In the recent past, Jagjit Singh developed this interpretation into a detailed theory of revolution: "The founding of the Sikh *Panth* outside the caste society in order to use it as the basis far combating the hierarchical set-up of the caste order, and the creation of the Khalsa for capturing the state in the interests of the poor and the suppressed, were only a projection, on the military and political plane, of the egalitarian approach of the Sikh religious thesis."[92]

Yet another theory of exegesis was offered by W. H. McLeod in *The Evolution of the Sikh Community* (1975), which explained the progressive development of the Panth not merely in terms of purposeful intention but also in terms of the influence of the social, economic, and historical environment. This specifically included such major features as the militant cultural traditions of the dominant group of the Jats (rural peasantry) within the Panth, the economic context within which it evolved, and the influence of contemporary events such as those produced by local political rivalry and foreign invasion.[93] This interpretation, however, came under vigorous attack within the Sikh scholarly circles. In his recent works, McLeod reassessed his earlier stance in light of criticisms and acknowledged the "intention of the Gurus as an important factor" in the gradual growth of the Sikh Panth, along with environmental factors that were overemphasized in his earlier analysis.[94]

Finally, in more recent studies "religion" is not considered a purely interior impulse secreted away in the human soul and limited to the private sphere, nor an institutional force separable from other nonreligious or secular forces in the public domain. Rather, all the public-private, religion-politics, and church-state dichotomies have come under the powerful critique of postmodern and postcolonial studies. It has been suggested that such dichotomies, rather than describing reality as it is, justify a certain configuration of power. The idea that "religion has a tendency to cause violence—and is therefore to be removed from public power— is one type of this essentialist construction of religion."[95] Not surprisingly, the Sikh doctrine of *miri-piri* explicitly affirms that religion and politics are bound together. That is, religious issues must be defended in the political arena and political activity must be conducted in accordance with traditional religious norms.[96]

Against the backdrop of these varying modes of exegesis, one can better understand the implications of the Punjab Crisis mentioned at the outset of this essay. Virginia Van Dyke has recently provided a summary of competing narratives of the Punjab crisis. Accordingly, the dominant narrative told by the Akali Dal and supported by academic and journalistic sources focuses on the malfeasance and vindictiveness of the state, more specifically the Congress Party and Indira Gandhi herself. In this narrative, the rise of a militant movement was a creation of Congress, as summed up succinctly in an article in *Tehelka:* "In 1978 Sikh radicals backed by Congress took centre stage and were able to successfully destabilize the Parkash Singh Badal government. That led to nearly two decades of strife."[97] In order to defeat the nefarious designs of Congress, so goes the narrative, there is a need for the coalition between the BJP (Bharatiya Janata Party, "Indian Peoples' Party") and the Akalis to preserve harmony and reassure the populace of continued peace. This coalition is also necessary for changing the image of the Sikhs as antinational.[98]

There are opposing narratives that explain the emergence of the ethnonationalist movement that focus on the desire of the Sikhs for autonomy or independence. There are also viewpoints opposing the argument that the coalition between the Akali Dal and the BJP is a statesmanlike intercommunal alliance to preserve the peace. According to these alternative voices, including from those few and dwindling number of Akalis who do not belong to the Badal faction, the alliance with BJP is completely self-serving on the part of the BJP and Badal and his supporters. These voices are relatively muted due to the widespread desire for peace, along with structural changes that support the main Akali faction's position.[99]

There is still another narrative of nonviolent Sikh militancy. The representation of Sikhs and Sikhism in violent and militant images has been pivotal in understanding Sikhism since colonial times. Sikh history is replete with the valor of the Sikh warrior in battle. However, there is less attention given to the Sikh warrior in equally and perhaps more demanding nonviolent actions. For instance, Paul Wallace makes the point that the Sikhs are not essentially violent but are militant where "militancy" does not mean violence in actions and reactions alone but also an aggressive and passionate stand for the cause of their religion and the Gurus. Through a study of the development of nonviolent militancy, Wallace argues that public demonstrations and political demands through nonviolent means have been more successful than violent ones. The three case studies of the Gurdwara Reform movement from 1920 to 1925, the Punjabi Suba (Province) movement from 1947 to 1966, and the movement against the emergency imposed by the Prime Minister Indira Gandhi from 1975 from 1977 highlight the strengths of nonviolent struggles and those of the actors within the Akali Dal. The violence during the 1980s in Punjab, Wallace argues, is now finding ways of closure through nonviolent democratic means, moving away from "anticentrism" to "cooperative federalism." Conflict resolution can be found through measures of democratic process and by accommodating the former militants in a peaceful manner along with initiating transparency and justice through the state structure.[100]

CONCLUSION

This study has analyzed the connection between Sikh sacred sources and the justification of violent acts as divinely mandated. Indeed, scriptural words can act as weapons to motivate people to battle against the temptations in the mind. In wars or other forms of collective violence, these words do inspire the killing of unjust and ruthless enemies who pose a danger to the very survival of the faith. Not surprisingly, militant interpretation of these texts has been seminal in generating a culture of violence in different historical periods. An analysis of the *Zafarnama* has revealed how its words can inspire the zealots to fight in a just war *(dharam yudh)* against evil forces. Further, the sword is central to the teachings and example of Guru Gobind Singh, and the text of the *Zafarnama* is explicit in declaring that it may be drawn only in defense of righteousness *(dharam)* and only when all other means of peaceful negotiations have failed. In other words, there is no sanction for indiscriminate, unrelenting, and insatiable violence in the Sikh tradition. In the face of tyranny, justice can be defended and maintained only through sacrifices. Most instructively, Torkel Brekke has remarked that "the Sikh tradition of *dharam yudh* has been kept alive by the Sikhs' keen sense of being a special people with a distinct identity and by recurrent conflicts with the central authorities in Delhi."[101]

Like all religious traditions, Sikhism has some violence in its history, especially in times of nationalistic or secessionist fervor. In fact, acts of violence or nonviolence are social phenomena that take place at particular historical junctures. They cannot be described as essential features of any community. The Punjab crisis of yesteryears reflected the multidimensionality of violence. On the one hand, the involvement of Sikh militants in random acts of violence and guerrilla warfare were "totally unwarranted and counterproductive and had the fully predictable result of bringing down the full power of the police and military on their own Sikh communities as well as the surrounding Hindu communities."[102] On the other hand, the state allowed the "chaos of insurgency to proliferate before brutally and clinically exterminating it almost at will."[103] Thus, one cannot overlook the sheer egregious and unjust acts of the state, killing in the name of order, security, and sheer power, especially when religious militants were the victims. Ultimately, all the principal actors in this spiral of violence had to pay the price with their lives. A considerable mythology gathered around Sant Jarnail Singh Bhindranwale during his lifetime. His death during the Indian army's assault on the Golden Temple in June 1984 assured that he will always be remembered as a great hero and martyr of the Sikh Panth.

NOTES

1. Mark Juergensmeyer, *Terror in the Mind of God* (Berkeley: University of California Press, 2000), 88.

2. Balbinder Singh Bhogal, "Text as Sword," in *Religion and Violence in South Asia,* ed. John R. Hinnells and Richard King (London: Routledge, 2007), 107.

3. Mark Juergensmeyer, *Global Rebellion* (Berkeley: University of California Press, 2008), 115.

4. Khushwant Singh, *A History of the Sikhs,* vol. 1, *1469–1839* (1963; New Delhi: Oxford University Press, 1999), 76–98.

5. Bhogal, "Text as Sword," 107–35; Navdeep Mandair, "An Approximate Difference," *Sikh Formations* 5, no. 2 (December 2009): 85–101.

6. Robin Rinehart, *Debating the Dasam Granth* (New York: Oxford University Press, 2011), 102–3.

7. Mandair, "An Approximate Difference," 94–95.

8. A. Walter Dorn and Stephan Gucciardi, "The Sword and the Turban: Armed Force in Sikh Thought," *Journal of Military Ethics* 10, no. 1 (2011): 67.

9. Laurie L. Patton, "Telling Stories about Harm," in Hinnells and King, *Religion and Violence in South Asia,* 11.

10. M1, *Var Majh* 2 (20), AG, 147. Key to this and subsequent references to sacred texts: the passage is the second *salok* (subsidiary stanza) of the twentieth stanza *(pauri)* of *Var* (Ballad) in the musical measure *Majh,* by Guru Nanak, on page 147 of the standard version of the Adi Granth (AG). The code word Mahala (or simply "M," meaning "King") with an appropriate number identifies the composition of each Guru. The works by Guru Nanak, Guru Angad, Guru Amar Das, Guru Ram Das, Guru Arjun, and Guru Tegh Bahadur are indicated by "M" 1, 2, 3, 4, 5, and 9, respectively. All the Gurus sign their compositions "Nanak" in the Adi Granth. The standard version of the Adi Granth has a pagination of 1,430-page text.

11. M1, *Japu* 17–18, AG, 3–4.

12. M1, *Var Majh* 1 (15), AG, 145.

13. M1, *Maru Solihe* 13, AG, 1034.

14. M1, *Asa* 39, *Asa Astapadi* 11, *Asa Astapadi* 12, and *Tilang* 5, AG, 360, 417–18, and 722–23.

15. M1, *Asa Astapadi* 11, AG, 417.

16. M1, *Asa* 39, AG, 360.

17. M1, *Asa Astapadi* 12, AG, 418.

18. Kanwarjit Singh, *Political Philosophy of the Sikh Gurus* (New Delhi: Atlantic Publishers, 1989), 116.

19. J. S. Grewal, *Guru Nanak in History* (Chandigarh: Panjab University, 1969), 163.

20. Bhogal, "Text as Sword," 119.

21. M1, *Tilang* 5, AG, 722.

22. M1, *Asa Astapadian* 11 (4–5), AG, 417.

23. M1, *Asa Astapadian* 11 (6), AG, 417.

24. W. H. McLeod, *Guru Nanak and the Sikh Religion* (New Delhi: Oxford University Press, 1976), 136. Originally published in 1968 by Clarendon Press.

25. W. H. McLeod, trans., *B40 Janam Sakhi* (Amritsar: Guru Nanak University Press, 1980), 78.

26. M1, *Tilang* 5, AG, 723.

27. *Shabadarath Sri Guru Granth Sahib Ji*, 5th ed. (Amritsar: SGPC, 1979), 723, n. 4.

28. McLeod, *Guru Nanak and the Sikh Religion*, 137, n. 3.

29. M1, *Ramakali Astapadian* 9, AG, 908.

30. M3, *Var Siri Ragu* 1 (11), AG, 86.

31. M5, *Gauri* 5, AG, 237.

32. M5, *Gauri Bavan Akhari* 39, AG, 258.

33. Patton, "Telling Stories about Harm," 13.

34. Bhat Salh, *Savayye Mahile Tejje Ke* 1, AG, 1396.

35. M4, *Var Gauri* 2 (21), AG, 312.

36. M1, *Salok Varan Te Vadhik* 20, AG, 1412.

37. M1, *Var Majh* 1 (10), AG, 142.

38. Louis E. Fenech, *Martyrdom in the Sikh Tradition* (New Delhi: Oxford University Press, 2000), 95–102. Dip Singh supernaturally carries his own decapitated head on his palm en route to Amritsar to fulfill his religious vow.

39. M1, *Vadahansu Alahanian* 2, AG, 579–80.

40. M1, *Asa* 3, AG, 9.

41. Ranbir Singh Sandhu, trans., *Struggle for Justice* (Dublin, Ohio: Sikh Educational and Religious Foundation, 1999), 88.

42. J. S. Grewal, *Sikh Ideology, Polity and Social Order* (New Delhi: Manohar, 1996), 30.

43. *Varan Bhai Gurdas*, 26:24.

44. *Varan Bhai Gurdas*, 26:25.

45. Ganda Singh, trans., "Nanak Panthis," *The Panjab Past and Present* 1 (1967): 63.

46. M9, *Salok* 16, AG, 1427.

47. *Shabadarath Dasam Granth Sahib* (Patiala: Punjabi University Press, 1973), 1:74.

48. DG, 39; W. H. McLeod, *The Sikhs: History, Religion, and Society* (New York: Columbia University Press, 1989), 52.

49. Mandair, "An Approximate Difference," 91.

50. Translation is taken from W. H. McLeod, *Essays in Sikh History, Tradition, and Society* (New Delhi: Oxford University Press, 2007), 69.

51. *Miri-piri*, "temporal-spiritual investiture," is the Sikh doctrine of the inseparability of religious and secular affairs.

52. Rinehart, *Debating the Dasam Granth*, 66–68.

53. W. H. McLeod, *Sikhism* (London: Penguin, 1997), 105.

54. Purnima Dhavan, *When Sparrows Became Hawks: The Making of the Sikh Warrior Tradition, 1699–1799* (New York: Oxford University Press, 2011), 3.

55. McLeod, *Sikhism*, 105.

56. Pashaura Singh, "Sikhism and Restorative Justice: Theory and Practice," in *The Spiritual Roots of Restorative Justice*, ed. Michael L. Hadley (Albany: SUNY Press, 2001), 206–9.

57. C. H. Loehlin, *The Granth of Guru Gobind Singh and The Khalsa Brotherhood* (Lucknow: n.p., 1971), 78.

58. *Zafarnama*, v. 44.

59. Ibid., v. 81.

60. Ibid., v. 69.

61. Timothy Gorringe, *God's Just Vengeance* (Cambridge: Cambridge University Press, 1996), 14.

62. Loehlin, *The Granth of Guru Gobind Singh*, 55.

63. Singh, *Political Philosophy of the Sikh Gurus*, 121.

64. *Zafarnama*, vv. 13–15, 47, and 55.

65. Ibid., vv. 50–51.

66. J. S. Grewal, "The *Zafarnama* of Guru Gobind Singh," in *From Guru Nanak to Maharaja Ranjit Singh* (Amritsar: Guru Nanak University Press, 1972), 66.

67. *Zafanama*, v. 22.

68. M. H. Tasbihi, ed., *The Persian-English Gulistan or Rose Garden of Sa'adi*, trans. Edward Rehatsek (Tehran: Shargh's, 1967), 575.

69. McLeod, *The Sikhs*, 56.

70. *Zafarnama*, v. 78.

71. Ibid., vv. 58–60.

72. Surjit Hans, *A Reconstruction of Sikh History from Sikh Literature* (Jalandhar: ABS Publication, 1988), 235.

73. *Zafarnama*, vv. 89–94.

74. Grewal, "The *Zafarnama* of Guru Gobind Singh," 64.

75. Ganda Singh, ed., *Ma'akhiz-i Tavarikh-i Sikhan jild avaval: Ahd-i Guru Sahiban* [Sources of Sikh history, vol. 1, the age of the Sikh Gurus] (Amritsar: Sikh History Society, 1949), 74.

76. *Gurzbardar* is a "mace-bearer," responsible for carrying messages to and from the Mughal emperor; *mansabdar* is a "rank-holder" in the *mansab* system of hierarchy in the organization of the nobility throughout the Mughal empire.

77. Grewal, "The *Zafarnama* of Guru Gobind Singh," 64.

78. Kharak Singh and Gurtej Singh, *Episodes from the Lives of the Gurus: Parchian Sewadas* (Chandigrah: Institute of Sikh Studies, 1995), 37, 133.

79. Online edition of Santokh Singh, *Gur-Pratap Suraj Granth*, ain 1, ansu 34, line 42.

80. McLeod, *Sikhism*, 129.

81. W. H. McLeod, *Sikhs of the Khalsa* (New Delhi: Oxford University Press, 2003), 65–73, 279–325.

82. Ibid., 284.

83. W. H. McLeod, trans., *The Chaupa Singh Rahit-nama* (Dunedin: University of Otago Press, 1987), 40 (8, a, iv).

84. Ibid., 40 (8, d, i–iii).

85. McLeod, *Sikhs of the Khalsa*, 300.

86. Singh, *A History of the Sikhs*, 76–98.

87. Ian J. Kerr, "Sikhs and State," in *Sikh Identity*, ed. Pashaura Singh and N. G. Barrier (New Delhi: Manohar, 1999), 164.

88. Richard G. Fox, *Lions of the Punjab* (Berkeley: University of California Press, 1985).

89. The Arya-Samaj (society of noble-ones) movement was started by Swami Dayanand Sarasvati (1824–83) in 1877 in the Punjab, attracting the Punjabi Hindus. This reform movement in colonial India redefined Hinduism as a well-defined system on Euro-centric lines much in the same way as the Singh Sabha movement redefined Sikh orthodoxy. Initially the Arya Samaj cooperated with the Sikhs, but soon they began aggressively assimilating the Rahitia or low-caste Sikhs in the Hindu

tradition through their *Shuddhi* (purification) rite. Soon this *Shuddhi* had driven a wedge between Hindu and Sikh communities, and propelled the Sikhs onward to a separate consciousness. In this change of self-perception may be found the seeds of Hindu-Sikh conflict in the Punjab which continues to the present.

90. Gokul Chand Nanrang, *Transformation of Sikhism* (1912; Ludhiana: Kalyani, 1998), 17.

91. J. D. Cunningham, *A History of the Sikhs* (1849; Delhi: S. Chand, 1955), 34.

92. Jagjit Singh, *Perspectives on Sikh Studies* (New Delhi: n.p., 1985), vii.

93. W. H. McLeod, *The Evolution of the Sikh Community* (New Delhi: Oxford University Press, 1975), chs. 1 and 3.

94. McLeod, *Sikhism*, 116.

95. R. Scott Appleby, "Fire and Sword: Does Religion Promote Violence?," *Commonweal* 137, no. 7 (April 9, 2010): 13.

96. McLeod, "The Role of Sikh Doctrine and Tradition in the Punjab Crisis," in *Essays in Sikh History, Tradition, and Society*, 99.

97. Virginia Van Dyke, "Politics in Punjab," *Sikh Formations* 5, no. 2 (December 2009): 126.

98. Ibid.

99. Ibid.

100. Paul Wallace, "Sikh Militancy and Non-Violence," in *Sikhism in Global Context*, ed. Pashaura Singh (New Delhi: Oxford University Press, 2011), 85–101.

101. Torkel Brekke, "The Dharam Yudh or Just War in Sikhism," in *Warfare and Politics in South Asia from Ancient to Modern Times*, ed. Kaushik Roy (New Delhi: Manohar Publications, 2011), 411.

102. Gerald James Larson, *India's Agony Over Religion* (Albany: SUNY Press, 1995), 244.

103. Arvind Mandair, "The Global Fiduciary," in Hinnells and King, *Religion and Violence in South Asia*, 220.

GLOSSARY OF NAMES AND TECHNICAL TERMS

Abū Bakr	Muhammad's companion and the future first caliph; reigned 632–634.
Adi Granth	"First Scripture" of the Sikh religion completed in 1604 and installed as the perpetual Guru of the Sikh faith in 1708.
Ahimsa	"Avoidance of violence"; a principle of the Hindu, Jain, and Buddhist religions.
Ahura Mazda	An ancient Iranian god whom Zarathushtra taught was uncreated and the principle deity of Zoroastrianism.
Akal Purakh	"Timeless, eternal one"; a common name for God in the Sikh tradition.
Akal Takhat	"Seat of the timeless one"; Seat of Sikh religious authority located in Amritsar, Punjab, India.
Angra Mainyu	"Destructive Spirit" or "Destructive Mind"; the primary antagonist in the cosmic struggle for good and order in Zoroastrianism.
Asbāb al-nuzūl	Occasions of qur'anic revelation.
Asha	Zoroastrian term that means "truth, existence, righteousness"; opposite of *drug*: "lie."
Atman	Sanskrit for "self," the liberation of which is the aim of Hinduism.
Avesta	The primary collection of sacred texts in the Zoroastrian religion.
Aws	A Non-Jewish tribe in Medina.
Āya	Arabic for "sign," the word is used technically to refer to the smallest sections of text in the Qur'an, comparable to "verses" of the Judeo-Christian Scriptures.

Baha'u'llah	Arabic for "the glory of God," title of the Baha'i tradition's foundational figure.
Banū al-Nadīr	A Jewish tribe in Medina.
Banū Qaynuqā'	A Jewish tribe in Medina.
Banū Qurayzā'	A Jewish tribe in Medina.
Al-Baydāwī	A medieval qur'anic exegete.
Bhakti	Sanskrit for "devotion," it is a cardinal religious virtue of Hinduism.
Bin Bāz, 'Abdullāh	Saudi religious scholar; grand mufti from 1993 to 1999.
Brahmanas	From the Sanskrit word for ultimate reality, these are normative commentaries on the Vedas or primary scriptures of Hinduism. Each is associated with its own Vedic school within the Hindu faith.
Cosmogony	An account of the origin(s) of the universe.
Darius I	Third king of the Achaemenid Empire, called also Darius the Great; reigned 522–486 B.C.E.
Dasam Granth	A seventeenth-century-C.E. Sikh scripture composed by the tenth Guru, Gobind Singh.
David	Second and greatest king of Israel, who, according to tradition, composed the Hebrew book of Psalms; regarded as a prophet in Islam.
Dead Sea Scrolls	A library of Hebrew, Aramaic, and Greek manuscripts of Jewish provenance dating from the second century B.C.E. to the first century C.E. and discovered in the middle of the twentieth century.
Dharma	Sanskrit meaning roughly "natural law"; in Hinduism it entails all of one's proper duty that contributes to personal fulfillment and the right ordering of the universe.
Drug	Avestan for "confusion," "lie," or "evil"; a term in Zoroastrianism opposed to *asha*.
Edom	Ancient nation south of Judea attested in the Hebrew Scriptures and said to be descended from Esau (see below).
Esau	According to Hebrew tradition, the son of Isaac and older brother of Jacob, from whom the Israelites descend.
Eschatology	Religious reflection on the end of history and the fulfillment of the divine plan.
Finhās	A Jewish elder in Medina.
Gāthās	Zoroastrian Scriptures, believed to have been composed by Zarathushtra himself.

Gentile	Jewish term for all non-Jews.
Golden Temple	Known also as the Harmandir Sahib (Punjabi for "abode of God"); largest Sikh gurdwara (place of worship), built by the fourth and fifth Gurus in Amritsar, Punjab, India.
Gospels	The first four books of the Christian New Testament, each of which offers a narrative of the life of Jesus Christ.
Guru	A Sanskrit word used in Hinduism commonly of specialists and teachers of religious knowledge and in Sikhism more specifically of the succession of ten teachers who founded and led the movement until the tenth enshrined as his successor the Sikh Scripture, the Granth Sahib.
Hadith	Arabic for "speech" or "information"; a term used in Islam for the several collections of recorded words and deeds of Muhammad used to contextualize and rightly interpret the Qur'an.
Henotheism	Worship of a single god without necessarily denying the existence of others.
Heretic	From the Greek for "choice"; a Christian term for teachers of unacceptable doctrine.
al-Hilālī, Taqiuddīn	Bin-Bāz-sponsored Qur'an translator.
Holy Week	The Christian observance of the week following Palm Sunday in which the events leading up to and including the Passion and Resurrection of Jesus are commemorated.
Ibn 'Abbās	A source of oral reports *(akhbār)* on *asbāb al-nuzūl* (circumstances of revelation).
Ibn al-Jawzī	A medieval qur'anic exegete.
Ibn Ishāq	Author of the *Sīra* (life and mission) of the Prophet; died 767.
Ibn Kathīr	A late medieval qur'anic exegete.
Ibn al-'Uthaymīn	Saudi religious scholar; died 2001.
'Ikrima	A source of oral reports *(akhbār)* on *asbāb al-nuzūl* (circumstances of revelation).
Jinn	Free, rational creatures (like humans and angels) in Arab folklore and Islamic belief created by Allah from "smokeless fire" (Q 55:14–15); better known to English speakers as a genie.
Josephus	First-century-C.E. Jewish historian.
Khalsa	From the Arabic for "pure"; an order of Sikhs founded by the tenth Guru as a governing and military body for the faith; initiates undergo a cleansing and baptismal ritual.

Khān, Muhsin	Bin-Bāz-sponsored Qur'an translator; born 1927.
Khazraj	A Non-Jewish tribe in Medina.
Krishna	Eighth and "complete" avatar of Vishnu, a principal Hindu deity; the main protagonist in the Bhagavad Gita.
Magi	Zoroastrian cult leaders or "priests."
Mahabharata	Ancient Sanskrit epic of which the Bhagavad Gita forms a part.
Mahdī	Arabic for "guided one"; eschatological figure in Islam who will appear before the Day of Judgment to establish justice on earth; details of his coming vary among Muslim sects.
Al-Māwardī	Exponent of the no-enigma interpretation of Muhammad and the Jews of Medina; ; died 1058.
Medina	City in modern Saudi Arabia where Muhammad spent the final years of his life and was interred; a major pilgrimage site of Muslims second only to Mecca in importance.
Messiah	Hebrew for "anointed"; a leader anticipated by the Jewish people understood by Christians to be Jesus of Nazareth.
Mishna	Written in 220 C.E.; the first major redaction of Rabbinic oral traditions.
Moses	Recipient of the Jewish Law from Yahweh and traditionally author of the Torah; listed among the major prophets of Islam.
Mughal Empire	Late medieval Muslim Empire, at its height (c. 1700) covering most of the Indian subcontinent.
Muqātil	A early medieval qur'anic exegete.
Al-Muslimūn	"The Muslims" (a nested or contested identity).
Al-Nasāra	"The Christians" (a nested or contested identity).
New Testament	Uniquely Christian scriptures containing the four canonical gospels, the Acts of the Apostles, a number of Epistles by first-century Christian leaders, and the Revelation (or Apocalypse).
Old Testament	Christian term for the Hebrew scriptures, authoritative for both Jews and Christians.
Pact of Medina	Agreement written by Muhammad that determined the relationships among all the tribes and religions in Medina.
Panth	Sanskrit for "path"; a Sikh religious community.
Pascha	Greek for "Passover"; used by Greek-speaking Christians for Easter.
Paul of Tarsus	First-century Jew of the school of Pharisees whose encounter with the risen Jesus prompted him to become Christianity's most successful early missionary; traditional author of most New Testament Epistles.

Pharisees	A school of late Second Temple Jewish thought characterized by teaching bodily resurrection and adhering to the oral traditions of Torah; precursors to Rabbinic Judaism.
Puja	Sanskrit for "adoration, worship"; used of various rituals (depending on the tradition) performed either at home or at a place of worship.
Qā'im	Arabic term for "one who arises," an eschatological figure in Shi'i Islam and Baha'i tradition.
Quraysh	The ruling tribe of Mecca.
Al-Qurtubī	A medieval qur'anic exegete.
Sayyid Qutb	Egyptian author of "Our Struggle with the Jews"; died 1966.
Rabbinic Judaism	The form Jewish religion took following the destruction of the Second Temple (70 C.E.); rabbis or teachers of the Law (in Hebrew, "my master") took leadership.
Sabbath	The seventh day of the week when, according to Genesis, Yahweh rested from his work of creation; observed by Jews as a day of rest.
Sadducees	A faction of late Second Temple Judaism identified with the ruling, priestly class at odds with the more popular Pharisees; known for rejecting the oral traditions of the Pharisees and the doctrine of the resurrection.
Safavid Empire	Late-medieval Muslim empire, at its height (c. 1630) covering all of modern Iran, Azerbaijan, and Armenia, most of Iraq as well as other territories; official religion was the minority Twelver Shi'i branch of Islam.
Samuel	According to the Hebrew scriptures, a prophet and the last judge of Israel, under whose leadership the kingdom was established first under Saul, then David.
Sanatan(a)	Sanskrit for "eternal"; Hinduism is called by its practitioners "Sanatan(a) Dharma"; Sanatan Sikhi is a Sikh school of thought that counts itself Hindu while abiding by the teachings of the Gurus.
Sanhedrin	Supreme court of Jewish law in ancient Israel; dissolved by the Roman Empire in 425.
Saul	First king of Israel, anointed by Samuel but found wanting by God in the exercise of his duties and replaced by David; known in the Qur'an as Tālūt.
Second Temple Judaism	Period in Jewish history from the construction of the second Temple in Jerusalem by the Persians in 515 B.C.E. to its destruction by the Romans in 70 C.E.
Septuagint	Collection of Greek translations of the Hebrew scriptures made in

	the third and second centuries B.C.E. that became the authoritative text of Greek-speaking Christians.
Shaivites	Oldest sect of Hinduism; reveres Shiva as the Supreme Being.
Shaktas	One of the four major sects of Hinduism; reveres Shaki (Sanskrit for "the goddess") as the Supreme Being.
Shās bin Qays	A Jewish elder in Medina.
Shi'i	Second largest sect of Islam; split from the majority Sunni sect over reckoning the succession of Imams from Muhammad.
Solomon	Son of David and king of Israel who built the first Temple in Jerusalem; known also for his wisdom and traditionally the author of the book of Proverbs in Hebrew scripture.
Al-Suddī	A source of oral reports *(akhbār)* on *asbāb al-nuzūl* (circumstances of revelation).
Sufism	Principal school of Islamic mystical thought; practitioners are known as Sufis or Dervishes.
Sura	Principal division of the Qur'an, sometimes called a chapter; suras are the individual revelations which were later collected in the Qur'an.
Al-Tabarī	An early medieval qur'anic exegete.
Al-Tabarsī	A medieval qur'anic exegete.
Tafsīr	Arabic for "interpretation"; Muslim term for exegetical commentaries on the Qur'an.
Talmud	Systematic compilation of successive waves of Jewish oral traditions, inclusive of earlier Mishna and Gamara traditions; two were made: the Babylonian Talmud and Palestinian Talmud.
Tannaim	From the Aramaic for "teachers"; term for the Jewish rabbis of the first two centuries C.E. whose teachings are recorded in the Mishna.
Theodicy	The endeavor to reconcile belief in a good, supreme deity with the manifest existence of the evil of the world.
Theogony	Title of an eighth-century B.C.E. poem of Hesiod; the word has come to connote any narrative account of the origins of divinity.
Theosophy	From the Greek for "divine wisdom"; esoteric investigation into the nature of existence, especially divine existence.
Twelver Shi'ism	A sect or "denomination" of Shi'ism that counts twelve legitimate successors to Muhammad before the last went into "occultation" or hiding, from whence he will return as the Madhi of Islamic eschatology.
Vaishnavites	One of the four major sects of Hinduism; reveres Vishnu as the Supreme Being.

Vedas	The four earliest Hindu scriptures, containing principally hymns and prayers: the Rigveda, Yajurveda, Samaveda, and Atharvaveda.
Al-Wāqidī	Author of the Book of *Maghāzī* (Battles); died 822.
Al-Yahūd	"The Jews" (a nested or contested identity).
Yazata	Avestan for "worthy of worship"; Zoroastrian title for divine beings.
YHWH	English transliteration of the Hebrew four-lettered name of God as it appears in the Hebrew scriptures.
Yogi	A Sanskrit word for a practitioner of Yoga or other ascetical, meditative practices in South Asian religions.
Al-Zamakhsharī	A medieval qur'anic exegete.
Zion	Originally the name of a mountain or hill around which Jerusalem was built; eventually used as a synonym for the city itself.
Zionism	Jewish political movement that originated in the late nineteenth century seeking to reestablish the state of Israel in Palestine as a Jewish nation.

CONTRIBUTORS

BERNHARD A. ASEN is Associate Professor of Biblical Languages and Literature in the Department of Theological Studies at Saint Louis University, where he teaches an introductory class on the Old Testament and graduate courses on the Psalms, Prophets, and Biblical Hermeneutics. He edited the journal *Theology Digest* for over twenty-five years.

JAMSHEED K. CHOKSY (BA, Columbia University; PhD, Harvard University) is Professor of Iranian Studies, Adjunct Professor of Religious Studies, and Affiliated Faculty Member of the Islamic Studies Program at Indiana University. He is the author of three books: *Evil, Good, and Gender* (Peter Lang Publishers, 2002); *Conflict and Cooperation* (Columbia University Press, 1997); and *Purity and Pollution* (University of Texas Press, 1989). He was an associate editor of the *Encyclopedia of Sex and Gender,* 4 vols. (Macmillan, 2007). Choksy also is a consulting editor of the *Encyclopedia Iranica* (Columbia University).

REUVEN FIRESTONE is Professor of Medieval Judaism and Islam at Hebrew Union College, Los Angeles, Senior Fellow of the Center for Religion and Civic Culture at the University of Southern California, and founder and codirector of the Center for Muslim-Jewish Engagement in Los Angeles. He has authored seven books and over eighty scholarly articles on Judaism, Islam, their relationship with each other and with Christianity, and religious phenomenology.

TODD LAWSON is Associate Professor of Islamic Thought at the University of Toronto, where he teaches courses on Islam, the Qur'an, Mysticism, and Shi'ism. He has published widely on Qur'an exegesis, Shi'i spirituality, and the emergence of the Babi and Baha'i religions. His study of the problem of the crucifixion of Jesus in Islamic thought, *The Crucifixion and the Qur'an,* appeared in 2009. His most recent book is *Gnostic Apocalypse & Islam: Qur'an, Tafsir, Messianism and the Literary Origins of the Babi Religions* (Routledge, 2012).

LEO D. LEFEBURE is the Matteo Ricci, S.J., Professor of Theology at Georgetown University. He is the coauthor with Peter Feldmeier of *The Path of Wisdom: A Christian Commentary on the Dhammapada,* which received the Frederick J. Streng 2011 Book Award from the Society for Buddhist-Christian Studies. He is also the author of *Revelation, the Religions, and Violence,* and of *The Buddha and the Christ.*

LAURIE L. PATTON is Professor of Religion and Dean of Arts and Sciences at Duke University. Until 2011, she was the Charles Howard Candler Professor of Early Indian Religions at Emory University. Her scholarly interests are in the interpretation of early Indian ritual and narrative, comparative mythology, literary theory in the study of religion, and women and Hinduism in contemporary India. In addition to over forty-five articles in these fields, she is the author or editor of seven scholarly books on early India and comparative mythology. Her translation of the Bhagavad Gita was published in 2008 in Penguin Classics Series.

JOHN RENARD is Professor of Theological Studies at Saint Louis University. Since receiving his Ph.D. in Islamic Studies (Harvard, NELC, 1978), he has been teaching and writing on Islamic studies, comparative theology, and medieval Mediterranean theological themes. His publications include *Islam and Christianity: Theological Themes in Comparative Perspective; Tales of God's Friends: Islamic Hagiography in Translation;* and *Friends of God: Islamic Images of Piety, Commitment and Servanthood* (California, 2011, 2009, and 2008).

MICHAEL A. SELLS is Professor at the University of Chicago Divinity School, where he writes and teaches in the areas of qur'anic studies; Sufi thought; Arabic poetry; mystical literature (Greek, Islamic, Christian, and Jewish); and religion and violence. He published *Early Muslim Mysticism: Sufi, Qur'an, Mi'raj, Poetic and Theological Writings* in Paulist Press's "Classics of Western Spirituality" series (1996). The new and expanded edition of his book *Approaching the Qur'an: The Early Revelations* appeared in 2007.

PASHAURA SINGH is Professor and Dr. Jasbir Singh Saini Endowed Chair in Sikh and Punjabi Studies at the University of California, Riverside. His publications include the following from Oxford University Press: *The Guru Granth Sahib: Canon, Meaning and Authority; The Bhagats of the Guru Granth Sahib: Sikh Self-Definition and the Bhagat Bani;* and *Life and Work of Guru Arjan: History, Memory and Biography in the Sikh Tradition.* In addition, he has edited four volumes, the most recent one being *Sikhism in Global Context* (Oxford, 2011).

INDEX

Aaron, 7, 65
Abd al-Baha' (Abbas Effendi), 14, 149, 151n2;
   Tablets of the Divine Plan, 14
Abhinavagupta, Kashmiri poet, philosopher,
   and mystical thinker, 183
Abiathar, priest, 64
Abraham: Old Testament, 6, 69, 82–83; Qur'an,
   10, 106; typological exegesis of, 6
Abrahamic traditions, 3, 16, 106, 127. *See also*
   Christianity; Islam; Judaism
Abū Bakr al-Siddīq, and Finhās, 102, 109, 112,
   113–15, 117–20, 130nn22,25
Achaemenids, 15, 16, 159, 164–69, 172–73
Acts of the Apostles, 8, 9, 22, 56, 71, 80–81, 88
Adam and Eve, fall, 10
Adi Granth, Sikh, 19, 20, 202–9
Advaita philosophy, 180
Aelia Capitolina, Jerusalem renamed as, 38
aesthetic theory: Indian, 179, 191–94. *See also*
   metaphorical imagery; poetics
Afghans, Sikhs and, 216, 217
Agag, King of Amalekites, 56, 59, 65
agamas (what has come down), 17–18
Agarwal, Pratap, 189
aggadah/haggadah, 5
ahimsa, principle of, 178, 189
Ahmad, Barakat, 131n30
Ahsa'i, Shaykh Ahmad al-, 157n60
Ahura Mazda, Zoroastrian, 15, 16, 158–72
'Ā'isha, a wife of Muhammad, 131n28;

Akali Dal, Sikh, 200, 220, 221
Akal Purakh, Sikh, 203–5, 208, 211, 212–13
Akal Takhat building, Sikh, 200, 209
Akbar, Emperor, 181, 209
akhbār, 136; Finhās, 102–3, 104, 107, 110
Akhbarat-i-Darbar-i-Mu'alla, 215
Akiba, Rabbi, 38–39, 51n43
Alcimus, Hellenizing Jewish priest, 35
Alexander, 34, 159, 166, 169
'Ali ibn Abi Talib, Muhammad's cousin and
   son-in-law, 136
allegorical exegesis, 8, 25–26, 190; Gita, 25, 177–
   78, 179–80, 183–90, 191, 194–95; Islamic, 12;
   Old Testament, 8–9, 25, 82–83; Zoroastrian-
   ism, 160. *See also* metaphorical imagery
Amalekites, 22, 25, 56–70; Agag King of, 56, 59,
   65; David vs., 64; modern day, 70; Saul vs.,
   56, 58–60, 63, 65, 66–67
Amar Das, Guru, 19, 206–7, 209
Ambrosiaster, unknown author, 87
Americans: Baha'i, 14; Civil War, 149; threat
   of religious vs. nonreligious enemy, 26;
   Transcendentalist, 185; Zoroastrian, 173
Ammonites, Milkom as tribal god of, 31
Amorites, Yahweh at war with, 60
Amos, 4, 66, 79
Amritsar, Sikh Golden Temple, 200, 209, 216,
   218, 222
anagogical exegesis, 8, 26. *See also* apocalyptic/
   eschatological exegesis